LAW *Is* JUSTICE

Notable Opinions of Mr. Justice Cardozo

WITH A FOREWORD BY

Hon. ROBERT F. WAGNER

United States Senator from New York

EDITED BY

A. L. SAINER, *LL.B., Ph.D.*

Member of the New York Bar

Instructor in Law at the College of the City of New York

Author of "The Adjective Law of New York"

"The Substantive Law of New York" etc.

THE LAWBOOK EXCHANGE, LTD.

Clark, New Jersey

ISBN 978-1-58477-010-7 (hardcover)
ISBN 978-1-61619-503-8 (paperback)

Lawbook Exchange edition 1999, 2014

The quality of this reprint is equivalent to the quality of the original work.

THE LAWBOOK EXCHANGE, LTD.
33 Terminal Avenue
Clark, New Jersey 07066-1321

Please see our website for a selection of our other publications and fine facsimile reprints of classic works of legal history:
www.lawbookexchange.com

Library of Congress Cataloging-in-Publication Data

Cardozo, Benjamin N. (Benjamin Nathan), 1870-1938.
Law is justice : notable opinions of Mr. Justice Cardozo / with a foreword by Robert F. Wagner ; edited by A.L. Sainer.
p. cm.
Originally published : New York : Ad Press, c1938.
Includes bibliographical references.
ISBN 1-58477-010-4 (cloth : alk. paper)
1. Judicial opinions—United States. I. Sainer, A.L. (Abraham Lawrence), 1900- . II. Title.

KF213.C33S2 1999
347.73'2634—dc21 99-34154
CIP

Printed in the United States of America on acid-free paper

LAW *Is* JUSTICE

Notable Opinions of Mr. Justice Cardozo

WITH A FOREWORD BY

Hon. ROBERT F. WAGNER

United States Senator from New York

EDITED BY

A. L. SAINER, *LL.B., Ph.D.*

Member of the New York Bar

Instructor in Law at the College of the City of New York

Author of "The Adjective Law of New York"

"The Substantive Law of New York" etc.

The AD PRESS Ltd.

New York

Dedicated to

JUSTICE THROUGH JUDICIAL PROCESS

Foreword

MORE revealing than anything that could be written about Mr. Justice Cardozo are his own judicial opinions and other writings, presented here in selected form. To dip into these pages is to share in a bequest that will live as long as law is a force in the life of man.

The layman will find here no legal mumbo jumbo, but a rich measure of the drama of litigated controversy, a comprehensive sweep of the human issues that underlie the jurist's art. The lawyer will review with deep satisfaction the work of the master craftsman, recognizing more clearly than all others the range of its genius and the self-restraint that marked perhaps its finest flowering. The student of society will thrill to the soaring spirit of one who, living in cloistered halls of justice, approached legal problems with the philosopher's breadth of vision.

Among the judges of his time, Benjamin Nathan Cardozo stood out from all the rest, mellow, not above but apart from the bustle of life, yet sensitive to its every current, doing his "little share," as he put it, "in translating into law the social and economic forces that throb and clamor for expression." Under his guiding influence, the New York Court of Appeals became the country's outstanding common law tribunal. Elevated to the Supreme Court of the United States during a critical period in history, his opinions on the broader state of national affairs reflected the maturity of his artistry and statesmanship. "Needs that were narrow or parochial a century ago may be interwoven in our day with the well-being of the nation. What is critical or urgent changes with the time." Thus did he sum up the basis of the Social Security Act, and find no constitutional obstacle to its fullest application in the world of today.

Justice Cardozo never sought popular acclaim or public favor. That he nevertheless won not only international renown but an invincible hold on the affections of our people is a living testimonial to his supreme worth. His work was unhappily cut short at its zenith. But the light of his genius continues after him to illumine the way for his own and future generations to the end of time.

ROBERT F. WAGNER.

Washington, D. C.

EDITOR'S NOTE

"If I begin to quote from the opinions of Mr. Justice Holmes, I can hardly know where I shall end, yet fealty to a master makes me reluctant to hold back. The sheaf will be a tiny one, made up haphazard, the barest sample of the riches which the gleaner may gather where he will."

These words, once written by Mr. Justice Cardozo, might well have been written by any member of the Bar, as a tribute to their author. One can hardly appreciate, much less overestimate, the respect and admiration felt for the former Chief Judge of the New York Court of Appeals, and later Associate Justice of the United States Supreme Court. To the student of the law, any decision by Mr. Justice Cardozo has been proof that "law" is synonymous with "justice". I have therefore chosen to call this collection "Law *is* Justice".

The cases selected have not been chosen for their legal and literary excellence alone. All of the opinions of the Justice are notable and do so excel. Those included in this book deal with matters of human and public interest and are such as, in my opinion, best illustrate the mind and heart of a great man. For the benefit of those who are not lawyers I have summarized the facts of the situations involved, omitted many case references and technical discussions. For that boldness, an apology is tendered.

I thank the Yale University Press for permitting me to quote from "Cardozo: The Nature of the Judicial Process" and from "The Growth of the Law"; the Columbia University Press, for the quotations from "Cardozo: Paradoxes of Legal Science"; and Harcourt, Brace & Co., for allowing me to quote from "Cardozo: Law and Literature".

CONTENTS

LAW *Is* JUSTICE:

Notable Opinions of Mr. Justice Cardozo

"THE LAW IS NOT LAX IN ITS FORFEITURE OF LIFE"

People v. *Galbo,* 218 N. Y. 283 (1916)

The chief characters in the tragedy are Domenico Galbo, his brother Joseph and Francesco Manzella. Domenico, a cripple who had lost both his legs, conducted a fruit store in partnership with his brother in Rochester. Unmarried, he made his living quarters above the store. In the rear of the store was a barn where the horses necessary for deliveries of fruit, were kept. Joseph was married and lived at the home of his father-in-law.

Francesco Manzella was a character of bad reputation and made blackmail his business. Physically he was strong and athletic. It seems that he knew the brothers well for he had on several occasions slept above the store with Domenico.

One Saturday afternoon Manzella requested a loan from Joseph but was definitely repulsed. Manzella then applied to Joseph's father-in-law and was told by the latter to return in the evening. Manzella did not keep the appointment.

Before dawn on Monday Domenico was seen by several marketmen driving his wagon from the city along Webster Road. In the rear of the wagon there seemed to be a barrel covered with canvas. Two hours later Domenico returned with the wagon. Those who saw it did not recall seeing the barrel then. By eight o'clock on that morning the body of Francesco Manzella was found at the bottom of a ravine along the Webster Road near the City of Rochester.

It was a gruesome sight. The head and legs had been cut off, and the body forced into a barrel. Twenty-two wounds and bruises were visible. That a violent struggle had taken place before death was evident. Whoever used the knife on the body did so with the skill of a surgeon.

That the body and the barrel had been placed there some time after three o'clock Sunday afternoon was proven by a young man who declared that he had been at the ravine on Sunday afternoon to set a trap for a skunk and that there was no barrel and no body then.

The barrel was a wine barrel with iron hoops and in the Galbo store were found four barrels of the same kind. It was shown that five barrels exactly like these had been delivered to the store seven months before by a Pittsburg wine dealer. Near the body in the ravine was found a printed time card exactly like some that had been seen on the ground of the Galbo yard only a week before. A blood-stained burlap sack found near the body and bearing the label of the Dickinson Company was shown to be exactly like six other bags of the same kind with the same label lying in the Galbo store.

Lest all this circumstantial evidence was not enough, the police traced the rope found near the blood-stained burlap sack to the store where rope of the same material and weight were suspended from hooks and carried bunches of bananas. The rope from two hooks was missing. The tailboard of Domenico's wagon showed traces of white paint and white paint was found on the fence which ran along the top of the ravine. Discolored wood shavings were found in the barrel and similar shavings were found in the Galbo barn.

That day, within thirty-six hours of the murder, Domenico Galbo was arrested. Not a scratch nor a blood-stain was found upon his person. The same was true of his brother Joseph. Not a trace of blood nor an implement of crime was found in the store. Domenico was indicted, tried and found guilty of murder in the second degree. Did the evidence sustain a verdict that he was a principal in the crime?

CARDOZO, J. * * *

The People say that these acts of possession and concealment stamp the defendant as the murderer. They do, we think, beyond question justify the inference that in some way and at some stage he became connected with this crime. But the question remains, in what way and at what stage? Was he a principal, and if so, did he himself commit the offense, or aid and abet its commission, or counsel or induce another to commit it? Was he, on the other hand, an accessory after the fact, aiding the offender to avoid arrest or punishment? Principals in the first and second degree at common law, and accessories before the fact are classed alike as principals today.[1] Accessories after the fact are classed simply as accessories. Which of these degrees of guilt attaches to the defendant?

It is the law that recent and exclusive possession of the fruits of crime, if unexplained or falsely explained, will justify the inference that the possessor is the criminal. That rule has most frequently been applied in cases of

[1]Penal Law of New York, Section 2.

burglary and larceny and receiving stolen goods; but it is not unknown in cases of murder. The highwayman kills his victim; the purpose of the murder is robbery; the same inference that identifies the robber identifies the murderer. Possession of the dead body—the subject of the crime itself—has much the same significance as possession of jewels or money or other fruits of crime. If there is any distinction, it is one chiefly of degree. The fruits of crime are themselves objects of desire; the possessor, at least presumably, has them because he wishes to enjoy them. But the possessor of the dead body wishes only to be rid of it. Its possession is thus associated more readily than that of money or jewels with the notion of concealment and thus with the form of guilt that attaches distinctively to the accessory after the fact. Often an attempt to secrete the body has played no other part than that of corroborative evidence. We do not say that it may not sometimes, if not explained or rebutted, be sufficient by itself. We must look to all the circumstances.

Only half of the problem, however, has been solved when guilty possession fixes the identity of the offender. There remains the question of the nature of his offense. Here again the facts must shape the inference. Is the guilty possessor the thief, or is he a receiver of stolen goods? Judges have said that if nothing more is shown, we may take him to be the thief. But as soon as evidence is offered that the theft was committed by someone else, the inference changes, and he becomes a receiver of stolen goods. Sometimes the circumstances may make it proper for a jury to say which inference is the true one. Learned commentators have said that in many cases the wrong inference has been drawn. Men whose crime was that they had received stolen property, have been convicted of stealing it themselves. A warning was sounded as long ago as the time of Lord Hale. These presumptive evidences, he said, "must be warily pressed, for it is better five guilty persons should escape unpunished, than one innocent person should die."[1] He couples the warning with instances drawn from his own experience where wrong had been done.

[1]Reported in Volume 2 Hale P. C. 289.

The problem is a hard one. To solve it we must steadily bear in mind that the inference of guilt to be drawn from possession is never one of law. It is an inference of fact. Other facts may neutralize it, or repel it, or render it so remote or tenuous or uncertain that in a given case we should reject it. The man who secretes a body and lies about it, may be found in most cases to be concealing his own crime, and, therefore, to be the murderer. That is so because personal guilt, unless the circumstances point to some other connection, is the reasonable inference. We are not to assume without evidence that someone else is implicated. He who conceals the crime may be taken to be the perpetrator. But how, if he proves an alibi? Are we then at liberty to infer that even if he did not commit the murder himself, he incited someone to do it, and thus, in spite of his proved absence, hold him as a principal? A is seen to shoot B, but C later has the body, and will not tell how he came by it. The law must say whether his silence is to condemn him as principal or as accessory. The same problem arises if a child or a frail woman secretes the body of a man who has been robbed and murdered on the highway. In these cases, the inference of actual perpetration is repelled. Even then, incriminating inferences remain possible; but unless other circumstances are shown, there is no principle of selection, aside from the presumption of innocence, to guide the choice between them. The guilty possessor of the body, though he did not use the weapon, may still have aided and abetted; but unless there are tokens that several joined in the affray, the likelihood of his presence is no greater than the likelihood of his absence. He may still be an accessory; whether before the fact or after is the problem. If the circumstances make one inference just as reasonable as the other, we must give the defendant the benefit of the conclusion that would mitigate his guilt.

In this case a legless cripple is charged to have murdered a strong man. The murder followed a fierce fight in which the strong man was beaten and wounded. It seems certain that the wounds were inflicted and the head severed as parts of a single combat. We cannot with reason say that the cripple did these things. Least of all can we say that he was able to do them and escape without a scratch or a blood stain. "Insufficient evidence is, in the eye of the law, no evidence"[1] and when we say that something is impossible, we do not mean impossible in the strictest sense, but so nearly impossible that a jury ought not to believe it. But as soon as we concede that the defendant did not kill Manzella, we lose ourselves in mystery when we attempt to measure the degree of his connection with the crime. We have no evidence, direct or circumstantial, that the actual perpetrator was assisted by any one. We have nothing to tell us when or where the crime occurred. We have no sign that it was committed in the defendant's presence. He may have known of it in advance, and planned or encouraged it. He may have learned of it later, and attempted to shield the criminal. The trial judge told the jury that the burden was on the People to prove beyond a reasonable doubt that the defendant, though he did not kill with his own hand, was none the less a principal; he must have become connected with the crime while Manzella was yet alive. If all that he did was to help the murderer to escape, he was not a principal, but an accessory, and the jury under the charge were then required to acquit him. The charge is sound, but it propounded to the jury a problem incapable of reasoned solution. Men do become accessories after the fact, and help others to cheat the law. Particularly is that so when they are related to the perpetrator. We have had to deal with such cases in this court. An accessory after the fact may be punished by imprisonment for not more than five years, or by a fine of not more than $500, or by both.[2] There is thus a serious penalty to be avoided. Moreover, the very fact that one becomes an accessory is proof of the strength of the desire to shield the principal.

In these circumstances we cannot see that the jury had

[1]*Matter of Case,* reported in volume 214 New York Reports 199, at page 203.

[2]Penal Law of New York, Section 1934.

any chart or compass by which to guide their judgment. A conviction upon circumstantial evidence is not to be sustained unless the circumstances are inconsistent with innocence. We may multiply inferences at times, but in multiplying them, we must not refine and rarefy them beyond measure. A body is hidden. The evidence forbids the inference that the hider is the slayer. That inference excluded, something more must be shown, some probability of time or place or circumstance, before the concealment of the body can be said to prove anything more than concealment of a crime. Small things may turn the scale. But something there must be.

We are thus led to the conclusion that the defendant was not proved to be a principal in the commission of this crime. He ought to have been indicted, and might then have been convicted, as an accessory. It is a mere accident that the jury found him guilty of murder in the second degree. To sustain their verdict they might have sent him to his death. The law is not so lax in its forfeiture of life. We cannot close this record with any sense of assurance that the defendant's connection with the crime preceded the event. The People charge in the indictment that the brother, Joseph, was one of the murderers. Like the defendant, he did not show a scratch or a blood stain. If the crime was his work, the defendant had a strong motive for concealment. If it was another's work, the mystery is deepened. We know that Manzella had led a life of crime in which bitter enmities must have been aroused; and we cannot say how the defendant was connected with the man or men by whom those enmities were avenged. In connecting him as a principal, conjecture has filled the gaps left open by the evidence, and the presumption of innocence has yielded to a presumption of guilt.

The judgment of conviction should be reversed, and a new trial ordered.[1]

WILLARD BARTLETT, *Ch. J.*, HISCOCK, CHASE, COLLIN and SEABURY, *JJ.*, concur; HOGAN, *J.*, concurs in result.

[1]It appears from the records in Monroe County, where this trial took place, that Domenico Galbo was never tried again.

"THE LAW EXACTS NO LICENSE FOR MINISTRATION BY PRAYER ALONE"

People v. *Vogelgesang*, 221 N. Y. 290 (1917)

In February, 1915, Albert Haldeman visited the office of Theodore J. Vogelgesang in Buffalo, hoping to be cured of heart disease. Accompanied by his wife he made four such visits and received three visits at his home. The efforts were futile. Haldeman died the following month. Vogelgesang did not pretend to be a doctor. He was a spiritualist. Yet he was indicted and convicted of the illegal practice of medicine. The treatment consisted of a massage with a liniment compounded of angle worms, turpentine, sweet oil and benzine, and a medicine for internal use compounded of wine, beef tea and citrate of iron was recommended. The same medicine was used for everyone who came to him and a fee was charged.

The real cure, according to Vogelgesang, was effected by his silent prayer indulged in by him while massaging his patient. His contention was that he was not practicing medicine but religion, having been commissioned by the Spiritualist Church as its spiritual healer. The fact was that that Church had so recognized him and that the practice of spiritual healing was a tenet of its faith. Vogelgesang was sentenced to imprisonment for six months. He appealed from his conviction.

CARDOZO, J.

The defendant has been convicted of the illegal practice of medicine. He says he is a spiritualist, and that he has practiced the religious tenets of his church. If that is all that he has done, he has acted within his rights. We think he has done more.

The statute prohibits the practice of medicine without a license, but excepts from its prohibition "the practice of the religious tenets of any church". We held in People v. Cole[1] that the exception protected the practitioners of Christian Science, who taught as part of their religion the healing power of mind. Even then we said that there were times when the question of their good faith must be submitted to a jury. But things were done by this defend-

[1]Reported in Volume 219 New York Reports 98.

ant which no good faith could justify. He combined faith with patent medicine. If he invoked the power of spirit, he did not forget to prescribe his drugs. "It is beyond all question or dispute," said Voltaire, "that magic words and ceremonies are quite capable of most effectually destroying a whole flock of sheep, if the words be accompanied by a sufficient quantity of arsenic." The law, in its protection of believers, has other cures in mind. The tenets to which it accords freedom, alike of practice and of profession, are not merely the tenets, but the religious tenets, of a church. The profession and practice of the religion must be itself the cure. The sufferer's mind must be brought into submission to the infinite mind, and in this must be the healing. The operation of the power of spirit must be, not indirect and remote, but direct and immediate. If that were not so, a body of men who claimed divine inspiration might prescribe drugs and perform surgical operations under cover of the law. While the healer inculcates the faith of the church as a method of healing, he is immune. When he goes beyond that, puts his spiritual agencies aside and takes up the agencies of the flesh, his immunity ceases. He is then competing with physicians on their own ground, using the same instrumentalities, and arrogating to himself the right to pursue the same methods without the same training.

The meaning of the act is made plain when we consider kindred legislation elsewhere. In varying phrases immunity is granted to those who practice their religious tenets, but always in such a form as to confine the exemption to spiritual ministrations. The statutes are collated in the briefs in People v. Cole (supra). Thus, in Maine, Massachusetts and Connecticut, the exemption is specifically declared to extend to those who practice Christian Science. In New Hampshire, it is declared to extend to "those who endeavor to prevent or cure disease or suffering by spiritual means or prayer." In Illinois the act does not apply to "any person who ministers to or treats the sick or suffering by mental or spiritual means without the use of any drug or material remedy." Nearly the same language is used in the statutes of New Jersey, North Carolina, Colorado, Virginia and Michigan. There are like provisions in other states. Through all this legislation there runs a common purpose. The law exacts no license for ministration by prayer or by the power of religion. But one who heals by other agencies must have the training of the expert.

If that is the true view of the meaning of this statute, the defendant on his own confession has violated the law. Errors which otherwise might be important, are thereby rendered harmless. The court charged the jury that the defendant had not the right to practice his religion for pay. There was doubtless error in the ruling. It is impossible, however, that the error should have affected the result, and we disregard it as immaterial.

The defendant was justly convicted, and the judgment should be affirmed.

HISCOCK, *Ch. J.*, POUND, CRANE and ANDREWS, *JJ.*, concur with CARDOZO, *J.*, and HOGAN, *J.*, concurs in result; CUDDEBACK, *J.*, reads dissenting memorandum.[1]

---

[1]Judge Cuddeback felt that the punishment was too severe and that the trial judge committed reversible error when he told the jury that a person has no right to practice his religious tenets for pay.

"THE MONEYS OF THE STATE BELONG TO THE PEOPLE OF THE STATE"

People v. *Crane*, 214 N. Y. 154 (1915)

Section 14 of the Labor Law was passed by the New York Legislature in 1909. By its terms only citizens of the United States were to be employed in the construction of state or municipal private works; and where laborers were employed in such work preference was to be given to citizens of the State of New York. Contracts for the construction of public works were to contain a clause rendering the contracts void if the provisions of Section 14 were not complied with.

A violation of this section constituted a misdemeanor and was punishable by a fine of not less than $50 nor more than $500 or by imprisonment for not less than 30 nor more than 90 days, or by both fine and imprisonment.

Clarence A. Crane was convicted of a misdemeanor for the violation of the foregoing statute in that he employed aliens as laborers in the performance of a contract executed by the president of the Borough of Manhattan for the construction of a catch basin in connection with the public sewer system. One of the employed laborers was an Italian. The nationality of the others is not shown.

Crane appealed from the conviction on the ground that the statute was unconstitutional in that its effect was (1) to deprive the excluded aliens of their liberty without due process of law since they were denied the right to labor on public works; (2) to deny to the excluded aliens the equal protection of the law; (3) to conflict with treaties between the United States and foreign countries; (4) to discriminate between aliens and citizens so as to give aid to private individuals in contravention of Article 8, of the New York State Constitution.

CARDOZO, J. * * *

The moneys of the state belong to the people of the state. They do not belong to the aliens. The state, through its legislature, has given notice to its agents, that in building its public works, it wishes its own moneys to be paid to its own citizens, and if not to them, then, at least, to citizens of the United States. The argument is made that

in thus preferring its own citizens in the distribution of its own wealth, it denies to the alien within its borders the equal protection of the laws.

The people viewed as an organized unit, constitute the state. The members of the state are its citizens. Those who are not citizens, are not members of the state. Society thus organized, is conceived of as a body corporate. Like any other body corporate, it may enter into contracts, and hold and dispose of property. In doing this, it acts through agencies of government. These agencies, when contracting for the state, or expending the state's moneys, are trustees for the people of the state. It is the people, *i.e.*, the members of the state, who are contracting or expending their own moneys through agencies of their own creation. Certain limitations on the powers of those agencies result from the nature of the trust. Since government, in expending public moneys, is expending the moneys of its citizens, it may not by arbitrary discriminations having no relation to the public welfare, foster the employment of one class of its citizens and discourage the employment of others. It is not fettered, of course, by any rule of absolute equality; the public welfare may at times be bound up with the welfare of a class; but public welfare, in a large sense, must, none the less, be the end in view. Every citizen has a like interest in the application of the public wealth to the common good, and the like right to demand that there be nothing of partiality, nothing of merely selfish favoritism, in the administration of the trust. But an alien has no such interest, and hence results a difference in the measure of his right. To disqualify citizens from employment on the public works is not only discrimination, but arbitrary discrimination. To disqualify aliens is discrimination indeed, but not arbitrary discrimination, for the principle of exclusion is the restriction of the resources of the state to the advancement and profit of the members of the state. Ungenerous and unwise such discrimination may be. It is not for that reason unlawful.

The power of a state to discriminate between citizens and aliens in the distribution of its own resources is sanctioned alike by decisions of the courts and by long-continued practice. Neither aliens nor the citizens of other states are invested by the constitution with any interest in the common property of the people of this state. It has been held, therefore, that a state may deny to aliens, and even to citizens of another state, the right to plant oysters or to fish in public waters. It may restrict to its own citizens the enjoyment of its game. It may discriminate between citizens and aliens in its charitable institutions, or in other measures for the relief of paupers. It may make the same discrimination in the distribution of its public lands; its forests; or other natural resources. It may deny to aliens the right to hold or inherit real estate, except where the right has been secured by treaty. The origin of this last disability is historical, but the policy underlying it is akin to the policy that underlies the others. The principle that justifies these discriminations is that the common property of the state belongs to the people of the state, and hence that, in any distribution of that property, the citizen may be preferred.

To defeat this law it must, therefore, be held that the constitution gives to the state a narrower liberty of choice in the expenditure of its own moneys than in the use or distribution of its other resources. I can find no justification for the supposed distinction. The construction of public works involves the expenditure of public moneys. To better the condition of its own citizens, and it may be to prevent pauperism among them, the legislature has declared that the moneys of the state shall go to the people of the state. The equal protection of the laws is due to aliens as to citizens; but equal protection does not mean that those who have no interest in the common property of the state, must share in that property on the same terms as those who have an interest.

In saying this, I assume that the purpose of the statute is not to promote efficiency in the doing of the work, but to discriminate in the distribution of the public wealth in favor of the citizen. There may be forms of employment where efficiency would be promoted by the employment of citizens, and if the statute were restricted to such employments, its validity would not be doubtful. Just as the state may confine to citizens the right to hold public office, so, on the same ground, it may confine to citizens the right to serve the state in any way, whenever there is a relation between the exclusion of aliens and the promotion of efficiency. There are many lines of service where it is conceivable that the employment of citizens will make for a stable administration. If the government were to take over the railroads, there would be force in the argument that the trains should be run by citizens on whose loyalty the government might depend in times of national disaster. We have grown accustomed to the government's administration of the mails, and none of us doubts that the service is one from which aliens may be excluded. In all these branches of employment, it is not difficult to discover some relation between citizenship and efficiency. The prohibition of alien labor in this statute is, however, unrestricted. It applies to the most temporary and occasional service, and to the lowest grades of labor. Even in those cases, it is for the legislature, according to the People's claim, to determine whether some relation exists between efficiency and citizenship; between loyalty in service, and service by the loyal. Such tests of fitness have a fair relation to permanent positions where a spirit of allegiance to the employer may be cultivated. It seems far fetched, however, to apply them to the task of day laborers excavating for sewers or digging trenches for a subway. The relation in such circumstances is so remote that we may consider it illusory. At least, I shall so assume for the purpose of this discussion. The statute has been frankly defended at our bar as a legitimate preference of citizens not to promote the efficiency of the work, but to promote the welfare of the men preferred; and from that aspect, it will be frankest and safest for us to view it.

To concede that such a preference was intended, is not to condemn the statute as invalid. The state in determining what use shall be made of its own moneys, may legitimately consult the welfare of its own citizens rather than that of aliens. Whatever is a privilege rather than a right, may be made dependent upon citizenship. In its war against poverty, the state is not required to dedicate its own resources to citizens and aliens alike. "The relief of the poor, the care of those who are unable to care for themselves, is among the unquestioned objects of public duty."[1] The modern state everywhere is mindful of that duty. It has extended its bounty in large measure, though not without some discrimination, to aliens; but it would not trench upon their rights under the constitution if it were to confine its bounty to its citizens. As it may discriminate between citizens and aliens in relief, so also it may discriminate in employment. When payment for public works is to be made from public funds, it may prefer in employment its own citizens, since to them the legislature may believe that the first duty is owing. Everywhere throughout the world the state, in its relation to the laborer, is assuming a larger obligation; but it cannot be that it owes this obligation to citizens and aliens in equal measure. In Great Britain there was enacted in 1908 a statute providing for old age pensions, restricted, it may be noted, to British subjects. In the same kingdom there was enacted in 1911 a statute providing for insurance against unemployment. In our own country the workmen's compensation laws that have been adopted in many states are phases of the same world-wide movement. We are not concerned at this time with the validity of these measures for the alleviation of the laborer's lot. We mention them as illustrations of an expanding consciousness in the modern state that relief against unemployment, both after the event and before it, is part of the state's function. How far the state will go beyond its own citizens in thus applying its own resources to the betterment of conditions, the legislature must say. Preferences to relieve against pauperism after it has become an accomplished fact do not violate the rights of aliens. Preferences to avert a threatened pauperism, or to render pauperism impossible,

[1]Brewer, *J.*, in *State ex rel. Griffith* v. *Osawkee Township,* reported in Volume 14 Kansas Reports 421.

stand on the same footing. In each instance the state announces as its public policy that the common property shall be used for the benefit of its common owners.

The argument is made, however, that there is a distinction between the right of government to exclude aliens from its own employment and the right to exclude aliens from employment by independent contractors. The ruling of the Supreme Court of the United States[1] goes far to invalidate the distinction. The first case considered a statute of Kansas prohibiting the employment of laborers for more than eight hours a day on any public work. The statute was held valid in its application to laborers in the service of contractors. The second case sustained a like statute, passed by Congress, to regulate employment on public works in the District of Columbia. The presence of an independent contractor, interposed between the state and the laborer, did not check the power of the government to prescribe the hours of labor. But without reference to those decisions, the distinction is inadequate. In a real and substantial sense, it is the money of the state that is paid to the laborers, though the distribution is made through the medium of contractors. That money constitutes the fund out of which the wages of laborers are payable. This is not only true as an economic and social fact. It is true also as a statement of the legal rights of those concerned. The state has given to any laborer employed by a contractor in the construction of a public improvement, a lien for the value of his labor upon the moneys of the state applicable to that improvement. The state has thus defined the channels through which the payment must be made. It has assumed a direct obligation not only to its own employees, but also to the employees of contractors on its works. To say that the latter class of employees receive, not the state's moneys, but those of the contractors, is to put form above substance. The great problems of public law do not turn upon these nice distinctions.

[1]The ruling appears in *Atkins* v. *Kansas,* reported in Volume 191 United States Reports 207 and in *Ellis* v. *United States,* Volume 206 United States Reports 246.

The fundamental powers of the state and the fundamental rights of man are built upon a broader basis. The truth and substance of the situation is that the contractor's employees are doing the state's work, and are paid out of the state's moneys; and this truth ought not to be obscured by distinctions between contractors and servants established to fix the gradations of civil liability.

It is now perceived that all persons engaged on the public works, from the highest officers to the lowest laborers, through all the gradations of contractors and subcontractors, are, in a very vital sense, in the service of the state. The state has a legitimate concern in the selection of the men to be employed from one extreme of the official hierarchy to the other. Whether they are called officers or employees does not matter. The power of the legislature depends upon the substance of things, and not upon names and labels.

To hold that this statute violates the federal constitution would be to ignore the contrary judgment expresed in the constitutions and legislation of many other states. There is a like provision in the constitution of Arizona, a constitution which was approved (so far as this provision is concerned) by joint resolution of congress. There are like provisions in the constitution of Idaho, and in that of Wyoming, which were also approved by congress. There is a like provision, restricted, however, to Chinese, in the constitution of California. There are like provisions applicable to all aliens in the statutes of Massachusetts, New Jersey, Pennsylvania and California. Legislation similar in purpose may be found in Montana, Nevada, Oregon and Hawaii. Unless the case against this statute is a clear one, the courts may not ignore this concurrence of opinion.

In thus holding that the power exists to exclude aliens from employment on the public works, we do not, however, commit ourselves to the view that the power exists to make arbitrary distinctions between citizens. We do not hold that the government may create a privileged caste among the members of the state. We do not hold that it may discriminate among its citizens on the ground of faith or color. A citizen may not be disqualified because of faith or color from service as a juror. For like reasons we assume that he may not be disqualified because of faith or color from serving the state in public office or employment. It is true that the individual, though a citizen, has no legal right in any particular instance to be selected as contractor by the government. It does not follow, however, that he may be declared disqualified from service, unless the proscription bears some relation to the advancement of the public welfare. The legislature has unquestionably the widest latitude of judgment in determining whether such a relation exists, but we are not required to hold that there is no remedy against sheer oppression. Where the line must be drawn, we do not now determine. We do not say that the legislature could single out A and B by name, and declare that, though citizens, they should never be employed on any public work. It may well be that such disqualification would be illegal under the fourteenth amendment of the federal constitution, in that it would deny to the citizens thus arbitrarily excluded the equal protection of the laws, and illegal also under our state constitution, which provides (Art. 1, sec. 1): "No member of this State shall be disfranchised, or deprived of any of the rights or privileges secured to any citizen thereof, unless by the law of the land, or the judgment of his peers." This opinion has failed of its purpose if it has failed to demonstrate that those provisions are without application to the exclusion of aliens from the enjoyment of the state's resources.

It must also be evident that nothing in this opinion gives countenance to the view that the government may deny to aliens the right to engage in any private trade or calling on terms of equality with citizens. If the calling is one that the state, in the exercise of its police power, may prohibit either absolutely, or conditionally by the exaction of a license, the fact of alienage may justify a denial of the privilege. There must, however, be some relation in such cases between the exclusion of the alien and the protection of the public welfare. But subject only to the exercise of the police power, it is true that in dealings between man and man, the alien and the citizen trade and labor on equal terms. It is a denial of the equal protection of the laws when the government, in its capacity as a lawmaker, regulating, not its own property, but private business, bars the alien from the right to trade and labor. It is not a denial of the equal protection of the laws when the government, in its capacity as proprietor, issuing a mandate to its own agents bars the alien from the right to share in the property which it holds for its own citizens.

Because the state may thus discriminate in favor of the citizen in regulating employment on its public works, it does not follow, however, that it may exclude aliens from the enjoyment of those works after they have been completed. Aliens may use the public highways as freely as citizens. Aliens may use the railroads and other agencies of transportation as freely as citizens. The reason is that the right to move about from place to place within the state is incidental to the right to live within the state. There are probably many other public works so intimately related, if not to life, at least to health and comfort, that merely arbitrary or oppressive discrimination against the alien in regulating their use, would be a denial by the state of the equal protection of the laws. To attempt to draw the line in advance is futile. The question must in each case be whether the use is one that is reasonably incidental to life under modern conditions in a civilized state, or whether it is rather a privilege which the state may grant or may withhold. To be employed by the state on the public works, and to receive payment out of the public purse is, I think, a privilege rather than a right.

The argument is made that if the statute is not invalid as in conflict with the fourteenth amendment of the constitution, it is invalid as in conflict with treaties between the United States and foreign nations. Typical of these treaties is the one with Italy. It provides: "The citizens of each of the high contracting parties shall have liberty to travel in the States and Territories of the other, to carry on trade, wholesale and retail, to hire and occupy houses and warehouses, to employ agents of their choice, and generally to do anything incident to, or necessary for trade, upon the same terms as the natives of the country, submitting themselves to the laws there established. The citizens of each of the high contracting parties shall receive, in the States and Territories of the other, the most constant protection and security for their persons and property, and shall enjoy in this respect the same rights and privileges as are, or shall be, granted to the natives, on their submitting themselves to the conditions imposed upon the natives." This treaty, in my judgment, does not limit the power of the state, as a proprietor, to control the construction of its own works and the distribution of its own moneys.

The argument is also made that discrimination between citizens and aliens may increase the cost of public works by limiting the supply of labor; and that to do this, in order to better the condition of our laborers, is to violate restrictions of the constitution of the state. Article VIII, section 9, of the state constitution provides that "neither the credit nor the money of the State shall be given or loaned to or in aid of any association, corporation or private undertaking." * * * The money that goes to laborers on public works is not given or loaned in aid of individuals within the meaning of these provisions. It is paid for service rendered. That is the direct and primary purpose of the payment. The primary and direct purpose being legal, the payment does not become illegal because a collateral and secondary purpose may be to protect a large class of the community against the peril of pauperism. In the long run, the payment may be found to have lessened the public burdens rather than to have increased them. The same argument was made against the validity of the statute for an eight-hour day. It was said that the result would be to increase the cost for the benefit of favored classes. The legislature is now empowered by the constitution to fix the wages and salaries of all employees upon the public works. This authority embraces the direct increase of expense by increasing salaries beyond the minimum fixed by competition. It must also embrace the indirect increase of expense by regulations of employment tending to diminish competition.

This statute must be obeyed unless it is in conflict with some command of the constitution, either of the state or of the nation. It is not enough that it may seem to us to be impolitic or even oppressive. It is not enough that in its making, great and historic traditions of generosity have been ignored. We do not assume to pass judgment upon the wisdom of the legislature. Our duty is done when we ascertain that it has kept within its power. "It must be remembered that legislatures are ultimate guardians of the liberties and welfare of the people in quite as great a degree as the courts."[1] If doubt exists whether there is a conflict between the statute and the constitution, the statute must prevail. These guiding principles are not to be honored by lip service only. Mischief and hardship, it is said, will follow the enforcement of this law. If that is so, we cannot help it. To correct those evils, if they shall develop, will be the province of legislation. The statute does not withhold from the alien the rights secured to him by the constitution; and we must enforce it as the law.

The judgment of the Appellate Division should be reversed, and the judgment of conviction affirmed.

WILLARD BARTLETT, *Ch. J.*, CHASE, HOGAN, MILLER and SEABURY, *JJ.*, concur with CARDOZO, *J.* COLLIN, *J.*, reads a dissenting opinion.[2]

---

[1]Holmes, *J.*, in *Missouri, Kansas & Texas Ry. Co.* v. *May*, reported in Volume 194 United States Reports 267, 270.

[2]Judge Collin expressed the view that any person who is banned by a statute from employment in public construction work, is deprived of liberty and property in violation of constitutional rights of aliens and citizens alike.

"FORESIGHT OF THE CONSEQUENCES INVOLVES THE CREATION OF A DUTY"

MacPherson v. *Buick Motor Company,* 217 N. Y. 382 (1916)

The Imperial Wheel Co. of Flint, Michigan, were reputable manufacturers of automobile wheels and had for a time been selling wheels to the Buick Motor Company which were put directly on the automobiles manufactured by the latter company. The Buick Company relied upon the wheel manufacturer to make all the necessary tests as to the strength of the material, and made no such tests itself.

An automobile was sold by the Buick Motor Company to a firm of automobile dealers in Schenectady, who, in turn, sold this car to Donald C. MacPherson. While MacPherson was driving this automobile at a speed of about eight miles an hour, a wheel collapsed. It was shown that this wheel had been defective when it was delivered to the Buick Company. There was no proof of actual knowledge of this defect on the part of the Buick Company.

Suit was commenced by MacPherson against the Buick Company because of its negligence in causing the damages sustained by him when the wheel collapsed. The defense argued that it owed no duty to a sub-vendee like MacPherson, who had bought the car from a dealer and not from the Buick Company.

The lower courts found for MacPherson and an appeal was taken to the Court of Appeals. The majority of the court affirmed the judgment, arguing that a sub-vendee may recover for negligence where the instrument ultimately sold is a dangerous instrumentality. Chief Judge Bartlett dissented, arguing that the liability of a seller of a manufactured article for negligence arising out of the existence of defects, does not extend to strangers but is confined to the immediate vendee, except where the article sold was of such a character that damage to life or limb was involved in the ordinary use thereof, and that an automobile was not such an inherently dangerous article.

The opinion of Judge Cardozo for the majority of the court follows:

CARDOZO, J. * * *

The question to be determined is whether the defendant owed a duty of care and vigilance to any one but the immediate purchaser.

The foundations of this branch of the law, at least in this state, were laid in Thomas v. Winchester.[1] A poison was falsely labeled. The sale was made to a druggist, who in turn sold to a customer. The customer recovered damages from the seller who affixed the label. "The defendant's negligence," it was said, "put human life in imminent danger." A poison falsely labeled is likely to injure any one who gets it. Because the danger is to be foreseen, there is a duty to avoid the injury. Cases were cited by way of illustration in which manufacturers were not subject to any duty irrespective of contract. The distinction was said to be that their conduct, though negligent, was not likely to result in injury to any one except the purchaser. We are not required to say whether the chance of injury was always as remote as the distinction assumes. Some of the illustrations might be rejected to-day. The principle of the distinction is for present purposes the important thing.

Thomas v. Winchester became quickly a landmark of the law. In the application of its principle there may at times have been uncertainty or even error. There has never in this state been doubt or disavowal of the principle itself. The chief cases are well known, yet to recall some of them will be helpful. Loop v. Litchfield[2] is the earliest. It was the case of a defect in a small balance wheel used on a circular saw. The manufacturer pointed out the defect to the buyer, who wished a cheap article and was ready to assume the risk. The risk can hardly have been an imminent one, for the wheel lasted five years before it broke. In the meanwhile the buyer had made a lease of the machinery. It was held that the manufacturer was not answerable to the lessee. Loop v. Litchfield was followed in Losee v. Clute[3], the case of the explosion of a steam boiler. That decision has been criticised but it must be confined to its special facts. It was put upon the ground that the risk of injury was too remote. The buyer in that

[1]Reported in Volume 6 New York Reports 397 (1852).
[2]Reported in Volume 42 New York Reports, 351 (1870).
[3]Reported in Volume 51 New York Reports 494 (1873).

case had not only accepted the boiler, but had tested it. The manufacturer knew that his own test was not the final one. The finality of the test has a bearing on the measure of diligence owing to persons other than the purchaser.

These early cases suggest a narrow construction of the rule. Later cases, however, evince a more liberal spirit. First in importance is Devlin v. Smith.[1] The defendant, a contractor, built a scaffold for a painter. The painter's servants were injured. The contractor was held liable. He knew that the scaffold, if improperly constructed, was a most dangerous trap. He knew that it was to be used by the workmen. He was building it for that very purpose. Building it for their use, he owed them a duty, irrespective of his contract with their master, to build it with care.

From Devlin v. Smith we pass over intermediate cases and turn to the latest case in this court in which Thomas v. Winchester was followed. That case is Statler v. Ray Mfg. Co.[2] The defendant manufactured a large coffee urn. It was installed in a restaurant. When heated, the urn exploded and injured the plaintiff. We held that the manufacturer was liable. We said that the urn "was of such a character inherently that, when applied to the purposes for which it was designed, it was liable to become a source of great danger to many people if not carefully and properly constructed."

It may be that Devlin v. Smith and Statler v. Ray Mfg. Co. have extended the rule of Thomas v. Winchester. If so, this court is committed to the extension. The defendant argues that things imminently dangerous to life are poisons, explosives, deadly weapons—things whose normal function it is to injure or destroy. But whatever the rule in Thomas v. Winchester may once have been, it has no longer that restricted meaning. A scaffold is not inherently a destructive instrument. It becomes destructive only if imperfectly constructed. A large coffee urn may have within itself, if negligently made, the potency of danger, yet no one thinks of it as an implement whose

---

1Reported in Volume 89 New York Reports 470 (1882).
2Reported in Volume 195 New York Reports 478 (1909).

normal function is destruction. We have mentioned only cases in this court. But the rule has received a like extension in our courts of intermediate appeal; it was applied to a builder who constructed a defective building; to the manufacturer of an elevator; to a contractor who furnished a defective rope with knowledge of the purpose for which the rope was to be used. We are not required at this time either to approve or to disapprove the application of the rule that was made in these cases. It is enough that they help to characterize the trend of judicial thought.

Devlin v. Smith was decided in 1882. A year later a very similar case came before the Court of Appeal in England.[1] We find in the opinion of BRETT, M. R., afterwards Lord ESHER (p. 510), the same conception of a duty, irrespective of contract, imposed upon the manufacturer by the law itself: "Whenever one person supplies goods, or machinery, or the like, for the purpose of their being used by another person under such circumstances that every one of ordinary sense would, if he thought, recognize at once that unless he used ordinary care and skill with regard to the condition of the thing supplied or the mode of supplying it, there will be danger of injury to the person or property of him for whose use the thing is supplied, and who is to use it, a duty arises to use ordinary care and skill as to the condition or manner of supplying such thing." He then points out that for a neglect of such ordinary care and skill whereby injury happens, the appropriate remedy is an action for negligence. The right to enforce this liability is not to be confined to the immediate buyer. The right, he says, extends to the persons or class of persons for whose use the thing is supplied. It is enough that the goods "would in all probability be used at once before a reasonable opportunity for discovering any defect which might exist," and that the thing supplied is of such a nature "that a neglect of ordinary care or skill as to its condition or the manner of supplying it would probably cause danger to the person or property of the person for whose use it was supplied, and who was about

[1] *Heaven* v. *Pender,* L. R. (Volume 11 Queens Bench Division 503).

to use it." On the other hand, he would exclude a case "in which the goods are supplied under circumstances in which it would be a chance by whom they would be used or whether they would be used or not, or whether they would be used before there would probably be means of observing any defect," or where the goods are of such a nature that "a want of care or skill as to their condition or the manner of supplying them would not probably produce danger of injury to person or property." What was said by Lord ESHER in that case did not command the full assent of his associates. His opinion has been criticised "as requiring every man to take affirmative precautions to protect his neighbors as well as to refrain from injuring them."[1] It may not be an accurate exposition of the law of England. Perhaps it may need some qualification even in our own state. Like most attempts at comprehensive definition, it may involve errors of inclusion and of exclusion. But its tests and standards, at least in their underlying principles, with whatever qualification may be called for as they are applied to varying conditions, are the tests and standards of our law.

We hold, then, that the principle of Thomas v. Winchester is not limited to poisons, explosives, and things of like nature, to things which in their normal operation are implements of destruction. If the nature of a thing is such that it is reasonably certain to place life and limb in peril when negligently made, it is then a thing of danger. Its nature gives warning of the consequences to be expected. If to the element of danger there is added knowledge that the thing will be used by persons other than the purchaser, and used without new tests, then, irrespective of contract, the manufacturer of this thing of danger is under a duty to make it carefully. That is as far as we are required to go for the decision of this case. There must be knowledge of a danger, not merely possible, but probable. It is possible to use almost anything in a way that will make it dangerous if defective. That is not enough to charge the manufacturer with a duty independ-

[1]Bohlen, Affirmative Obligations in the Law of Torts, Volume 44 American Law Register (New Series) 341.

ent of his contract. Whether a given thing is dangerous may be sometimes a question for the court and sometimes a question for the jury. There must also be knowledge that in the usual course of events the danger will be shared by others than the buyer. Such knowledge may often be inferred from the nature of the transaction. But it is possible that even knowledge of the danger and of the use will not always be enough. The proximity or remoteness of the relation is a factor to be considered. We are dealing now with the liability of the manufacturer of the finished product, who puts it on the market to be used without inspection by his customers. If he is negligent, where danger is to be foreseen, a liability will follow. We are not required at this time to say that it is legitimate to go back of the manufacturer of the finished product and hold the manufacturers of the component parts. To make their negligence a cause of imminent danger, an independent cause must often intervene; the manufacturer of the finished product must also fail in his duty of inspection. It may be that in those circumstances the negligence of the earlier members of the series is too remote to constitute, as to the ultimate user, an actionable wrong. We leave that question open. We shall have to deal with it when it arises.[1] The difficulty which it suggests is not present in this case. There is here no break in the chain of cause and effect. In such circumstances, the presence of a known danger, attendant upon a known use, makes vigilance a duty. We have put aside the notion that the duty to safeguard life and limb, when the consequences of negligence may be foreseen, grows out of contract and nothing else. We have put the source of the obligation where it ought to be. We have put its source in the law.

---

[1]The Court of Appeals was faced with the situation here left open in the case of *Smith* v. *Peerless Glass Company* (reported in Volume 259 New York Reports 292 and decided in 1932). The plaintiff lost the sight of an eye by the explosion of a soda water bottle made by the Peerless company. A different company had bought the empty bottle from the defendant, filled it with carbonated water and sold it to the public. Thus the defendant was in the same position as the maker of the wheel in the *Buick* case. It was held by a unanimous court that if there was negligence in the manufacture of the bottle, it could be held liable. At the time this decision was rendered, Judge Cardozo was no longer a member of this court.

From this survey of the decisions, there thus emerges a definition of the duty of a manufacturer which enables us to measure this defendant's liability. Beyond all question, the nature of an automobile gives warning of probable danger if its construction is defective. This automobile was designed to go fifty miles an hour. Unless its wheels were sound and strong, injury was almost certain. It was as much a thing of danger as a defective engine for a railroad. The defendant knew the danger. It knew also that the car would be used by persons other than the buyer. This was apparent from its size; there were seats for three persons. It was apparent also from the fact that the buyer was a dealer in cars, who bought to resell. The maker of this car supplied it for the use of purchasers from the dealer just as plainly as the contractor in Devlin v. Smith supplied the scaffold for use by the servants of the owner. The dealer was indeed the one person of whom it might be said with some approach to certainty that by him the car would not be used. Yet the defendant would have us say that he was the one person whom it was under a legal duty to protect. The law does not lead us to so inconsequent a conclusion. Precedents drawn from the days of travel by stage coach do not fit the conditions of travel to-day. The principle that the danger must be imminent does not change, but the things subject to the principle do change. They are whatever the needs of life in a developing civilization require them to be.

* * *

There is nothing anomalous in a rule which imposes upon A, who has contracted with B, a duty to C and D and others according as he knows or does not know that the subject-matter of the contract is intended for their use. We may find an analogy in the law which measures the liability of landlords. If A leases to B a tumbledown house he is not liable, in the absence of fraud, to B's guests who enter it and are injured. This is because B is then under the duty to repair it, the lessor has the right to suppose that he will fulfill that duty, and, if he omits to do so, his guests must look to him. But if A leases a building to be used by the lessee at once as a place of public entertainment, the rule is different. There injury to persons other than the lessee is to be foreseen, and foresight of the consequences involves the creation of a duty.

In this view of the defendant's liability there is nothing inconsistent with the theory of liability on which the case was tried. It is true that the court told the jury that "an automobile is not an inherently dangerous vehicle." The meaning, however, is made plain by the context. The meaning is that danger is not to be expected when the vehicle is well constructed. The court left it to the jury to say whether the defendant ought to have foreseen that the car, if negligently constructed, would become "imminently dangerous." Subtle distinctions are drawn by the defendant between things inherently dangerous and things imminently dangerous, but the case does not turn upon these verbal niceties. If danger was to be expected as reasonably certain, there was a duty of vigilance, and this whether you call the danger inherent or imminent. In varying forms that thought was put before the jury. We do not say that the court would not have been justified in ruling as a matter of law that the car was a dangerous thing. If there was any error, it was none of which the defendant can complain.

We think the defendant was not absolved from a duty of inspection because it bought the wheels from a reputable manufacturer. It was not merely a dealer in automobiles. It was a manufacturer of automobiles. It was responsible for the finished product. It was not at liberty to put the finished product on the market without subjecting the component parts to ordinary and simple tests. The obligation to inspect must vary with the nature of the thing to be inspected. The more probable the danger, the greater the need of caution.

The judgment should be affirmed with costs.

HISCOCK, CHASE and CUDDEBACK, *JJ.*, concur with CARDOZO, *J.*, and HOGAN, *J.*, concurs in result; WILLARD BARTLETT, *Ch. J.*, reads dissenting opinion; POUND, *J.*, not voting.

"THE HONORABLE FULFILLMENT OF ENGAGEMENTS"

De Cicco v. *Schweizer*, 221 N. Y. 431 (1917)

Count Oberto Giacomo Giovanni Francesco Mario Gulinelli of Ferrara, Italy was affianced to and was to be married to Blanche Josephine Schweizer the daughter of Joseph and Ernestine Schweizer. On January 16, 1902 Mr. Schweizer had his attorney prepare a document which in substance was a promise on his part to pay annually to his daughter "who is now affianced to and is to be married to the above said Count", the sum of $2500 beginning January 20, 1902. On January 20, 1902 the couple were married and left for Italy.

The father made the promised payments every year until 1912 and when that instalment was not forthcoming the plaintiff who held an assignment executed by the daughter in which the Count joined, commenced suit.

The defense resisted solely upon the ground that Mr. Schweizer's promise could not be enforced because under the law it was necessary that consideration be given in exchange for the promise, i.e., a legal right had to be given up in exchange for the father's promise. Since at the time the promise was made the couple were under a binding obligation to marry, the actual marriage was merely the execution of their obligation. The promise to pay the annuity was asserted to be merely a gratuitous promise.

CARDOZO, J. * * *

That marriage may be a sufficient consideration is not disputed. The argument for the defendant is, however, that Count Gulinelli was already affianced to Miss Schweizer, and that the marriage was merely the fulfillment of an existing legal duty. For this reason, it is insisted, consideration was lacking. The argument leads us to the discussion of a vexed problem of the law which has been debated by courts and writers with much subtlety of reasoning and little harmony of results. There is general acceptance of the proposition that where A is under a contract with B, a promise made by one to the other to induce performance is void. The trouble comes when the promise to induce performance is made by C, a stranger. Distinctions are then drawn between bilateral and unilateral contracts; between a promise by C in return for a new promise by A, and a promise by C in return for performance by A. Some jurists hold that there is consideration in both classes of cases. Others hold that there is consideration where the promise is made for a new promise, but not where it is made for performance. Others hold that there is no consideration in either class of cases.

The storm-centre about which this controversy has raged is the case of Shadwell v. Shadwell,[1] which arose out of a situation similar in many features to the one before us. Nearly everything that has been written on the subject has been a commentary on that decision. There an uncle promised to pay his nephew after marriage an annuity of £150. At the time of the promise the nephew was already engaged. The case was heard before ERLE, *Ch. J.*, and KEATING and BYLES, *JJ.* The first two judges held the promise to be enforcible. BYLES, *J.*, dissented. His view was that the nephew, being already affianced, had incurred no detriment upon the faith of the promise, and hence that consideration was lacking. Neither of the two opinions in Shadwell v. Shadwell can rule the case at bar. There are elements of difference in the two cases, which raise new problems. But the earlier case, with the literature which it has engendered, gives us a point of departure and a method of approach.

The courts of this state are committed to the view that a promise by A to B to induce him not to break his contract with C is void. If that is the true nature of this promise, there was no consideration. We have never held, however, that a like infirmity attaches to a promise by A, not merely to B, but to B and C jointly, to induce them not to rescind or modify a contract which they are free to abandon. To determine whether that is in substance the promise before us, there is need of closer analysis.

The defendant's contract, if it be one, is not bilateral. It is unilateral. The consideration exacted is not a promise, but an act. The Count did not promise anything.

[1]Reported in Volume 9 Common Bench (New Series) 159 (English Reports).

In effect the defendant said to him: If you and my daughter marry, I will pay her an annuity for life. Until marriage occurred, the defendant was not bound. It would not have been enough that the Count remained willing to marry. The plain import of the contract is that his bride also should be willing, and that marriage should follow. The promise was intended to affect the conduct, not of one only, but of both. This becomes the more evident when we recall that though the promise ran to the Count, it was intended for the benefit of the daughter. When it came to her knowledge, she had the right to adopt and enforce it. In doing so, she made herself a party to the contract. If the contract had been bilateral, her position might have been different. Since, however, it was unilateral, the consideration being performance, action on the faith of it put her in the same position as if she had been in form the promisee. That she learned of the promise before the marriage is a legitimate inference from the relation of the parties and from other attendant circumstances. The writing was signed by her parents; it was delivered to her intended husband; it was made four days before the marriage; it called for a payment on the day of the marriage; and on that day payment was made, and made to her. From all these circumstances, we may infer that at the time of the marriage the promise was known to the bride as well as the husband, and that both acted upon the faith of it.

The situation, therefore, is the same in substance as if the promise had run to husband and wife alike, and had been intended to induce performance by both. They were free by common consent to terminate their engagement or to postpone the marriage. If they forebore from exercising that right and assumed the responsibilities of marriage in reliance on the defendant's promise, he may not now retract it. The distinction between a promise by A to B to induce him not to break his contract with C, and a like promise to induce him not to join with C in a voluntary rescission, is not a new one. It has been suggested in cases where the new promise ran to B solely, and not to B and C jointly. The criticism has been made that in such circumstances there ought to be some evidence that C was ready to withdraw. Whether that is true of contracts to marry is not certain. Many elements foreign to the ordinary business contract enter into such engagements. It does not seem a far-fetched assumption in such cases that one will release where the other has repented. We shall assume, however, that the criticism is valid where the promise is intended as an inducement to only one of the two parties to the contract. It may then be sheer speculation to say that the other party could have been persuaded to rescind. But where the promise is held out as an inducement to both parties alike, there are new and different implications. One does not commonly apply pressure to coerce the will and action of those who are anxious to proceed. The attempt to sway their conduct by new inducements is an implied admission that both may waver; that one equally with the other must be strengthened and persuaded; and that rescission or at least delay is something to be averted, and something, therefore, within the range of not unreasonable expectation. If pressure, applied to both, and holding both to their course, is not the purpose of the promise, it is at least the natural tendency and the probable result.

The defendant knew that a man and a woman were assuming the responsibilities of wedlock in the belief that adequate provision had been made for the woman and for future offspring. He offered this inducement to both while they were free to retract or to delay. That they neither retracted nor delayed is certain. It is not to be expected that they should lay bare all the motives and promptings, some avowed and conscious, others perhaps half-conscious and inarticulate, which swayed their conduct. It is enough that the natural consequence of the defendant's promise was to induce them to put the thought of rescission or delay aside. From that moment, there was no longer a real alternative. There was no longer what philosophers call a "living" option. This in itself permits the inference of detriment. "If it is proved that the defendants with a view to induce the plaintiff to enter into a contract made a statement to the plaintiff of such a nature as would be likely to induce a person to enter into the contract, it is a fair inference of fact that he was induced to do so by the statement".[1] The same inference follows, not so inevitably, but still legitimately, where the statement is made to induce the preservation of a contract. It will not do to divert the minds of others from a given line of conduct, and then to urge that because of the diversion the opportunity has gone by to say how their minds would otherwise have acted. If the tendency of the promise is to induce them to persevere, reliance and detriment may be inferred from the mere fact of performance. The springs of conduct are subtle and varied. One who meddles with them must not insist upon too nice a measure or proof that the spring which he released was effective to the exclusion of all others.

One other line of argument must be considered. The suggestion is made that the defendant's promise was not made *animo contrahendi*. It was not designed, we are told, to sway the conduct of any one; it was merely the offer of a gift which found its *motive* in the engagement of the daughter to the Count. Undoubtedly, the prospective marriage is not to be deemed a consideration for the promise "unless the parties have dealt with it on that footing".[2] "Nothing is consideration that is not regarded as such by both parties".[3] But here the very formality of the agreement suggests a purpose to affect the legal relations of the signers. One does not commonly pledge one's self to generosity in the language of a covenant. That the parties believed there was a consideration is certain. The document recites the engagement and the coming marriage. It states that these are the "consideration" for the promise. The failure to marry would have made the promise ineffective. In these circumstances we cannot say that the promise was not intended to control the conduct of those whom it

---

[1]BLACKBURN, *L.J.*, in *Smith* v. *Chadwick*, reported in Volume 9 Appeals Cases 196 (English case).

[2]Holmes, Common Law, page 292.

[3]*Philpot* v. *Gruninger*, reported in Volume 14 Wall. 570 (United States Supreme Court).

was designed to benefit. Certainly we cannot draw that inference as one of law. Both sides moved for the direction of a verdict,[1] and the trial judge became by consent the trier of the facts. If conflicting inferences were possible, he chose those favorable to the plaintiff.

The conclusion to which we are thus led is reinforced by those considerations of public policy which cluster about contracts that touch the marriage relation. The law favors marriage settlements, and seeks to uphold them. It puts them for many purposes in a class by themselves. It has enforced them at times where consideration, if present at all, has been dependent upon doubtful inference. It strains, if need be, to the uttermost the interpretation of equivocal words and conduct in the effort to hold men to the honorable fulfilment of engagements designed to influence in their deepest relations the lives of others.

The judgment should be affirmed with costs.

HISCOCK, *C.J.*, and CUDDEBACK, POUND and ANDREWS, *JJ.*, concur with CARDOZO, *J.*, and CRANE, *J.*, concurs in opinion. COLLIN, *J.*, not voting.

---

[1]Where a trial is conducted before a jury, the jury determines what the facts really were. Each side, however, may ask the court to direct the jury to find a verdict in his favor. Where that is done and no subsequent request is made to let the jury decide, the judge rather than the jury, decides the facts.

"THERE IS NO SAFETY IN IGNORANCE IF PROPER INQUIRY WOULD AVAIL"

People v. *Sheffield Farms-Slawson-Decker Co.,* 225 N. Y. 25 (1918)

The Sheffield Farms-Slawson-Decker Co. was engaged in the sale of milk and employed 125 drivers to make deliveries to their many customers. One of the State's inspectors found a boy of thirteen years helping a driver named Schmidt in his work by sitting on the wagon to prevent the theft of milk bottles. The driver paid this boy. A charge was thereupon entered against the Sheffield Company for violating Section 162 of the Labor Law which in substance declared that no child under the age of fourteen years shall be employed or permitted to work in connection with certain listed mercantile establishments which included businesses similar to that of the Sheffield Company. The Penal Law (Section 1275), provided that a violation of the Labor Law constituted a misdemeanor and was punishable, if a first offense, by a fine of not less than twenty nor more than fifty dollars and repetition of the offense incurred a heavier fine and even imprisonment. In this case a fine of twenty dollars was imposed upon the company and an appeal was taken upon the ground that there was no evidence to warrant a conviction under the Labor Law.

The Sheffield Company showed that its rule was that drivers were not allowed to have any one not in the employ of the company aid them in their work or even ride on their wagons. It sent out inspectors occasionally to check up on the drivers. Offenders discovered had been reprimanded but had not been discharged. The people showed that one driver who had been convicted on a similar charge was still in the company's service. The people also showed that this very boy employed by Schmidt had been helping him for six months, but there was no definite proof of knowledge of that fact by the Sheffield Company.

CARDOZO, J. * * *

There are two statutes to be construed: the Labor Law, which imposes the duty, and the Penal Law, which attaches the penalty. The Labor Law, standing by itself, is not a criminal statute. The purpose of most of its provisions is not penal, but remedial. But a separate statute supplements its mandates and prohibitions by attaching penal consequences. For many years, they were attached to the violation of certain enumerated provisions and those only. Included in that enumeration were the provisions relating to factories and the employment of children therein; those relating to the manufacture of articles in tenements; and those relating to mercantile establishments and the employment therein of women and children. But an amendment passed in 1913 has imported into the domain of the law of crimes a vast body of rules which grew up in other fields of law. The statute now contains the sweeping declaration that "any person who violates or does not comply with any provisions of the labor law, * *, any rule or regulation of the industrial board of the department of labor, or any lawful order of the commissioner of labor," shall be guilty of a crime. These penal consequences, imposed by a separate statute, do not of necessity affect the meaning that the Labor Law would have without them. The scope of the duty is one problem; the extent to which the breach may be visited with punishment, another.

At the outset, therefore, we turn to the Labor Law itself. Section 162 is directed primarily against the employer, and only secondarily against others as they may aid and abet him. He must neither create nor suffer in his business the prohibited conditions. The command is addressed to him. Since the duty is his, he may not escape it by delegating it to others. He breaks the command of the statute if he employs the child himself. He breaks it equally if the child is employed by agents to whom he has delegated "his own power to prevent". What is true of employment, must be true of the sufferance of employment. The personal duty rests on the employer to inquire into the conditions prevailing in his business. He does not rid himself of that duty because the extent of the business may preclude his personal supervision, and compel reliance on subordinates. He must then stand or fall with those whom he selects to act for him. He is in the same plight, if they are delinquent, as if he had failed to abate a nuisance on his land. It is not an instance of *respondeat superior*. It is the case of the non-performance of a non-delegable duty. There are a host of other provisions of the Labor Law where the duty must be held personal, or we nullify the statute.

The employer, therefore, is chargeable with the sufferance of illegal conditions by the delegates of his power. But to say that does not tell us how sufferance may be implied. We do not construe the statute with all the rigor urged by counsel for the People. Not every casual service rendered by a child at the instance of a servant is "suffered" by a master. If a traveling salesman employed by a mercantile establishment in New York gives a dime to a boy of thirteen who has carried his sample case in Buffalo, the absent employer is not brought within the grip of the statute. Sufferance as here prohibited implies knowledge or the opportunity through reasonable diligence to acquire knowledge. This presupposes in most cases a fair measure at least of continuity and permanence. But the duty to inquire existing, there is no safety in ignorance if proper inquiry would avail. Whatever reasonable supervision by oneself or one's agents would discover and prevent, that, if continued, will be taken as suffered. Within that rule, the cases must be rare where prohibited work can be done within the plant, and knowledge or the consequences of knowledge avoided. But where work is done away from the plant, the inference of sufferance weakens as the opportunity for supervision lessens. No one would say that an employer had suffered the continuance of a wrong because some pieceworker, working at home on a garment had been aided by a child. In such a case, the true implications of sufferance would be almost instinctively perceived. On the other hand, we think the statute draws no distinction between sufferance and permission. This is apparent from its scheme as revealed in related sections. The two words are used indiscriminately. In such circumstances, each may take some little color from the other. Permission, like sufferance, connotes something less than consent. Sufferance, like permission, connotes some opportunity for knowledge. Thus viewed, the scheme of the statute becomes consistent and uniform.

From the Labor Law itself, and the definition of the statutory duty, we pass to the Penal Law, and the determination of the statutory penalties. It is only in their application to section 162 of the Labor Law that those penalties concern us. What the Penal Law means in its application to other sections, we do not attempt to say. Such cases must be dealt with as they arise. Slight differences in the mischief to be remedied or in the wording of the law or in the presumable purpose of the lawmakers may work a change of meaning. When the problem is thus limited, the answer is not doubtful. Any act or omission that will charge an employer with a breach of section 162 of the Labor Law becomes by force of this section 1275 a breach of the Penal Law as well. That is the plain meaning, and we are not at liberty to detract from it. There was power in the legislature to impose this stringent penalty and to punish offenders by fines moderate in amount. We have recently sustained the exercise of a like power where the fine was recoverable through the form of a civil action. The substance of constitutional power is not changed though the remedy for the collection of the fine is by information or indictment. Prosecutions and fines for nuisances, created by an agent in the absence of the owner, have long been known to the law. In these and like cases, the duty to make reparation to the state for the wrongs of one's servants, when the reparation does not go beyond the payment of a moderate fine, is a reasonable regulation of the right to do business by proxy. That right is not strictly absolute any more than any other. In such matters, differences of degree are vital. Even a fine may be immoderate. But in sustaining the power to fine, we are not to be understood as sustaining to a like length the power to imprison. We leave that question open. That there may be reasonable regulation of a right is no argument in favor of regulations that are extravagant. Exceptional principles apply to callings of such a nature that one may be excluded from them altogether. Of these it may be true that by engaging in them at all, one accepts the accompanying conditions. We speak rather of callings pursued of common right, where restrictions must be reasonable. This case does not require us to decide that life or liberty may be forfeited without tinge of personal fault through the acts or omissions of others. The statute is not void as a whole though some of its penalties may be excessive. The good is to be severed from the bad. The valid penalties remain.

Our conclusion is that there is some evidence of the defendant's negligence in failing for six months to discover and prevent the employment of this child; that the omission to discover and prevent was a sufferance of the work; and that for the resulting violation of the statute, a fine was properly imposed.

The judgment should be affirmed.

HISCOCK, *Ch. J.*, COLLIN, CUDDEBACK and ANDREWS, *JJ.*, concur with CARDOZO, *J.*; POUND and CRANE, *JJ.*, each in memorandum, also concur.

"THE FUNCTION FULFILLED IS THE ESSENCE OF THE PRIVILEGE ENJOYED"

Holmes Electric Protective Co. v. *Williams,* 228 N. Y. 412 (1920)

The Holmes Burglar Alarm Telegraph Company and the American District Telegraph Company maintained systems of overhead wires for the detection of burglary in the City of New York. This system had been made popular by one Edward Holmes who in 1872 conducted a business which consisted of the manufacture and sale of electrical alarm devices. He managed what he called the "Central Office System of Burglar Alarm." This involved the connecting of premises with a wired apparatus which would register electrically an alarm at the central office when unlawfully interfered with. In the case of an authorized entry a code signal is given the central office. In the absence of such code signal the entry is assumed to be unauthorized. The wires were run over housetops, over private property and across public streets. As an important part of this service watchmen patroled and inspected the protected premises and checked the apparatus. The customers' properties were in the main, banks, lofts, stores, residences and office buildings.

In 1874 Holmes incorporated the Holmes Burglar Alarm Telegraph Company under the General Manufacturing Act and it took over the Holmes' Central office system. The American District Telegraph Company which maintained a similar business had been incorporated under the Telegraph Act of 1848 three years before. They competed until the two companies were purchased by the Holmes Electric Protective Company in 1883. The latter corporation had just been incorporated under the Telegraph Act.

When the Holmes Electric Protective Company took over the two companies in 1883, 927 customers were being served. The business prospered and in 1917 the company was serving over 2520 customers.

In 1891 pursuant to an order from the board of electrical control of the City of New York the overhead wires were placed in electrical conduits underground. Suddenly, in 1910, the city began to question the right of the company to maintain its wires in the city streets or in the subway conduits. It threatened to remove the wires. An action was therefore commenced to restrain William Williams as Commissioner of Water Supply, Gas & Electricity of the City of New York from interfering with the wires.

The City was successful in the lower courts on the ground that the Company not having obtained a franchise from the City of New York to use the streets or electric subways for its wires it could not so continue its business. The company appealed to the Court of Appeals and based its case on the assertion that its having been incorporated under the Telegraph Act automatically gave it a franchise or authority to maintain its wires and carry on its burglar alarm system as above described.

Four opinions were written in the decision of the Court of Appeals. Judges Crane and Andrews wrote for the majority and Judges Pound and Cardozo wrote dissenting opinions. The majority held that the business of the company was a public utility. It assisted in the preservation of law and order. Furthermore it was exactly like the other telegraph companies which had franchises and for whose benefit the power of condemnation could be exercised, for did it not string wires over which messages were to pass? Though the wording of the Telegraph Act would seem to apply solely to telegraph companies as then understood, yet when the telephone was perfected so as to transmit the human voice over wires, the Telegraph Act was held to be the authority for the incorporation of telephone company with franchise rights. Finally the acts of the city in permitting the use for over 25 years and requiring the removal of overhead wires to the underground conduits, while not enough to estop the city, showed that a practical interpretation had been given to the Telegraph Act so as to enable the company to have franchise rights.

Judge Pound in his dissent pointed out that the company did not do a business of transmitting messages like a telephone and telegraph company; that the messages were only a means to warn the watchmen who were the important part of the service; that its business was entirely private; that the order of the commissioners in 1891 requiring the removal of overhead wires to subway conduits was of no consequence as these commissioners really had no power to execute their order as it was not in their domain to determine whether the company's use of the streets was for a public purpose. The separate dissenting opinion of Judge Cardozo follows:

CARDOZO, J. (dissenting)

I concur in Judge POUND'S conclusions, and in the reasoning which supports them.

The plaintiff did not get the right to occupy the highway unless it also got the right of eminent domain. The same sentence of the statute which says that telegraph companies shall have the one right, says also that they shall have the other. We must determine whether the plaintiff's business is so affected with a public use as to justify a holding that it comes by implication within the grant of these extraordinary privileges. I think the question is not strictly whether the legislature could confer such privileges by words clearly sufficient to indicate that intent. I think the question rather is whether the public use, if any, is so related to that served by the telegraph or the telephone generally as to make the inference of intent a fair one.

The purpose of the telegraph or telephone as commonly employed is not to carry information to the telegraph company itself. The purpose is to disseminate information among the public indiscriminately. The common welfare is served by freedom of communication, whether men or things or thoughts be the subjects of transmission. The telegraph and the telephone like the railroads and the post are agencies of commerce. They spread abroad the knowledge without which life could be ill maintained in a complex order of society.

The plaintiff is not organized to disseminate information indiscriminately among the members of the public in aid of the myriad interests which touch the lives of men. It is organized for the conveyance of a particular form of intelligence to a particular member of the public, i.e., to itself, in aid of a particular and private business. A railroad organized with the restriction that it should carry the products of the organizer and nothing else, would be a railroad in name, but not one organized for public service. A telephone company organized by a caterer or a jeweler or a department store with the restriction that it must carry no messages except orders for the wares or services of the organizer would meet with difficulty if it should attempt to exercise the power of eminent domain. This plaintiff seeks to exercise a like power in aid of its business as a private watchman. I do not think it is an answer to say that the business is a useful one and tends to the preservation of the peace and order of society. Private in its essential purpose, if not in the range or degree of its utility, it, none the less, remains. I do not say that the range or degree of its utility would not justify the legislature in investing it with special rights by special or explicit grant. That question is not here. I say merely that the private and selfish limits of its purposes forbid the implication of such a grant from words of doubtful import. The plaintiff is not a subordinate governmental agency like a volunteer fire department organized for the public good and supplying protection in a field where government has not entered. In a settled community, with an organized power of the state, it undertakes to supplement the protection of the police by the use of private watchmen furnished by itself. I speak of them as private watchmen though they may be sworn in as special officers. The company procures this rank for them in no spirit of public helpfulness, but merely to increase the effectiveness of service to subscribers. It does not come under a duty to watch the property of persons not subscribers, to warn them of impending danger, or to respond with relief to their summons of distress. Protection is restricted to those who pay the price.

I think we should be slow to hold that the legislature intended by words of general import to delegate the power of eminent domain in aid of such a purpose. These telegraphic signals are not employed as a means whereby the company's subscribers may communicate with one another and thus potentially with all the world. They are merely signals to the company that something has happened to call for investigation by a watchman in fulfillment of its contract. The signal may mean a burglar or a forgetful householder or a window broken by a storm. I can discover only a remote connection between the good to be attained by signaling a contractor in aid of the fulfillment of his contract, and the good resulting from the free interchange of ideas among the members of the community by telegram or telephone or post in aid of the multifarious needs and interest of life in organized society. Private detective agencies are not organs of government. The state is still the primary guardian of the peace and order of its members. Its power to condemn the property of the citizen is not to be extended by doubtful inference and remote analogy to agencies organized for private gain which supplement its action. In the peace of the state, most men pass their lives, and find repose in its protection. Those who wish a special protection beyond that which most of us find necessary and which government supplies, have not yet been given the right to obtain it by the occupation of the land of others or by encroachment on the public ways.

I think the history of the statute confirms this estimate of its purpose. If we carry ourselves back in thought to 1848, we cannot doubt that the extraordinary powers conferred upon telegraph companies by the general statute of that year went to them in their capacity as surveyors of intelligence, fulfilling functions akin to those of common carriers, like the railroads and the post. They were authorized to construct lines of telegraph along the public roads and highways and (upon payment of just compensation) over lands in private ownership, and they were required to receive dispatches from any member of the public, and to transmit them with impartiality and in the order of receipt. The wording of the statute, in so far as it confers the right to occupy the highways, is substantially the same as that of the Post Roads Act of Congress, adopted July 24, 1866 which gave to every telegraph company the right to construct, maintain and operate its lines along the post roads of the nation. The end in view was the same under one statute as under the other, the fostering, for the public good, of the public agencies of commerce. It is true that by a ruling of the Supreme Court, telephone companies do not enjoy the protection of the Federal act and that by a ruling of this court now confirmed by legislation they do enjoy like privileges with telegraph companies of the older form under the statutes of the state. That ruling found its basis in the fact that the telephone, like the telegraph, is a purveyor of intelligence by electricity, and thus fulfils a like function as an instrumentality of commerce.

But even under our statute, the function fulfilled is the essence of the privilege enjoyed. No one, I think, would assert that the plaintiff, even though it transmits electric signals by methods not unknown in 1866, is an instrumentality of commerce entitled as of right to occupy the highways of the nation. I see no better reason to believe that it is entitled as of right to occupy the highways of the state.

I do not forget that the plaintiff has been incorporated under the Telegraph Act, and that the legislature has recognized the regularity of its corporate existence. That is not equivalent to recognition of its right to obstruct the highways of the public, or to condemn the lands of private owners, irrespective of the purpose served by condemnation or obstruction. Any seven men may make themselves a telegraph company by filing a certificate. When they go farther, and attempt to occupy the highways or condemn the property of their neighbors, they must show something more than regularity of corporate existence. They must show that they are acting in aid of public purposes, and not merely that, but in aid of the public purposes which the legislature had in view when it said that telegraph companies might exercise as its delegate an important attribute of sovereignty. It is true that section 102 of the Statute (Transp. Corp. Law) says that every "such corporation," i. e., every telegraph and telephone company, may occupy and condemn. It is also true, however, that section 103 of the statute says that "every such corporation," shall receive dispatches from the public and transmit them as received. Duty and privilege are imposed and granted in terms of equal generality. Construction of the statute, if permissible to exclude the plaintiff from the duty, is equally permissible to exclude it from the privilege. I think that sections 102 and 103 of the present statute, like the corresponding section of the act of 1848, must be limited in their application to corporations serving the public as instrumentalities of commerce. The readiness of the legislature to clothe with extraordinary powers the telegraph companies which it knew in

1848 and which fulfilled the function of common carriers of intelligence, and even to clothe telephone companies with like powers since they fulfill a like function, is little evidence of its readiness to extend the same powers to corporations which are not common carriers of intelligence, and which, if they serve any public use, serve one that is doubtful and limited and indisputably different.

The plaintiff lays much stress on section 105 of the Transportation Corporations Law. Its history is, I think, significant. It goes back to 1880. By chapter 90 of the Laws of 1880, authority was given for the appointment of special policemen, not exceeding two hundred, in aid of a telegraphic system of signaling to a central office. That was the statute regulating the subject at the time of the incorporation of the plaintiff in 1883. It was not an amendment of the act of 1848, under which telegraph companies were organized. It was not a term of the charter. It was an independent grant of power. The legislature knew that signal companies existed; but we have no reason to suppose that it also knew under what statutes they had been incorporated, or whether they had strung their wires under the claim of a perpetual franchise, or under temporary or special license. In point of fact, the plaintiff's predecessor, then the owner of this plant, was not organized under the Telegraph Act at all, but under the act for the formation of business corporations. The act of 1880, first adopted as an independent statute, did not come into the Transportation Corporations Law till 1890 and there it has since remained. If it did not have the effect, when it stood alone, of clothing the plaintiff with the power of eminent domain, I do not think it gained that effect when in the course of revision it was brought into a different context. Something more must be shown to sustain the claim of title to a privilege so extraordinary. In the process of the consolidation of a multitude of scattered statutes, there have come into the Transportation Corporations Law fragments of legislation which, if related to every preceding section, might bring the plaintiff and like companies within the letter of the grant. The problem is not solved so easily. It remains in the end a problem in the reading of the legislature's intention, with a larger problem of constitutional power ever in the background. The nature of the use determines the nature of the privilege.

I find little force in the argument of practical construction. If there has been practical construction in favor of the company, there has also been practical construction against it, and that by the one person best acquainted with the situation, the company itself. The Public Service Commissions Law requires every telegraph and telephone company to file schedules of its charges and to make yearly reports to the commission. No schedules or reports have been filed by the plaintiff, though the failure to file them, if they are due, has subjected it to heavy penalties. I think that telegraph and telephone companies within the purview of the Public Service Commissions Law are those that would be so recognized in the common speech of men. The plaintiff has rightly acted on the assumption that it does not come within that class. By the same token it does not come within the class of telegraph or telephone companies invested with the power of eminent domain. I lay slight stress on the circumstance that public officers did not attempt to disturb the wires when they were strung across the housetops. We may get some notion of the slight significance of silence and inaction when we recall that the wires were strung in the beginning by the plaintiff's predecessor, organized as a business corporation, and, therefore, without shadow of right, in default of special license, to occupy the public ways.

I am not free from doubt by any means. The principle, however, is fundamental that "every public grant of property, or of privileges or franchises, if ambiguous, is to be construed against the grantee and in favor of the public".[1] It is in favor of the public that my doubts are now resolved.

---

[1] *Central Transportation Co.* v. *Pullman's Palace Car Co.*, reported in Volume 139 United States Reports 24.

"WE DO NOT CONFISCATE THE LANDS OR GOODS OF THE STRANGER WITHIN OUR GATES"

Techt v. *Hughes,* 229 N. Y. 222 (1920)

On December 7, 1917 war was declared between Austria-Hungary and the United States. Twenty days later James J. Hannigan, a citizen of the United States, died a resident in the City of New York. Part of his property consisted of a piece of real estate in the City of New York.

He left him surviving two daughters, Sara E. Techt and Elizabeth L. Hughes. In 1911 Sara had married Frederick E. Techt, a resident of the United States, but a citizen of Austria-Hungary. Under the law as it existed at that time the marriage made Sara an alien, for Congress had enacted that "any American woman who marries a foreigner shall take the nationality of her husband."

Since James J. Hannigan had left no will, the real property descended to his children, but Elizabeth contested the right of her sister to share, claiming the law to be that aliens though they could take lands by purchase could not take by descent.

It was conceded that the loyalty of both Sara and her husband had never been questioned by the United States Government.

CARDOZO, J. * * *

The rule at common law was that aliens might take lands by purchase, and hold until office found, but could take nothing by descent. "If an alien could acquire a permanent property in lands, he must owe an allegiance equally permanent with that property to the King of England, which would probably be inconsistent with that which he owes to his own natural liege lord; besides that thereby the realm might in time be subject to foreign influence, and feel many other inconveniences".[1] Blackstone was repeating the explanation which was already traditional in his day. Inheritance by aliens, says Coke, would "tend to the destruction of the realm." And if it be demanded "wherein doth that destruction consist," his answer is: "first, it tends to destruction tempore belli;

[1]Volume 1 Blackstone Commentaries 372.

for then strangers might fortify themselves in the heart of the realm and be ready to set fire on the commonwealth," for all which he finds example and warning in the legend of the Trojan horse. Artificial and far-fetched may seem to-day this defense of the policy of the rule. We may even doubt whether it is sound in history. There is little to the point. The rule, whatever its origin, is inveterate and undoubted. It survives today except as statute or treaty may have abrogated or changed it.

The plaintiff is indisputably an alien. Congress has enacted that "any American woman who marries a foreigner shall take the nationality of her husband." That statute was considered in Mackenzie v. Hare[1] where an American-born woman, married to a British subject, and residing in California, was held, by force of her marriage, to have lost the right to vote. Marriage to an alien is voluntary expatriation. The plaintiff is in the same position as if letters of naturalization had been issued to her in Austria. She is in the same position as her husband. She is without capacity to inherit unless statute or treaty has removed the disability.

Both statute and treaty are invoked in her behalf. The statute says that "a citizen of the United States is capable of holding real property within this state, and of taking the same by descent, devise or purchase," and that "alien friends are empowered to take, hold, transmit and dispose of real property within this state in the same manner as native born citizens, and their heirs and devisees take in the same manner as citizens."[2] Alien enemies, therefore, have such rights and such only as were theirs at common law. The treaty says that "where, on the death of any person holding real property, or property not personal, within the territories of one party, such real property would, by the laws of the land, descend on a citizen or subject of the other, were he not disqualified by the laws of the country where such real property is situated, such citizen or subject shall be allowed a term of two

[1]Reported in Volume 239 United States Reports 299.

[2]Real Property Law, section 10.

years to sell the same; which term may be reasonably prolonged, according to circumstances; and to withdraw the proceeds thereof, without molestation, and exempt from any other charges than those which may be imposed in like cases upon the inhabitants of the country from which such proceeds may be withdrawn." (Art. II of Convention between United States and Austria.)

Statute and treaty will be separately considered.

(1) If the plaintiff's capacity to inherit depended solely on the statute, I should feel constrained to hold against her. I cannot follow the Appellate Division in its view that she is in law an "alien friend." The wisdom or fairness of the statute, I make no attempt to vindicate. Our duty is done when we enforce the law as it is written. In the primary meaning of the words, an alien friend is the subject of a foreign state at peace with the United States; an alien enemy is the subject of a foreign state at war with the United States. This primary meaning must be taken to be the true one unless evidence is at hand that some other meaning was intended. There are times, indeed, when alien enemies are relieved of disabilities, and treated in the same way or nearly the same way as friends. Unless they are present in the hostile territory or are found adhering to the enemy, they retain, by express or implied license of the sovereign, many of the privileges that belong to them in peace. Sometimes, though loosely, we speak of them as friends for the purpose of characterizing their status when they are brought within the range of exemption, tacit or proclaimed. The truth is that they are enemies, who, within the limits placed by the sovereign upon a revocable license, enjoy the privileges of friends. Their identification with friends is never complete. They are subject to one restriction or another betokening their enemy character. No doubt there is a growing tendency to narrow the field of disability. The day may come when the movement will have spread so far that the subject of a hostile power residing within our territory and yielding obedience to our laws will be ranked as a friend, not for some purposes, but for all. But in construing a statute

we assume that the legislature has spoken in the light of the law as it is, and not as it may hereafter be. The law as declared in New York when this statute was enacted, held fast to the old moorings. Its history, briefly followed, may make the solution of the problem clearer.

In the beginnings of English law, the bodies of alien enemies found within the realm were seized and their goods were forfeit to the crown. The first relaxation was in favor of the merchant class. We read in Magna Charta that "if in time of war merchants of the country at war with us shall be found in our country at the outbreak of the war, they shall be attached without damage to their bodies, or their goods, until it is known to us or to our chief justice how merchants of our country who are then found in the country at war with us are treated; and if ours are safe there, the others shall be safe in our country". From foreign merchants, protection spread to others. They were still enemies, however, and were far from remaining in the realm on terms of equality with friends. Coke, writing in 1608 tells us that an alien friend may acquire goods personal as an Englishman, and may maintain an action for the same. "But if this alien become an enemy (as all alien friends may), then he is utterly disabled to maintain any action, or get anything within this realm. And this is to be understood of a temporary alien, that being an enemy may be a friend, or becoming a friend, may be an enemy."[1] In time the courts held that alien enemies, if permitted to remain within the realm, might sue in English courts. They were within the protection of the King's license, either tacit or express.

TREBY, *Chief Justice,* said that "wars at this day are not so implacable as heretofore, and therefore, an alien enemy, who is here in protection, may sue his bond or contract; but an alien enemy abiding in his own country cannot sue here."[2] So the law has since remained for aliens within the realm. Even so, they were enemies, and not to

---

[1]Calvin's Case, reported in Volume 7, Coke's Reports (Eng.) 1.

[2]*Wells* v. *Williams,* (1697) reported in Volume 1 Lord Raymond's Reports 282.

be confused with friends. A prisoner of war might sue, though assuredly an enemy. So might an interned alien under the English statute though we express no opinion whether he has a like right under ours. The concession of these privileges to enemies resident within the realm neither transformed them into friends, nor put the two classes on a parity. That is true of enemies in our day as of enemies in the past. Their presence is permitted "subject to various arbitrary regulations". They have no "general license" to live on the same footing as Englishmen and friends.

A like development has taken place in the United States. Kent, writing in 1813, held that alien enemies, if permitted to remain in the United States, could maintain actions in our courts. He will have none of the new doctrine, inspired by the teachings of Rousseau that war is a relation solely between bodies politic, and not between individuals. He holds that "a war on the part of the government, is a war on the part of all the individuals of which that government is composed." Other courts took the same ground.[1] It is not a question of personal sentiments or friendship. It is a question of the allegiance due from the subject to the sovereign. I do not stop to inquire whether international law should put aside this conception of war as involving a relation between individuals, and substitute Rousseau's conception of a relation solely between states. The legislature of New York cannot have supposed, when it passed this statute in 1913, that the change had yet been made. The words alien friend and alien enemy had come down through the centuries, freighted with a significance which they had gained under the old order. The plaintiff has the burden of showing that, as used in this statute, they were filled with a new content.

I think the content is unchanged. At the threshold is met the evidence supplied by kindred legislation. This statute is one of a type. Throughout the type, the phraseology varies. The thought back of it is constant. In New York the first statute regulating the rights of aliens in re-

[1]The Rapid, reported in Volume 8 Cranch (U. S.) 155.

spect of lands was passed in 1798. Its language is that "all and every conveyance or conveyances hereafter to be made or executed to any alien or aliens, not being the subject of some foreign state or power which is or shall be at the time of such conveyance at war with the United States of America, shall be deemed valid to vest the estate thereby granted in such alien or aliens". In other states, we find a like restriction. New Jersey says that it shall be lawful for "any alien, not being the subject of any state or power which shall be at war with the United States" to take by purchase and descent. Georgia gives a like right to aliens, the subjects of governments at peace with the United States. Maryland, Kentucky and West Virginia speak of "aliens not enemies". I am persuaded that these statutes, whatever the differences of phraseology, reveal the same policy, and mean the same thing.

Acts of Congress having relation to different but kindred topics help to fix the meaning. Section 2171 of the United States Revised Statutes declares in substance that "alien enemies" shall not be naturalized. The courts have applied the prohibition to citizens of Austria-Hungary. Another act of Congress declares that all male citizens or male persons "not alien enemies" who have declared their intention to become citizens between the ages of 21 and 30, shall be subject to the draft. Other legislative bodies use the same words with the same meaning. Texas and Connecticut have passed laws that "alien enemies" must register. Great Britain in the Alien Restriction Order issued under the authority of the British Alien Restriction Act of 1914, has said that "the expression 'alien friend' means an alien whose sovereign or state is at peace with his Majesty, and the expression alien enemy means an alien whose sovereign or state is at war with his Majesty."

I find nothing that overbears the cumulative force of all this statutory definition either in the President's proclamation of December 11, 1917, issued under the authority of section 4067 of the United States Revised Statutes, or in the act of October 6, 1917 (40 U. S. Stat. p. 411, ch.

106) "to define, regulate and punish trading with the enemy."

Section 4067 of the United States Revised Statutes as in force in December, 1917, provided that in case of war, all "subjects of the hostile nation or government, being males of the age of fourteen years and upward, who shall be within the United States, and not actually naturalized, shall be liable to be apprehended, restrained, secured, and removed, as alien enemies," and "the President is authorized, in any such event, by his proclamation thereof, or other public act to direct the conduct to be observed, on the part of the United States, toward the aliens who become so liable; the manner and degree of the restraint to which they shall be subject, and in what cases, and upon what security their residence shall be permitted, and to provide for the removal of those who, not being permitted to reside within the United States, refuse or neglect to depart therefrom; and to establish any other regulations which are found necessary in the premises and for the public safety."

An amendment of the statute in April, 1918, extended its scope to women. On April 6, 1917, at the outbreak of the war with Germany, and again on November 16, 1917, the President issued proclamations regulating the conduct of German subjects resident in the United States. On December 11, 1917, he issued a proclamation regulating the conduct of subjects of Austria-Hungary resident in the United States. After the amendment of section 4067 in April, 1918, a supplemental proclamation of May 31, 1918, brought women within the scope of the regulations then applicable to men. The restrictions laid upon German subjects, remaining in the United States were many and minute. They were subject to summary arrest and internment by order of the President. They could not possess firearms or explosives. They could not approach forts, or arsenals, or munition factories. They could not depart from the United States without the permit of the President or the order of a court. They were excluded from the District of Columbia. They could not enter railroad depots, yards, or terminals without license. They were commanded to register, and their presence in the United States, its territories and possessions, became unlawful without registration cards upon their persons. Restrictions imposed upon the subjects of Austria-Hungary were fewer and less burdensome, yet the proclamations did not leave them on an equality with friends. They were not at liberty to depart from the United States without permit of the President or the order of a court. They could not land in or enter the United States except under such restrictions and at such places as the President might prescribe. They were subject to summary arrest and internment whenever there was reasonable cause for the belief that their presence at large was a menace to the peace and safety of the country. No doubt they retained many of the privileges that had been theirs in times of peace. That was true of Germans also. The courts were open to them. Keeping within the law, they might live their lives and pursue their callings unmolested. Overnight, however, a proclamation of the President might subject them to new burdens. The great immunities of the Constitution were not theirs in undiminished force. What others did confidently and of right, they did by sufferance and doubtfully, uncertain of the restrictions of the morrow. They were alien enemies, treated with liberality, but watched with a suspicious eye as enemies, and never identified with friends.

The Trading with the Enemy Act[1] did not invest them with a different status. Its definition of an enemy was "for the purposes of such trading and of this act," and for no other. Trade was prohibited with any one resident within the hostile territory, even though a citizen of the United States, and with such other persons, wherever resident, if subjects of the hostile nation, as might be brought within the term enemy by proclamation of the President. The prohibition in its main features is in line with the restrictions which would have been imposed in default of any statute. But the disability of aliens in respect of the

[1]Volume 40 United States Statutes, Chapter 106.

ownership of lands has no connection with their disabilities in respect of the privileges of trade. If the state of New York had declared that all aliens should have capacity to acquire ownership by descent, neither the Trading with the Enemy Act, nor any rule of the common law, would read into the statute an implied exception in the contingency of war, and withhold the right of succession from alien enemies whether resident in hostile territory or here. The nation by act of Congress might declare their lands forfeit but in the absence of such a forfeiture title would be theirs. To argue, that alien enemies, resident in the United States, may inherit because they may trade is to assume that disabilities must have identity of duration though they have diversity of origin.

Trade in aid of the enemy's resources, since it tends to prolong the combat, is illegal for everyone within our jurisdiction, whether enemy or friend. The prohibition does not run against the alien as an incident of the disabilities of alienage. It runs against citizen and alien as an incident of the necessities of war. The sovereign will not permit its military operations to be hampered by those whom it controls. Much of the obscurity which surrounds the rights of aliens has its origin in this confusion of diverse subjects. Disabilities are confounded with prohibitions; the incidents of alienage with incidents that are common to alienage and citizenship. Sometimes we are told in loose and sweeping terms that there may be no trade with alien enemies. The statement is inaccurate for commercial domicile, and not alienage, determines the enemy character of commerce. Then, to supply the needed correction, a new definition of alien enemies is put forward for the purpose of the rule, and finally what is a definition for one purpose is erroneously assumed to be a definition for all others. The truth is that the right to trade, since it does not follow lines of citizenship, should not be formulated in terms of alienage. If a citizen of the United States does business in a hostile territory, trade is prohibited with him as much as with an alien. To bring him within the compass of a rule imperfectly stated at the outset, he is sometimes characterized by courts as an alien enemy himself. In reality, of course, he is not an alien, either enemy or friend. What is meant is that trade with him is as unlawful as if he were alien enemy. But plainly the statute of New York does not speak of alien friends, in this special and unnatural sense. There was no thought of taking from our own citizens the right of purchase and inheritance when resident in hostile lands. The definition of enemies for the purpose of trade is thus in some features too wide and in others too narrow when fitted to this statute. It is too wide in that it includes citizens as well as aliens, abroad. It is too narrow in that it excludes the alien at home.

General statements in such cases as Porter v. Freudenberg[1], that the test of an alien enemy is not his nationality, but the place in which he resides or carries on business, are for the same reason misleading and erroneous if dislocated from their setting. Read in the light of the context, they become consistent and intelligible. "What did that case decide? It decided that for the purpose of trading, it is not a person's nationality that determines whether he is an alien enemy".[2] Subjects of a belligerent power are thus classified for a particular purpose as no longer alien enemies, when all that is meant is that they are relieved to that extent and for that purpose of the disabilities of enemies. The German-born subject, resident within the British realm, who found himself interned in a war camp, though with the right to trade and sue, was probably under no delusion that he was in law an alien friend.

The case under the statute of New York comes down, then, to this: The question, "What are the rights of alien enemies in the absence of statutory restriction?" is distinct from the question, "Who are alien enemies within the scope of such restriction?" Alien enemies, resident within our borders, retain by implied license many of the civil rights of friends. Implication ceases, however, to be legiti-

---

1Reported in volume 1 King's Bench (Eng.) 857 (1915).

2*Schaffenius* v. *Goldberg*, reported (1916) in Volume 1 King's Bench 284, 299.

mate when an express and conflicting prohibition occupies the field. *Expressum facit cessare tacitum.* The civil rights which belong to alien enemies by implied license of the Federal government do not include the right to purchase or inherit land. That is a subject which every state, in the absence of inconsistent treaty, may regulate for itself. The civil rights which belong to alien enemies by implied license of the states, do not include in New York the right to purchase and inherit land, for the field is occupied by statute, and there is, therefore, nothing to be implied. The legislature might have refused to draw a distinction between enemies and friends. It might have given capacity to all aliens alike, and in that event capacity would not have ended with the outbreak of the war. It chose a policy less liberal. It gave the privilege to friends and withheld the privilege from enemies. I find no ground for the belief that it intended the definition of enemies to wait upon the varying terms of proclamations of future presidents, to be enlarged today, and restricted tomorrow, with the changing fortunes of a war. For the same reason, I cannot think that there was willingness to impair the security of titles by substituting the uncertain and fluid test of loyalty in act and speech for the certain and historic test of allegiance to the sovereign. In the law of land, more than in any other branch of law, words are used as terms of art. Here, more than in any other field, the method of history supplies the organon of interpretation for the work of legislators and judges. Deep into the soil go the roots of the words in which the rights of the owners of the soil find expression in the law. We do not readily uproot the growths of centuries.

(2) The support of the statute failing, there remains the question of the treaty. The treaty, if in force, is the supreme law of the land[1] and supersedes all local laws inconsistent with its terms. Judicial construction has already fixed its meaning. The right which it secures is in form a right of sale. In substance, it is a right of ownership. The fee descends subject to the condition that it

[1]United States Constitution, Article VI.

shall be disposed of within the "term of two years, which term may be reasonably prolonged according to circumstances". We do not need to determine the effect of a breach of the condition. In this instance there was none. Judgment of partition and sale was entered within the term of two years. The plaintiff has an estate of inheritance if the treaty is in force.

The effect of war upon the existing treaties of belligerants is one of the unsettled problems of the law. The older writers sometimes said that treaties ended ipso facto when war came. The writers of our own time reject these sweeping statements. International law today does not preserve treaties or annul them regardless of the effects produced. It deals with such problems pragmatically, preserving or annulling as the necessities of war exact. It establishes standards, but it does not fetter itself with rules. When it attempts to do more, it finds that there is neither unanimity of opinion nor uniformity of practice. "The whole question remains as yet unsettled" (Oppenheim). This does not mean, of course, that there are not some classes of treaties about which there is general agreement. Treaties of alliance fall. Treaties of boundary or cession, "dispositive" or "transitory" conventions, survive. So, of course, do treaties which regulate the conduct of hostilities. Intention in such circumstances is clear. These instances do not represent distinct and final principles. They are illustrations of the same principle. They are applications of a standard. When I ask what the principle or standard is, and endeavor to extract it from the long chapters in the books, I get this, and nothing more, that provisions compatible with a state of hostilities, unless expressly terminated, will be enforced, and those incompatible rejected. "Treaties lose their efficacy in war only if their execution is incompatible with war." *"Les traités ne perdent leur efficacité en temps de guerre que si leur exécution est incompatible avec la guerre elle-même."*[1] That in substance was Kent's view, here as often in advance of the thought of his day. "All those duties

[1]Bluntschli, "Droit International Codifie", sec. 538.

of which the exercise is not necessarily suspended by the war, subsist in their full force. The obligation of keeping faith is so far from ceasing in time of war, that its efficacy becomes increased, from the increased necessity of it."[1] That, also, more recently, is the conclusion embodied by the Institute of International Law in the rules voted at Christiania in 1912 which defined the effects of war on International Conventions. In these rules, some classes of treaties are dealt with specially and apart. Treaties of alliance, those which establish a protectorate or a sphere of influence, and generally treaties of a political nature, are, it is said, dissolved. Dissolved, too, are treaties which have relation to the cause of war. But the general principle is declared that treaties which it is reasonably practicable to execute after the outbreak of hostilities, must be observed then as in the past. The belligerents are at liberty to disregard them only to the extent and for the time required by the necessities of war. *"Les traités restés en vigueur et dont l'execution demeure, malgré les hostilités, pratiquement possible doivent être observés comme par le passé. Les Etats belligérants ne peuvent s'en dispenser que dans la mesure et pour le temps commandés par les necessités de la guerre."*[2]

This, I think, is the principal which must guide the judicial department of the government when called upon to determine the progress of a war whether a treaty shall be observed in the absence of some declaration by the political departments of the government that it has been suspended or annulled. A treaty has a twofold aspect. In its primary operation, it is a compact between independent states. In its secondary operation, it is a source of private rights for individuals within states. Granting that the termination of the compact involves the termination of the rights, it does not follow because there is a privilege to rescind that the privilege has been exercised. The question is not what states may do after war has supervened, and this without breach of their duty as members

[1]Volume 1 Kent Commentaries, page 176.

[2]Institut de droit international, annuaire 1912, p. 648.

of the society of nations. The question is what courts are to presume that they have done. "Where the department authorized to annul a voidable treaty shall deem it most conducive to the national interest that it should longer continue to be obeyed and observed, no right can be incident to the judiciary to declare it void in a single instance."[1] President and senate may denounce the treaty, and thus terminate its life. Congress may enact an inconsistent rule, which will control the action of the courts. The treaty of peace itself may set up new relations, and terminate earlier compacts either tacitly or expressly. The proposed treaties with Germany and Austria give the victorious powers the privilege of choosing the treaties which are to be kept in force or abrogated. But until some one of these things is done, until some one of these events occurs, while war is still flagrant, and the will of the political departments of the government unrevealed, the courts, as I view their function, play a humbler and more cautious part. It is not for them to denounce treaties generally, en bloc. Their part it is, as one provision or another is involved in some actual controversy before them, to determine whether, alone, or by force of connection with an inseparable scheme, the provision is inconsistent with the policy or safety of the nation in the emergency of war, and hence presumably intended to be limited to times of peace. The mere fact that other portions of the treaty are suspended or even abrogated is not conclusive. The treaty does not fall in its entirety unless it has the character of an indivisible act. *"Le traité tombe pour le tout quand il présente le caractère d'un acte indivisible."* To determine whether it has this character, it is not enough to consider its name or label. No general formula suffices. We must consult in each case the nature and purpose of the specific articles involved. *"Il faut * * * examiner dans chaque cas, si la guerre constitue par sa nature même un obstacle à l'exécution du traité."*[2]

I find nothing incompatible with the policy of the gov-

---

[1]Jay, *Ch. J.*, in *Jones* v. *Walker,* Volume 2 Paine, 688, 701.
[2]Bluntschli, *supra.*

ernment, with the safety of the nation, or with the maintenance of the way in the enforcement of this treaty so as to sustain the plaintiff's title. We do not confiscate the lands or goods of the stranger within our gates. If we permit him to remain, he is free during good behavior to buy property and sell it. He is to be "undisturbed in the peaceful pursuit" of his life and occupation and "accorded the consideration due to all peaceful and law-abiding persons".[1] If we require him to depart, we assure to him, for the recovery, disposal and removal of his goods and effects and for his departure, the full time stipulated by any treaty then in force between the United States and the hostile nation of which he is a subject; and where no such treaty is in force, such time as may be declared by the President to be consistent with the public safety and the dictates of humanity and national hospitality. A public policy not outraged by purchase will not be outraged by inheritance. The plaintiff is a resident; but even if she were a non-resident, and were within the hostile territory, the policy of the nation would not divest her of the title whether acquired before the war or later. Custody would then be assumed by the alien property custodian. The proceeds of the property, in the event of sale, would be kept within the jurisdiction. Title, however, would be unchanged, in default of the later exercise by Congress of the power of confiscation, now seldom brought into play in the practice of enlightened nations. Since the argument of this appeal, Congress has already directed, in advance of any treaty of peace, that property in the hands of the custodian shall be returned in certain classes of cases to its owners, and in particular where the owner is a woman who at the time of her marriage was a native-born citizen of the United States and prior to April 6, 1917, intermarried with a subject or citizen of Germany or Austria-Hungary (Act of June 5, 1920). It follows that even in its application to aliens in hostile territory, the maintenance of this treaty is in harmony with the nation's policy and consistent with the nation's welfare.

[1]President's Proclamation of December 11, 1917.

To the extent that there is conflict between the treaty and the statute we have the same situation that arises whenever there is an implied repeal of one law by another. To the extent that they are in harmony, both are still in force. There is in truth no conflict here except in points of detail. In fundamental principle and purpose, the treaty remains untouched by later legislation. In keeping it alive, we uphold the policy of the nation, revealed in acts of Congress and proclamations of the President, "to conduct ourselves as belligerents in a high spirit of right and fairness"[1] without hatred of race and without taint of self-seeking.

I do not overlook the statements which may be found here and there in the works of authors of distinction, that treaties of commerce and navigation are to be ranked in the class of treaties which war abrogates or at least suspends. Commerce is friendly intercourse. Friendly intercourse between nations is impossible in war. Therefore, treaties regulating such intercourse are not operative in war. But stipulations do not touch commerce because they happen to be embodied in a treaty which is styled one to regulate or encourage commerce. We must be on our guard against being misled by labels. Bluntschli's warning, already quoted, reminds us that the nature and the name of covenants determines whether they shall be disregarded or observed. There is a line of division, fundamental in importance, which separates stipulations touching commerce between nations from those touching the tenure of land within the territories of nations. Restrictions upon ownership of land by aliens have a history all their own, unrelated altogether to restriction upon trade. When removed, they cease to exist for enemies as well as friends, unless the statute removing them enforces a distinction. More than that, the removal, when effected by treaty, gives reciprocal privileges to the subjects of each state, and is thus of value to one side as much as to the other. For this reason, the inference is a strong one, as was pointed out by the Master of the Rolls in Sutton v.

[1]President Wilson's Address to the Congress, April 2, 1917.

Sutton[1] that the privileges, unless expressly revoked, are intended to endure. There, as in Society for the Propagation of the Gospel v. Town of New Haven,[2] the treaty of 1794 between the United States and England protecting the citizens of each in the enjoyment of their landed property, was held not to have been abrogated by the war of 1812. Undoubtedly there is a distinction between those cases and this in that there the rights had become vested before the outbreak of the war. None the less, alike in reasoning and in conclusion, they have their value and significance. If stipulations governing the tenure of land survive the stress of war though contained in a treaty which is described as one of amity, it is not perceived why they may not also survive though contained in a treaty which is described as one of commerce. In preserving the right of inheritance for citizens of Austria when the land inherited is here, we preserve the same right for our citizens when the land inherited is there. Congress has not yet commanded us, and the exigencies of war, as I view them, do not constrain us, to throw these benefits away.

No one can study the vague and wavering statements of treaties and decision in this field of international law with any feeling of assurance at the end that he has chosen the right path. One looks in vain either for uniformity of doctrine or for scientific accuracy of exposition. There are wise cautions for the statesman. There are few precepts for the judge. All the more, in this uncertainty, I am impelled to the belief that until the political departments have acted, the courts, in refusing to give effect to treaties, should limit their refusal to the needs of the occasion; that they are not bound by any rigid formula to nullify the whole or nothing; and that in determining whether this treaty survived the coming of war, they are free to make choice of the conclusion which shall seem the most in keeping with the traditions of the law, the policy of the statutes, the dictates of fair dealing, and the honor of the nation.

HISCOCK, *Ch. J.*, CHASE, HOGAN, MCLAUGHLIN and CRANE, *JJ.*, concur; ELKUS, *J.*, concurs in result.

[1]Reported in Volume 1, Russell & Mylne Reports (Eng.) 664, 675.
[2]Reported in Volume 21 United States Reports 464, 494.

"THE COURT MUST CONSIDER THE REASON OF A RULE AND THE EVILS WHICH IT AIMS TO REMEDY"

Matter of Fowles, 222 N. Y. 222 (1918)

Charles Frederick Fowles and his wife, Frances May, planned to make a trip to Europe on the "Lusitania" in May, 1915. German submarine warfare was then at its height, and rumors apparently well founded, were spread abroad that attempts would be made to sink the ship before it reached its European destination.

Realizing these dangers, Mr. and Mrs. Fowles prepared their respective wills on April 29, 1915.

The will of Mr. Fowles made certain definite bequests, and by the 8th Article thereof, he gave his residuary estate to certain trustees, to be divided into three parts. The first part consisted of 45% of that residue and the income thereof was to be paid to his wife during her life, and upon her death this 45% was to be divided by giving one-half of it to certain other trustees in accordance with the provisions of the will of his wife. If she failed to make provisions in her will for the one-half of this portion, it was to be held in trust for his daughters by a former wife.

The provisions of the will of Mr. Fowles were very clear, but an added article (the 9th) created a difficulty. That article declared that in the event he and his wife should die simultaneously or under such circumstances as to render it impossible to determine who predeceased the other, it was his declaration that his death should be considered as having occurred first. The fears of Fowles were fully justified when the "Lusitania" was sunk on May 7, 1915. Fowles and his wife were both lost at sea and there was nothing to show which was the survivor. The wife left a will made at the same time as the husband's, and provision was made therein for the trust of the one-half of the portion of the residuary estate mentioned in her husband's will. It was given to trustees for the use of a sister during her life, and provisions made for its distribution upon the sister's death.

The validity of this gift in the wife's will in so far as it applied to the husband's estate was questioned on the ground that the 9th article directing a presumption of survivorship could not be considered effective. If Mr. Fowles had predeceased his wife, her estate would be larger and the beneficiaries under her will would get more. The difficulty alleged to stand in the way was the rule of law that no instrument outside the very will itself could be used to enlarge or diminish the terms of a will. The 9th article, it was claimed, incorporated by reference the will of his wife and since the will of his wife was not executed by him, it could not be considered part of his will.

Judge Cardozo in his opinion felt that the rule against incorporation by reference was not applicable to the situation at hand.

Chief J. Hiscock, Judges Chase and Andrews concurred. Judge Crane dissented in an opinion with which Judge Cuddeback concurred, and Judge McLaughlin read a separate dissenting opinion.

CARDOZO, J. * * *

Of his intention, there can be no doubt. In that, we all agree. He was about to set sail with his wife upon a perilous journey. He knew that disaster was possible. He knew that if death came, there would be no presumption to whom it had come first. He told the courts what he wished them to do if all other tests of truth should fail. They were to distribute his estate as they would if his wife were the survivor. We cannot know whether she was in truth the survivor or not: there is no break in the silence and obscurity of those last hours. The very situation which was foreseen has thus arisen. If intention is the key to the problem, the solution is not doubtful. We are now asked to hold that under the law of the state of New York, a testator may not lawfully declare that a power executed by one who dies under such conditions shall be valid to the same extent as if there were evidence of survivorship.

Two rules of law are supposed to stand in the way. One is the rule that a power created by will lapses if the donee dies before the will takes effect. The other is the rule that wills must be executed in compliance with statutory formalities, and are not to be enlarged or diminished by reference to extrinsic documents which may not be authentic. A testator is not permitted at his pleasure to violate these rules. He does violate them, it is said, by indirection, if he may dispense with evidence of survivorship and still sustain the gift which purports to execute the power. If the wife had survived a single second, the gift would certainly be valid. That would be so though she had signed her will while her husband was yet alive and before the power took effect. It is possible that she did survive, but it is also possible that she did not. The latter possibility, it is said, renders the gift void. We do not think it does.

It is true that a power created by will lapses if the donee of the power dies before the maker of the will. That is because a will has no effect till the death of the testator. Whatever power it creates, comes into being at that time. But to say this, does not answer the question before us. The question is not whether this power of appointment lapsed. The question is whether the testator has avoided the consequences of a lapse. More concretely, it is whether the law permits him to provide that if the donee's survivorship is incapable of proof, he will give his estate none the less to whomever she has named. This is what this testator said, not in words, but in effect. His will in this respect has a parallel in the one construed in Matter of Greenwood[1]. There gifts were made to relatives, with the provision that if the legatees died leaving issue, the benefits of the gifts should not lapse, "but should take effect as if his or her death had happened immediately after mine". These words were held equivalent to a gift to the personal representatives of the legatees named. So here, there is by implication a gift to the legatees named by the wife, and a ratification of any execution of the power, however premature. The intent to avert the consequences of a lapse is clear. The only question is whether the intent is one to which the law will give effect. One obstacle, and one only, can be thought of. That is the rule against the incorporation of extrinsic documents, testamentary in character but not themselves authenticated in accordance with the statute. It is said that this rule is violated when a testator, to keep a power alive, ratifies its execution, adopts the will which executes it as his own, and thus in effect averts a lapse. We do not share that view.

---

[1]Reported in 1912 Reports (England) Volume 1 Chancery Division 392.

Everything that this testator did is justified by our decision in Matter of Piffard.[1] The distinction between that case and this is purely verbal. There is none in substance. In that case the testator authorized his daughter to dispose of a share of his estate by will. If she died before him, leaving a will in execution of the power, he directed his executors to transfer the share to her executors or trustees. We upheld the validity of that provision. We said that it might not be "possible to sustain the power of appointment as such". We held, however, that the daughter's will might be referred to "not as transferring the property by an appointment, but to define and make certain the persons to whom and the proportions in which the one-fifth should pass by the father's will in case of the death of the daughter in his lifetime". There was a like decision upon like facts in Condit v. De Hart.[2] The argument is made that the express direction to transfer the share to the daughter's executors or trustees distinguishes the Piffard case from the one at bar. But in another form of words, this testator gave the same direction. He directed his executor to turn over his estate to the persons named by his wife. There is no distinction between a direction to pay the *trustees* named in another will, and a direction to pay the *legatees* named in a will. The daughter's trustees in the Piffard case were not to take as individuals. They had no beneficial interest. They were to take as trustees. Only by reference to the will which appointed them could the nature of the trust and the names and interests of the beneficiaries be learned. If there was a violation of the rule against incorporation here, there was equally a violation there.

Piffard's case cannot be distinguished. It ought not to be overruled. Only the clearest error would warrant us in baffling the just hopes and purposes of this testator by disregarding a decisive precedent. But there are substantial reasons to support the view that the decision was right. The reasons may appeal with different strength to

---

[1]Reported in Volume 111 New York Reports 410.

[2]Reported in Volume 62 New Jersey Law Reports 78.

different minds. For our present purposes, it is enough that they are at least substantial. The rule against incorporation has not been set aside. It has been kept within bounds which were believed to be wise and just. The rule is sometimes spoken of as if its content had been defined by statute, as if the prohibition were direct and express, and not inferential and implied. But the truth is that it is the product of judicial construction. Its form and limits are malleable and uncertain. We must shape them in the light of its origin and purpose. All that the statute says is that a will must be signed, published and attested in a certain way. From this the consequence is deduced that the testator's purpose must be gathered from the will, and not from other documents which lack the prescribed marks of authenticity. It is a rule designed as a safeguard against fraud and mistake. In the nature of things, there must be exceptions to its apparent generality. Some reference to matters extrinsic is inevitable. Words are symbols, and we must compare them with things and persons and events. It is a question of degree. Sometimes the distinction is said to be between documents which express the gift and documents which identify it. But the two classes of cases run into each other by almost imperceptible gradations. One may ratify assumptions of power, extinguish debts, wipe out wrongs, confirm rights, by the directions of one's will. In these and other cases, the expressions of the gift and the description of its subject matter must often coalesce. No general formula can tell us in advance where the line of division is to be drawn.

It is plain, therefore, that we are not to press the rule against incorporation to "a drily logical extreme". We must look in each case to the substance. We must consider the reason of the rule, and the evils which it aims to remedy. But as soon as we apply that test, the problem solves itself. There is here no opportunity for fraud or mistake. There is no chance of foisting upon this testator a document which fails to declare his purpose. He has not limited his wife to any particular will. Once identify the document as *her* will; it then becomes his own. He authorizes her to act, and confirms her action. For the purpose of the rule against incorporation, the substance of the situation is thus the same as it always is when a will creates a power. The substance is that a power which would otherwise have lapsed, has been kept alive by the declaration that its execution, however premature, is ratified and approved. But the execution of a power does not violate the rule against incorporation. It can make no difference for that purpose whether the execution is authorized in advance or made valid by relation. There is no greater impairment in the one case than in the other of the principle of the integrity and completeness of testamentary expression. The source of title may be in one case the appointment, and in the other the confirmatory will. But if we go beneath the form and reach realities, the truth is that under the sanction of the will, a power has been executed. That is the principle which underlies the ruling in Matter of Piffard and Condit v. De Hart. We reaffirm it now. To hold that the purpose of this testator has been adequately or inadequately declared according to the accident of time at which death came to him or his wife in the depths of the ocean, is to follow the rule against incorporation with blind and literal adherence, forgetful of its origin, its purpose, and its true and deep significance. * * *

HISCOCK, *Ch. J.*, CHASE and ANDREWS, *JJ.*, concur with CARDOZO, *J.*; CRANE, *J.*, reads dissenting opinion, except as to specific legacies, and CUDDEBACK, *J.*, concurs; MCLAUGHLIN, *J.*, reads dissenting opinion.[1]

Ordered accordingly.

[1]This dissenting opinion expressed the view that there was nothing in the will of Mr. Fowles which referred to her will, and to read his wife's will into his would violate the rule against incorporation by reference. Furthermore, there was no reference in his will to the legatees named in hers nor any proof that he knew what was in his wife's will.

"THE LAW DOES NOT INSIST THAT AN EMPLOYEE SHALL WORK WITH HIS EYE UPON THE CLOCK"

Matter of Grieb v. *Hammerle,* 222 N. Y. 382 (1918)

Grieb was a cigar packer and was paid at the rate of $1.25 for packing 1,000 cigars. When not busy packing, he would deliver cigars for his employer to various customers. It was not infrequent that these deliveries were made after working hours. One Saturday afternoon Grieb left the factory after the day's work and spent the early part of the evening with two friends. He happened to pass by the factory and saw a light, whereupon he went upstairs with his two friends. They found the employer tying up two boxes of cigars. They all chatted for a while, when his employer asked Grieb to deliver the boxes to a customer at the Amos Hotel, and to collect for them. He left his employer and his two friends in the factory. On his way downstairs he fell and died from the injuries.

Death benefits under the Workmen's Compensation Law were sought for the widow and the minor child. It was opposed on the ground that the injury to Grieb did not arise in the course of his employment, and therefore was not within the application of the Workmen's Compensation Law.

Could the death benefits be recovered?

CARDOZO, J. * * *

The argument is made that the injury did not arise out of or in the course of the servant's employment. I think that is too narrow a view. If Grieb had been injured during working hours, it would make no difference that his service was gratuitous. If the service was incidental to the employer's business and was rendered at the employer's request, it would be part of the employment within the meaning of this statute. Any other ruling would discourage helpful loyalty (Hartz v. Hartford Faience Co., 90 Conn. 539). In that case a shipping clerk whose duty was to keep the books, lent a hand of his own motion in the delivery of merchandise. His claim for compensation was sustained. We do not need to go so far. We cannot doubt that in the case cited the claim would have been valid if custom or special request had established the approval of the employer. To hold otherwise would lead to strange conclusions. It cannot be that an employer may ask a clerk to assist mechanics in repairing dangerous machinery, and then be heard to say that because the service was gratuitous, the employee, if injured, is outside the pale of the employment. *Pro hac vice,* by force of custom or request, the employment is enlarged. We have already held that in determining the relation of employer and employee, the payment of wages is not the sole test. We should hold the same thing now.

It is plain, therefore, that Grieb's service, if it had been rendered during working hours, would have been incidental to his employment. To overturn this award, it is necessary to hold that the service ceased to be incidental because rendered after hours. That will never do. The law does not insist that an employee shall work with his eye upon the clock. Services rendered in a spirit of helpful loyalty, after closing time has come, have the same protection as the services of the drone or the laggard. But the argument is that because the employee had left for the day, and had then returned, his rights are different. Why he returned, we do not know. Perhaps it was idle curiosity. Perhaps the unexpected light which he saw in the factory after closing, made him feel that investigation was due in the interest of his employer. At all events, when he reached there, he found business in progress. His employer had prepared cigars for delivery, and was writing out the bill. What Grieb then undertook to do with his employer's approval was just as much a part of the business as if it had been done in the noonday sun. He was not only to deliver the cigars. He was also to collect the money. That is the plain implication of the request that he should take the bill with him. Moreover, it is a fair inference that he expected to return, and bring the money back, for he did not take his companions with him, but left them behind. How far he had to go we do not know. There is no evidence where the Amos Hotel is situated. There is nothing to show that the employee would have passed it in going to his home. I do not say that the case would be different if such things had been proved. It is enough to say that they are not here. This case is not one where the servant goes out primarily on his own business or for his personal convenience, and only incidentally and by the way does something for the master. All the circumstances point to the conclusion that Grieb left the factory on the fatal errand for the sole purpose of helping the master in the transaction of the master's business. It was not mere friendship, it was the relation of employer and employee, that led the one to request the service and the other to render it. If such a service is not incidental to the employment within the meaning of this statute, loyalty and helpfulness have earned a poor reward.

To reach this conclusion, there is no need to attempt a precise or comprehensive definition of the term employment. One must leave such problems to be worked out by the process of exclusion and inclusion in particular cases, rather than by "a fixed standard of measurement". It is enough that here the employee was in the general service of the employer; that the service rendered was incidental to the business; that it was one which this employee had been accustomed to render upon request; and that the errand was the cause of his presence on the stairway. The inference is legitimate that it was not the comradeship of friends, but the tacit sanctions of a relation of power and dependence which prompted the master's request and the servant's acquiescence.

HISCOCK, *Ch. J.*, CUDDEBACK, POUND, CRANE and ANDREWS, *JJ.*, concur; COLLIN, *J.*, not voting.

"FOR THE PHYSICIST ONE THING IS THE CAUSE; FOR THE JURIST ANOTHER"

Bird v. *St. Paul Fire & Marine Ins. Co.,* 224 N. Y. 47 (1918)

The St. Paul Fire & Marine Insurance Company had issued a policy of insurance to Henry Bird covering the body, tackle, apparel and other furniture of his canal boat the "Henry Bird Jr." The policy specifically provided that the company was to indemnify Bird against loss resulting from the perils of "the Sounds, Harbors, Bays, Rivers, Canals & Fires". It did not mention damage from explosion.

On the night of July 30, 1916 a fire broke out near some freight cars in the freight yards of the Lehigh Valley Railroad Company situated at Black Tom in the harbor of New York. Its cause was unknown. The freight cars were loaded with explosives and when the fire reached them they exploded. This explosion caused the fire to spread to other freight cars also loaded with explosives and another and more terrific explosion occurred.

The last explosion caused a concussion of the air which damaged the "Henry Bird Jr.", then about 1,000 feet away, to the extent of $675. No fire actually reached the boat. The insurance company refused to pay arguing that the damage was not caused by fire within the meaning of the policy. The Appellate Division gave judgment to Bird, interpreting the policy to cover the loss as here sustained under the fire clause. An appeal was taken to the Court of Appeals.

CARDOZO, J. * * *

There is no doubt that when fire spreads to an insured building that there causes an explosion, the insurer is liable for all the damage. We assume that, in the absence of some exception in the policy, a like liability follows when an explosion caused by fire occurs in neighboring buildings. But the question here is whether space is a factor in the solution of the problem. The Appellate Division says that it is not; no matter how great the distance, the insurer remains liable. Other courts have held otherwise. The question came before the English Court of Common Pleas in Evereet v. London Assurance Co.[1] There

[1]Reported in Volume 19 Common Bench Reports (New Series) 126.

gunpowder ignited and exploded. The plaintiff's building, half a mile away, was damaged by concussion. The court gave judgment for the defendant. "Speaking of this injury, no person would say that it was occasioned by fire. It was occasioned by a concussion or disturbance of the air caused by fire elsewhere." A like ruling was made in Louisiana by a divided court.[1] In Tennessee, the ruling was the same: "Legal conclusions cannot always be safely reached by pressing the processes of logical illation to their ultimate results."[2]

The problem before us is not one of philosophy. If it were, there might be no escape from the conclusion of the court below. General definitions of a proximate cause give little aid. Our guide is the reasonable expectation and purpose of the ordinary business man when making an ordinary business contract. It is his intention, expressed or fairly to be inferred, that counts. There are times when the law permits us to go far back in tracing events to causes. The inquiry for us is how far the parties to this contract intended us to go. The causes within their contemplation are the only causes that concern us. A recent case in the House of Lords gives the true method of approach.[3] LORD SHAW refers in his opinion to the common figure of speech which represents a succession of causes as a chain. He reminds us that the figure, though convenient, is inadequate. "Causation is not a chain, but a net. At each point, influences, forces, events, precedent and simultaneous, meet, and the radiation from each point extends infinitely." From this complex web, the law picks out now this cause and now that one. The same cause producing the same effect may be proximate or remote as the contract of the parties seems to place it in light or shadow. That cause is to be held predominant which they would think of as predominant. A common-sense appraise-

---

[1] *Caballero* v. *Home Mutual Ins. Co.*, reported in Volume 15 Louisiana Annual Reports 217.

[2] *Hall* v. *National Fire Ins. Co.*, reported in Volume 115 Tennessee Reports 513, 521.

[3] *Leyland Shipping Co.* v. *Norwich Fire Ins. Society*, reported in Volume 118 Law Times, 120, 125.

ment of every-day forms of speech and modes of thought must tell us when to stop. It is an act of "judgment as upon a matter of fact".

This view of the problem of causation shows how impossible it is to set aside as immaterial the element of proximity in space. The law solves these problems pragmatically. There is no use in arguing that distance ought not to count, if life and experience tell us that it does. The question is not what men ought to think of as a cause. The question is what they do think of as a cause. We must put ourselves in the place of the average owner whose boat or building is damaged by the concussion of a distant explosion, let us say a mile away. Some glassware in his pantry is thrown down and broken. It would probably never occur to him that within the meaning of his policy of insurance, he had suffered loss by fire. A philosopher or a lawyer might persuade him that he had, but he would not believe it until they told him. He would expect indemnity, of course, if fire reached the thing insured. He would expect indemnity, very likely, if the fire was near at hand, if his boat or his building was within the danger zone of ordinary experience, if damage of some sort, whether from ignition or from the indirect consequences of fire, might fairly be said to be within the range of normal apprehension. But a different case presents itself when the fire is at all times so remote that there is never exposure to its direct perils, and that exposure to its indirect perils comes only through the presence of extraordinary conditions, the release and intervention of tremendous forces of destruction. A result which in other conditions might be deemed a mere incident to a fire and, therefore, covered by the policy, has ceased to be an incident, and has become the principal. The distinction is no less real because it involves a difference of degree. In such a case, the damage is twice removed from the initial cause. It is damage by concussion; and concussion is not fire nor the immediate consequence of fire. But there is another stage of separation. It is damage by concussion traveling over a distance so remote that exposure to peril is not within the area of ordinary prevision, the range of probable expectation. The average man who speaks of loss by fire does not advert to the consequences of this play of catastrophic forces.

Precedents are not lacking for the recognition of the space element as a factor in causation. This is true even in the law of torts where there is a tendency to go farther back in the search for causes than there is in the law of contracts. Especially in the law of insurance, the rule is that "you are not to trouble yourself with distant causes". But even in tort, where responsibility is less dependent on intention, space may break the chain of causes. The wrongdoer who negligently sets fire to a building, is not liable without limit for the spread of the flames. In our own state, there is a fixed and somewhat arbitrary restriction.[1] But even in jurisdictions where the liability is broader, its bounds are the reasonable and the probable. The wrongdoer may be charged with those consequences and those only within the range of prudent forethought. It is not enough that what happens is in the course of nature. It must be in the probable course of nature. Others would have us say that reasonable probability of injury is important, not so much in measuring the extent of liability for wrong, as in determining whether there has been a wrong. *Quo ad* the owner of distant buildings there may be no negligence in acts which involve a breach of duty to one's neighbor. We need not go into these refinements. For our present purposes, it is enough that alike in contract and in tort, contiguity or remoteness in space may determine either the existence or the measure of liability. In doubtful situations a jury must say where the line is to be drawn.

The case comes, therefore, to this: Fire must reach the thing insured, or come within such proximity to it that damage, direct or indirect, is within the compass of reasonable probability. Then only is it the proximate cause because then only may we suppose that it was within

[1]The liability is limited to damage caused to the premises which catch flames directly from the building in which the fire started.

the contemplation of the contract. In last analysis, therefore, it is something in the minds of men, in the will of the contracting parties, and not merely in the physical bond of union between events, which solves, at least for the jurist, this problem of causation. In all this, there is nothing anomalous. Everything in nature is cause and effect by turns. For the physicist, one thing is the cause; for the jurist, another. Even for the jurist, the same cause is alternately proximate and remote as the parties choose to view it. A policy provides that the insurer shall not be liable for damage caused by the explosion of a boiler. The explosion causes a fire. If it were not for the exception in the policy, the fire would be the proximate cause of the loss and the explosion the remote one. By force of the contract, the explosion becomes proximate. A collision occurs at sea, and fire supervenes. The fire may be the proximate cause and the collision the remote one for the purpose of an action on the policy. The collision remains proximate for the purpose of suit against the colliding vessel. There is nothing absolute in the legal estimate of causation. Proximity and remoteness are relative and changing concepts.

It may be said that these are vague tests, but so are most distinctions of degree. On the one hand, you have distances so great that as a matter of law the cause becomes remote; on the other, spaces so short that as a matter of law the cause is proximate. The boat moored to the pier is damaged by fire when dynamite about to be loaded from the piers is ignited by a falling match. Fire destroys the city building when the wall of an adjoining building, weakened by the flames, collapses. Between these extremes, there is a borderland where juries must solve the doubt.

In this case, the facts are not disputed. The inferences to be drawn from them are not doubtful. The damage was not a loss by fire within the meaning of the policy.

The judgment should be reversed, and judgment ordered for the defendant.

HISCOCK, *Ch. J.*, COLLIN, CUDDEBACK, POUND, CRANE and ANDREWS, *JJ.*, concur.

"WHERE THE TEST OF THE PERTINENT IS VAGUE, THERE MUST BE SOME CHECK UPON CALUMNY"

Andrews v. *Gardiner,* 224 N. Y. 440 (1918)

Champe S. Andrews was attorney for the County Medical Society. One Dr. Conrad was suspected of performing abortions and Andrews prepared a trap for him. A woman acting as ally for Andrews visited Dr. Conrad and pretended to need his services. The doctor was arrested in the act of examining her. Indictment followed and Conrad was convicted of the crime of attempted abortion. He served his term in prison.

Upon his release Conrad petitioned to Governor Higgins for his pardon so that he might be restored to citizenship and resume the practice of his profession. The County Medical Society vigorously opposed the petition, charging that Conrad had practiced a business of abortion for many years in New York and New Jersey. The opposing papers were signed by the Medical Society and by Andrews' firm as counsel. The petition for clemency was denied.

Six years later (1911) Conrad renewed his application, this time to Governor Dix. His petition was signed by Asa B. Gardiner, his attorney. The petition contained a bitter assault against Andrews. It charged that the latter had inflamed the medical society through false complaints; that he had framed an innocent man; that he had used his position as counsel for the society to manufacture cases and extort money from the victims; that he was a blackmailer and a depraved scoundrel.

A second document attached to the foregoing petition and signed by Gardiner declared that the petition had been prepared by him and received his heartiest concurrence. It also contained a statement of his friendship for Conrad and his faith in Conrad's innocence.

As a matter of fact, before Gardiner had signed the petition, he had gone over the situation with Conrad, his client. The attack upon Andrews had been deemed necessary in order to break the force of the opposition of the medical society, which was under the control of Andrews. Gardiner had no personal knowledge of the truth of the libelous matter in the petition. He admitted that readily to the Governor.

Although there was no general publication of the petition as it was handed to the governor and no one else, Andrews brought suit for libel against Gardiner. The litigation dragged and there were several trials. The defense of Gardiner was that his statements made as an attorney in a *judicial proceeding* were privileged and he could therefore not be held liable. On the first trial the court agreed with the defendant and Andrews' complaint was dismissed. The Appellate Division reversed the dismissal and ordered a new trial holding that some of the libelous statements were not relevant to the application for the pardon and therefore were not privileged. On the second trial the complaint was again dismissed at the end of Andrews' evidence. Once more the Appellate Division reversed and ordered a new trial holding that it was not necessary to inquire into the character of Andrews until there was denial of the truth of Andrews' statements. Upon the third trial Gardiner and Conrad testified and they furnished the denials. The trial judge held that Gardiner's assault was not relevant to the proceedings before the governor and so was not privileged. Damages, therefore, were to be assessed. The Appellate Division affirmed. The defendant appealed.

Were the statements of Gardiner relevant? If they were relevant were they absolutely privileged? If they were irrelevant would lack of malice excuse the defendant? These questions were answered by Judge Cardozo in his opinion which follows:

CARDOZO, J. * * *

The rule is that counsel are privileged in respect of any statements, oral or written, made in judicial proceedings, and pertinent thereto. In England, the immunity is broader. There the privilege exists whether the statements are relevant or not. With us the condition is added that the privilege will be lost if the libel is irrelevant. But while counsel keep within those bounds, their immunity is absolute. For the moment, we put aside the question whether there is any difference in that respect between statements in judicial proceedings and statements to the governor in a petition for clemency. We view the case provisionally as if the statements had been made in court.

We think it was error to rule that the defamatory charges were not pertinent to the appeal for mercy. There is no room in such matters for any strict or narrow test. Much must be left to the discretion of the advocate. The privilege embraces anything that may possibly be pertinent. We cannot say that the plaintiff's reputation was so plainly foreign to the issue that counsel should have refused to join a client in attacking it. The client took the ground that the plaintiff had planned the prosecution, had used it as a means of winning profit and reputation, and had blocked an earlier petition for pardon by overwhelming his victim under an avalanche of charges. Counsel was assured that those charges were false. If the governor believed them, pardon was almost certain to be refused. They revealed Conrad, not as an offender in one instance, but as a hardened criminal. The argument was that the governor should not believe them. They had been put forward, it was said, by the plaintiff, who was the head and front of the conspiracy; he had hoodwinked the society into adopting them; in fact they were his work; and his character was such that he was unworthy of belief. Those statements may have been false, but they were not impertinent. To appreciate their pertinency, we may ask ourselves what the duty of counsel would have been, had they been true. The answer is not doubtful.

The question remains whether the defendant's privilege is qualified or absolute. The difference is that malice destroys the one and does not change the other. If the statements had been made in court, there is no doubt, since they were pertinent, that the privilege would have been absolute. We assume that the privilege would be the same if the statements had been made before tribunals having attributes similar to those of courts. There is no difference in respect of degree between the privilege of counsel and that of parties and witnesses. They are phases of the same immunity. "Neither party, witness, counsel, jury or judge, can be put to answer, civilly or criminally, for words spoken in office."[1] The courts have refused, however, to apply the rule of absolute privilege to proceedings which, though official and public, are not in substance judicial. In such cases the privilege is the qualified one that attaches to the honest assertion of a right of fulfilment of a duty.

---

[1]Lord Mansfield in *Rex* v. *Skinner*, Lofft Reports (Eng.) 55.

The question, therefore, is whether absolute privilege ought now to be extended to an application for a pardon. It was so extended by the Court of Civil Appeals of Texas in Connellee v. Blanton;[1] but we think erroneously. Such an application is not a proceeding in court, nor one before an officer having "attributes similar" to a court's. It is a petition for mere grace and mercy. It may be made by anyone, and without the convict's knowledge. It grows out of the action of the courts, but it seeks to reverse their action by an appeal to motives and arguments which are not those of jurisprudence. There are no clearly defined issues. There is often a most informal hearing. Sometimes there is argument by counsel. As often, the plea for mercy is made by wife or kin or friends. Whatever privilege belongs to counsel, should belong also to them; the right to plead for clemency is not a monopoly of the bar. Even if counsel speaks, his words are not "spoken in office". Nor are they subject to like restraints. At such a time anything is pertinent that may move the mind to doubt or the heart to charity. It is not necessary that reason be convinced; it is enough that compassion is stirred. The range of possible inquiry gives warning that the privilege should be confined within the limits of good faith. Where the test of the pertinent is so vague, there must be some check upon calumny. While convict and counsel act in good faith, they are immune; the privilege is lost when they defame with malice. There is no license under cover of such an occasion, to publish charges known to be false or put forward for revenge. We are not dealing here with statements made by witnesses required to attend a hearing: there is a distinction between the testimony of witnesses and voluntary complaints. We do not go beyond the case before us. Our ruling is in harmony with the tendency of courts to restrict the scope of absolute privilege in libel. It is in harmony with rulings made where petitions have been submitted to the governor or the legislature for relief against oppression or the redress of other wrongs: the oppression of a harsh or unjust judgment is

[1]Reported in 163 Southwestern Reporter 404.

not to be distinguished in this respect from any other abuse of power. The ruling gives just protection alike to suitor and to counsel, and charges them with liability only when the privilege is abused.

The judgment should be reversed, and a new trial granted.

HISCOCK, *Ch. J.*, COLLIN, CUDDEBACK, POUND and CRANE, *JJ.*, concur; ANDREWS, *J.*, not sitting.

"A BARGAIN MUST EXHIBIT A MEASURABLE DEGREE OF PROVIDENCE IN THE ADJUSTMENT OF REWARD TO SERVICE"

Matter of Reisfeld, 227 N. Y. 137 (1919)

The infant child of Morris and Clara Nacht was run over and killed by a truck operated by the Nathan Manufacturing Company. The law firm of Reisfeld & Cymberg was thereupon retained by the father to bring an action for damages. The retainer signed only by Morris Nacht provided that the compensation of the attorneys was to be fifty per cent. of any recovery either by settlement or verdict.

Their first step in the suit was to arrange for the appointment of an administrator for the estate of the infant and the father was duly appointed and qualified. Thereafter a summons was served upon those who had caused the death of the child. Before anything further was done the action was settled by the parents without the knowledge of the attorneys and $1,000 was paid. This sum the parents divided between themselves. As a matter of law, whatever was recovered did belong to the parents in equal shares.

The attorneys started a proceeding against the Nathan Manufacturing Company in which they sought to charge the company with the sum of $500 on the ground that pursuant to the Judiciary Law the Company destroyed their lien in that amount when it paid the $1,000 directly to their clients.

Upon the hearing in the lower court (Special Term) it was held that the lien was to be restricted to the reasonable value of the services, found to be $150. An appeal was taken and the Appellate Division held that the lien was to be measured by the contract and the law firm was allowed $500. The Nathan Manufacturing Company appealed to the Court of Appeals.

CARDOZO, J. * * *

We think the modification goes too far. The petitioners were dealing with an administrator. The proceeds of the cause of action belonged equally to the father and the mother. Upon his own interest in the cause of action, the father might impose any lien that he pleased. Upon the interest of his wife, he could not lay a charge beyond the limits of the reasonable. There is evidence justifying a finding that the administrator had ignored that restraint upon his power. The Appellate Division reversed upon the law and the determination of the Special Term must stand if it has any basis in the facts. By this contract, the half of any settlement, no matter how made or when, was to go to the attorneys. Whether they did much or little or substantially nothing, their reward was to be the same. The result, if the contract stands, is to give them $500 for some preliminary investigation of the accident and the service of a summons. Had the settlement been larger, they would have a claim for even more. We cannot say that the Special Term was under a duty to approve as reasonable a contract leading to such results. The father is bound, because he assented, and there is no finding of mistake or fraud. The mother is free, because she did not assent, and hence the contract must be reasonable when it imposes a charge upon her right. The fee may be contingent; its size may be increased because of the contingency; but none the less, the bargain must exhibit a measurable degree of providence in the adjustment of reward to service. If such providence is lacking, the administrator will not bind others, even though he binds himself. The test to be applied should be substantially the same as that applied under section 474 of the Judiciary Law to contracts with a guardian.

These principles determine the extent of the lien and the distribution of its burdens. The share of the father in the cause of action and its proceeds is subject to a lien of $250, one-half of the promised fee. If he is liable for more, the remedy is against him personally. He did not charge his share with the whole fee, but only with his proportion of the fee which he attempted to charge upon the cause of action as a whole. The interest of the mother is subject to a lien of $75. That is her proportion of the reasonable value. Those are the amounts which the surrogate or the Supreme Court would have charged against the shares of the parents if application had been made in advance of the completed settlement to adjust the lien of the attorneys. Those, therefore, are the payments that must be made to the petitioners now.

We think it unimportant that the father fixed the terms of the retainer before his appointment as administrator. By prosecuting the action after appointment he approved and continued the arrangement.

The order of the Appellate Division should be modified by reducing the lien to the sum of $325.

HISCOCK, *Ch. J.*, CHASE, HOGAN, POUND and ANDREWS, *JJ.*, concur; MCLAUGHLIN, *J.*, dissents and votes to affirm the order of the Special Term.[1]

[1]No dissenting opinion was written.

"THERE WILL BE NO ASSUMPTION OF A PURPOSE TO VISIT VENIAL FAULTS WITH OPPRESSIVE RETRIBUTION"

Jacobs & Young v. *Kent*, 230 N. Y. 239 (1921)

In June, 1914 Jacobs & Young, Inc., builders, completed the building of a country residence for George E. Kent and the latter then began to occupy the dwelling. The total contract price was over $77,000. of which $3,483.86 remained unpaid.

One of the specifications for the plumbing work provided that all wrought-iron piping was to be of Reading manufacture. As a result of an oversight on the part of the subcontractor, piping other than of Reading manufacture was installed and when in March of the following year Kent learnt of this he refused to pay the unpaid balance without the installation of the Reading piping. This meant the demolition of a good portion of the completed structure at great expense to the builders and the latter left the work untouched.

Upon the trial for the sum due, the builders tried to show that the brands installed, though made by other manufacturers, were the same in quality, in appearance, in market value and in cost as the Reading brand. This evidence was excluded and it is with the propriety of this exclusion that the opinion deals.

CARDOZO, J. * * *

We think the evidence, if admitted, would have supplied some basis for the inference that the defect was insignificant in its relation to the project. The courts never say that one who makes a contract fills the measure of his duty by less than full performance. They do say, however, that an omission, both trivial and innocent, will sometimes be atoned for by allowance of the resulting damage, and will not always be the breach of a condition to be followed by a forfeiture. The distinction is akin to that between dependent and independent promises, or between promises and conditions. Some promises are so plainly independent that they can never by fair construction be conditions of one another. Others are so plainly dependent that they must always be conditions. Others, though dependent and thus conditions when there is departure in point of subtance, will be viewed as independent and collateral when the departure is insignificant. Considerations partly of justice and partly of presumable intention are to tell us whether this or that promise shall be placed in one class or in another. The simple and the uniform will call for different remedies from the multifarious and the intricate. The margin of departure within the range of normal expectation upon a sale of common chattels will vary from the margin to be expected upon a contract for the construction of a mansion or a "skyscraper." There will be harshness sometimes and oppression in the implication of a condition when the thing upon which labor has been expended is incapable of surrender because united to the land, and equity and reason in the implication of a like condition when the subject-matter, if defective, is in shape to be returned. From the conclusion that promises may not be treated as dependent to the extent of their uttermost minutiae without a sacrifice of justice, the progress is a short one to the conclusion that they may not be so treated without a perversion of intention. Intention not otherwise revealed may be presumed to hold in contemplation the reasonable and probable. If something else is in view, it must not be left to implication. There will be no assumption of a purpose to visit venial faults with oppressive retribution.

Those who think more of symmetry and logic in the development of legal rules than of practical adaptation to the attainment of a just result will be troubled by a classification where the lines of division are so wavering and blurred. Something, doubtless, may be said on the score of consistency and certainty in favor of a stricter standard. The courts have balanced such considerations against those of equity and fairness, and found the latter to be the weightier. The decisions in this state commit us to the liberal view, which is making its way, nowadays, in jurisdictions slow to welcome it. Where the line is to be drawn between the important and the trivial cannot be settled by a formula. "In the nature of the case precise boundaries are impossible."[1] The same omission may take

[1]Williston on Contracts, Volume 2, Section 841.

on one aspect or another according to its setting. Substitution of equivalents may not have the same significance in fields of art on the one side and in those of mere utility on the other. Nowhere will change be tolerated, however, if it is so dominant or pervasive as in any real or substantial measure to frustrate the purpose of the contract. There is no general license to install whatever, in the builder's judgment, may be regarded as "just as good." The question is one of degree, to be answered, if there is doubt, by the triers of the facts and, if the inferences are certain, by the judges of the law. We must weigh the purpose to be served, the desire to be gratified, the excuse for deviation from the letter, the cruelty of enforced adherence. Then only can we tell whether literal fulfillment is to be implied by law as a condition. This is not to say that the parties are not free by apt and certain words to effectuate a purpose that performance of every term shall be a condition of recovery. That question is not here. This is merely to say that the law will be slow to impute the purpose, in the silence of the parties, where the significance of the default is grievously out of proportion to the oppression of the forfeiture. The willful transgressor must accept the penalty of his transgression. For him there is no occasion to mitigate the rigor of implied conditions. The transgressor whose default is unintentional and trivial may hope for mercy if he will offer atonement for his wrong.

In the circumstances of this case, we think the measure of the allowance is not the cost of replacement, which would be great, but the difference in value, which would be either nominal or nothing. Some of the exposed sections might perhaps have been replaced at moderate expense. The defendant did not limit his demand to them, but treated the plumbing as a unit to be corrected from cellar to roof. In point of fact, the plaintiff never reached the stage at which evidence of the extent of the allowance became necessary. The trial court had excluded evidence that the defect was unsubstantial, and in view of that ruling there was no occasion for the plaintiff to go farther with an offer of proof. We think, however, that the offer, if it had been made, would not of necessity have been defective because directed to difference in value. It is true that in most cases the cost of replacement is the measure. The owner is entitled to the money which will permit him to complete, unless the cost of completion is grossly and unfairly out of proportion to the good to be attained. When that is true, the measure is the difference in value. Specifications call, let us say, for a foundation built of granite quarried in Vermont. On the completion of the building, the owner learns that through the blunder of a subcontractor part of the foundation has been built of granite of the same quality quarried in New Hampshire. The measure of allowance is not the cost of reconstruction. "There may be omissions of that which could not afterwards be supplied exactly as called for by the contract without taking down the building to its foundations, and at the same time the omission may not affect the value of the building for use or otherwise, except so slightly as to be hardly appreciable."[1] The rule that gives a remedy in cases of substantial performance with compensation for defects of trivial or inappreciable importance has been developed by the courts as an instrument of justice. The measure of the allowance must be shaped to the same end.

The order should be affirmed, and judgment absolute directed in favor of the plaintiff.[2]

---

[1]*Handy* v. *Bliss,* reported in Volume 204 Massachusetts Reports, pages 513, 519.

[2]The court was divided 4 to 3 on this decision. Chief Judge Hiscock, Judges Hogan and Crane agreed with Judge Cardozo. The dissenting opinion of Judge McLaughlin concurred in by Judges Pound and Andrews is interesting for its "symmetry and logic." The pith of the dissent is this:

> "The defendant had a right to contract for what he wanted. He had a right before making payment to get what the contract called for. It is no answer to this suggestion to say that the pipe put in was just as good as that made by the Reading Manufacturing Company, or that the difference in value between such pipe and the pipe made by the Reading Manufacturing Company would be either "nominal or nothing". Defendant contracted for pipe made by the Reading Manufacturing Company. What his reason was for requiring this kind of pipe is of no importance. He wanted that and was entitled to it."

"THE DIFFERENCE IS NO LESS REAL, BECAUSE A DIFFERENCE OF DEGREE"

Heidemann v. *American District Telegraph Co.,* 230 N. Y. 305 (1921)

Carl V. Heidemann was employed as a night watchman by the American District Telegraph Company, whose business it was to protect the property of its subscribers against burglary. It was Heidemann's duty to patrol a certain district in Brooklyn, try the doors of the customers' premises and otherwise keep watch until relieved.

At about 3 o'clock in the morning of September 22nd, 1919 a police officer, patrolling his beat in the section covered by Heidemann, observed some burglars and started in pursuit after them. He fired into the air but they kept running and passed by Heidemann. A second shot struck and killed Heidemann.

His widow claimed an award under the Workmen's Compensation Act. The Appellate Division held that she was not entitled to any relief under the act because death did not arise "out of" the employment even though it did occur "in the course of" the employment. An appeal was taken to the Court of Appeals.

CARDOZO, J. * * *

We reach a different conclusion. Heidemann's duties involved exposure to something more than the ordinary perils of the street, with its collisions, its pitfalls, and the like. For him, in a measure not common to the public generally, there was exposure to the perils that come from contact with the criminal and lawless. Other men, if the ill fortune was theirs to be close to an affray, might, indeed, encounter a like fate. His calling multiplied the chance that he would be near when trouble came, and in multiplying the chance increased exposure to the risk. "He was brought by the conditions of his work 'within the zone of special danger.' "[1]

We are told that the death was unrelated to the employment, because the burglars had not entered a building which the employer was protecting. The incidents of service may not be limited so narrowly. It was not only

[1]*Matter of Leonbruno* v. *Champlain Silk Mills,* reported in Volume 229 New York Reports 470.

in repelling attack upon the property of his employer's patrons that Heidemann had to face the perils of his calling. He faced them at all times while abroad upon his duties. His employment put him upon the street at night, and put him there in search of trouble. If shots were heard, or cries of distress, or the sounds of an affray, others might run to shelter. His duty was to search the cause. The disturbance might have its origin in the homes and stores and offices intrusted to his care. He could not know unless he looked. Crimes of violence flourish under cover of the night and darkness. That was the very reason why Heidemann was there to guard.

The sudden brawl, the "chance medley" are dangers of the streets, confronting with steady menace the men who watch while others sleep. Casual and irregular is the risk of the belated traveler, hurrying to his home. Constant, through long hours, was the risk for Heidemann, charged with a duty to seek, where others were free to shun. The difference is no less real, because a difference of degree. The tourist on his first voyage may go down with the ship, if evil winds arise. None the less, in measuring his risk, we do not class him with the sailor for whom the sea becomes a home. The night, too, has its own hazards, for watchman and for wayfarer. Death came to Heidemann in the performance of his duty, face to face with a peril to which the summons of that duty called him.

The order of the Appellate Division should be reversed.

HOGAN, POUND, CRANE, and ANDREWS, *JJ.*, concur. HISCOCK, *C.J.*, and MCLAUGHLIN, *J.*, dissent.[1]

---

[1]The dissenters did not write any opinion.

"IN A TANGLE OF MISCONCEPTIONS, THE TRUTH MAY HAVE BEEN SMOTHERED"

People v. *Hattie Dixon*, 231 N. Y. 111 (1921)

On November 16, 1918 the dead body of Margaret Hooper, a colored girl of 17, was found in a park in Bronx County lying between two hills of rock. It was obvious that she had been strangled to death as six strands of cord were tightly tied around her neck and her hands were tied behind her back. Where she was discovered a rock as big as a fist was resting on her head as she lay face downward. No signs of a struggle were visible. A hat and a piece of paper with an address was found beside her. The people at this address knew the girl but had no motive for the death.

For about two months before her death Margaret had been living with Hattie Dixon, a negro woman, and her 16 year old son Theodore who were in no way related to her. A friend of Theodore, one Henry Scott, a boy of extremely base sensibilities, was a frequent visitor to the house.

It was soon learned that Hattie had an insurance policy on Margaret's life payable to Hattie, that she had about $100 of Margaret's money under her control and that Margaret was about to leave for Richmond, Virginia, her native town.

Hattie, her son and Scott were jointly indicted for the murder. Hattie was separately tried and Scott was a witness for the people. The first trial resulted in a disagreement and she was tried again. Scott narrated how Hattie had arranged for the murder. The boys were to take Margaret over the 138th Street Bridge and have sexual intercourse with her. Scott was then to hit her on the head with a rock, choke her, turn her on her face, put a rock on her head and put the paper with the address on it in her hat. She was to furnish the cord. For this Scott and Theodore were to receive $200.

The plan, according to Scott, was executed exactly as planned. Margaret agreed to spend the evening with the boys as they had been very friendly. Scott swore that he had had previous sexual relations with Margaret. This story was uncorroborated except by some circumstances which tended to connect Hattie with the crime. Testimony was given by one Cruse, a friend of Scott that he saw Hattie give Scott money on the night of the killing. Also that Hattie had told of the details of Margaret's death, ***especially*** *of the fact that Margaret had been hit on the head with a stone before she could have known it from any one except Scott.* Hattie denied any connection with the plan or the killing. She explained her knowledge of the fact that Margaret had been hit on the head with a stone by stating that when she went to the police station before going to the morgue to identify the body the day after the murder a policeman behind the desk had so told her. This was not contradicted. The jury brought back a verdict of guilty of murder in the first degree against Hattie.

Upon appeal, the conviction was affirmed. Four judges (Hiscock, *C. J.,* Chase, Pound and Andrews) voted for affirmance, declaring through Judge Pound's written opinion that after a careful review of the record of the case, they were unable to find any legal error of substance or justification for the belief that the defendant did not have a fair trial.

Judges Hogan, Cardozo and Crane dissented, the latter two writing opinions. These opinions dealt primarily with an incident which occurred upon the trial. One of the jurors asked "Is there any evidence that Mrs. Dixon was told at the police station on Saturday that the girl had been hit on the head with a stone?" The court told the jury that she was informed in the *detective bureau* that Margaret was dead. "That's all. That is all my minutes show." At this point Hattie Dixon's attorney stated:

> "If your honor please, my understanding is that the juror asked whether there was anything to contradict the testimony of Hattie Dixon to the effect that the man behind the desk at the police station told her that the girl had been found with a rope around her neck and a stone on her head * * *
>
> The Court: Well, I don't remember any such testimony. If there was any such testimony and you invite my attention to it, I will have it read.
>
> Mr. Smith: Yes, sir; I can invite your attention to it".

But the Court failed to give the attorney his chance.

The dissenting opinion of Judge Cardozo follows:

CARDOZO, J. * * * (dissenting)

I think a new trial should be ordered in furtherance of justice. We are slow to reverse upon the facts a verdict of guilt rendered by intelligent jurors with understanding of the evidence. The measure of our faith is in some sense the measure of our duty to see to it that faith is justified. We lose the right to put so much of the responsibility on others than ourselves, to lean so heavily on verdicts, if understanding of the evidence may be poisoned, and the verdict held as truth.

This jury wished to know whether there was any testimony that the defendant had been told at the police station that the girl had been hit on the head with a stone. The prevailing opinion makes it plain how significant in support of innocence such testimony would be. The trial judge said in effect that no such testimony was in the case. He read the testimony of a detective that the defendant was informed that the girl was dead, and, after reading that, he added, "That is all my minutes show." The defendant's counsel then tried to direct attention to other testimony. The defendant herself had testified that the man behind the desk at the station had said that the girl was found lying with a stone on her head. Not only had the defendant so testified, but no one had contradicted her. To this suggestion, the court responded: "Well, I don't remember any such testimony, and if you invite my attention to it, I will have it read." Counsel replied: "Yes, sir; I can invite your attention to that." Before he had a chance to do so, in the midst almost of his protesting words, "Just a moment now, if your honor please," and upon the suggestion of the district attorney that enough had been read, the jury was sent back.

We are told, in belittlement of all this, that when the trial judge said, "I don't remember any such testimony," he was not referring to the defendant's testimony, which counsel was seeking to recall to him. He was referring, it is said, to the existence of something in contradiction of her testimony. The words that follow, in which he invited counsel to direct attention to the testimony if it existed, and counsel's response to the invitation, show this construction to be untenable. The court was not inviting counsel to point out testimony prejudicial to the defendant which the court could not remember. Counsel was not asserting his ability to invite the court's attention to testimony prejudicial to his client which in fact did not exist. Invitation and response both demonstrate that court and counsel were in accord in their interpretation of each other's meaning. The one denied and the other asserted that the defendant had made the statements on the witness stand which counsel wished the court to place before the jury. The fact is that the statements had been made, and that the officer behind the desk, who could have contradicted them if false, was not a witness for the people.

In this tangle of misconceptions, I am fearful that the truth may have been smothered. A jury eager for light upon a point of crucial moment, avows itself in darkness, and for answer is confirmed in error. Ignorance, admitted at the beginning by the request for information, is heightened and deepened by a response intended to dispel it. I think we should do wrong in upholding a verdict thus rooted in uncertainty. We do not help the case by saying that a judge is not required to state his recollection of the facts. The judgment, if it is to be sustained, must pass a deeper scrutiny. It is not enough to show that by the test of error of law there is no flaw in the instructions. What concerns us more profoundly is whether there is justice in the verdict. Justice is not there unless there is also understanding.

My vote is for reversal.

HISCOCK, *C.J.*, and CHASE and ANDREWS, *JJ.*, concur with POUND, *J.*

CRANE, *J.*, reads dissenting opinion, and HOGAN, *J.*, concurs with him.

CARDOZO, *J.*, reads dissenting memorandum, concurring with CRANE, *J.*

Judgment of conviction affirmed.[1]

---

[1]Hattie Dixon was not electrocuted. Her death sentence was commuted to life imprisonment.

"THE DANGERS OF A JURISPRUDENCE OF CONCEPTIONS"

Hynes v. New York Central Railroad Co., 231 N. Y. 229 (1921)

One hot July day in 1916, James Harvey Hynes, a boy of 16, swam with two companions from the Manhattan to the Bronx side of the Harlem River, a navigable stream. The New York Central Railroad had a right of way on the Bronx side and operated its trains at that point by high-tension wires strung on poles and cross-arms.

About 5 years before, a plank had been placed under a rock on the railroad's property and was being used by swimmers as a diving board, without permission of the railroad but at the same time without protest or obstruction. Only 7½ feet of this plank was beyond the line of the railroad's property over the public waterway.

On the day mentioned Hynes climbed on the defendant's property, ran therefrom to the front of this springboard and poised for his dive. At that moment a cross-arm with an electric wire fell from one of the railroad's poles, hit the boy and plunged him to his death in the water. His mother, as administratrix sued the railroad company for damages.

The courts below refused recovery on the ground that Hynes was a trespasser on the land of the railroad and that therefore, the only duty owing him was to abstain from wilfull or wanton injury, an element not here present.[1] The Court of Appeals (three judges, Hiscock, Chase and McLaughlin dissenting), reversed and ordered a new trial in accordance with the following opinion of Judge Cardozo:

CARDOZO, J. * * *

Thus far the courts have held that Hynes at the end of the springboard above the public waters was a trespasser on the defendant's land. They have thought it immaterial that the board itself was a trespass, an encroachment on the public ways. They have thought it of no significance that Hynes would have met the same fate if he had been below the board and not above it. The board, they have said, was annexed to the defendant's bulkhead. By force of such annexation, it was to be reckoned as a fixture,

[1]Under the law of New York the owner of premises owes no duty to a trespasser except to abstain from intentional, reckless and wanton injury.

and thus constructively, if not actually, an extension of the land. The defendant was under a duty to use reasonable care that bathers swimming or standing in the water should not be electrocuted by wires falling from its right of way. But to bathers diving from the springboard, there was no duty, we are told, unless the inquiry was the product of mere willfulness or wantonness—no duty of active vigilance to safeguard the impending structure. Without wrong to them, cross-arms might be left to rot; wires highly charged with electricity might sweep them from their stand and bury them in the subjacent waters. In climbing on the board, they became trespassers and outlaws. The conclusion is defended with much subtlety of reasoning, with much insistence upon its inevitableness as a merely logical deduction. A majority of the court are unable to accept it as the conclusion of the law.

We assume, without deciding, that the springboard was a fixture, a permanent improvement of the defendant's right of way. Much might be said in favor of another view. We do not press the inquiry for we are persuaded that the rights of bathers do not depend upon these nice distinctions. Liability would not be doubtful, we are told, had the boy been diving from a pole, if the pole had been vertical. The diver in such a situation would have been separated from the defendant's freehold. Liability, it is said has been escaped because the pole was horizontal. The plank when projected lengthwise was an extension of the soil. We are to concentrate our gaze on the private ownership of the board. We are to ignore the public ownership of the circumambient spaces of water and of air. Jumping from a boat or a barrel, the boy would have been a bather in the river. Jumping from the end of a springboard, he was no longer, it is said, a bather, but a trespasser on a right of way.

Rights and duties in systems of living are not built upon such quicksands.

Bathers in the Harlem River on the day of this disaster were in the enjoyment of a public highway, entitled to reasonable protection against destruction by the defendant's wires. They did not cease to be bathers entitled to the same protection while they were diving from encroaching objects or engaging in the sports that are common among swimmers. Such acts were not equivalent to an abandonment of the highway, a departure from its proper uses, a withdrawal from the waters, and an entry upon land. A plane of private right had been interposed between the river and the air, but public ownership was unchanged in the space below it and above. The defendant does not deny that it would have owed a duty to this boy if he had been leaning against the springboard with his feet upon the ground. He is said to have forfeited protection as he put his feet upon the plank. Presumably the same result would follow if the plank had been a few inches above the surface of the water instead of a few feet. Duties are thus supposed to arise and to be extinguished in alternate zones or strata. Two boys walking in the country or swimming in a river stop to rest for a moment along the side of the road or the margin of the stream. One of them throws himself beneath the overhanging branches of a tree. The other perches himself on a bough a foot or so above the ground. Both are killed by falling wires. The defendant would have us say that there is a remedy for the representatives of one and none for the representatives of the other. We may be permitted to distrust the logic that leads to such conclusions.

The truth is that every act of Hynes from his first plunge into the river until the moment of his death was in the enjoyment of the public waters, and under cover of the protection which his presence in those waters gave him. The use of the springboard was not an abandonment of his rights as bather. It was a mere by-play, an incident, subordinate and ancillary to the execution of his primary purpose, the enjoyment of the highway. The by-play, the incident, was not the cause of the disaster. Hynes would have gone to his death if he had been below the springboard or beside it. The wires were not stayed by the presence of the plank. They followed the boy in his fall, and overwhelmed him in the waters.

The defendant assumes that the identification of ownership of a fixture with ownership of land is complete in every incident. But there are important elements of difference. Title to the fixtures, unlike title to the land, does not carry with it rights of ownership *usque ad coelum.*[1] There will hardly be denial that a cause of action would have arisen if the wires had fallen on an aeroplane proceeding above the river, though the location of the impact could be identified as the space above the springboard. The most that the defendant can fairly ask is exemption from liability where the use of the fixture is itself the efficient peril. That would be the situation, for example, if the weight of the boy upon the board had caused it to break and thereby throw him into the river. There is no such causal connection here between his position and his injuries. We think there was no moment when he was beyond the pale of the defendant's duty—the duty of care and vigilance in the storage of destructive forces.

This case is a striking instance of the dangers of "a jurisprudence of conceptions", the extension of a maxim or a definition with relentless disregard of consequences to "a dryly logical extreme." The approximate and relative become the definite and absolute. Landowners are not bound to regulate their conduct in contemplation of the presence of travelers upon the adjacent public ways. There are times when there is little trouble in marking off the field of exemption and immunity from that of liability and duty. Here structures and ways are so united and commingled, superimposed upon each other, that the fields are brought together. In such circumstances, there is little help in pursuing general maxims to ultimate conclusions. They have been framed *alio intuitu.* They must be reformulated and readapted to meet exceptional conditions. Rules appropriate to spheres which are conceived of as separate and distinct cannot both be enforced when the spheres become concentric. There must then be readjust-

---

[1]Under the old theory, an owner of land owns everything above his land in a straight line upwards "to the sky". This rule has been somewhat broken by decisions involving the rights of aircraft to fly over the property of others.

ment or collision. In one sense, and that a highly technical and artificial one, the diver at the end of the springboard is an intruder on the adjoining lands. In another sense, and one that realists will accept more readily, he is still on public waters in the exercise of public rights. The law must say whether it will subject him to the rule of the one field or of the other, of this sphere or of that. We think that considerations of analogy, of convenience, of policy, and of justice, exclude him from the field of the defendant's immunity and exemption, and place him in the field of liability and duty.

The judgment of the Appellate Division and that of the Trial Term should be reversed, and a new trial granted.[1]

HOGAN, POUND, and CRANE, *JJ.*, concur.

HISCOCK, *C.J.*, and CHASE and MCLAUGHLIN, *JJ.*, dissent.

---

[1]The first trial of this case took place in 1917 and resulted in a verdict for the plaintiff in the sum of $8,000. The judge set aside the verdict on the ground that the plaintiff was a trespasser and he ordered a new trial. An appeal from this order was taken and the Appellate Division affirmed by a vote of 3 to 2. A second trial was had in 1919. This time the case was dismissed at the end of the plaintiff's evidence. The plaintiff appealed but the Appellate Division affirmed, 4 to 1. It was on appeal from this affirmance that the above opinion was written in the Court of Appeals. Upon the third trial, in 1921, the plaintiff was awarded a verdict in the sum of $10,000, and a judgment was entered for $14,482.62 including interest, costs and disbursements. This time the defendant appealed, but the Appellate Division affirmed unanimously. Thus ended the case.

"SACRIFICE AND SERVICE WILL SEEK NO REWARD SAVE IN CONFORMITY TO LAW"

Barthelmess v. *Cukor,* 231 N. Y. 435 (1921)

The state legislature on April 19, 1920, adopted an amendment to the Military Law which provided that entrance to the United States military and naval service was to give a preference in promotion to employees in the civil service of the state. On May 10 of the same year the enactment was repealed but with the proviso that the repeal was not to impair any rights theretofore accrued thereunder.

While the statute was in effect, a vacancy existed in the grade of police sergeant in the City of New York. One George W. Cook, a soldier in the late war and who had taken a promotion examination while in the military service, was No. 524 on the eligible list. He as well as some other war veterans on the list claimed a preference on April 27, 1920, thirteen days before the statute was repealed. The three highest names on the list were those of men who had had no military or naval record.

The state constitution (Art. 5, Section 9) provided that promotions among civil service employees were to be made according to merit and fitness to be ascertained as far as practicable by competitive examinations. Honorably discharged soldiers and sailors from the army and navy in the *Civil War* were to be given preference.

The Municipal Service Commission in the case we are discussing was about to certify to the police commissioner as eligible for promotion not the names of the three highest on the list but the names of three World War Veterans. The statute of 1920 was thereupon attacked as unconstitutional.

CARDOZO, J. * * *

The preference which it (the Constitution) concedes is restricted to veterans of the Civil War. The statute gives, or attempts to give, a like preference to veterans of other wars. The restriction embodied in the Constitution was no hasty inadvertence. It was established after long debate. The convention was reminded that other wars or other emergencies might come. With this reminder it conceded one preference, and one only. Neither Legislature nor court is competent to add another. The Legislature may, indeed, say, if for reasons not merely arbitrary its judgment shall so dictate, that in one calling or another examination is not practicable. Even when it does not say this, it may say that military or naval service (whether in the Civil War or elsewhere) is something to be counted by the examiners, like experience in other fields, whenever service or experience qualifies for office or employment. Service so considered does not override the results of competitive examination, but enters into the results as a contributory factor. A different situation arises when service controls selection, irrespective of qualifying value. It is the difference between an appraisal of merit, an estimate of fitness, and a preference or bonus. The Constitution circumscribes the field of privilege and favor.

This statute is not an estimate of capacity. It is the expression of a preference. The Legislature has not said that the test of competitive examination is impracticable, no matter what the position, whenever soldiers or sailors are among the candidates for promotion. It has said, in effect, that, even though the test of competitive examination be practicable, soldiers and sailors shall be eligible in advance of others. The statute was so construed at the Appellate Division, and its entire scheme and framework exclude another meaning. Mere entrance into army or navy, and that whether voluntary or involuntary, is made sufficient for preferment. Neither the kind nor the quality nor the duration of the service is important. There is not even the requirement of an honorable discharge. Service for a month or a day as cook or as hostler counts as much as service throughout the war, and the winning of a cross of honor. The preference is not confined to callings or positions where efficiency might be thought to be promoted by the discipline of camp or ship. The clerk or the bookkeeper is subjected to the same tests as the policeman or the fireman. The myriad offices and employments in the civil service of the state and of hundreds of municipal corporations, with all the countless exactions and variations of their duties, are classified as one, and governed by a single rule. If more is needed to disclose the purpose of the statute, we may find it in the repealing act and the proviso there attached. The Legislature in that act has, in effect, construed its own meaning; has exhibited and declared its plan. As the result of the repeal, a small class, and one arbitrarily chosen, has been clothed with special privileges. A line is drawn between veterans who went upon the eligible list before May 10, 1920, the date of the repeal, and the host of other veterans who will go upon the list hereafter. The former receive the preference which the latter are denied. No one will assert that there is any difference between these classes that makes competitive examination less practicable for the one than for the other. If practicable in the future, it was practicable in the past. If impracticable once, it is impracticable now. The discrimination points the motive, and confirms the preference.

In determining the purpose of the lawmakers, we have gone far toward determining their power. Neither expressly nor by implication is the statute a pronouncement that the presence of a soldier among the candidates makes competitive examination futile. Only when the test is futile does the Constitution suffer its rejection. We do not mean to say that if such a pronouncement had been made it would control the judgment of the courts. The duty would still be theirs, while giving efficacy to the statute within the field of legislative discretion, to exercise a supervisory judgment in circumstances of evasion or abuse. It is one thing to say that heroism shall count for more than knowledge in offices and employments where heroism, more than knowledge, is the test and evidence of fitness. It is another thing to say that, in all the humdrum work of life, the daily routine of shop and of office, of counter and of desk, soldier and sailor, irrespective of the extent and quality of their service, must be presumed to have qualifications sufficient to advance them from the bottom to the top. The discipline of army and navy, to justify this exaltation of its significance, must bear something more than a remote or fanciful relation to the duties of office or employment. If that were not so, there might be discrimination without measure. Ex-legislators, and ex-officeholders generally, as well as countless other classes, might plead the discipline of the past as creating a presumption of fitness for the duties of the future. There is no need, however, to dwell upon the consequences of an explicit declaration by the Legislature that the test of competitive examination is impracticable for some candidates though practicable for others, suitors for the same position. The statute makes no such declaration in terms, and the breadth of its extension, its undiscriminating generality, these, and other features, make it impossible that the declaration be implied. In such circumstances, the condemnation of the act is written in the Constitution in words too plain to be misread. Competitive examination must be the test if practicable. Competitive examination has not been found to be impracticable. The Legislature has substituted a preference for a test.

We are referred to precedents in other jurisdictions where there is nothing in the Constitution to regulate the formation of the civil service. They can have little significance for us. They show that preference of veterans is not the denial to others of the equal protection of the law. They do not show the range of preference under the Constitution of New York. Reward for military or naval service may seem to foster love of country. It may be an expression of gratitude and patriotism. We have said by our Constitution that valor is not to be rewarded, nor patriotism stimulated, unless in submission to the restraints which we have imposed upon the choice of public servants. The mandate of the people has excluded sentiments and motives that may guide the judgment of the lawmakers in jurisdictions where discretion is unfettered. It has subordinated flexibility and discretion to regularity and system.

The argument is made, however, that the Constitution is satisfied if candidates must pass an examination before their names are entered on the list, and that if only this is done the Legislature is at liberty to shuffle the places as it will. Preferences or favored classes, it is said, may be created without limit if confined to those who pass. In that view, the eligible list in truth consists of two lists, one primary and the other secondary, one general and the other special. Competition must regulate the one, but favor may constitute the other. We do not so read the simple words in which the Constitution phrases its command. The test is competitive examination. Competition is useless if favor may reverse the verdict. Eligiblity counts for little if grades of eligibility may be established without restriction. Sublists may then be made up of one political party or another. The three lowest names upon the list may be directed to be certified in advance of the three highest. The victory may go to one class, and the prizes to another. We construed the civil service section of the Constitution in the light of another section (article 10, Sec. 2) which says that local officers shall be chosen by the local authorities. We said that this implied some privilege of selection on the part of the public officer who was to exercise the appointing power. The Legislature might require him to make a choice among the three highest on the list, but could not exclude judgment altogether by restricting him to the one that was the highest of the three. This statute has another aim. It is not addressed exclusively to the power that appoints. It is addressed to the power that certifies the names of those eligible for appointment. It does not enlarge the range of selection available to the police commissioner in the exercise of his power to promote. It circumscribes the list of those whom the examining officers are to return to him as eligible for promotion. This is not to preserve the power of the local authorities to appoint the local officers. It is to set at naught the test of competitive examination while imposing new restrictions upon freedom of appointment. The command of the Constitution is not obeyed by such devices. The proviso that permits standing to be inverted in favor of veterans of the Civil War is significant of the prohibition that would have attached if the proviso had been omitted. Competition, as far as practicable, is the test for one list as for another, for sublist as for principal.

The members of the court are not oblivious of the debt of gratitude that is due to the soldiers and sailors of the nation for sacrifice and service. If discharge of that debt requires a preference in the civil service, the people can so declare. An amendment of the Constitution extending to veterans of all wars the privilege now enjoyed by veterans of the Civil War has been proposed by concurrent resolution of the Legislature, and at the coming election will go before the voters. This statute as it now stands is an attempt by imperfect and hasty legislation to anticipate the process of orderly amendment. If sustained, it would benefit, not veterans generally, but a small and arbitrary number. Those who went upon the list before May 10, 1920, and whose rights had then accrued, would be entrenched behind a preference in which their own comrades in arms, going upon the list thereafter, would be incompetent to share. At the same time, in return for this dubious and partial gain, there would have been conceded to the Legislature a power of discrimination that might undermine the civil service by injecting beneath its foundations an ever-widening stream of favor. Sacrifice and service will seek no reward save in conformity to law, and none other can be theirs.

The court is constrained to adjudge that chapter 282 of the statutes of 1920 ignores the limitations of the Constitution, and that the preference which it concedes is void.[1]

HISCOCK, *C.J.*, and HOGAN, POUND, CRANE and ANDREWS, *JJ.*, concur.

[1]By an amendment approved by the people at the 1925 general election, the Constitution (Article 5, section 6) provides that honorably discharged soldiers, sailors, marines and nurses disabled in the performance of duty in any war, are to be entitled to preference in civil service appointment or promotion.

"THE PARENT DOES NOT LISTEN UNMOVED TO THE NECESSITIES OF HER SONS WHO HAVE FOUGHT IN HER DEFENSE"

People v. *Westchester County National Bank*, 231 N. Y. 465 (1921)

An Act of the Legislature of 1920 provided for the issue of $45,000,000 of bonds by the state the proceeds of which were to be paid into the state treasury and expended only for a bonus to persons who were honorably discharged after having served in the military or naval service during the World War for a period longer than two months and who were both at the time they entered service and at the time the act became effective, residents of New York. It was further required that the act was to be approved by the electorate before taking effect. It was approved by a vote of 1,454,940 against 673,292.

The Westchester County National Bank was the successful bidder for $25,000 of bonds issued under the authority of this act. It later refused to accept them and justified its refusal by the assertion that the act was unconstitutional. The Appellate Division held the statute to be constitutional. On appeal, the Court of Appeals reversed and held the statute unconstitutional. The majority opinion by Judge Andrews pointed out that the bonus was not merely for the wounded but was to include even those who had had safe clerical jobs. He warned that the sum of $45,000,000 would prove inadequate and there might be no limit to the indebtedness with which the state would be burdened.

Arguing the legal questions, the opinion admitted that the act tended to serve a public purpose, for the payment of a bonus showing the gratitude of the people for those who had made sacrifices for it, is an incitement to patriotism and an encouragement to defend the country in future conflicts. Nevertheless, argued Judge Andrews, the statute is unconstitutional. It runs counter to Section 1 of Article 7 of the State Constitution which declares "The credit of the state shall not in any manner be given or loaned to or in the aid of any individual, association or corporation," as well as to Section 9, Article 8 which reads "Neither the credit nor the money of the state shall be given or loaned to or in aid of * * * any private undertaking."

It is true enough, wrote Judge Andrews, that it has been held that a payment to an individual is not a gift if it be made in recognition of a claim, moral or equitable, which he may have against the state. But all such have been cases where the state has received benefits or where injuries have been suffered in its service. The soldiers were not servants of the state. They did not serve under its authority.

Two dissenting opinions were written, one by Judge Pound who very briefly argued that since such payment of a bonus is for a public purpose the State may borrow money for that purpose, "so long as no association, corporation or private undertaking, acting as a quasi-state agency, receives the money."

The other dissenting opinion, by Judge Cardozo, reads as follows:

CARDOZO, J. (dissenting)

"The credit of the state shall not in any manner be given or loaned to or in aid of any individual, association or corporation." Constitution of New York, art. 7, Sec. 1. The purpose of prohibition is revealed in its history. The purpose was to put an end to the use of the credit of the state in fostering the growth of private enterprise and business. That is the mischief which gives understanding of the remedy. I do not mean that the prohibition is to be limited to the particular evil that inspired it. It *is* limited, however, to evils of a kindred nature. The credit of the state may not be pledged in aid of an individual who has no claim in justice or morals to relief or compensation. It *may* be pledged in recognition of an honorable obligation to effect a proportionate and equitable distribution of the burdens of public service. Payments so made or promised are in one sense gifts, for they are the voluntary assumption of liabilities not theretofore imposed by law. They are not gifts, however, in the sense of the prohibition under discussion, for their animating purpose is not benefaction, but requital.

We are told that requital, if due at all, is due, not from the state, but from the nation, which summoned the host to service. I find myself unable to define by bounds so artificial the claims of equity and honor. The service that preserved the life and safety of the nation preserved at the same time the life and safety of the states. If something is still due beyond the letter of the bond, state, as well as nation, will not rest till justice has been done. Neither can silence conscience by referring the claimant to the other. I am not convinced by the argument that reparation, if due from our Legislature to residents of New York, is due in equal measure to residents of Maine and California. Each state may fairly be left to take care of its own. Most have already done so. One finds it hard to believe that they have, all of them, been meddling in matters not of their concern. It is the state rather than the nation—possessing as the state does the residuary powers of government—which in our federal system is to be viewed as *parens patriae.* The parent does not listen unmoved to the necessities of her sons who have fought in her defense.

I pass, then, to the question whether the Legislature might reasonably hold that men who in greatly serving had also greatly suffered gained thereby a claim to reparation for their suffering. I mean, of course, a claim in justice or equity or morals or honor. Great achievement and great sacrifice have been meagerly rewarded. The perils of battle, the hardships of camp and trench, may be poorly paid at any price; few will assert that they are recompensed at the rate of $1 a day. Even for those who did not reach the firing line, there were the pangs of separation from home and kindred, the anxieties and the strain of a new and hazardous adventure. Legislature and people, beneficiaries of this devotion, have heard the call of a moral duty to mitigate the disparity between suffering and requital. But the catalogue of suffering does not end with pain of mind and body. There was money loss as well, or so at least a Legislature, looking at average conditions, might not unreasonably believe. Its judgment in such matters must prevail unless wholly arbitrary and baseless. Labor in the market was paid with no such modest stipend as these men received for labor in submarine and trench. Even with food and housing added to the stipend, we cannot say that there is mere caprice in a finding of the lawmakers that compensation was inadequate. Often the stipend was sent home for the benefit of relatives who, if not wholly dependent on the absent one, had need of something more if they were to be maintained in his absence according to the standards of the past. Lost also were indefinite opportunities for profit and advancement. While soldiers and sailors risked their lives abroad, wages abnormally high were the reward of those who stayed behind. The losses did not end with peace. Men who had left their callings overnight, breaking up the old relations of business and employment, found on their return that business must be rebuilt, and employment sought anew. Then, too, the shock and strain provoked a period of reaction, in which idleness was inevitable. New losses must be suffered till work could be resumed, and life adjusted to the ways of peace. It is significant, I think, that the statute limits the bonus to soldiers and sailors of the lower grades; *i.e.*, to those whose pay was smallest, and who are most in need of aid. Of these, some may bear a loss more easily than others, but for many, if not for all, there will be loss in some degree. Legislation in such matters must take note of average conditions. The problem is too complex, the difficulty of proof too great, for investigation of the individual case, and adjustment of reward accordingly. We take judicial notice, too, that since the beginnings of our history a sense of the moral obligation to give aid to the returning soldier has been felt and acted on by government. The call of these and kindred equities has been heard and answered in the past. Are the equities so feeble, is their summons so plainly an illusion, that we may answer them no more?

We have held that the Legislature is still free, with all the restrictions imposed by the Constitution upon gifts of money or of credit, to assume liability in law when liability may be found in equity or honor. Equity and honor are the same as in olden days. The Constitution does not define them, nor seek to circumscribe their content. An employee in a state hospital was injured by the assault of a patient confided to his care.[1] A statute after the event declared that upon a finding by the Court of Claims

[1] *Munro* v. *State*, reported in Volume 223 New York Reports 208.

that the injuries "were so sustained" damages therefor should "constitute a legal and valid claim against the state." We held that the right to reparation was so rooted in equity and fairness that the Legislature was free to recognize it by assuming liability. We did not put our decision, as the Legislature did not base the statute, upon any theory of negligence in the conduct of the enterprise. The claimant has been injured by an "unforeseen accident" as the result of service to the state, and that was thought enough, though the state was not at fault. If a hospital attendant, serving in times of peace, has a moral claim to be indemnified against the risks of an employment which he was free to accept or to reject, the soldier injured in a war has at least an equal equity. I cannot doubt that under Munro v. State of New York, supra, a bonus or pension to the maimed or incapacitated would be the recognition and fulfillment of a moral obligation, and not a largess or donation, the dole of charity or benevolence. The conscience of the state would listen with little patience to the argument that wounded and disabled had no claim upon its bounty because wounds and disabilities were suffered in the service of the nation. This the prevailing opinion apparently concedes, though I cannot reconcile the concession with the logic of its theorem. Relief in such circumstances would not rest upon the narrow ground that the injured or disabled might be in danger of becoming paupers. It would be due. If so, the Legislature should read the promptings of morality, though all were self-supporting. Aid to men thus stricken is not benevolence to the poor. It is an attempt, however feeble, with sacrifice outweighing payment, to set the balance true.

If the account may be recast by adjusting recompense to suffering when the disparity disturbs the conscience, it is for the Legislature to declare when conscience is disturbed. Not this form of sacrifice or that to the exclusion of another, but merely sacrifice unrequited, is the basis of its power. I cannot say that there is an equity in unrequited wounds, and none in other suffering of body or of mind. The grip is, indeed, weaker, and yet it can be felt.

I cannot say, if there is an equity in suffering of body or of mind, that there is none in economic suffering, the loss of money or money's worth. Few would doubt this if the soldiers had received no pay at all. Pay so inadequate as to be almost nominal does not greatly change the balance. A. has saved the life of B., or of B.'s child, and in so doing has suffered loss. Many a man in B.'s case would feel that the loss should be repaired. We deal here with a like service, not of one man, but of an army. "That which would have been merely a charity or a gift is not such by reason of the service given, the consideration rendered, the honorable obligation incurred."[1] We err when we envisage the soldier's relation to the government in the category of contract. Contract in the true sense there is none, but service conscripted, rewarded at its will. That is why payment of the wage does not always satisfy the conscience that there has been payment of the debt. The Constitution does not silence these mutterings of spiritual disquiet when sacrifice unevenly distributed oppresses those who profit by it with the sense of a burden undischarged. Our ruling in Matter of Borup,[2] was founded in that truth. We held that it was in the power of the Legislature by a retroactive statute to assume liability to a landowner injured by a change of grade, though at the time of the change the impairment of value was damage without wrong. Under the law before the statute, the loss was one of the incidents of life in organized society. It was part of the price which the citizen must pay for the benefits of government. We held that the Legislature might readjust the incidence of the burden, might establish a more equitable distribution between the individual and the public, through the voluntary acceptance of liability for a loss which was without a remedy when suffered. I cannot yield to an appraisal of values that would find the basis of an equity there, and a mere cobweb, an illusion, here. In neither case is there legal liability unless the Legislature assumes one. In each there is an unequal

---

[1] *Trustees of Exempt Firemen's Benev. Fund* v. *Roome,* reported in Volume 93 New York Reports 326.

[2] Reported in Volume 182 New York Reports 222.

pressure of the burdens and the power of government upon one man and upon others. The readjustment of these burdens along the lines of equality and equity is a legitimate function of the state as long as justice to its citizens remains its chief concern.

I am led, therefore, to the conclusion that the payment of this bonus, as money earned, but not received, is not wholly without support in something which the Legislature might estimate as a moral or honorary obligation. If there is any reasonable basis for such an estimate, for such a conception of equity and justice, the courts must yield to the judgment of the Legislature that it is worthy of recognition. The question is then one that the Legislature must determine for itself. Some may think the service so far beyond requital that the attempt should be surrendered for mere futility. Others may think that high and unselfish sacrifice is cheapened when repaid in money. Others again may think that for the sake of the economic or financial stability of the commonwealth losses already suffered should be left to lie where they have fallen. These are questions of political or legislative expediency. I make no attempt to answer them. I am not to substitute my judgment for the judgment of the lawmakers. The act, moreover, was either valid or invalid at the date of its enactment. Its validity cannot turn upon the hope or expectation that aid, at some indefinite period hereafter, may be granted by the nation. Impressive is the list of like statutes to be found in other states (California, Connecticut, Maine, Massachusetts, Michigan, Minnesota, Montana, Nevada, New Jersey, New Hampshire, North Dakota, Oregon, Rhode Island, South Dakota, Vermont, Washington, Wisconsin, and Wyoming), as well as in foreign countries (Italy, France, Great Britain, Canada, and Australia). Impressive, too, is the vote in favor of our own statute, when submitted to the electors. I cannot bring myself to believe that all these concurring acts were unmoved by any conception of honor or of duty, or that the conception, if held, had no basis in reality. If there be the possibility of conflicting motives, those that vitiate are to be rejected, and those that validate presumed.

We are warned that the recognition of this equity may be followed by the recognition of others still weaker and more rarefied. All sorts of hypothetical situations are suggested in the briefs of counsel, and held before us *in terrorem*. I am not swerved by these forebodings. I do not know the equity that is incapable of being reduced to an absurdity when extended by some process of analogy to varying conditions. Here, as often in the law, the difference between right and wrong is a difference of degree. Most of these imaginary problems will never in fact arise. They assume a Legislature and an electorate without responsibility or conscience. The public credit is not pledged in these cases by the Legislature alone. The pledge is invalid unless ratified by the vote of the electors. Const. art. 7, Sec. 4. I find little opportunity here for the charlatan or the cheat. Something more than a bizarre and shadowy pretense, some service stirring the deep currents of public gratitude and loyalty, will be needed before these protecting dykes and dams are overcome and flooded. But the existence of a power is not refuted by demonstrating the opportunity for its abuse. The abuse must be dealt with when it arises. We may not nullify a statute from mere mistrust of the capacity of Legislature and people to use their power wisely. I am persuaded that hundreds of thousands of earnest men and women believe that justice and equity demand the payment of this bonus. They may be wrong. I do not know. It is enough that I cannot characterize their belief as a vagary of the mind, an idle dream or phantasy, an irrational pretense.

There is a difference, not to be ignored, between profit and indemnity. If the soldiers had not suffered, and the sole purpose of the bonus were to reward them above others, the reward might be said to have no basis except gratitude, a free offering of thanksgiving, untouched by the admixture of any sentiment of justice. Their service has been coupled with sacrifice, and from the union of the two there is born the equity that prompts to reparation.

The judgment should be affirmed with costs.

"THE LAW DOES NOT DISCRIMINATE BETWEEN THE RESCUER OBLIVIOUS OF HIS PERIL AND THE ONE WHO COUNTS THE COST"

Wagner v. *International Railway*, 232 N. Y. 176 (1922)

The International Railway Company operated an electric railway between Buffalo and Niagara Falls. At one point there was a sharp turn to the left over a bridge which was about 158 feet long from one abutment to the other. Early one evening Arthur Wagner and his cousin Herbert Wagner boarded a car at a station situated before the aforementioned bridge. Other passengers entering the car at the same time so filled it that Arthur and Herbert were compelled to stand near the edge of the car's platform. Though this platform was provided with doors, the conductor did not close them.

The car approached the curve before the bridge without slackening its speed, then about 8 miles an hour. There was a violent lurch just as the car reached the bridge and Herbert was thrown out of the car. The cry of "Man overboard" was raised but the car continued to the end of an incline past the end of the bridge before it stopped. Arthur immediately jumped off the car and walked along the trestle until he arrived at the spot where he thought he would find his cousin's body. He groped around and found his cousin's hat. As he continued his search he missed his footing and fell. Suit was commenced by Arthur Wagner against the railway company for the injuries sustained.

Upon the trial Arthur Wagner claimed that before he started to walk the trestle, he had been invited to do so by the conductor who followed with a lantern. This was denied by the conductor. In the court's charge to the jury, he stated that the fact that the car company was negligent toward Herbert did not charge it with liability for injuries suffered by the plaintiff Arthur unless it actually believed that the conductor asked Arthur to go with him and followed him with a lantern. The jury apparently did not believe Arthur in his assertion about the conductor and accordingly brought in a verdict for the car company.

Arthur Wagner appealed claiming that the limitation set out by the court was erroneous and that the case did not hinge upon the conductor's invitation. When the Appellate Division affirmed the judgment, Wagner appealed to the Court of Appeals.

CARDOZO, J. * * *

Danger invites rescue. The cry of distress is the summons to relief. The law does not ignore these reactions of the mind in tracing conduct to its consequences. It recognizes them as normal. It places their effects within the range of the natural and probable. The wrong that imperils life is a wrong to the imperiled victim; it is a wrong also to his rescuer. The state that leaves an opening in a bridge is liable to the child that falls into the stream, but liable also to the parent who plunges to its aid. The railroad company whose train approaches without signal is a wrongdoer toward the traveler surprised between the rails, but a wrongdoer also to the bystander who drags him from the path. The rule is the same in other jurisdictions. The risk of rescue, if only it be not wanton, is born of the occasion. The emergency begets the man. The wrongdoer may not have foreseen the coming of a deliverer. He is accountable as if he had.

The defendant says that we must stop, in following the chain of causes, when action ceases to be "instinctive." By this is meant, it seems, that rescue is at the peril of the rescuer, unless spontaneous and immediate. If there has been time to deliberate, if impulse has given way to judgment, one cause, it is said, has spent its force, and another has intervened. In this case, the plaintiff walked more than 400 feet in going to Herbert's aid. He had time to reflect and weigh; impulse had been followed by choice; and choice, in the defendant's view, intercepts and breaks the sequence. We find no warrant for thus shortening the chain of jural causes. We may assume, though we are not required to decide, that peril and rescue must be in substance one transaction; that the sight of the one must have aroused the impulse to the other; in short, that there must be unbroken continuity between the commission of the wrong and the effort to avert its consequences. If all this be assumed, the defendant is not aided. Continuity in such circumstances is not broken by the exercise of volition. So sweeping an exception, if recognized, would leave little of the rule. "The human mind," as we have said,[1] "acts with celerity which it is sometimes impossible to measure." The law does not discriminate between the rescuer oblivious of peril and the one who counts the cost. It is enough that the act, whether impulsive or deliberate, is the child of the occasion.

The defendant finds another obstacle, however, in the futility of the plaintiff's sacrifice. He should have gone, it is said, below the trestle with the others; he should have known, in view of the overhang of the cars, that the body would not be found above; his conduct was not responsive to the call of the emergency; it was a wanton exposure to a danger that was useless. We think the quality of his acts in the situation that confronted him was to be determined by the jury. Certainly he believed that good would come of his search upon the bridge. He was not going there to view the landscape. The law cannot say of his belief that a reasonable man would have been unable to share it. He could not know the precise point at which his cousin had fallen from the car. If the fall was from the bridge, there was no reason why the body, caught by some projection, might not be hanging on high, athwart the tie rods or the beams. Certainly no such reason was then apparent to the plaintiff, or so a jury might have found. Indeed, his judgment was confirmed by the finding of the hat. There was little time for delay, if the facts were as he states them. Another car was due, and the body, if not removed, might be ground beneath the wheels. The plaintiff had to choose at once, in agitation and with imperfect knowledge. He had seen his kinsman and companion thrown out into the darkness. Rescue could not charge the company with liability if rescue was condemned by reason. "Errors of judgment," however, would not count against him if they resulted "from the excitement and confusion of the moment."[2] The reason that was exacted of him was not the reason of the morrow. It was reason fitted and proportioned to the time and the event.

---

[1]*People* v. *Majone,* reported in Volume 91 New York Reports 211, 212.

[2]*Corbin* v. *Philadelphia,* reported in Volume 195 Pennsylvania Reports 461.

Whether Herbert Wagner's fall was due to the defendant's negligence, and whether plaintiff, in going to the rescue, as he did, was foolhardy or reasonable in the light of the emergency confronting him, were questions for the jury.

The judgment of the Appellate Division and that of the Trial Term should be reversed, and a new trial granted.

HISCOCK, *C. J.*, and HOGAN, POUND, MCLAUGHLIN, CRANE, and ANDREWS, *JJ.*, concur.

"THE PASSENGER WHO OMITS TO READ TAKES THE RISK OF THE OMISSION"

Murray v. *Cunard S. S. Co.,* 235 N. Y. 162 (1923)

Luke J. Murray, a second cabin passenger on the Cunard steamship Mauretania, fell upon the deck of the ship and broke his kneecap. His statement was that he caught his foot in a rope attached to a canvas curtain which was blown by the wind because it had been left unfastened and though the steamship company denied that the event occurred in that manner and claimed that he had fallen while jumping over ropes which separated the deck for one class of passengers from the deck of another, the court decided the case on the assumption that Murray's version was the true one.

The Mauretania reached Southampton on May 2, 1920, four days after the above accident. Murray went ashore with the aid of a crutch and was taken by train to London. From London he went to Dublin and he spent 6 weeks in a hospital. After leaving the hospital trouble developed in his knee and he was again confined to bed, this time for several months. Finally an operation was performed and several pieces of bone removed from his knee. His final discharge from the hospital was in November. He sailed for New York in January and the action against the Cunard Steamship Company was begun in February, 1921, about 10 months after the accident.

The steamship company asserted that the rights of the parties were controlled by the terms of the ticket issued to him before the departure of the vessel. This ticket was described in large type as a "cabin passage contract ticket" and declared also in large type that "This contract ticket is issued by the company and accepted by the passenger on the following terms and conditions." One of the terms that followed was that no action was to be maintained for personal injury to the passenger unless the action was begun within one year after the termination of the voyage and written notice of the claim was delivered to the company within 40 days after debarkation. The first requirement was followed but no written claim had been delivered within 40 days.

Murray had judgment in the courts below but the steamship company appealed to the Court of Appeals.

CARDOZO, J. * * *

We assume, without intending to decide, that the plaintiff's narrative, if accepted, would sustain a finding by the jury that the defendant had been negligent. We assume also that a contract exonerating the defendant altogether from liability for negligent injury to a passenger would be ineffective and void because opposed to public policy. Exoneration, however, is not to be confused with regulation. "A stipulation for written notice within a reasonable time stands on a different footing, and of this there is no doubt." (Gooch v. Oregon Short Line Ry. Co.).[1] There the contract called for notice within 30 days. The plaintiff was in a hospital for about 30 days under the care of a doctor employed by the defendant, but was not disabled from giving the notice. The court enforced the contract. "Very probably," it was said, "an exception might be implied if the accident made notice within the time impracticable". There is no evidence that this plaintiff was physically or mentally unable to give notice of the injury. Even if we were to assume in his favor that there was incapacity for a time, with a resulting extension of the period for notice, he did not make a move within 40 days thereafter. Limitations of this kind have their justification in the need of some safeguard to protect the carrier against fraud. Passengers on steamships scatter in all directions when the voyage is at an end. If claims may be presented at any time within the term of years permitted by the statute of limitations, the opportunity for investigation will often be lost beyond recall. "The practice of fraud is too common to be ignored."[2]

The plaintiff argues that he is not bound by the conditions of the ticket because he did not read them. The omission does not help his case. The law is settled in this state that a ticket in this form, issued by a steamship company for a voyage across the ocean, is more than a mere token or voucher. It is a contract, creating the obligation and defining the terms of carriage. The ruling is in accord with judgments in other jurisdictions. This is not a case of a mere notice on the back of a ticket, separate either in substance or in form from the body of

---

[1]Reported in Volume 258 United States Supreme Court Reports 22.
[2]*Gooch* v. *Oregon Short Line Ry. Co., supra.*

the contract. Here the condition is wrought into the issue, the two inseparably integrated. This ticket, to the most casual observer, is as plainly a contract, burdened with all kinds of conditions, as if it were a bill of lading or a policy of insurance. "No one who could read could glance at it without seeing that it undertook * * * to prescribe the particulars which should govern the conduct of the parties until the passenger reached the port of destination." In such circumstances, the act of acceptance gives rise to an implication of assent. The passenger who omits to read takes the risk of the omission.

The plaintiff is not helped by his surrender of the ticket when he went aboard the ship, after he had then held it several days with ample time to read it. A contract valid and reasonable in its inception does not become invalid and unreasonable thereafter because the passenger who has assented is unable, when the voyage is over, to recall the terms of the assent. If some aid to memory is required, his business is to make for himself a note of the conditions, or to procure from the carrier a copy, which doubtless would be given for the asking. There is little ground for the belief that this plaintiff would have examined his ticket within the period of 40 days, though he had taken it ashore on the termination of the voyage. If we accept his own testimony, he paid no heed to the conditions, and the thought of any need to refer to them did not enter his mind. He had abundant opportunity both on the ship and later to inquire about the terms of carriage, if he supposed them to be important. We should indulge in the merest speculation if we were to say that the surrender of the ticket was the cause of the omission of the notice. Whether it was or not, his contract remained the same. He is charged as if he had signed. The obligation of one who signs is not defeated by proof that the document has been lost or that its contents have been forgotten.

Some argument is made that the limitation does not apply where the injury is aggravated after the date of debarkation, since the suffering thereby occasioned is part of the damage which the passenger may claim. A like point was made in Gooch v. Oregon Short Line Ry. Co., supra, as will appear from an inspection of the record, but the court did not sustain it. The notice was to be warning to the carrier of an event that would expose it to a claim of liability, irrespective of the amount.

The judgment of the Appellate Division and that of the Trial Term should be reversed, and the complaint dismissed.

HISCOCK, *C.J.*, and POUND, MCLAUGHLIN, and CRANE, *JJ.*, concur. HOGAN, *J.*, not voting. ANDREWS, *J.*, absent.

"THE TESTS TO BE APPLIED ARE THOSE OF COMMON UNDERSTANDING AS REVEALED IN COMMON SPEECH"

Connelly v. *Hunt Furniture Co.*, 240 N. Y. 83 (1925)

Harry Connelly was employed by an undertaker as an embalmer's helper. One day he was required to handle a corpse which because of a leg amputation had become decayed and full of gangrenous matter. Some of this poison entered a little cut in his hand and spread to his neck. When he scratched a pimple on his neck with the infected finger, general blood poisoning set in and he soon died.

His dependent mother Martha Connelly sought an award under the Workmen's Compensation Act. The claim was opposed on the ground the injury spoken of in the statute was only "an accidental injury arising out of and in the course of employment and such disease or infection as may naturally and unavoidably result therefrom."

Judge Cardozo wrote the court's opinion allowing the award, Judges Pound, Crane and Lehman concurring. Three judges (Hiscock, C. J., McLaughlin and Andrews) dissented on the ground that the injury causing the disease was not accidental, since the contact made was intended to be made and did not involve an occurrence which was sudden or unexpected. Was the contact with the corpse in and of itself an injury?

The opinion of Judge Cardozo follows:

CARDOZO, J. * * *

A trifling scratch was turned into a deadly wound by contact with a poisonous substance. We think the injection of the poison was itself an accidental injury within the meaning of the statute. More than this, the contact had its occasion in the performance of the servant's duties. There was thus not merely an accident, but one due to the employment. We attempt no scientifically exact discrimination between accident and disease, or between disease and injury. None perhaps is possible, for the two concepts are not always exclusive, the one of the other, but often overlap. The tests to be applied are those of common understanding as revealed in common speech.

We have little doubt that common understanding would envisage this mishap as an accident, and that common speech would so describe it. Germs may indeed be inhaled through the nose or mouth, or absorbed into the system through normal channels of entry. In such cases their inroads will seldom, if ever, be assignable to a determinate or single act, identified in space or time. For this as well as for the reason that the absorption is incidental to a bodily process both natural and normal, their action presents itself to the mind as a disease and not an accident. Our mental attitude is different when the channel of infection is abnormal or traumatic, a lesion or a cut. If these become dangerous or deadly by contact with infected matter, we think and speak of what has happened as something catastrophic or extraordinary, a mishap or an accident, though very likely a disease also. "A common-sense appraisement of everyday forms of speech and modes of thought must tell us when to stop."[1]

If Connelly's death was the outcome of an accident, as we think indisputably it was, only a strained and artificial terminology would refuse to identify the accident with the pernicious contact and its incidents, and confine that description to the scratch or the abrasion, which had an origin unknown. On the contrary, when a scratch or abrasion is of itself trivial or innocent, the average thought, if driven to a choice between the successive phases of the casualty, would find the larger measure of misadventure in the poisonous infection. The choice, however, is one that is needless and misleading. The whole group of events, beginning with the cut and ending with death, was an accident, not in one of its phases, but in all of them. If any of those phases had its origin in causes engendered by the employment, the act supplies a remedy.

We think this reading of the statute is well supported by authority. The earlier cases on the subject are decisions by the House of Lords. Brintons, Ltd. v. Turvey,[2] held that there was an "injury by accident" where a bacillus passed from wool to the eye of a workman, and infected him with anthrax. That judgment, in some of its aspects, was

---

[1]*Bird* v. *St. Paul F. & M. Ins. Co.,* reported in Volume 224 New York Reports 47, 51. See also *supra,* page 75.

[2](1905) Appeals Cases 230.

quoted with approval by this court in Lewis v. Ocean Accident & G. Corp.,[1] where the controversy had to do, however, not with a claim under the statute, but with a policy of insurance. In our own court, Horrigan v. Post Standard Co.[2] was a case where a workman who had cut one of his fingers was poisoned through an infection suffered while cleaning out a urinal, and Hart v. Wilson & Co.,[3] a case where a puller of wool, suffering from eczema of the hands, became a sufferer from tetanus as the result of germs which entered the system through the cracks in his skin.

Matter of Jeffreyes v. Sager Co.[4] is cited to the contrary, but it differs in important features. There the employee of a photographer, who dipped her hand in a developing solution many times a day for more than a week, was poisoned and lost a finger through the gradual action of the chemicals. The claim was disallowed. The contacts were voluntary, and the process of absorption was through channels of entry both natural and normal. More important, however, "the injuries resulted from no occurrence which is referable to any particular moment of time which is definite." The ensuing injuries were thought to be an occupational disease.

We make little progress when, viewing infection as an isolated concept, and ignoring its channels of attack or the manner of its coming, we say, upon the authority of science, that infection is a disease. It may be this, and yet an accident, too. Sunstroke, strictly speaking, is a disease, but the suddenness of its approach and its catastrophic nature have caused it to be classified as an accident. Tuberculosis is a disease, yet, if it results from the sudden inhalation of poisonous fumes, it may also be an accident. A like ruling has been made where some extreme and exceptional exposure has induced pneumonia or rheumatism.

---

[1]Reported in Volume 224 New York Reports 18.

[2]Reported in Volume 224 New York Reports 620.

[3]Reported in Volume 227 New York Reports 554.

[4]Opinion written in the first appellate court and reported in Volume 198 Appellate Division Reports 446 and affirmed by the Court of Appeals in Volume 233 New York Reports 535.

Nor does it clarify the problem much to characterize the act as voluntary, unless we can also say of the volition that involved in it there was foresight of the peril and acceptance of the consequences. If Connelly had knowingly injected a germ into the cut, then indeed there would have been a volition inconsistent with an accident. A finding might then be made that there was a "willful intention of the injured employee to bring about the injury." As it is, there is no evidence of his appreciation of the danger, and none that the contacts, so far at least as they included the scratch and the pimple, were designed and deliberate, rather than heedless or inadvertent. The range of accident would be reduced, indeed, to vanishing dimensions, if we were to take out of the category every case in which the physical movement had been willed without adverting to the consequences. The laborer who cut the poison ivy and was awarded compensation[1] intended to cut grass, though he did not know that it was poisoned. The undertaker's helper intended to embalm a corpse, and found to his undoing that he had been impregnated by putrefying matter adhering to his hand.

An argument is built upon the wording of the statute. Workmen's Compensation Law, Sec. 2, subd. 7. The statute speaks, as we have seen, of "accidental injuries arising out of and in the course of the employment," and also of "such disease or infection as may naturally and unavoidably result therefrom." The point is made that infection is here coupled with disease as something other than an accident or an injury, though a possible concomitant. We think the intention was by the addition of these words to enlarge and not to narrow. Infection like disease, may be gradual and insidious, or sudden and catastrophic. It may be an aggravation of injuries sustained in the course of the employment and arising therefrom, in which event it enters into the award, though its own immediate cause was unrelated to the service. It may be an aggravation of injuries which in their origin or primary form were apart

[1]*Plass* v. *Central N. E. R. R. Co.*, reported in Volume 169 Appellate Division Reports 826.

from the employment, in which event, if sudden and catastrophic and an incident of service, it will supply a new point of departure, a new starting point in the chain of causes, and be reckoned in measuring the award as an injury itself.

POUND, CRANE, and LEHMAN, *JJ.*, concur.

HISCOCK, *C.J.*, and MCLAUGHLIN and ANDREWS, *JJ.*, dissent.

"JUSTICE TO THE STRANGER AS WELL AS JUSTICE TO THE RESIDENT"

Dean v. *Dean*, 241 N. Y. 240 (1925)

Robert J. Dean and his wife Amelia resided in Ontario, Canada, where they had married, and of which country they were citizens. In February, 1919 Dean abandoned his wife and their two children and failed to make provision for their support. He lived for a time in Buffalo, N. Y. and then moved to Erie, Pennsylvania. While in the latter state he brought suit against his wife for divorce charging desertion on her part.

No summons in the Pennsylvania action was served upon Mrs. Dean personally. Upon the false statement that he did not know her whereabouts, the husband obtained an order from the Pennsylvania court which permitted the service to be effected by publication in the newspapers. Mrs. Dean did not appear in the action nor was she aware of its existence. The result was that the husband obtained a decree of divorce by default in 1923. He remarried in Pennsylvania and returned to Buffalo.

In 1924 Mrs. Dean still believing herself to be married to Robert J. Dean, moved to Buffalo and then for the first time learned the truth. She started an action for divorce which was granted. The husband appealed arguing that Amelia F. Dean had no standing in court as she was no longer his wife because of the Pennsylvania decree which had dissolved their marriage.

CARDOZO, J. * * *

The situation then is this: The husband, after deserting his wife in the matrimonial domicile in Ontario, obtained, upon constructive service of process, a divorce in Pennsylvania. The full faith and credit clause of the Constitution of the United States[1] does not command us to accord recognition to a judgment so procured. The only question is whether comity or public policy, or, to put it differently, our own interpretation of the conflict of laws, should prompt us to concede a recognition that we are at liberty to refuse. We do not need to inquire what our conclusion would be if the issue of abandonment had been resolved in favor of the husband. In that event, the

[1]Article 4, Section 1. Full Faith and Credit shall be given in each State to the public Acts, Records, and judicial Proceedings of every other State.

wife, though she remained in Ontario, would have been under a duty to live with her husband wherever he offered her a home. In the view of the law, his domicile would have been hers. A different problem would be before us for solution if it thus appeared that the Pennsylvania court, in decreeing a divorce, was adjudicating the status of parties whose domicile was there. We do not even have to forecast the decision that would be made if they had been living separate by consent. We confine ourselves to the facts as found. The wife, having been deserted by her husband, might maintain a domicile of her own, and she chose to maintain one in Ontario, till later she changed it to New York. She has never consented that her husband acquire a home apart from her, nor barred herself by misconduct from objecting to his doing so. In these circumstances, the incapacity of the divorce decree of Pennsylvania to affect the status of the abandoned wife does not depend upon some local policy established by New York for the protection of citizens or residents. It does not have its origin in the need of preserving the domestic law against evasion by one spouse to the prejudice of the other. It results from the general principles that govern the extra-territorial recognition of jurisdiction in actions of divorce.

We do not mean that these principles have validity as law, *ex proprio vigore,* irrespective of conflicting conceptions of expediency or justice. The policy behind them is always local in the sense that each state, aside from constitutional restrictions, may formulate its own conception for itself. The like may be said of the conflict of laws generally. The conception of justice prevalent at home will override an opposing conception prevalent abroad, but the conception prevalent at home may exact justice to the stranger as well as justice to the resident. So we think it does. The wife, domiciled in Canada, and there abandoned by her husband, became by her marriage a party to a relation which the courts of Pennsylvania have attempted to destroy. They have done this, though there has been no submission to the jurisdiction by her, upon the basis of a domicile which the erring husband has wrongfully set up apart from her. We think the judgments of this court leave no escape from the conclusion that, according to the standards of justice prevalent among us, injustice would be done if that attempt were to prevail. This being so, the divorce decree of Pennsylvania ought not to be recognized as valid in New York, unless it would have been recognized as valid in the country in which the wife was domiciled at the time when the decree was made. If the courts of her domicile were satisfied, we might follow where they led. But Canada does not recognize the binding force of the decree. The law of Ontario to that effect was proved upon the trial. We find nothing in our public policy to justify a holding that the wife, who remained a wife while she kept her domicile in Ontario, should be deemed to have ceased to be one when she changed her domicile to New York.

If there is need of other support for this conclusion, it is given by the husband's fraud. He obtained an order for the publication of the summons in local newspapers of Erie County, Pa., upon the false suggestion that the wife's whereabouts were unknown. The purpose as well as the effect of this misstatement was to keep her in ignorance of the suit. We do not need to say that for such a fraud alone the judgment would be disregarded, if jurisdiction, as recognized internationally, were otherwise complete. At least the fraud will help us to determine whether a recognition dependent upon conceptions of public policy and justice shall be granted or withheld. An abandoned and defrauded wife asks us to maintain her status as it was fixed by the law of her domicile at the date of the fraudulent decree. We cannot say that conceptions of public policy and justice require us to change it.

The judgment should be affirmed, with costs.

HISCOCK, *C.J.*, and POUND, MCLAUGHLIN, and ANDREWS, *JJ.*, concur with CRANE and CARDOZO, *JJ.* LEHMAN, *J.*, dissents.[1]

[1]The basis of the dissent was that the public policy of New York places no obstacle to giving force to a decree of divorce of another State which dissolved a marriage of one of its own residents, when New York at no time had any jurisdiction over that marriage.

"SHALL THE CRIMINAL GO FREE BECAUSE THE CONSTABLE HAS BLUNDERED?"

People v. *Defore,* 242 N. Y. 13 (1926)

John Defore was arrested by a policeman charged with petit larceny, the complainant having accused Defore of stealing an overcoat valued at less than $50.[1] The arrest took place in the hall of Defore's boarding house and the officer, after making the arrest, entered Defore's room and searched it. A blackjack, a bag and hat were found. Defore was indicted for the possession of the weapon. The trial on the larceny charge resulted in acquittal.

Defore then moved before the trial on the indictment for the possession of the blackjack, to suppress the evidence obtained by the arresting officer in his search of the room without a warrant. The court denied the application. The objection to the receipt of the blackjack in evidence was again raised upon the trial. The objection was overruled.

Defore claimed upon this appeal that through the rulings of the court he suffered

(a) A denial of his rights under the statute (Civil Rights Law, Sec. 8), against unreasonable search and seizure, which reads:

"The right of the people to be secure in their persons, houses, papers and effects, against unreasonable searches and seizures shall not be violated; and no warrants can issue but upon probable cause supported by oath or affirmation, and particularly describing the place to be searched, and the persons or things to be seized."

(b) A denial of his rights under Article 1, Section 6, of the State Constitution which gives immunity against compulsory self-incrimination and reads:

"No person * * * shall be compelled in any criminal case to be a witness against himself."

(c) A denial of his rights under the Fourteenth Amendment of the Constitution of the United States, which declares that

"Nor shall any State deprive any person of life, liberty, or property, without due process of law."

---

[1]If the value had been over $50 the charge would have been grand larceny under the then existing statute. Penal Law Sections 1296, 1298.

CARDOZO, J. * * *

The search was unreasonable "in the light of common-law traditions." A different conclusion might be necessary if the defendant had been lawfully arrested. As an incident to such an arrest, his person might have been searched for the fruits or evidences of crime. So, it seems, might the place where the arrest was made. But the arrest was not lawful. One who, acting without a warrant, arrests for a misdemeanor exceeds the bounds of privilege, whether he be a private person or an officer, unless the crime has been committed or attempted in his presence. The defendant had neither committed the crime or petit larceny in the presence of the officer nor there attempted to commit it. He had not committed nor attempted it anywhere. There was no lawful arrest to which the search could be an incident.

The people stress the fact that the weapon was contraband, a nuisance subject to destruction. This might have justified the seizure, the abatement of the nuisance, if the weapon had been exposed to view. It might even have justified the refusal to return the weapon, though discovered by unlawful means. It did not justify the search. There is no rule that homes may be ransacked without process to discover the fruits or the implements of crime. To make such inquisitions lawful, there must be the support of a search warrant issued upon probable cause. Search even then is "confined under our statute to property stolen or embezzled, or used as the means of committing a felony, or held with the intent to use it as an instrument of crime." The warrant does not issue for things of evidential value merely. What would be a wrong with a warrant is not innocent without one. To dispense with process in the pursuit of contraband is to dispense with it in the one case in which it may ever issue in the pursuit of anything. Means unlawful in their inception do not become lawful by relation when suspicion ripens into discovery.

We hold, then, with the defendant that the evidence against him was the outcome of a trespass. The officer might have been resisted, or sued for damages, or even prosecuted for oppression. He was subject to removal or other discipline at the hands of his superiors. These consequences are undisputed. The defendant would add another. We must determine whether evidence of criminality, procured by an act of trespass, is to be rejected as incompetent for the misconduct of the trespasser.

The question is not a new one. It was put to us more than 20 years ago in People v. Adams[1] and there deliberately answered. A search warrant had been issued against the proprietor of a gambling house for the seizure of gambling implements. The police did not confine themselves to the things stated in the warrant. Without authority of law, they seized the defendant's books and papers. We held that the documents did not cease to be competent evidence against him though the seizure was unlawful. In support of that holding, we cited many authorities, and notably a series of decisions by the courts of Massachusetts.

"A trespasser may testify to pertinent facts observed by him, or may put in evidence pertinent articles or papers found by him while trespassing. For the trespass he may be held responsible civilly, and perhaps criminally; but his testimony is not thereby rendered incompetent."[2]

The ruling thus broadly made is decisive, while it stands, of the case before us now. It is at variance, however, with later judgments of the Supreme Court of the United States. Those judgments do not bind us, for they construe provisions of the federal Constitution, the Fourth and Fifth Amendments, not applicable to the states. Even though not binding, they merit our attentive scrutiny. Weeks v. United States[3] held that articles wrongfully seized by agents of the federal government should have been returned to the defendant or excluded as evidence, if a timely motion to compel return had been made before the trial. Silverthorne Lumber Co. v. United States and Amos

---

[1]Reported in Volume 176 New York Reports 351. [The Supreme Court of the United States affirmed the judgment in Volume 192 United States Reports 585.]

[2]Quoted from *Commonwealth* v. *Tibbetts,* reported in Volume 157 Massachusetts Reports 519.

[3]Reported in Volume 232 United States Reports 383.

v. United States[1] held that a motion before trial was unnecessary if the defendant had no knowledge until the trial that an illegal seizure had been made. Burdeau v. McDowell[2] held that a federal prosecutor might make such use as he pleased of documents or other information acquired from a trespasser, if persons other than federal officers were guilty of the trespass. Hester v. United States and Carroll v. United States[3] drew a distinction between search and seizure in a house and search and seizure in the fields or in automobiles or other vehicles. Finally Agnello v. United States[4] held that the evidence must be excluded, though the things seized were contraband, and though there had been no motion before trial if the facts were undisputed. This means that the Supreme Court has overruled its own judgment in Adams v. People of State of New York, for the facts were undisputed there. The procedural condition of a preliminary motion has been substantially abandoned, or, if not enforced at all, is an exceptional requirement. There has been no blinking the consequences. The criminal is to go free because the constable has blundered.

The new doctrine has already met the scrutiny of courts of sister states. The decisions have been brought together for our guidance through the industry of counsel. In 45 states (exclusive of our own) the subject has been considered. Fourteen states have adopted the rule of the Weeks Case either as there laid down or as subsequently broadened. Thirty-one have rejected it. The controversy, starting with the courts, has been taken up by the commentators, and with them has been the theme of animated argument. For the most part, there has been adherence to the older doctrine. With authority thus divided, it is only some overmastering consideration of principle or of policy that should move us to a change. The balance is not

---

[1]Reported in Volume 251 United States Reports 298 and 255 United States Reports 313, respectively.

[2]Reported in Volume 256 United States Reports 465.

[3]Reported in Volume 265 United States Reports 57 and 267 United States Reports 132 respectively.

[4]Reported in Volume 269 United States Reports 20.

swayed until something more persuasive than uncertainty is added to the scales.

We find nothing in the statute (Civil Rights Law, Sec. 8) whereby official trespasses and private are differentiated in respect of the legal consequences to follow them. All that the statute does is to place the two on an equality. In times gone by, officialdom had arrogated to itself a privilege of indiscriminate inquisition. The statute declares that the privilege shall not exist. Thereafter, all alike, whenever search is unreasonable, must answer to the law. For the high intruder and the low, the consequences become the same. Evidence is not excluded because the private litigant who offers it has gathered it by lawless force. By the same token, the state, when prosecuting an offender against the peace and order of society, incurs no heavier liability.

The federal rule as it stands is either too strict or too lax. A federal prosecutor may take no benefit from evidence collected through the trespass of a federal officer. The thought is that, in appropriating the results, he ratifies the means. He does not have to be so scrupulous about evidence brought to him by others. How finely the line is drawn is seen when we recall that marshals in the service of the nation are on one side of it, and police in the service of the states on the other. The nation may keep what the servants of the states supply. We must go farther or not so far. The professed object of the trespass rather than the official character of the trespasser should test the right of government. The incongruity of other tests gains emphasis from the facts of the case before us. The complainant, the owner of the overcoat, co-operated with the officer in the arrest and the attendant search. Their powers were equal, since the charge was petit larceny, a misdemeanor. If one spoke or acted for the state, so also did the other. A government would be disingenuous, if, in determining the use that should be made of evidence drawn from such a source, it drew a line between them. This would be true whether they had acted in concert or apart. We exalt form above substance when we hold that the use is made lawful because the intruder is without a badge of office. We break with precedent altogether when we press the prohibition farther.

The truth, indeed, is that the statute says nothing about consequences. It does no more than deny a privilege. Denying this, it stops. Intrusion without privilege has certain liabilities and penalties. The statute does not assume to alter or increase them. No scrutiny of its text can ever evoke additional consequences by a mere process of construction. We must attach them, if at all, because some public policy, adequately revealed, would otherwise be thwarted. But adequate revelation of such a policy it is surely hard to see. This would have been true in the beginning before the courts had spoken. It is more plainly true today. In this state the immunity is the creature, not of Constitution, but of statute.[1] The Legislature, which created, has acquiesced in the ruling of this Court that the prohibition of the search did not anathematize the evidence yielded through the search. If we had misread the statute or misconceived the public policy, a few words of amendment would have quickly set us right. The process of amendment is prompt and simple. It is without the delays or obstructions that clog the change of Constitutions. In such circumstances silence itself is the declaration of a policy. We scan the statute in vain for any token of intention that search by intruders wearing a badge of office shall have any different consequences in respect of the law of evidence than search by intruders generally.

We are confirmed in this conclusion when we reflect how far-reaching in its effect upon society the new consequences would be. The pettiest peace officer would have it in his power, through overzeal or indiscretion, to confer immunity upon an offender for crimes the most flagitious. A room is searched against the law, and the body of a murdered man is found. If the place of discovery may not be proved, the other circumstances may be insufficient to connect the defendant with the crime. The privacy of the home has been infringed, and the murderer goes free. An-

[1] Civil Rights Law, Section 8.

other search, once more against the law, discloses counterfeit money or the implements of forgery. The absence of a warrant means the freedom of the forger. Like instances can be multiplied. We may not subject society to these dangers until the Legislature has spoken with a clearer voice. In so holding, we are not unmindful of the argument that, unless the evidence is excluded, the statute becomes a form and its protection an illusion. This has a strange sound when the immunity is viewed in the light of its origin and history. The rule now embodied in the statute was received into English law as the outcome of the prosecution of Wilkes and Entick.[1] Wilkes sued the messengers who had ransacked his papers, and recovered a verdict of £4,000 against one and £1,000 against the other. Entick, too, had a substantial verdict. We do not know whether the public, represented by its juries, is today more indifferent to its liberties than it was when the immunity was born. If so, the change of sentiment without more does not work a change of remedy. Other sanctions, penal and disciplinary, supplementing the right to damages, have already been enumerated. No doubt the protection of the statute would be greater from the point of view of the individual whose privacy had been invaded if the government were required to ignore what it had learned through the invasion. The question is whether protection for the individual would not be gained at a disproportionate loss of protection for society. On the one side is the social need that crime shall be repressed. On the other, the social need that law shall not be flouted by the insolence of office. There are dangers in any choice. The rule of the Adams Case strikes a balance between opposing interests. We must hold it to be the law until these organs of government by which a change of public policy is normally effected shall give notice to the courts that the change has come to pass.

There remains a second claim of privilege. "No person shall be * * * compelled in any criminal case to be a wit-

---

[1]*Wilke's* case is reported in Volume 19 State Trials, at page 1405, and *Entick* v. *Carrington* is in the same volume at page 1030.

ness against himself."[1] This immunity, like the statutory one against unreasonable search and seizure, was considered in the Adams Case. We limited it to cases where incriminatory disclosure had been extorted by the constraint of legal process directed against a witness. The Supreme Court agreed with us.[2] Other courts and learned commentators have taken the same ground. Unless that ruling is to be changed, the conclusion is not doubtful.

We put the question aside whether in some other situation differing from the one before us there may be need to qualify or soften a ruling so comprehensive. In putting it aside, we would not be understood as expressing, even by indirection, a belief that change is called for. Enough for present purposes to decide the case at hand. The weapon discovered through this search was an implement of crime. It was not the kind of thing to be protected against prying inquisition. It was a thing to be ferreted out and brought to light and, when found, wrested from the holder. There is no relation in such circumstances between the absence of a search warrant and the constitutional immunity against involuntary disclosure. The production of the weapon would have been just as incriminatory and just as involuntary if a warrant had been issued. The law, in providing for the warrant, does not proceed upon the theory that the defendant will thereby be protected against disclosing his own crime. On the contrary, the very object of the warrant is to compel him to disclose it. Things outlawed or contraband, possessed without right, and subject upon seizure to forfeiture or destruction, may be offered in evidence without trenching upon the privilege in respect of self-incrimination whether seizure has been made with warrant or without.

The defendant makes the point that, though the blackjack was contraband, the bag and hat were not. Error in admitting these in evidence, even if error were found, might be disregarded as harmless. But in truth the question is not here. All three articles were offered in evidence

---

[1]New York Constitution, art. 1 Sec. 6.

[2]*Adams* v. *People*, reported in Volume 192 United States Reports 585.

together. The objection did not discriminate between them. It was a general one to all alike. If any were admissible, the objection fails.

In this state of the record, we are not required to determine the application of the constitutional privilege to things lawfully possessed. We know that there are times when such things, not contraband at all, may be seized and placed in evidence. In this very case, if the overcoat had been worth $51, instead of $50 only, the arrest (for all that appears) would have been lawful, since the officer might arrest the defendant if a felony had been committed, and there was reasonable cause to believe that the defendant was the perpetrator.[1] In that event, there might have been search of the place where the arrest was made to discover the fruits or even the evidence of larceny. The use of things thus seized would be lawful in any ensuing prosecution either for that crime or for another, yet it would none the less be used against the will of the accused. Seizure, whether legitimate or a trespass, is not voluntary surrender. There is strong support in this for the ruling of the Adams Case that force is not the test, but rather force accompanied by process aimed against a witness and compelling action on his part. In the words of Baker, *J.*, writing for the Circuit Court of Appeals:[2] "'Witness' is the keyword." A defendant is "protected from producing his documents in response to a subpoena duces tecum, for his production of them in court would be his voucher of their genuineness." There would then be "testimonial compulsion." The keyword is disregarded, however, when compulsion not testimonial is brought within the orbit of the privilege. People ex rel. Ferguson v. Reardon[3] went upon the theory that the inspection there permitted by a statute was in effect a proceeding for a discovery or an examination before trial.

---

[1]The New York law provides that an officer may arrest without a warrant and not be subject to liability for arresting the wrong person, if the arrest is for a felony actually committed by someone and the officer has reasonable ground to suspect that the one arrested committed the crime.

[2]*Haywood* v. *United States,* reported in Volume 268 Federal Reporter 795, 802.

[3]Reported in Volume 197 New York Reports 236.

The distinctions are indeed close. But the line of division will not be drawn with finality till there is before us a record which requires us to trace it.

As a last resort, the defendant invokes the Fourteenth Amendment and the requirement of "due process."

The Fourteenth Amendment would not be violated, though the privilege against self-incrimination were abolished altogether. The like must be true of the immunity against search and seizure without warrant in so far as that immunity has relation to the use of evidence thereafter.

The judgment of conviction should be affirmed.

HISCOCK, *C.J.*, and POUND, MCLAUGHLIN, CRANE, ANDREWS, and LEHMAN, *JJ.*, concur.

"SENTIMENTS AND USAGES, DEVOUTEDLY HELD, MAY NOT BE FLOUTED FOR CAPRICE"

Yome v. *Gorman*, 242 N. Y. 395 (1926)

John D. Yome was very sick. He called to his sick bed a Catholic priest and the last rites and sacraments of the Catholic Church were administered to him. A few days later (February 5, 1925) he died. His wife, Anna, caused a public funeral mass to be held for her deceased husband in a church and then caused his body to be buried in the Holy Cross Cemetery in Brooklyn.

The legal difficulties which followed are closely bound with the history of this cemetery ground. In 1886 a seventeen-month-old infant of John and Anna had been buried in that cemetery. Three years after that another child, less than 3 years old, had been there buried. As old age approached, John and Anna decided to provide a final resting place for themselves and for those close to them, and so in 1916 they bought an eight-grave plot in Holy Cross Cemetery where their two infant children had been buried.

Holy Cross Cemetery was maintained by the Roman Catholic Diocese of Brooklyn and burial within the cemetery was a privilege reserved only to those who died in communion with the Roman Catholic Church, and was always subject to the rules of the Bishop of the Diocese. The certificate of ownership delivered to the Yomes so provided. One of the rules forbade the removal of a body from consecrated ground to ground that was unconsecrated or consecrated to another faith.

One year after the purchase of the burial ground John caused the body of his deceased mother-in-law to be buried therein. Two years later his wife's brother was therein buried. When John died he was survived by his widow, two adult daughters and one adult son.

Soon after the death of her husband, Anna had a change of heart and became the owner of a plot in a non-Catholic cemetery. She made a demand upon John B. Gorman as Supervisor of Roman Catholic Cemeteries for permission to remove the bodies of her husband and the other members of her family who were buried in the Holy Cross Cemetery. The permission was refused on the ground that disinterment for the purpose of removal to a cemetery of another faith would be an act of desecration.

Anna, seeking to justify her position, insisted that her husband, mother and brother had been without devotion to the tenets of the Church; that her husband did not care where he was buried if only he was close to her. The surviving children all supported their mother in her requests.

When the officials remained firm, Anna Yome obtained an injunction restraining them from preventing the removal. They appealed.

CARDOZO, J. * * *

Upon the record before us, one may draw conflicting inferences of duty and propriety. The wishes of wife and next of kin are not always supreme and final though the body is yet unburied. Still less are they supreme and final when the body has been laid at rest and the aid of equity is invoked to disturb the quiet of the grave. There will then be "due regard to the interests of the public, the wishes of the decedent, and the rights and feelings of those entitled to be heard by reason of relationship or association."[1] A benevolent discretion, giving heed to all those promptings and emotions that men and women hold for sacred in the disposition of their dead, must render judgment as it appraises the worth of the competing forces.

To the making of that appraisal many factors will contribute. One may not fix their values in advance, for in so doing one would overlook the varying force of circumstance. One can do little more than offer the suggestion of example. The wish of the deceased, even though legal compulsion may not attach to it, has at least a large significance. Especially is this so when the wish has its origin in intense religious feeling.

Only some rare emergency could move a court of equity to take a body from its grave in consecrated ground and put it in ground unhallowed if there was good reason to suppose that the conscience of the deceased, were he alive, would be outraged by the change. Subordinate in importance, and yet at times not wholly to be disregarded, are the sentiments and usages of the religious body which confers the right of burial. We do not interpret the terms of this certificate of purchase as importing a contract between the cemetery and the owners of the plot that there shall be no disinterment at any time if forbidden by

[1]*Pettigrew* v. *Pettigrew,* reported in Volume 207 Pennsylvania Reports 313.

the tenets of the Church or the orders of the Bishop. How far such a contract, if made, would call for enforcement by injunction there is no occasion to determine. Even without contract, sentiments and usages, devoutly held as sacred, may not be flouted for caprice. They must be weighed in the balance with the motives and feelings that sway the acts of the survivors. Removal at the instance of a wife or of kinsmen near in blood to satisfy a longing that those united during life shall not be divided after death may seem praiseworthy and decorous when removal at the instance of distant relatives or strangers would be arbitrary or cruel. The dead are to rest where they have been laid unless reason of substance is brought forward for disturbing their repose.

We have sought, not to declare a rule, but to exemplify a process. The considerations we have instanced and others of like order may move a court of equity to keep a grave inviolate against the will of the survivors. They are none of them so absolute, however, that they may not be neutralized by others. The wish expressed during life may have been declared casually or lightly. The bond of religion may have been weak, and the bond of marriage or of kinship may have been strong. Separation after death from the resting place of wife or child may have seemed an evil more poignant than separation after death from the faithful of the church. We are told by Mrs. Yome that so her husband would have felt. Her statement does not control us. To some extent, though not at all conclusively, it is contradicted by his acts. The trier of the facts must probe his state of mind. With this, when it is ascertained and the intensity of his feelings measured, must be compared the sentiments and wishes of wife and kin surviving. A like process must be followed before the other graves may be disturbed. Right must then be done as right would be conceived of by men of character and feeling.

The order of the Appellate Division and that of the Special Term should be reversed with costs.

HISCOCK, *C.J.*, and POUND, McLAUGHLIN, LEHMAN, and CRANE, *JJ.*, concur. ANDREWS, *J.*, not voting.

"IF DUAL INTERESTS ARE TO BE SERVED THE DISCLOSURE MUST LAY BARE THE TRUTH"

Wendt v. *Fischer,* 243 N. Y. 439 (1926)

Edmund C. Wendt, the owner of a piece of property in the city of New York, engaged Fischer, Hammond & Heinrich, real estate brokers, to find a buyer who would purchase the property for $75,000 of which at least $10,000 would be in cash. They later represented to him that they had a client who would pay $80,000 but only $7,500 would be cash. Wendt agreed and sold the property at the proposed figure. The property was taken in the name of a "dummy" but the broker's customer was the Hosmer Realty Corporation which took the property from this "dummy".

Unknown to Wendt, the president, treasurer and manager of the Hosmer Realty Corporation was Hammond, a member of the firm of brokers. Hammond and his fiancee were the record and beneficial owners respectively of all the corporation's stock. The real facts were discovered when a few weeks later the Hosmer Realty Corporation resold the property for $87,500, making a $7,500 profit.

Wendt commenced an action for an accounting, maintaining that the broker's failure to disclose Hammond's connection with the real purchaser was a breach of their duty and justified his claim.

CARDOZO, J. * * *

We think the sale was voidable at the option of the seller. Hammond, employed to sell, was under a disability to buy without full and frank disclosure of his relation to the purchase. We are told that the sale may be upheld because his ownership of the stock was nominal and the profits of the transaction would benefit another. Even so, the conflict was not reconciled between divided claims to fealty. As broker for the seller, the duty of this fiduciary was to make the terms as favorable to his employer and the price as high as possible. As president and manager of the buyer corporation, its sole representative in the transaction, his duty was just the opposite. We are told that the corporation is to be blotted out of the picture, and the case viewed as if the equitable owner of the shares who supplied the corporation with the money for the purchase, had taken title in her own name. The difficulty is that she preferred for reasons sufficient to herself to vest the title in another. The courts are not at liberty to nullify her choice and remake the transaction into something other than it was. We are told that the conflict of interest was sufficiently revealed when the brokers informed the plaintiff that the sale was to be made to a client of their office. Disclosure so indefinite and equivocal does not set the agent free to bargain for his own account or for the account of a corporation which acts through him alone.

If dual interests are to be served, the disclosure to be effective must lay bare the truth, without ambiguity or reservation, in all its stark significance. Finally, we are told that the brokers acted in good faith, that the terms procured were the best obtainable at the moment, and that the wrong, if any, was unaccompanied by damage. This is no sufficient answer by a trustee forgetful of his duty. The law "does not stop to inquire whether the contract or transaction was fair or unfair. It stops the inquiry when the relation is disclosed, and sets aside the transaction or refuses to enforce it, at the instance of the party whom the fiduciary undertook to represent, without undertaking to deal with the question of abstract justice in the particular case."[1] Only by this uncompromising rigidity has the rule of undivided loyalty been maintained against disintegrating erosion.

A question remains as to the remedy available. The defendant Hosmer Realty Corporation must account for the profits of the resale. It got no title to the property except one that was subject to a trust, for in the acceptance of its title it was acting through the trustee and no one else. When the property was resold, the trust was impressed upon the proceeds. The defendants Fischer, Hammond & Heinrich, the brokers, are accountable for the moneys paid to them for commissions. Commissions were not earned unless duty had been done. We think

---

[1]*Munson* v. *Syracuse G. & C. R. Co.,* reported in Volume 8, Northeastern Reporter 355.

the judgment goes too far, however, in declaring the brokers to be accountable for profits. We do not need to consider what their liability would be if the plaintiff were limiting his claim of recovery to the reasonable value. That is not the theory of the action or the judgment. The plaintiff elects to charge the Hosmer Realty Corporation with the profits that have come to it as upon a sale for his account. The brokers took no part in effecting the resale and had no share in the profits realized therefrom. The corporation resold and collected and enjoyed the proceeds. It, and no one else, as to this increment of value, is to be charged as a trustee.

The judgment should be modified by providing that the defendants Fischer, Hammond & Heinrich shall be accountable only for their commissions.

HISCOCK, *C.J.*, and POUND, MCLAUGHLIN, CRANE and ANDREWS, *JJ.*, concur. LEHMAN, *J.*, absent.

"IN THE COMPLEXITIES OF MODERN LIFE, ONE DOES NOT KNOW WHERE THE ORDINARY ENDS AND THE EXTRAORDINARY BEGINS"

Kerr S. S. Co. v. *Radio Corporation of America,* 245 N. Y. 284 (1927)

The Kerr Steamship Company, Inc. delivered to the Radio Corporation of America, a 29-word telegram in cipher to be transmitted to Manila, Philippine Islands. The telegram was written on one of the blanks of the Radio Corporation which was prefaced by printed words in this way:

> "Send the following radiogram via R. P. A., subject to terms on back hereof which are hereby agreed to."

The Radio Company had no direct circuit for the transmission of messages to Manila, but its most inexpensive way of sending messages to the Philippines was to forward them over the line of the Commercial Cable Company which transmitted them by cable.

When messages were thus sent, a copy was made for the cable company and a copy kept in the radio company's files. Through some inadvertence the copy intended for the cable company was mislaid and never delivered and the steamship company's telegram never reached Manila.

The message, translated from cipher, contained instructions to one Macondray as to the loading of a ship. Untranslated the message was unintelligible. As a result of the failure to deliver the message the cargo was not laden and the freight was lost to a damage of over $6,000.

Upon the trial the Kerr Company was allowed to recover the entire amount that was lost because of the non-delivery of the message on the ground that the cipher, though it could not be read by the radio company, must have been understood as having relation to some transaction of a business nature and that from this understanding alone there followed a liability for the damages that would have been recognized as natural if the details of the transaction had been known.

The radio company asserted that the limit of its liability was $26.78, the price of sending the message.

CARDOZO, C. J. * * *

The settled doctrine of this court confines the liability of a telegraph company for failure to transmit a message within the limits of the rule in Hadley v. Baxendale.[1] Where the terms of the telegram disclose the general nature of the transaction which is the subject of the message, the company is answerable for the natural consequences of its neglect in relation to the transaction thus known or foreseen. On the other hand, where the terms of the message give no hint of the nature of the transaction, the liability is for nominal damages or for the cost of carriage if the tolls have been prepaid.

We are now asked to hold that the transaction has been revealed within the meaning of the rule if the length and cost of the telegram or the names of the parties would fairly suggest to a reasonable man that business of moment is the subject of the message. This is very nearly to annihilate the rule in the guise of an exception. The defendant upon receiving from a steamship company a long telegram in cipher to be transmitted to Manila would naturally infer that the message had relation to business of some sort. Beyond that it could infer nothing. The message might relate to the loading of a cargo, but equally it might relate to the sale of a vessel or to the employment of an agent or to any one of myriad transactions as divergent as the poles. Notice of the business, if it is to lay the basis for special damages, must be sufficiently informing to be notice of the risk.

At the root of the problem is the distinction between general and special damage as it has been developed in our law. There is need to keep in mind that the distinction is not absolute, but relative. To put it in other words, damage which is general in relation to a contract of one kind may be classified as special in relation to another. If A. and B. contract for the sale of staple goods, the general damage upon a breach is the difference between the market value and the price. But if A. delivers to X. a telegram to B. in cipher with reference to the same sale, or a letter in a sealed envelope, the general damage upon the default of X. is the cost of carriage and no more. As to him the difference between price and value is damage

---

[1]Reported in Volume 9 Exchequer Reports (Eng.) 341.

to be ranked as special, and therefore not recoverable unless the message is disclosed. The argument for a larger liability loses sight of this distinction. It misses a sure foothold in that it shifts from general damage in one relation to general damage in another. The bearer of a message who infers from the surrounding circumstances that what he bears has relation to business of some kind is liable, we are told, for any damages that are natural with reference to the character of the business as to which knowledge is imputed. When we ask, however, to what extent the character of the business will be the subject of imputed knowledge, we are told that it is so much of the business only as will make the damage natural. Thus we travel in a circle, what is natural or general being adapted to so much of a putative business as is constructively known, and what is constructively known being adapted to what is general and natural. One cannot build conclusions upon foundations so unstable. The loss of a cipher message to load a vessel in the Philippines may mean to one the loss of freight, to another an idle factory, to another a frustrated bargain for the sale or leasing of the cargo. We cannot say what ventures are collateral till we know the ventures that are primary. Not till we learn the profits that are direct can we know which ones are secondary. There is a *contradictio in adjecto* when we speak of the general damages appropriate to an indeterminate transaction.

The key to Hadley v. Baxendale is lost if we fail to keep in mind the relativity of causation as a concept of the law. The argument for the plaintiff mistakenly assumes that the test of what is general damage in a controversy between the sender of a message and the receiver is also the test between the sender and the carrier. To unify the two relations is to abandon Hadley v. Baxendale in its application to contracts for the transmission of a message. If knowledge that a message is concerned with business of some kind is by imputation knowledge of those forms of business, and those only, that are typical and normal, there must be search for a definition of the normal and the typical. The quest is obviously futile. Every effect is natural when there is complete knowledge of the cause. Every damage becomes natural when the transaction out of which it arises has been fully comprehended. Imputed knowledge cannot stop with imputed notice of transactions that are standardized by usage. In the complexities of modern life, one does not know where the ordinary ends and the extraordinary begins. Imputed knowledge, if it exists, must rest upon an assumption less timid and uncertain. The assumption cannot be less than this, that whatever a carrier could ascertain by diligent inquiry as to the nature of the undisclosed transaction, this he should be deemed to have ascertained, and charged with damages accordingly. We do not need to consider whether such a rule might wisely have been applied in the beginning, when the law as to carriers of messages was yet in its infancy. Most certainly it is not the rule announced in our decisions. We cannot accept it now without throwing overboard the doctrine that notice is essential. Notice may indeed be adequate though the transaction is indicated in outline only. The carrier must draw such reasonable inferences in respect of the character of the business as would be drawn by men of affairs from condensed or abbreviated dispatches. Something, however, there must be to give warning that the subject of the message is not merely business in general, but business of a known order.

We are not unmindful of the force of the plaintiff's assault upon the rule in Hadley v. Baxendale in its application to the relation between telegraph carrier and customer. The truth seems to be that neither the clerk who receives the message over the counter nor the operator who transmits it nor any other employee gives or is expected to give any thought to the sense of what he is receiving or transmitting. This imparts to the whole doctrine as to the need for notice an air of unreality. The doctrine, however, has prevailed for years, so many that it is tantamount to a rule of property. The companies have regulated their rates upon the basis of its continuance. They have omitted precautions that they might have thought it necessary to adopt if the hazard of the business was to be indefinitely increased. Nor is the doctrine without other foundation in utility and justice. Much may be said in favor of the social policy of a rule whereby the companies have been relieved of liabilities that might otherwise be crushing. The sender can protect himself by insurance in one form or another if the risk of nondelivery or error appears to be too great. The total burden is not heavy since it is distributed among many, and can be proportioned in any instance to the loss likely to ensue. The company, if it takes out insurance for itself, can do not more than guess at the loss to be avoided. To pay for this unknown risk, it will be driven to increase the rates payable by all, though the increase is likely to result in the protection of a few. We are not concerned to balance the considerations of policy that give support to the existing rule against others that weigh against it. Enough for present purposes that there are weights in either scale. Telegraph companies in interstate and foreign commerce are subject to the power of Congress. If the rule of damages long recognized by state and federal decision is to give way to another, the change should come through legislation.

POUND, CRANE, ANDREWS, LEHMAN, KELLOGG, and O'BRIEN, *JJ.*, concur.

Judgment accordingly.

"A CRIMINAL, HOWEVER SHOCKING HIS CRIME, IS NOT TO ANSWER FOR IT WITH FORFEITURE OF LIFE OR LIBERTY TILL TRIED AND CONVICTED IN CONFORMITY WITH LAW"

People v. *Moran*, 246 N. Y. 100 (1927)

Thomas Moran and four companions were riding in an automobile in Brooklyn, New York, when a Police Department car containing two officers, Byrns and Daskiewicz, ordered them to stop. The driver, La Curto, obeyed despite Moran's call that he continue driving. The officers stepped out of the police car and Moran and some of his companions did likewise. As Moran stepped down from the car he quickly drew his revolver and shouted "Stick them up." Officer Daskiewicz made a movement as if to draw his own gun and Moran fired two shots at him, and as Byrns made a jump to seize him, a third shot was fired and hit Byrns. Both officers died as a result of their wounds.

Moran fled and hid after this affray, but a few days later surrendered and made a full confession, and with bravado declared his wish to go to the electric chair. He refused any assistance even from his counsel, but the latter asserted the defense of insanity and upon that issue Moran was convicted of murder in the first degree in connection with the death of Byrns.

An appeal was automatically taken to the Court of Appeals and the main ground of appeal asserted was an error in the charge. The trial judge had put the case to the jury upon the single theory of a homicide committed by one who was at the time of the homicide engaged in the commission of a felony which, if true, constituted murder in the first degree. This theory necessarily confined the jury to a choice between a verdict of acquittal and one of murder in the first degree. The judge refused to submit the other degrees of homicide or to permit counsel in summing up to speak about the other degrees. The trial judge's theory was that if Moran after shooting Daskiewicz, which was one felony, shot and killed Byrns in an effort to escape, there was a homicide while engaged in the commission of a felony and, therefore, murder in the first degree, irrespective of intent. The jury were not to consider whether Moran had fired with deliberate and premeditated design to kill.

The Court of Appeals in an opinion by Chief Judge Cardozo unanimously concurred in by the other Judges, reversed the conviction,

CARDOZO, C. J. * * *

The judgment must be reversed because of basic error in the charge.

Repeated decisions of this court bear witness to the fact that such (the charge as given) is not the law. Homicide is murder in the first degree when perpetrated with a deliberate and premeditated design to kill, or, without such design, while engaged in the commission of a felony. To make the quality of the intent indifferent, it is not enough to show that the homicide was felonious, or that there was a felonious assault which culminated in homicide. Such a holding would mean that every homicide, not justifiable or excusable, would occur in the commission of a felony, with a result that intent to kill and deliberation and premeditation would never be essential. The felony that eliminates the quality of the intent must be one that is independent of the homicide and of the assault merged therein, as, e. g., robbery or larceny or burglary or rape. Cases are found at times where the inculpatory facts are susceptible of one interpretation only: Either the one accused was engaged in an independent felony at the time of the killing, or he did not kill at all. In such conditions the law does not say that other forms or grades of homicide shall be submitted to the jury. If, however, the facts are susceptible of varying interpretations, there must be a submission of whatever forms and grade comport with the proofs and the indictment. The statute is explicit. "Upon the trial of an indictment, the prisoner may be convicted of the crime charged therein, or of a lesser degree of the same crime, or of an attempt to commit the crime so charged, or of an attempt to commit a lesser degree of the same crime."[1] Whenever intent becomes material, its quality or persistence—the deranging influence of fear or sudden impulse or feebleness of mind or will—is matter for the jury if such emotions or disabilities can conceivably have affected the thought or purpose of the actor.

This killing was not done in circumstances excluding every possible hypothesis except one of homicide while

[1]Penal Law, Section 610.

engaged in another or independent felony. The trial judge told the jury that the defendant was engaged in such a felony, if, before he had been placed in the lawful custody of an officer, he shot Officer Byrns in an effort to escape. We have held exactly to the contrary. The very meaning of flight is desistance or abandonment, unless, indeed, in special circumstances as in cases where a thief is fleeing with his loot. If the defendant was trying to escape, then the first felony, the assault upon Daskiewicz, was over. A second felony had begun, a felonious assault on Byrns. The felony then begun was not independent of the homicide. It was the homicide itself.

We are told that Byrns grappled with the defendant to save his brother officer from the threat of fresh attack, or that so a jury might determine. Reference is then made to People v. Wagner[1] as authority for a holding that a struggle thus begun is one connected with another felony so that intent is unimportant. In all this, there is a futile attempt to split into unrelated parts an indivisible transaction. The attack upon Daskiewicz was not separate and distinct in motive or origin from the one upon Byrns. The summons by the defendant to surrender was aimed equally at each, and so was the threat of the revolver which he drew from his pocket to emphasize his words. At that very moment there began a felonious assault directed against both, against one as plainly as the other. Byrns did not plunge into a fight to which he had hitherto been a stranger, intent upon rescue and nothing else. He was in the fight from the beginning, a sharer of its perils from the moment the assault began. We can only guess at the motive with which he grappled with his assailant, and a jury could do no more. The testimony for the people is that Daskiewicz at that stage of the affray had already been shot twice. There is nothing in such evidence to show that another shot at him was planned or that Byrns so supposed. The inference is just as reasonable that Byrns was trying to defend his own life, or to foil an escape by arresting the assailant. Indeed, there seems to

[1]Reported in Volume 245 New York Reports 143.

have been no thought upon the trial that his motive, whether rescue or something else, would affect the nature of the crime. The jurors were never asked to say whether he had joined in the struggle with one motive or another. They were told, on the contrary, that a shot to escape after an attack upon another was a shot by one engaged in the commission of a felony.

Applied to such facts, our ruling in People v. Wagner (supra), recently decided, is far from an authority to sustain the people's judgment. Wagner was engaged in an assault upon a woman when Basto, another occupant of the same house, came to the woman's rescue, and in the ensuing fight was killed. We held that the trial judge did not err in permitting the jury to say that the homicide was by one engaged in a separate or independent felony, the assault upon the woman. The other grades of homicide were charged. The jury were not told that the evidence was susceptible of one interpretation and no other. The case was put to them in all its phases, with instructions appropriate to each. There is little need to elaborate distinctions. They appear upon the surface. Basto, a stranger to the fight, plunged into it while it was yet in progress, to stay the commission of a felony upon the person of another.

This court has given warning more than once that the conditions justifying submission of the "felony" grade of manslaughter to the exclusion of all others, must be understood to be "exceptional." Such a submission is proper only where there is "no possible view of the facts which would justify any other verdict except a conviction of the crime charged or an acquittal." Apparently the warning has need to be repeated. Evidence uncertain in its implications must not be warped or strained to force a jury into the dilemma of choosing between death and freedom. We do not say that this jury, with choice unconstrained, would have chosen otherwise than it did. There was ample evidence to justify a verdict of deliberate and premeditated murder if that issue had been submitted. It never was. The reason it never was is that the jurors must then have been informed of the range and measure of their power. We may not "sustain a conviction erroneously secured on one theory on the conjecture that it would have followed just the same if the correct theory had been applied."[1] A criminal, however shocking his crime, is not to answer for it with forfeiture of life or liberty till tried and convicted in conformity with law.

The judgment of conviction should be reversed and a new trial ordered.[2]

POUND, CRANE, ANDREWS, LEHMAN, KELLOGG, and O'BRIEN, *JJ.*, concur.

---

[1]Chief Judge Hiscock in People v. Smith, reported in Volume 232 New York Reports 239, 244.

[2]Thomas Moran was retried the following year. On this trial the defendant claimed insanity and feebleness of mind as a defense. The jury, however, found that he knew the nature and quality of his act and that it was wrong. He was convicted of murder in the first degree. The conviction was affirmed in the Court of Appeals and Moran was executed in December 1928.

"THE HALF TRUTHS OF ONE GENERATION TEND AT TIMES TO PERPETUATE THEMSELVES IN THE LAW AS THE WHOLE TRUTH OF ANOTHER"

Alleghany College v. *National Chautauqua County Bank,* 246 N. Y. 369 (1927)

Alleghany College of Meadville, Pa., commenced a drive to secure an additional endowment of $1,250,000. Among the many who were solicited was Mary Yates Johnston of Jamestown, N. Y. In response to an appeal she signed a pledge card which in part read as follows:

> "In consideration of my interest in Christian education, and in consideration of others subscribing, I hereby subscribe and will pay to the order of the treasurer of Alleghany College, Meadville, Pennsylvania, the sum of Five Thousand Dollars."

A further declaration in this pledge card made the amount payable thirty days after her death and she also indorsed the writing with a proviso that the gift was to be known as the Mary Yates Johnston memorial fund and the proceeds of the fund to be used to educate students preparing for the ministry.

Mary Johnston anticipated the due date by paying $1,000 during her lifetime and the college set the money aside to be held as a scholarship fund as requested by the donor. Seven months later she notified the college that she repudiated the promise.

Mary Johnston died. Thirty days passed and the $4,000 balance was not paid to the College. Thereupon this action was commenced against the executor of her will, the National Chautauqua County Bank of Jamestown, to recover that sum.

The defense offered was that the promise of Mary Yates Johnston was a gratuitous promise, nothing other than a gift being intended. The College as promisee did not accept the offer made. It gave no consideration, surrendered no legal right at the request of the promisor in exchange for her promise.

CARDOZO, C. J. * * *

The law of charitable subscriptions has been a prolific source of controversy in this state and elsewhere. We have held that a promise of that order is unenforceable like any other if made without consideration. On the other hand, though professing to apply to such subscriptions the general law of contract, we have found consideration present where the general law of contract, at least as then declared, would have said that it was absent.

A classic form of statement identifies consideration with detriment to the promisee sustained by virtue of the promise. So compendious a formula is little more than a half truth. There is need of many a supplementary gloss before the outline can be so filled in as to depict the classic doctrine. "The promise and the consideration must purport to be the motive each for the other, in whole or at least in part. It is not enough that the promise induces the detriment or that the detriment induces the promise if the other half is wanting."[1] If A promises B to make him a gift, consideration may be lacking, though B has renounced other opportunities for betterment in the faith that the promise will be kept.

The half truths of one generation tend at times to perpetuate themselves in the law as the whole truth of another, when constant repetition brings it about that qualifications, taken once for granted, are disregarded or forgotten. The doctrine of consideration has not escaped the common lot. As far back as 1881, Judge Holmes in his lectures on the Common Law (page 292), separated the detriment, which is merely a consequence of the promise from the detriment, which is in truth the motive or inducement, and yet added that the courts "have gone far in obliterating this distinction." The tendency toward effacement has not lessened with the years. On the contrary, there has grown up of recent days a doctrine that a substitute for consideration or an exception to its ordinary requirements can be found in what is styled "a promissory estoppel." Whether the exception has made its way in this state to such an extent as to permit us to say that the general law of consideration has been modified accordingly, we do not now attempt to say. Cases such as Siegel

[1]Langdell, "Summary of the Law of Contracts," pp. 82-88.

v. Spear & Co.[1] may be signposts on the road. Certain, at least, it is that we have adopted the doctrine of promissory estoppel as the equivalent of consideration in connection with our law of charitable subscriptions. So long as those decisions stand, the question is not merely whether the enforcement of a charitable subscription can be squared with the doctrine of consideration in all its ancient rigor. The question may also be whether it can be squared with the doctrine of consideration as qualified by the doctrine of promissory estoppel.

We have said that the cases in this state have recognized this exception, if exception it is thought to be. Thus, in Barnes v. Perine[2] the subscription was made without request, express or implied, that the church do anything on the faith of it. Later, the church did incur expense to the knowledge of the promisor, and in the reasonable belief that the promise would be kept. We held the promise binding, though consideration there was none except upon the theory of a promissory estoppel. In Presbyterian Society v. Beach[3] a situation substantially the same became the basis for a like ruling. So in Roberts v. Cobb[4] and Keuka College v. Ray[5] the moulds of consideration as fixed by the old doctrine were subjected to a like expansion. Very likely, conceptions of public policy have shaped, more or less subconsciously, the rulings thus made. Judges have been affected by the thought that "defenses of that character" are "breaches of faith towards the public, and especially towards those engaged in the same enterprise, and an unwarrantable disappointment of the reasonable expectations of those interested."[6] The result

[1]Reported in Volume 234 New York Reports 479. In that case the defendant took the plaintiff's furniture for safe-keeping and promised to obtain a fire insurance policy to cover the furniture. The defendant failed to do so and when loss by fire was sustained, the plaintiff was permitted to recover though no consideration had been given by the plaintiff for the defendant's promise to obtain the insurance.

[2]Reported in Volume 12 New York Reports 18.

[3]Reported in Volume 74 New York Reports 72.

[4]Reported in Volume 103 New York Reports 600.

[5]Reported in Volume 167 New York Reports 96.

[6]Allen, *J.*, in *Barnes* v. *Perine, supra.*

speaks for itself irrespective of the motive. Decisions which have stood so long, and which are supported by so many considerations of public policy and reason, will not be overruled to save the symmetry of a concept which itself came into our law, not so much from any reasoned conviction of its justice, as from historical accidents of practice and procedure. The concept survives as one of the distinctive features of our legal system. We have no thought to suggest that it is obsolete or on the way to be abandoned. As in the case of other concepts, however, the pressure of exceptions has led to irregularities of form.

It is in this background of precedent that we are to view the problem now before us. The background helps to an understanding of the implications inherent in subscription and acceptance. This is so though we may find in the end that without recourse to the innovation of promissory estoppel the transaction can be fitted within the mould of consideration as established by tradition.

The promisor wished to have a memorial to perpetuate her name. She imposed a condition that the "gift" should "be known as the Mary Yates Johnston Memorial Fund." The moment that the college accepted $1,000 as a payment on account, there was an assumption of a duty to do whatever acts were customary or reasonably necessary to maintain the memorial fairly and justly in the spirit of its creation. The college could not accept the money and hold itself free thereafter from personal responsibility to give effect to the condition. More is involved in the receipt of such a fund than a mere acceptance of money to be held to a corporate use. The purpose of the founder would be unfairly thwarted or at least inadequately served if the college failed to communicate to the world, or in any event to applicants for the scholarship, the title of the memorial. By implication it undertook, when it accepted a portion of the "gift," that in its circulars of information and in other customary ways when making announcement of this scholarship, it would couple with the announcement the name of the donor. The donor was not at liberty to gain the benefit of such an undertaking upon the payment of a part and disappoint the expectation that there would be payment of the residue. If the college had stated after receiving $1,000 upon account of the subscription, that it would apply the money to the prescribed use, but that in its circulars of information and when responding to prospective applicants it would deal with the fund as an anonymous donation, there is little doubt that the subscriber would have been at liberty to treat this statement as the repudiation of a duty impliedly assumed, a repudiation justifying a refusal to make payments in the future. Obligation in such circumstances is correlative and mutual. A case much in point is New Jersey Hospital v. Wright, 95 N. J. Law, 462, where a subscription for the maintenance of a bed in a hospital was held to be enforceable by virtue of an implied promise by the hospital that the bed should be maintained in the name of the subscriber. A parallel situation might arise upon the endowment of a chair or a fellowship in a university by the aid of annual payments with the condition that it should commemorate the name of the founder or that of a member of his family. The university would fail to live up to the fair meaning of its promise if it were to publish in its circulars of information and elsewhere the existence of a chair or a fellowship in the prescribed subject, and omit the benefactor's name. A duty to act in ways beneficial to the promisor and beyond the application of the fund to the mere uses of the trust would be cast upon the promisee by the acceptance of the money. We do not need to measure the extent either of benefit to the promisor or of detriment to the promisee implicit in this duty. "If a person chooses to make an extravagant promise for an inadequate consideration, it is his own affair." It was long ago said that "when a thing is to be done by the plaintiff, be it never so small, this is a sufficient consideration to ground an action."[1] The longing for posthumous remembrance is an emotion not so weak as to justify us in saying that its gratification is a negligible good.

[1]Holdsworth, "History of English Law", Volume 8, page 17.

We think the duty assumed by the plaintiff to perpetuate the name of the founder of the memorial is sufficient in itself to give validity to the subscription within the rules that define consideration for a promise of that order. When the promisee subjected itself to such a duty at the implied request of the promisor, the result was the creation of a bilateral agreement. There was a promise on the one side and on the other a return promise, made, it is true, by implication, but expressing an obligation that had been exacted as a condition of the payment. A bilateral agreement may exist though one of the mutual promises be a promise "implied in fact," an inference from conduct as opposed to an inference from words. We think the fair inference to be drawn from the acceptance of a payment on account of the subscription is a promise by the college to do what may be necessary on its part to make the scholarship effective. The plan conceived by the subscriber will be mutilated and distorted unless the sum to be accepted is adequate to the end in view. Moreover, the time to affix her name to the memorial will not arrive until the entire fund has been collected. The college may thus thwart the purpose of the payment on account if at liberty to reject a tender of the residue. It is no answer to say that a duty would then arise to make restitution of the money. If such a duty may be imposed, the only reason for its existence must be that there is then a failure of "consideration." To say that there is a failure of consideration is to concede that a consideration has been promised, since otherwise it could not fail. No doubt there are times and situations in which limitations laid upon a promisee in connection with the use of what is paid by a subscriber lack the quality of a consideration, and are to be classed merely as conditions. "It is often difficult to determine whether words of condition in a promise indicate a request for consideration or state a mere condition in a gratuitous promise. An aid, though not a conclusive test in determining which construction of the promise is more reasonable is an inquiry whether the happening of the condition will be a benefit to the promisor. If so, it is a fair inference that the happening was requested as a consideration."[1] Such must be the meaning of this transaction unless we are prepared to hold that the college may keep the payment on account, and thereafter nullify the scholarship which is to preserve the memory of the subscriber. The fair implication to be gathered from the whole transaction is assent to the condition and the assumption of a duty to go forward with performance. The subscriber does not say: I hand you $1,000 and you may make up your mind later, after my death, whether you will undertake to commemorate my name. What she says in effect is this: I hand you $1,000 and if you are unwilling to commemorate me, the time to speak is now.

The conclusion thus reached makes it needless to consider whether, aside from the feature of a memorial, a promissory estoppel may result from the assumption of a duty to apply the fund, so far as already paid, to special purposes not mandatory under the provisions of the college charter (the support and education of students preparing for the ministry)—an assumption induced by the belief that other payments sufficient in amount to make the scholarship effective would be added to the fund thereafter upon the death of the subscriber.

The judgment of the Appellate Division and that of the Trial Term should be reversed, and judgment ordered for the plaintiff as prayed for in the complaint.

POUND, CRANE, LEHMAN and O'BRIEN, *JJ.*, concur with CARDOZO, *Ch. J.;* KELLOGG, *J.*, dissents[2] in opinion in which ANDREWS, *J.*, concurs.

---

[1]Williston, "Law of Contracts" Sec. 112.

[2]The dissenting opinion found nothing in the offeror's writing which showed any intent on her part to make a contract with Alleghany College. The latter, it said, was not asked to do anything. She merely expressed a desire. At most, her offer could be accepted by the college by doing what she asked for and then only after her death. But upon her death her offer also terminated as a matter of law. There could not then possibly be an acceptance of that offer.

"NOT WHAT HAS BEEN DONE UNDER A STATUTE, BUT WHAT MAY BE DONE, IS THE TEST OF ITS VALIDITY"

Connolly v. *Justice Scudder*, 247 N. Y. 401 (1928)

Rumors concerning dishonesty among public officials in the County of Queens impelled a citizen to file charges with Governor Alfred E. Smith on December 15, 1927 against Maurice E. Connolly, the President of the Borough of Queens. The charges were filed with a view to his removal from office. On the following day the Governor, pursuant to Section 34 of the Public Officers Law, directed Justice Townsend Scudder, one of the Justices of the Supreme Court, to take evidence concerning these charges and to report his findings and his conclusions to the Governor.

Two weeks later, Justice Scudder gave notice to Connolly that he would commence the taking of evidence at the County Courthouse in Long Island City, on February 1, 1928. This notice was signed by the Justice with the addition of his official title as Justice of the Supreme Court.

Preparations had in the meantime been begun and Emory R. Buckner, a New York attorney, was designated as counsel in the proceeding. Seven associate counsels, two engineers, a firm of accountants, many process servers and clerical assistants were appointed and a suite of offices obtained for these assistants. It was planned to hold secret hearings, at which neither Connolly nor his counsel were to be present and Justice Scudder was to select such evidence as in his opinion seemed credible. This evidence was then, in turn, to be presented in public in the presence of Connolly and his counsel.

Witnesses were immediately summoned under subpoena to attend before Justice Scudder in the preliminary secret investigations and their testimony taken under oath.

The activities of Justice Scudder soon met with opposition. In the early part of January, 1928, several witnesses who had been subpoenaed to attend one of these preliminary sessions applied to the Supreme Court for an order to vacate the subpoenas served upon them on the ground that they had been issued without warrant of law. The court upheld the validity of the subpoenas and an appeal was immediately filed to the Court of Appeals on the claim that constitutional rights of these witnesses had been violated.

In the first week of February, Connolly obtained from the Appellate Division an order which commanded Justice Scudder to refrain from any further proceeding except at a hearing at which Connolly was afforded an opportunity to be present. This decision was based upon the ruling that Section 34 of the Public Officers Law did not warrant the proceedings ruled against.

The legislature of New York which was then in session immediately amended Section 34 so as to provide that in any proceeding for the removal of a public officer the Governor may direct his delegate, whether a judge or a commissioner, to conduct an investigation into the charges, and that neither the officer proceeded against nor his counsel was to have any right to be present unless expressly so permitted. The investigating officer was authorized to employ counsel and the amendment further provided that all acts theretofore performed by one designated by the Governor in a pending proceeding were legalized and confirmed.

Upon the adoption of this amendment to the statute, the Appellate Division vacated its previous order.

The two appeals, one by the witnesses whose application to vacate the subpoenas served upon them had been denied, and the other by Connolly whose attempt to stop the proceedings was rendered unsuccessful by the second ruling of the Appellate Division, were heard together by the Court of Appeals.

The following is the opinion of Chief Judge Cardozo which was concurred in by all the Judges of the Court.

CARDOZO, C. J. * * *

We think there has been an attempt by section 34 of the Public Officers Law, both in its original and in its amended form, to charge a justice of the Supreme Court with the mandatory performance of duties nonjudicial. He is made the delegate of the Governor in aid of an executive act, the removal of a public officer. At the word of command he is to give over the work of judging, and set himself to other work, the work of probing and advising. His findings when made will have none of the authority of a judgment. To borrow Bacon's phrase, they will not "give the rule or sentence." They will not be preliminary or ancillary to any rule or sentence to be pronounced by the judiciary in any of its branches. They will be mere advice to the Governor, who may adopt them, or modify them, or reject them altogether. From the beginnings of our history, the principle has been enforced that there is no inherent power in Executive or Legislature to charge the judiciary with administrative functions except when reasonably incidental to the fulfillment of judicial duties. The exigencies of government have made it necessary to relax a merely doctrinaire adherence to a principle so flexible and practical, so largely a matter of sensible approximation, as that of the separation of powers. Elasticity has not meant that what is of the essence of the judicial function may be destroyed by turning the power to decide into a pallid opportunity to consult and recommend. The question arose as far back as 1792. An act of Congress required the Circuit Courts of the United States to examine into the pension claims of soldiers and seamen of the Revolution, and to certify their opinion to the Secretary of War with a view to corrective legislation. The judges of the several circuits concurred in a determination that the duty was not judicial.[1] In 1851 the Supreme Court of the United States considered that determination and approved it, declining jurisdiction under an act not widely different.[2] There was an opinion by Taney, *C.J.*, which has become a landmark of the law. Nowhere has the doctrine thus established been applied more steadily or forcefully than in the courts of New York.[3] The function of the judges "is to determine controversies between litigants." They are not adjuncts or advisers, much less investigating instrumentalities, of other agencies of government. Their pronouncements are not subject to review by Governor or Legislature. They speak "the rule or sentence."

The statute was thus an encroachment upon the independence of judicial power even in the form in which it stood until recently amended. Still more clearly is it such an encroachment in its form as now reframed. The judge is made a prosecutor. He is to have his counsel and assistant counsel and experts and detectives. He is to follow trails of suspicion, to uncover hidden wrongs, to

---

[1] *Hayburn's Case,* Reported in Volume 2 Dallas (United States) 409.

[2] *United States* v. *Ferreira,* Reported in Volume 13 Howard (United States) 40.

[3] *Matter of Davies,* reported in Volume 168 New York Reports 89.

build up a case as a prosecutor builds one. If he were the district attorney of the county, he would do no more and no less. What he learns is not committed to a record available to all the world. It is locked within his breast to be withheld or disclosed as his discretion shall determine. No doubt he is to act impartially, neither presenting from malice nor concealing from favor. One might say the same of any prosecutor. The outstanding fact remains that his conclusion is to be announced upon a case developed by himself. Centuries of common-law tradition warn us with echoing impressiveness that this is not a judge's work. We should be sorry to weaken that tradition by any judgment of this court.

Superficial analogies are suggested, but superficial only. A magistrate before whom there is laid an information of the commission of a crime may take the depositions of the informant and prosecutor and of any witnesses produced. His inquiry is judicial. If he finds that a crime has been committed and that there is reasonable cause to believe that the defendant has committed it, he issues a warrant of arrest. He does not keep to himself the knowledge thus acquired, but embodies it in depositions which are exhibited to the defendant like any other public record. A justice of the Supreme Court, upon proof by affidavit that the moneys of a town or village have been unlawfully or corruptly expended, shall make a summary investigation of the affairs of such town or village, and the accounts of such officers, and in his discretion may appoint experts to make such investigation and may cause the result thereof to be published in such manner as he may deem proper. The validity of that statute has been assumed, though never questioned or determined. There are adversary parties. On the one side are the taxpayers, not less than 25 in number, submitting the petition; on the other the suspected officers, to whom notice must be given. Like an examination by a magistrate, the inquiry is preliminary or ancillary to action unmistakably judicial. "If such justice shall be satisfied" that any of the moneys of such town or village are wasted or misapplied, "he shall forthwith grant an order" restraining such unlawful use. An Appellate Division, charged with a duty to supervise the conduct of its officers, the members of the bar, orders an inquiry into abuses believed to have developed. It may act of its own motion upon a showing of wrongdoing by one member of the bar. There is authority for the view that it may act upon a like showing of wrongdoing by an indeterminate group, whether the group be large or small. Once more, as with an examining magistrate, inquiry is pursued in aid of a judicial function. We have no occasion to determine with finality whether jurisdiction was legitimately assumed in all these cases or in any of them. However far they go, they do not reach the case at hand. No doubt there are peripheral zones where the judicial and the administrative merge into each other. The hinterland may be plain when the frontier is uncertain.

The range of our decision will not be misapprehended. We deny the power of the Legislature to charge a justice of the Supreme Court with the duties of a prosecutor in aid of the Executive. We do not question its power to lay such duties on the Executive himself or on a commissioner appointed as his agent or adviser. Just as the Governor may investigate and afterwards remove, so his commissioner may investigate and later recommend removal. Neither the one nor the other is subject to the supervision of the courts. The argument is made that by a provision of the charter,[1] a president of a borough is not to be removed without "an opportunity of being heard in his defense".[2] Nothing in that requirement amounts to a direction that in the performance of an executive act, the function of inquisition shall be divorced from that of hearing and decision. Other answers are available, but they do not have to be developed.

We reach the final stage in the course of the respondent's argument. Granting that functions nonjudicial may not be cast upon a judge so as to impose a duty of acceptance, the privilege, we are told, is his to assume the per-

---

[1]Greater New York Charter, Sections 122, 382.

[2]Constitution of the State of New York, Article 10, Section 1.

formance of the duty, not in his capacity of judge, but in his private or individual capacity as if named as a commissioner. The action of the circuit judges who refused to hold themselves bound by the act of Congress of 1792 is cited as a precedent. Some of the judges, declining to serve in the capacity of judges, "agreed to construe the power as conferred on them individually as commissioners," and as commissioners reported to the Secretary of War.

The Constitution of New York provides:[1]

> "The judges of the Court of Appeals and the justices of the Supreme Court shall not hold any other public office or trust, except that they shall be eligible to serve as members of a constitutional convention."

There is no equivalent provision in the Constitution of the United States. The appellants maintain that service as commissioner in removal proceedings under section 34 of the statute, if not the acceptance of an office, is the acceptance of a public trust.

The prohibition has an ancient history. It goes back for its origin to the Constitution of 1777. At that time it was limited to the acceptance of an "office." "That the chancellor and judges of the Supreme Court shall not, at the same time, hold any other office, excepting that of Delegate to the general Congress, upon special occasions; and that the first judges of the County Courts in the several counties, shall not, at the same time, hold any other office, excepting that of Senator or Delegate to the general Congress."[2] The next Constitution, that of 1821, broadened the prohibition, at least in terms, so as to include not only an office, but any public trust. "Neither the chancellor nor justices of the Supreme Court, nor any circuit judge, shall hold any other office or public trust. All votes for any elective office, given by the Legislature or the people, for the chancellor or a justice of the Supreme Court, or circuit judge, during his continuance in his

[1]Article 6, Section 19.

[2]Constitution of 1777, Article 25.

judicial office, shall be void."[1] The depth of feeling on the subject can be gathered from the form of the resolution as first proposed to the convention by the judiciary committee:

> "They (the chancellor and the judges) shall not, on any pretense, hold any other office or public trust, whether created under this Constitution, or otherwise; and their acceptance thereof, shall vacate their judicial offices: Nor shall they be eligible to the office of Governor, or Lieutenant Governor, within two years after the expiration or resignation of their judicial offices."[2]

The Constitution of 1846 continued the prohibition without substantial change from that of 1821. "They (the judges of the Court of Appeals and the justices of the Supreme Court) shall not hold any other office or public trust." A new prohibition was added: "They shall not exercise any power of appointment to public office."[3] This latter prohibition was dropped in the amendment of 1874, very likely in the belief that it was sufficiently embodied in the clause prohibiting the acceptance of any other public trust. No change was made in respect of these provisions by the Constitution of 1894, and none of importance by the revision of the judiciary article of 1926.

The decisions construing the prohibition are halting and obscure. One has difficulty finding the common denominator that will bring them into harmony.

People ex rel. Washington v. Nichols[4] brought before the court a provision of the appropriation bill of 1871. The sum of $20,000 was to be paid for relics of George Washington upon the certificate of Martin Grover and two others that the relics were in their opinion genuine. Martin Grover was then a judge of this court, though the statute did not so describe him. He refused to join in a

---

1Constitution of 1821, Article 5, Section 7.

2Journal of Convention of 1821, pp. 101, 108; see, also, p. 296.

3Constitution of 1846, Article 6, Section 8.

4Reported in Volume 52 New York Reports 478.

certificate of approval, and the question came up whether he was competent to act. The court defined an office as "an employment on behalf of the government, in any station or public trust, not merely transient, occasional, or incidental." Office was thus a species of which a public trust was the genus. The court went on to rule that the "doing of such an act, a single act like this," did not involve the "holding" either of an office or a trust within the fair intendment of the constitutional provision. The Legislature had not said that annexed to the judicial office there should be a continuing duty to certify or audit at the request of the Executive or of others. The power was exhausted by the performance of "a single act."

Matter of Hathaway[1] brought before the court an act of 1830, empowering the Supreme Court to appoint a commissioner to serve as a surrogate for the purpose of a particular proceeding, when the surrogate, and other officers having the power of a surrogate, appeared to be disqualified. The case was decided by a closely divided court. No reference was made in the opinions to this provision of the Constitution. The only question considered was the effect of another provision, whereby the judges were prohibited from exercising any "power of appointment to public office." The ruling was that since the office of surrogate was not vacant, the designation of a substitute to serve in a single case was not an appointment to "office" any more than an appointment of a referee or a commissioner of appraisal. The term office "embraces the idea of tenure, duration, emolument and duties fixed by law."[2] A "trust" is not an "office," unless clearly so recognized by Constitution or statute, if it lacks the quality of permanence.

People ex rel. Welch v. Bard[3] brought before the court the provision of the Military Law of 1908 authorizing a justice of the Supreme Court to execute a certificate or order calling upon the military authorities for aid in case

---

[1]Reported in Volume 71 New York Reports 238.

[2]Per Stone, *J.*, in *Metcalf & Eddy* v. *Mitchell*, reported in Volume 269 United States Reports 514, 520.

[3]Reported in Volume 209 New York Reports 304.

of any breach of the peace, riot, tumult, etc. Plainly there was here no office or public trust apart from that of judge. The certificate or order was incidental to the duty of a magistrate in the preservation of the peace. With equal reason the point might have been made that a magistrate should be denied the power of a peace officer in making an arrest. "The performance of administrative duties as to matters incidental to the exercise of judicial powers or which have some reasonable connection with a judicial purpose has repeatedly been sanctioned."

The foregoing are the chief decisions invoked by the respondent to sustain his assumption of the duties of a commissioner. We pass to the cases invoked by the appellants.

Matter of Davies[1] brought before the court the monopoly act of 1899 empowering a justice of the Supreme Court on the petition of the Attorney General to make an order, in advance of any suit, for the examination of a witness. The statute was analyzed in an elaborate opinion. We upheld it for the reason that the examination was incidental to a judicial proceeding, prospective, if not pending. Except for this feature, the duties would be administrative, and the order could not stand. If the willingness of a judge to accept administrative trusts could avail without more to validate his action, the elaborate opinion was in the main a waste of effort. Enough that the order had been made, and the trusts had been accepted. The opinion is instinct with a ruling that acceptance would have been futile unless the duties were judicial.

People v. Hall[2] brought before the court the statute empowering the justices of the Appellate Division to appoint a commissioner of jurors. We upheld it on the ground that the power, though a public trust, is one reasonably incidental to the performance of judicial duties. It is analogous to the one so often exercised by courts of appointing clerks and other officers "necessary to the trans-

---

[1]*Supra.*.
[2]Reported in Volume 169 New York Reports 184.

action of their business." Such a power involves a public trust, because it is intrusted to public officers, to be exercised in behalf of the public, by clothing a private citizen with the powers and duties of public office."[1]

Matter of Gilroy,[2] a decision by the Appellate Division, is to the effect that one elected a justice of the Supreme Court vacates through his acceptance of the office an earlier appointment as commissioner of appraisal since by retaining it he would be holding another public trust.

The Case of the Supervisors of Election[3] was decided by the Supreme Judicial Court of Massachusetts under a provision of the Massachusetts Constitution substantially the same as ours. It held void a statute whereby a justice of the Supreme Judicial Court was to be permitted, in term time or vacation, to appoint two supervisors of election for each of the city wards. "We cannot exercise this power as judges, because it is not a judicial function; nor as commissioners, because the Constitution does not allow us to hold any such office."

The problem now before us must be viewed in the background of authority supplied by this summary of the precedents. So viewing it, we think that within the constitutional prohibition there was an acceptance of a "public trust."

The statute annexes or seeks to annex to the office of a judge, not a temporary power to be exhausted by a single act (as in the case of the Washington relics), but a continuing power to be exercised whenever occasion shall arise. As often as the Governor commands, the judge is to obey. As often as the need arises, the call is to be met. He is to be a standing commissioner whose function is to serve when summoned. In such circumstances, the public trust does not cease to be continuing and permanent because the judge may be willing to fulfill it on one occasion and unwilling on another. As well might one urge that a power conferred upon the judges to fill vacancies in office

---

[1]Per Vann, *J.*, in *People* v. *Hall,* reported in Volume 169 New York Reports, at page 195.

[2]Reported in Volume 11 New York Appellate Division Reports 65.

[3]Reported in Volume 114 Massachusetts Reports 247.

whenever they occurred would be something other than a public trust because the judges might act as to one office and refuse to act as to another. As well might one say that the order reviewed by this court in Matter of Davies, supra, would be upheld, though the statute had been read as conferring administrative powers, on the theory that when separate applications are separately considered, there is involved in respect of each the acceptance of a separate trust. In determining the quality of the trust, regard must be had to the intention of the Legislature in directing its creation. If the intention was, as here, to annex a permanent duty as an incident to the judicial office, a public trust has been created though the occasions for discharging it may be irregular or fitful.

The policy at the root of the constitutional prohibition reinforces this conclusion. The policy is to conserve the time of the judges for the performance of their work as judges, and to save them from the entanglements, at times the partisan suspicions, so often the result of other and conflicting duties. Some of these possibilities find significant illustration in the very cases before us now. Here is an inquiry which has already separated the respondent for more than two months from the discharge of his judicial duties, and which is likely to continue for many weeks to come. The charges as first submitted involved a scrutiny of the acts of the accused official in multifarious transactions for 15 years or more. Supplemental charges have now been filed with the result that the issues are more involved than ever. The great staff of counsel and assistants engaged upon the work is a token of its complexity and its probable duration. Interference so prolonged with assignments to judicial duty is the very evil that was meant to be hit by the prohibitions of the Constitution directed against dual office. True indeed it is that there may be times when the duties of a commissioner will be less onerous and protracted. Even so, the nature of the trust must be measured by its reasonable possibilities. Not what has been done under a statute, but what may reasonably be done under it, is the test of its validity.

The content of the duties tends with as much significance as their duration to point to performance as the acceptance of a public trust. A commissioner in these proceedings is more than a referee or an arbitrator, whose duties touch the parties affected by his decision, and concern the public interests remotely if at all. Here the very subject of the inquiry is one distinctively public, the tenure of a public officer. In pursuing that inquiry, the commissioner is authorized from time to time, so long as he functions as commissioner, to incur bills for his expenses and the expenses of his staff. These bills, subject to audit, will be payable from the public purse. If the power to incur such expenses and charge them on the public treasury is not a public trust, one is at a loss to understand how such a trust can be created.

We hold that the respondent is disqualified, while retaining the office of judge, to act as the delegate of the Governor under one name or another. The prohibitions of the Constitution are not to be evaded through the form of accepting as an individual what the judge must reject. At least, that is so when what is done is official and not personal in its quality and incidents. In this instance neither Legislature nor Executive nor judge had any thought of evasion. The Legislature did not intend when a commission was directed to a judge that he should act as an individual, his title as judge being mere *descriptio personae.* It annexed the duty to the office. The Governor in issuing the commission did not intend to invite co-operation by a private citizen as an act of grace or favor. The language of the designation is not the language of request or of appointment. It is the language of command, addressed by the Executive to a member of the judiciary who is expected to obey. Above all, the respondent himself had no thought to accept the designation in any new capacity. From first to last he has assumed to act as judge and nothing else. He has made his return and affidavits as a justice of the Supreme Court. He has issued his notices and subpoenas with recitals that describe him as a justice of the Supreme Court, and with the addition of his title as such justice he has signed his name thereto. We were informed by his counsel that in case of need he will exercise the power to punish a contumacious witness for a contempt of his authority, though such power does not exist unless the subpoena has been issued by a justice of the court.[1] Equivocal acts will be so interpreted as to escape a violation of the constitutional command, and even the risk of violation, when conduct, though permissible, is close to the line of danger. Here the acts are not equivocal. Nothing has been said and nothing has been done with the will to serve in any other capacity than that of a justice of the court.

We are satisfied that in so holding we do not misread the respondent's thought and purpose. The Governor, in selecting a judge so distinguished and experienced, was animated by a high sense of public duty, the desire to name a delegate of unquestioned ability and character. Mr. Justice Scudder was animated by a like sense of public duty in responding to a call to service. He thought, beyond a doubt, that the effect of the statute was to annex the duty to the office. If he was uncertain of its validity, he preferred to wait to condemn it until invalidity had been adjudged after argument and deliberation in appropriate proceedings. He supposed that he was discharging his duty as a judge in assuming a heavy burden incidental to the office. There is no reason to believe that his choice would have been the same if he had supposed that he was abandoning, pro tanto, his duty as a judge. His conduct is misinterpreted if we read it as evidencing an election to step aside from his judgeship and take upon himself, with all the chances of illegality, the duties of a commissioner. He has been the judge throughout.

Upon the appeal by Richardson and others, the order of the Special Term should be reversed, and the motion to vacate the subpoenas granted.

Upon the appeal by the petitioner Connolly, the order of the Appellate Division should be reversed, and an order of prohibition granted commanding the respondent to desist from further action as a justice of the Supreme Court

[1] Civil Practice Act, Section 406.

in the investigation or hearing of the subject-matter of these charges.[1]

POUND, CRANE, ANDREWS, LEHMAN, KELLOGG, and O'BRIEN, *JJ.*, concur.

[1] After this decision was rendered, Governor Alfred E. Smith appointed Honorable C. J. Shearn to conduct the inquiry. Connolly resigned as president of the borough of Queens. The political favorites, who had obtained lucrative contracts at exorbitant figures to construct sewers, were indicted for income tax evasions. Connolly and Phillips, the latter the apparent chief beneficiary, were indicted for conspiracy. Phillips died before the trial got under way. Connolly was convicted.

"THERE ARE DUTIES, TOO, FOR THE DESERTED SPOUSE AS WELL AS THE DESERTER"

Mirizio v. *Mirizio,* 248 N. Y. 175 (1928)

Cosmo Mirizio and Fannie Mirizio became husband and wife by means of a civil ceremony in September, 1921. They were observers of the Catholic religion and entered into an agreement that they would not live together as husband and wife until the performance of a religious ceremony. The ceremony, however, never occurred as Cosmo refused to join in it. Any sexual relationship without a religious ceremony violated the wife's conscientious and religious scruples and she refused to yield. Cosmo, on his part, refused to support his wife unless she agreed to and did share his home and board. The result was an action commenced by him to annul the marriage, which was dismissed. Then an action was brought by Fannie against her husband alleging abandonment and non-support and demanding a judgment of separation with provision for her support.

The litigation was carried from the Supreme Court of the State of New York, through the Appellate Division and to the Court of Appeals. Cosmo's defense was sustained in all courts, the Court of Appeals rendering its decision on January 26, 1926 to the effect that a wife seeking affirmative relief under her marriage contract must show that she is willing to discharge her obligations under it and that one of her obligations is to participate in the ordinary physical marriage relations with her husband, however much this relationship may be distasteful to her.[1]

The day after the decision of the Court of Appeals was handed down, Fannie Mirizio wrote a letter to her husband offering to live with him as a wife in every sense, but his answer was that though he would once have greeted the offer with joy, his love had vanished with the years. Subsequent attempts on the part of the wife met with no response.

Fannie Mirizio then commenced a new action for separation and for support. The trial judge decided in her favor, but the Appellate Division on appeal dismissed her complaint on the ground that she had so definitely abandoned her husband that her repentance after a five-year delay was too late. She appealed.

[1]This first Mirizio decision is reported in Volume 242 of the New York Reports 74.

Two judges of the Court of Appeals (Crane and Lehman) dissented. Judge Cardozo did not sit in the case and therefore did not vote on the decision.

CARDOZO, C. J. * * *

The question therefore is whether the refusal to cohabit with the defendant upon the grounds and in the conditions stated is an abandonment so definitive as to be unaffected by repentance. The plaintiff acted on advice of counsel and under a claim of legal right. She believed that she was not recreant to her duty as a wife when she declined to live with a husband who had shamelessly repudiated a promise to appease her conscience and his own by sanctifying the marriage with the blessing of the church. She had probable cause for that belief, as is sufficiently attested by the close division in this court. It turns out that she was in error. The moment she was so advised, she gave notice to the defendant that she would yield submission to the law. We are told that her error has barred his door to her forever.

Not every separation is an abandonment beyond annulment or recall. One must look to all the circumstances. Of these, time will commonly be the weightiest, yet not always so decisive that it cannot be neutralized by others. We have refused to compress within a formula the extenuating possibilities of behavior in all its myriad diversities. "What is reasonable will depend on the circumstances of the case and the conduct of the parties."[1] Lawless repudiation of duty, an attitude and spirit of mere rebellion or defiance, maintained without repentance after cooling time has passed, may exact a finding of definitive abandonment though the interval is short. Mistake and provocation and hardship and reservations will permit another finding though the interval is long. There are duties, too, for the deserted spouse as well as the deserter. One who is chargeable with fault contributing to the breach, palliating and explaining it, though not excusing it altogether, may not stand back indifferent, refusing the concessions to be expected of gentleness and honor. Separation, to be abandonment, must be obstinate and hardened.

We are to measure the plaintiff's conduct by these and cognate tests of right dealing and humanity. She was the

---

[1]*Bohmert* v. *Bohmert,* reported in Volume 241 New York Reports 446.

victim of mistake. She acted, as we have seen, in accordance with the advice of counsel and with probable cause. She was the victim, besides, of provocation and oppression. The defendant had treated her with indifference to her feelings and in wanton disregard of his solemn words of honor. His refusal to fulfill the promise that would have made her his at once gives color to the belief that he was scheming to be rid of her. He could not have acted differently if he had been seeking from the beginning to provoke her to a course of conduct that would free him from the performance of his duty as her husband. With all these affronts, she maintained her wifely station. In declining to live with him, she did so with reservations and conditions: She would live apart till he kept faith with her, and then she would be his. We have said that she was wrong. The adjudication then made binds us, however emphatic the dissent. We have no thought to depart from it. Plainly, however, she was not wrong in such a sense or in such a degree as to betoken defiance of duty, a "rebellious and unrepentant" spirit, a will to live apart whether the law approved or frowned. She invoked the law to aid her. The moment it condemned her, she bowed to its command.

We think a term of separation may not be said to constitute, as a matter of law, a definitive abandonment when it is bounded by a lawsuit, maintained upon reasonable grounds and with sincerity of conviction for the very purpose of determining whether the separation shall continue. No doubt the interval has been a long one, nearly five and a half years, between marriage and submission. At first the husband was the plaintiff in an unfounded action for annulment. The wife postponed, it seems, her suit for separation until his had been dismissed. But if the time has been long, the defendant could have made it short. There has never been a day in all these years when he might not have had the plaintiff as his own if he had done what a man of honor and a gentleman should have been prompt and glad to do. One is not aggrieved by a separation thus fostered and prolonged.

A plea of former judgment has been urged. It has no basis in the record. There was no holding in the former suit that the plaintiff's conduct toward her husband had the force of an abandonment. There was not even a holding that she had refused to make her home with him. The holding was merely this, that in refusing him the privilege of sexual intercourse she was guilty of such misconduct as to bar her claim for support while the misconduct continued. The defendant did not counterclaim for a separation either on the ground of abandonment or on any other. If a decree for separation had been given him, another question would be here.

Whatever her errors may have been, the plaintiff is the defendant's wife. He has never offered her a home, nor paid a dollar to maintain her. Not yet has the law released him from the duty of support.

The judgment of the Appellate Division should be reversed, and that of the Special Term affirmed.

POUND, CRANE, ANDREWS, and LEHMAN, *JJ.*, concur.
KELLOGG and O'BRIEN, *JJ.*, dissent.[1]

[1]The dissenters wrote no opinion.

"THE RISK REASONABLY TO BE PERCEIVED DEFINES THE DUTY TO BE OBEYED"

Palsgraf v. *Long Island Railroad Company,* 248 N. Y. 339 (1928)

Helen Palsgraf was waiting for a train on the Long Island Railroad Station which would take her to Rockaway Beach. A train stopped at the station which was bound for another place and Helen Palsgraf remained standing on the platform while it pulled out. Suddenly two men ran forward to get into the train before it could leave the station. One of them reached the platform of the car even though the train was already moving. The other man, carrying a package, just managed to reach the car but seemed unsteady as if about to fall. The guard on the car who had held the door open for the two men running toward the train reached forward to help him in and another guard on the platform ran along with the train and pushed this passenger from behind.

The pulling and pushing of this passenger caused the package from under his arm to fall down upon the rails. The package was about fifteen inches long and was covered with a newspaper and seemed harmless enough. The fact was that it contained fireworks and as they hit the ground they exploded. The shock of the explosion caused a scale which was standing on the platform many feet away and near Helen Palsgraf to fall down. The scale struck Helen Palsgraf, causing her injuries, and she commenced suit against the Long Island Railroad Company. A judgment in her favor was affirmed by the Appellate Division by a divided court, and an appeal was taken by the railroad company to the Court of Appeals.

The Court of Appeals was divided four to three. The minority in an opinion written by Judge Andrews, in which Judges Crane and O'Brien concurred, took a view that the acts of the company's guards were part of the chain which directly led to the injuries of Helen Palsgraf. Since there was no remoteness in time and little in space, it needed no great foresight to predict that, given such an explosion as here, the natural result would be to injure one on the platform at no greater distance from the scene than was Miss Palsgraf.

The majority, however, in an opinion by Chief Judge Cardozo, ruled that none of the intervening acts which led up to the injuries were part of a direct chain constituting proximate cause.

CARDOZO, C. J. * * *

The conduct of the defendant's guard, if a wrong in its relation to the holder of the package, was not a wrong in its relation to the plaintiff, standing far away. Relatively to her it was not negligence at all. Nothing in the situation gave notice that the falling package had in it the potency of peril to persons thus removed. Negligence is not actionable unless it involves the invasion of a legally protected interest, the violation of a right. "Proof of negligence in the air, so to speak, will not do."[1] The plaintiff, as she stood upon the platform of the station, might claim to be protected against intentional invasion of her bodily security. Such invasion is not charged. She might claim to be protected against unintentional invasion by conduct involving in the thought of reasonable men an unreasonable hazard that such invasion would ensue. These, from the point of view of the law, were the bounds of her immunity, with perhaps some rare exceptions, survivals for the most part of ancient forms of liability, where conduct is held to be at the peril of the actor. If no hazard was apparent to the eye of ordinary vigilance, an act innocent and harmless, at least to outward seeming, with reference to her, did not take to itself the quality of a tort because it happened to be a wrong, though apparently not one involving the risk of bodily insecurity, with reference to some one else. "In every instance, before negligence can be predicated of given act, back of the act must be sought and found a duty to the individual complaining, the observance of which would have averted or avoided the injury."[2] The plaintiff sues in her own right for a wrong personal to her, and not as the vicarious beneficiary of a breach of duty to another.

A different conclusion will involve us, and swiftly, too, in a maze of contradictions. A guard stumbles over a package which has been left upon a platform. It seems to be a bundle of newspapers. It turns out to be a can of dynamite. To the eye of ordinary vigilance the bundle is

---

[1]Pollock, "Torts" (11th Ed.) page 455.

[2]McSherry, C. J., in *West Virginia Central & P. R. Co.* v. *State,* reported in Volume 96 Maryland Reports 652, 666.

abandoned waste, which may be kicked or trod on with impunity. Is a passenger at the other end of the platform protected by the law against the unsuspected hazard concealed beneath the waste? If not, is the result to be any different, so far as the distant passenger is concerned, when the guard stumbles over a valise which a truckman or a porter has left upon the walk? The passenger far away, if the victim of a wrong at all, has a cause of action, not derivative, but original and primary. His claim to be protected against invasion of his bodily security is neither greater nor less because the act resulting in the invasion is a wrong to another far removed. In this case, the rights that are said to have been violated, the interests said to have been invaded, are not even of the same order. The man was not injured in his person nor even put in danger. The purpose of the act, as well as its effect, was to make his person safe. If there was a wrong to him at all, which may very well be doubted, it was a wrong to a property interest only, the safety of his package. Out of this wrong to property, which threatened injury to nothing else, there has passed, we are told, to the plaintiff by derivation or succession a right of action for the invasion of an interest of another order, the right to bodily security. The diversity of interests emphasizes the futility of the effort to build the plaintiff's right upon the basis of a wrong to some one else. The gain is one of emphasis, for a like result would follow if the interests were the same. Even then, the orbit of the danger as disclosed to the eye of reasonable vigilance would be the orbit of the duty. One who jostles one's neighbor in a crowd does not invade the rights of others standing at the outer fringe when the unintended contact casts a bomb upon the ground. The wrongdoer as to them is the man who carries the bomb, not the one who explodes it without suspicion of the danger. Life will have to be made over, and human nature transformed, before provision so extravagant can be accepted as the norm of conduct, the customary standard to which behavior must conform.

The argument for the plaintiff is built upon the shifting meanings of such words as "wrong" and "wrongful," and shares their instability. What the plaintiff must show is "a wrong" to herself; i.e., a violation of her own right, and not merely a wrong to some one else, nor conduct "wrongful" because unsocial, but not "a wrong" to any one. We are told that one who drives at reckless speed through a crowded city street is guilty of a negligent act and therefore of a wrongful one, irrespective of the consequences. Negligent the act is, and wrongful in the sense that it is unsocial, but wrongful and unsocial in relation to other travelers, only because the eye of vigilance perceives the risk of damage. If the same act were to be committed on a speedway or a race course, it would lose its wrongful quality. The risk reasonably to be perceived defines the duty to be obeyed, and risk imports relation; it is risk to another or to others within the range of apprehension. This does not mean, of course, that one who launches a destructive force is always relieved of liability, if the force, though known to be destructive, pursues an unexpected path. "It was not necessary that the defendant should have had notice of the particular method in which an accident would occur, if the possibility of an accident was clear to the ordinarily prudent eye."[1] Some acts, such as shooting, are so imminently dangerous to any one who may come within reach of the missile, however unexpectedly, as to impose a duty of prevision not far from that of an insurer. Even today, and much oftener in earlier stages of the law, one acts sometimes at one's peril. Under this head, it may be, fall certain cases of what is known as transferred intent, an act willfully dangerous to A resulting by misadventure in injury to B. These cases aside, wrong is defined in terms of the natural or probable, at least when unintentional. The range of reasonable apprehension is at times a question for the court, and at times, if varying inferences are possible, a question for the jury. Here, by concession, there was nothing in the situation to suggest to the most cautious mind that the parcel wrapped in newspaper would spread wreckage through the station. If the guard had thrown it down knowingly and willfully,

---

[1]*Munsey* v. *Webb,* reported in 231 United States Reports 150, 156.

he would not have threatened the plaintiff's safety, so far as appearances could warn him. His conduct would not have involved, even then, an unreasonable probability of invasion of her bodily security. Liability can be no greater where the act is inadvertent.

Negligence, like risk, is thus a term of relation. Negligence in the abstract, apart from things related, is surely not a tort, if indeed it is understandable at all. Negligence is not a tort, unless it results in the commission of a wrong, and the commission of a wrong imports the violation of a right, in this case, we are told, the right to be protected against interference with one's bodily security. But bodily security is protected, not against all forms of interference or aggression, but only against some. One who seeks redress at law does not make out a cause of action by showing without more that there has been damage to his person. If the harm was not willful, he must show that the act as to him had possibilities of danger so many and apparent as to entitle him to be protected against the doing of it though the harm was unintended. Affront to personality is still the keynote of the wrong. Confirmation of this view will be found in the history and development of the action on the case. Negligence as a basis of civil liability was unknown to medieval law. For damage to the person, the sole remedy was trespass, and trespass did not lie in the absence of aggression, and that direct and personal. Liability for other damage, as where a servant without orders from the master does or omits something to the damage of another, is a plant of later growth. When it emerged out of the legal soil, it was thought of as a variant of trespass, an offshoot of the parent stock. This appears in the form of action, which was known as trespass on the case. The victim does not sue derivatively, or by right of subrogation, to vindicate an interest invaded in the person of another. Thus to view his cause of action is to ignore the fundamental difference between tort and crime. He sues for breach of a duty owing to himself.

The law of causation, remote or proximate, is thus foreign to the case before us. The question of liability is always anterior to the question of the measure of the consequences that go with liability. If there is no tort to be redressed, there is no occasion to consider what damage might be recovered if there were a finding of a tort. We may assume, without deciding, that negligence, not at large or in the abstract, but in relation to the plaintiff, would entail liability for any and all consequences, however novel or extraordinary. There is room for argument that a distinction is to be drawn according to the diversity of interests invaded by the act, as where conduct negligent in that it threatens an insignificant invasion of an interest in property results in an unforseeable invasion of an interest of another order, as, e.g., one of bodily security. Perhaps other distinctions may be necessary. We do not go into the question now. The consequences to be followed must first be rooted in a wrong.

"IF THE HOUSE IS TO BE CLEANED, IT IS FOR THOSE WHO OCCUPY AND GOVERN IT, RATHER THAN FOR STRANGERS, TO DO THE NOISOME WORK"

People ex rel. Karlin v. *Culkin,* 248 N. Y. 465 (1928)

It was rumored in the City of New York that "ambulance chasing" was spreading to a demoralizing extent. The allegations were that members of the bar were commencing actions in order to collect damages for injuries to property and persons in accidents which never had occurred; that injuries were deliberately exaggerated in order to force larger settlements with defendants or their insurers; that poor clients who had legitimate claims did not receive their full share of the monies actually collected; that many attorneys had a large staff of "runners" whose duty it was to learn of any accidents and to have the injured sign a retainer for their employer, an attorney whom the injured may never have heard of; that these "runners" who were not attorneys obtained a share of the fee despite the fact that this was prohibited by the Canons of Ethics; that the retainers were drawn on extravagant terms; that these cases, very often maintained without probable cause and as weapons of extortion, congested the calendars, resulting in delay to litigants who had legitimate disputes to settle.

These reports and accusations resulted in a petition being drawn and presented by three leading bar associations to the Appellate Division for the First Judicial Department (covering New York and Bronx Counties) in January, 1928. The court was asked to inquire into the practices charged in the petition and any other improper practices which might be discovered in the course of the proposed investigation and to so act that a recurrence of the evils would be avoided and the honor of the bar maintained.

The Appellate Division announced that it would exercise its supervisory and disciplinary powers even in cases where specific charges were not made against a named attorney and that it would act of its own motion whenever it had reasonable cause to believe that there had been professional misconduct. Justice Isador Wasservogel, one of the Justices of the Supreme Court, was designated by the Appellate Division to conduct the investigation, with full authority to summon witnesses, compel the giving of testimony and the production of books and documents. The bar associations with the court's authorization appointed Isidor J. Kresel as counsel in aid of the inquiry.

The investigation proceeded. Lawyers were called and so were their clients. Among those subpoenaed to appear was Alexander Karlin, a member of the New York bar of 25 years' standing. It had been discovered that his practice involved the trial of many actions for personal injuries and it was sought to question him concerning his conduct in the procurement of these cases. He appeared in court pursuant to the subpoena but he refused to be sworn.

When he persisted in his stand, Justice Wasservogel adjudged him in contempt and committed him to jail until he should submit to be sworn and examined. Karlin then sued out a writ of habeas corpus and petitioned for his release, claiming that he was being detained illegally. The petition was dismissed and on appeal the Appellate Division affirmed the contempt order and the one dismissing the writ of habeas corpus. Thereupon an appeal was taken to the Court of Appeals.

CARDOZO, C. J. * * *

The precise question to be determined is whether there is power in the Appellate Division to direct a general inquiry into the conduct of its own officers, the members of the bar, and in the course of that inquiry to compel one of those officers to testify as to his acts in his professional relations. The grand jury inquires into crimes with a view to punishment or correction through the sanctions of the criminal law. There are, however, many forms of professional misconduct that do not amount to crimes. Even when they do, disbarment is not punishment within the meaning of the criminal law. Inquisition by the court with a view to the discipline of its officers is more than a superfluous duplication of inquisition by the grand jury with a view to the punishment of criminals. The two fields of action are diverse and independent. True, indeed, it is that disbarment may not be ordered without notice of specific charges. So also, an indictment must precede a conviction of a felony. We cannot know to-day whether charges will be laid against the relator as an outcome of his testimony or of the testimony of others. If preferred, they will be the subject of a separate proceeding, as separate as proceedings, before and after an indictment. The requirements of the law as to the formulation of a charge are inapplicable to an inquisition in advance of the preferment of the charge.

"Membership in the bar is a privilege burdened with conditions."[1] The appellant was received into that ancient fellowship for something more than private gain. He became an officer of the court, and, like the court itself, an instrument or agency to advance the ends of justice. His co-operation with the court was due, whenever justice would be imperiled if co-operation was withheld. He might be assigned as counsel for the needy, in causes criminal or civil, serving without pay. He might be directed by summary order to make restitution to a client of moneys or other property wrongfully withheld. He might be censured, suspended, or disbarred for "any conduct prejudicial to the administration of justice."[2] All this is undisputed. We are now asked to hold that, when evil practices are rife to the dishonor of the profession, he may not be compelled by rule or order of the court, whose officer he is, to say what he knows of them, subject to his claim of privilege if the answer will expose him to punishment for crime. Co-operation between court and officer in furtherance of justice is a phrase without reality, if the officer may then be silent in the face of a command to speak. There are precedents of recent date, decisions in Wisconsin and Ohio, upholding the power of the court by a general inquisition to compel disclosure of the truth. Precedents far more ancient, their roots deeply set in the very nature of a lawyer's function, point the same way.

"The Supreme Court shall have power and control over attorneys and counselors at law."[3] The first Constitution of the state declared a like rule in terms not widely different. Provision was there made that "all attorneys, solicitors, and counselors at law hereafter to be appointed, be appointed by the court, and licensed by the first judge of the court in which they shall respectively

[1]*Matter of Rouss,* reported in Volume 221 New York Reports 84.
[2]Judiciary Law, section 88, subd. 2.
[3]Judiciary Law, section 88, subd. 2.

plead or practice, and be regulated by the rules and orders of the said courts."[1] What was meant by this provision that lawyers should be "regulated by the rules and orders of the said courts"? Would the men who framed the Constitution of 1777 have been in doubt for a moment that a rule or order might be made whereby lawyers would be under a duty, when so directed by the court, to give aid by their testimony in uncovering abuses? We find the answer to these questions when we view the history of the profession in its home across the seas.

The barrister, unlike the attorney, was not in the strict sense an officer of the court where he was privileged to speak. He was called to the bar upon the nomination of the inns of court, whose members exercised that power as the delegates of the judges. If a barrister was suspected of misconduct, the benchers of his inn might inquire of his behavior. We can hardly doubt that refusal to answer would have been followed by expulsion. There was thus little occasion for controversies as to discipline to be brought before the judges, unless the benchers failed in the performance of their duties. In case they did fail, a supervisory power was ever in reserve. The inns, being unincorporated associations, were not subject to mandamus. They were subject, however, to visitation by the judges. What the court could not do by the instrument of a writ, the judges did by orders in their capacity as visitors. They were not diffident or chary in announcing their pleasure or displeasure. Dugdale's Origines Juridicales contains a record of the orders of the judges in the exercise of their control over members of the inns. The conduct of the barristers was regulated with minute particularity, even in matters so personal as the growth of their beards or the cut of their dress. Short shrift would there have been for the barrister who refused to make answer as to his professional behavior in defiance of the visitors.

The attorney, unlike the barrister, was not a member of an inn, but an officer of the court, and subject to its

---

[1]Constitution of 1777, section 27.

orders. These orders might be general, not directed to a single attorney as the outcome of a controversy, but announcing rules of conduct to be adhered to in the future. Many prohibitions now imbedded in our law, often with the added sanction of a legislative enactment, came into being through regulations or orders adopted by the court of its own motion to put an end to some abuse. Thus, by section I of an order made in Michaelmas Term, 1654, by the Court of Common Pleas, as well as by a like order of the Court of Upper or King's Bench, attorneys were required to give notice of their chambers of habitations "under pain of being put off the roll"; no one, under like penalty, was to practice in another's name, nor was any one knowingly to permit another to practice in his name, excepting in warrants of attorney for common recoveries; "for the prevention of maintenance and brocage, no attorney was to be lessee in an ejectment nor bail for a defendant in this court in an action."

The plenitude of the control thus asserted over the behavior of attorneys would lead us to infer that there was power to compel them to submit to an inquisition as to professional misconduct, even if precedent more precise were lacking for such an exercise of power. The curious thing is, however, that precedents more precise exist. More than three centuries ago evils not unlike those revealed in this petition disturbed the English courts. They met the situation in much the same way, by an inquest under oath as to the conduct of their officers.

In Easter Term (9 Eliz. 1567), the Lord Chief Justice of the Common Pleas delivered a charge to a jury made up of officers, clerks and attorneys, who had been summoned by special writ to inquire into wrongdoing by officers of the court. This was not a grand jury in the usual sense, for the Common Pleas was not a court of criminal jurisdiction. The ordinary courts of criminal jurisdiction were the King's or Queen's Bench and the Courts of the Justices of Assize, Oyer and Terminer and Gaol Delivery. The special jury was instructed to inquire into falsities, erasures, contempts and misprisions, *"de omnibus falsitatibus, de rasuris, de contemptibus, et de mis-*

prisionibus." Those guilty of falsities were the ambulance chasers of the day. A falsity, said the Lord Chief Justice, is "where a man outwardly will set a shew, a face and countenance that he doth well, and truly knowing inwardly and to himself that it is not so, but mere subtlety and falsehood, as, for example, if he will sue forth of purpose false process, or wittingly of himself will minister a false and foreign plea, not taking it of his client." An erasure, as its name imports, is a wrongful alteration of a record of the court. A contempt is committed by "such as contemn and break our orders and rules, and will not obey the orders of this court; within this are not only officers, clerks and attorneys contained, but also any other stranger that contemneth the same." A misprision "is where a man knoweth treason or felony to be done, and yet doth conceal it and keep it close."

This might seem, if it had been left unqualified, to be a license to inquire into misprisions generally. A qualification swiftly followed. "The misprision you are to inquire of is misprisio clerici," as where writs have been fraudulently put in without the seals required by law. The offense was thus linked to the jurisdiction of the court. The charge closes with an arraignment of disloyal or negligent attorneys, and an appeal to the jury to hold them to their duty. Our court is "slandered and evil spoken of, our cares and labors made void and frustrate" by the "negligence of clerks and ministers;" the client "beginneth to think evil of us that are judges, to suspect our skill," and to speak evil of the law. "Of these and like negligence" the jury shall inquire; and also of such attorneys "as be late and slack comers to the term by reason whereof their clients' matters go not forward." "We shall deprive such of their attorneyship." The end of the inquisition was, not punishment, but discipline. "I will appoint you no time certain," said the Lord Chief Justice in conclusion, "but that you may do it at your leisure in time convenient between this and Michaelmas Term; if you will have such as give evidence to be sworn, we shall find the means that they shall be sworn." The inquest was not to lack the sanction of an oath.

In Michaelmas Term, 1654, both the Common Pleas and the King's Bench resorted to a like expedient for the discipline of attorneys as well as other officers.[1]

The order of the Common Pleas is divided into sections. Section III bears the title "concerning the reformation and punishment of abuses in general." It is—

"ordered that a jury of able and credible officers, clerks and attorneys once in three years be impaneled and sworn to inquire:

"1. Of the points usually inquirable by the writ, viz., falsities, contempts, misprisions and offences.

"2. Of such who have been admitted attorneys or clerks and are notoriously unfit, their names to be presented to the court, and they to be punished or removed, as the case shall require.

"3. Of new or exacted fees, and of those that have taken them under whatsoever pretense, and to prepare and present a table of the due and just fees that the same may be fixed and continue in every office, and likewise for the Fleet.

"And that some persons be enjoined and sworn to give evidence, viz., some clerks of the court, and some attorneys in every county, not excluding others."

A system was thus established for a continuing inquiry into the conduct of attorneys, with a view to their discipline and removal by a court of civil jurisdiction.

Supplementary to this system are the provisions of section IV, "concerning the better preservation of order among the officers and clerks, and observation of breach of orders and misdemeanors." By this section it was ordered "that the court do once every year in Michaelmas Term nominate twelve or more able and credible practisers in the court to continue for the year coming from these purposes hereafter limited"; that "they give information to the court from time to time of breaches of orders and miscarriages of officers, attorneys and clerks."

---

[1]Cooke's Rules, "Orders and Notices in the Court of Common Pleas and in the Court of King's Bench".

Orders similar to those set forth in sections III and IV were made at the same term by the Court of Upper or King's Bench.

With this background of precedent there is little room for doubt as to the scope and effect of the provision in the Constitution of 1777 that attorneys might be regulated by rules and orders of the courts. The provision was declaratory of a jurisdiction that would have been implied, if not expressed. The next Constitution, that of 1821, was silent as to the whole subject, containing no reference either to regulation or to appointment. Promptly, to avoid misapprehension, the Legislature passed a statute,[1] which continued in the same words the provision formerly contained in the Constitution of 1777. There was a revision of the statutes in 1827, in which the provision was omitted, but the courts continued to act upon the theory that the power of regulation was either inherent or implied. The question does not now concern us whether the power may be withdrawn or modified by statute. Instead of being withdrawn, it has been explicitly confirmed. In 1912, by an amendment of section 88 of the Judiciary Law, the jurisdiction was removed from the realm of implication. The earlier statutes were restored through a renewed declaration that lawyers are subject to the control and power of the court. We are back to the law as it existed in 1777.

The argument from history is reinforced by others from analogy and policy. The power of the court in the discipline of its officers is in truth a dual one. It prefers the charges, and determines them. Preliminary inquiry there must be, at least to some extent, before a decision can be reached whether to prosecute at all. Voluntary affidavits or even unsworn statements will often be enough. Occasions may arise where the probe must be more searching if justice is not to fail. The power to inquire imports by fair construction the power to inquire by methods appropriate and adequate, and so by compulsory process if search would otherwise be thwarted. Analogies are at

---

[1]Laws of 1823, Chapter 182, section 19.

hand to give support to that conclusion. A legislative body may act upon common knowledge or information voluntarily contributed. At times it stands in need of more. There is then power to investigate by subpeona under the sanction of an oath. "The right to pass laws necessarily implies the right to obtain information upon any matter which may become the subject of a law."[1] Such analogies are not decisive, yet they reinforce in some degree the structure of the argument. A curious anomaly would be here, if the courts with all their writs and processes could do less in regulating and controlling the conduct of their officers than a legislative body can do in relation to a stranger.

The argument is pressed that, in conceding to the court a power of inquisition, we put into its hands a weapon whereby the fair fame of a lawyer, however innocent of wrong, is at the mercy of the tongue of ignorance or malice. Reputation in such a calling is a plant of tender growth, and its bloom, once lost, is not easily restored. The mere summons to appear at such a hearing and make report as to one's conduct may become a slur and a reproach. Dangers are indeed here, but not without a remedy. The remedy is to make the inquisition a secret one in its preliminary stages. This has been done in the first judicial department, at least, in many instances, by the order of the justice presiding at the hearing. It has been done in the second judicial department, where a like investigation is in progress by order of the Appellate Division directing the inquiry.

A preliminary inquisition, without adversary parties, neither ending in any decree nor establishing any right, is not a sitting of a court within the fair intendment of section 4 of the Judiciary Law, whereby sittings of a court are required to be public. It is a quasi administrative remedy whereby the court is given information that may move it to other acts thereafter. The closest analogue is an inquisition by the grand jury for the discovery of crime. There secrecy of counsel is enjoined upon the jurors by

---

[1] *Briggs* v. *MacKellar,* reported in Volume 2 Abbott's Practice Reports 30.

an oath of ancient lineage. It would be strange if disclosure were a duty upon an inquisition by the court. There is a practice of distant origin by which disciplinary proceedings, unless issuing in a judgment adverse to the attorney, are recorded as anonymous. The need of secrecy is the greater when the proceeding is in the stage of preliminary investigation. Full protection against publicity was accorded to the relator, if he had chosen to avail of it. Publicity came to him through his refusal to be sworn.

We conclude that the refusal was a contempt and that the investigation must proceed. In so holding we place power and responsibility where in reason they should be. No doubt the power can be abused, but that is true of power generally. In discharging a function so responsible and delicate, the courts will refrain, we may be sure, from a surveillance of the profession that would be merely odious or arbitrary. They will act considerately and cautiously, mindful at all times of the dignity of the bar and of the resentment certain to be engendered by any tyrannous intervention. No lack of caution or consideration can be imputed to them here. They did not move of their own prompting, but at the instance of the very bar whose privacy and privilege they are said to have infringed. In the long run the power now conceded will make for the health and honor of the profession and for the protection of the public. If the house is to be cleaned, it is for those who occupy and govern it, rather than for strangers, to do the noisome work.

The orders are affirmed.

POUND, CRANE, ANDREWS, LEHMAN, KELLOGG and O'BRIEN, *JJ.*, concur.

"A TRUSTEE IS HELD TO SOMETHING STRICTER THAN THE MORALS OF THE MARKET PLACE"

Meinhard v. *Salmon*, 249 N. Y. 458 (1928)

In April, 1902 Louisa M. Gerry, the owner of the Hotel Bristol located at the northwest corner of 42nd Street and Fifth Avenue, in the City of New York, leased the premises to Walter J. Salmon, a real estate operator, for a period of 20 years commencing May 1, 1902. Salmon was to have alterations made changing the hotel building for use as shops and offices at a cost of $200,000.

Not possessing the necessary funds, Salmon entered into a contract with Morton H. Meinhard, a woolen merchant, whereby the latter was to pay Salmon half the moneys needed for the alteration and operation of the property. In return for this Meinhard was to receive 40% of the net profits for the first five years and 50% after that. Losses were to be borne equally. It was definitely agreed that Salmon was to have sole power to manage, lease and operate the building.

In 1921, when the lease was near its end, the landlord was Elbridge T. Gerry. He was the owner not alone of the property which formerly had been the Hotel Bristol but of one lot adjoining the Bristol Building on Fifth Avenue and four adjoining lots on Forty-second Street. It was his plan to lease the entire tract, tear down the existing buildings and erect a large structure in their place. He approached several men but the idea did not find favor. In January 1922, four months before the termination of the lease, Gerry, who did not know Meinhard, discussed the matter with Salmon. The conferences resulted in the execution of a lease for a 20-year period with option for renewals between Gerry as landlord and the Midpoint Realty Company as tenant. This corporation was owned and controlled by Salmon. In these dealings Salmon acted without any fraudulent intent to hide anything from his partner.

The arrangements under the new lease called for the destruction of the buildings then on the premises at the end of seven years and a new building to cost $3,000,000 was to be erected. Salmon told Meinhard nothing about his dealings with Gerry nor of the execution of the new lease. When the news came to Meinhard's attention in February he demanded that the lease be held in trust as an asset of their joint venture. He offered to share equally with Salmon any personal obligations the new lease required. The offer was refused.

CARDOZO, C. J. * * *

The two were coadventurers, subject to fiduciary duties akin to those of partners. As to this we are all agreed. The heavier weight of duty rested, however, upon Salmon. He was a coadventurer with Meinhard, but he was manager as well. During the early years of the enterprise, the building, reconstructed, was operated at a loss. If the relation had then ended, Meinhard as well as Salmon would have carried a heavy burden. Later the profits became large with the result that for each of the investors there came a rich return. For each the venture had its phases of fair weather and of foul. The two were in it jointly, for better or for worse.

Joint adventurers, like copartners, owe to one another, while the enterprise continues, the duty of the finest loyalty. Many forms of conduct permissible in a workaday world for those acting at arm's length, are forbidden to those bound by fiduciary ties. A trustee is held to something stricter than the morals of the market place. Not honesty alone, but the punctilio of an honor the most sensitive, is then the standard of behavior. As to this there has developed a tradition that is unbending and inveterate. Uncompromising rigidity has been the attitude of courts of equity when petitioned to undermine the rule of undivided loyalty by the "disintegrating erosion" of particular exceptions. Only thus has the level of conduct for fiduciaries been kept at a level higher than that trodden by the crowd. It will not consciously be lowered by any judgment of this court.

The owner of the reversion, Mr. Gerry, had vainly striven to find a tenant who would favor his ambitious scheme of demolition and construction. Baffled in the search, he turned to the defendant Salmon in possession of the Bristol, the keystone of the project. He figured to himself beyond a doubt that the man in possession would prove a likely customer. To the eye of an observer, Salmon held the lease as owner in his own right, for himself and no one else. In fact he held it as a fiduciary, for himself and another, sharers in a common venture. If this fact had been proclaimed, if the lease by its terms had run in favor of a partnership, Mr. Gerry, we may fairly assume, would have laid before the partners, and not merely before one of them, his plan of reconstruction. The pre-emptive privilege, or, better, the pre-emptive opportunity, that was thus an incident of the enterprise, Salmon appropriated to himself in secrecy and silence. He might have warned Meinhard that the plan had been submitted, and that either would be free to compete for the award. If he had done this, we do not need to say whether he would have been under a duty, if successful in the competition, to hold the lease so acquired for the benefit of a venture then about to end, and thus prolong by indirection its responsibilities and duties. The trouble about his conduct is that he excluded his coadventurer from any chance to compete, from any chance to enjoy the opportunity for benefit that had come to him alone by virtue of his agency. This chance, if nothing more, he was under a duty to concede. The price of its denial is an extension of the trust at the option and for the benefit of the one whom he excluded.

No answer is it to say that the chance would have been of little value even if seasonably offered. Such a calculus of probabilities is beyond the science of the chancery. Salmon, the real estate operator, might have been preferred to Meinhard, the woolen merchant. On the other hand, Meinhard might have offered better terms, or reinforced his offer by alliance with the wealth of others. Perhaps he might even have persuaded the lessor to renew the Bristol lease alone, postponing for a time, in return for higher rentals, the improvement of adjoining lots. We know that even under the lease as made the time for the enlargement of the building was delayed for seven years. All these opportunities were cut away from him through another's intervention. He knew that Salmon was the manager. As the time drew near for the expiration of the lease, he would naturally assume from silence, if from nothing else, that the lessor was willing to extend it for a term of years, or at least to let it stand as a lease from year to year. Not impossibly the lessor would have done so, whatever his protestations of unwillingness, if Salmon had not given assent to a project more attractive. At all events, notice of termination, even if not necessary, might seem, not unreasonably, to be something to be looked for, if the business was over and another tenant was to enter. In the absence of such notice, the matter of an extension was one that would naturally be attended to by the manager of the enterprise, and not neglected altogether. At least, there was nothing in the situation to give warning to any one that while the lease was still in being, there had come to the manager an offer of extension which he had locked within his breast to be utilized by himself alone. The very fact that Salmon was in control with exclusive powers of direction charged him the more obviously with the duty of disclosure, since only through disclosure could opportunity be equalized. If he might cut off renewal by a purchase for his own benefit when four months were to pass before the lease would have an end, he might do so with equal right while there remained as many years. He might steal a march on his comrade under cover of the darkness, and then hold the captured ground. Loyalty and comradeship are not so easily abjured.

Little profit will come from a dissection of the precedents. None precisely similar is cited in the briefs of counsel. What is similar in many, or so it seems to us, is the animating principle. Authority is, of course, abundant that one partner may not appropriate to his own use a renewal of a lease, though its term is to begin at the expiration of the partnership. The lease at hand with its many changes is not strictly a renewal. Even so, the standard of loyalty for those in trust relations is without the fixed divisions of a graduated scale. There is indeed a dictum in one of our decisions that a partner, though he may not renew a lease, may purchase the reversion if he acts openly and fairly. It is a dictum, and no more, for on the ground that he had acted slyly he was charged as a trustee. The holding is thus in favor of the conclusion that a purchase as well as a lease will succumb to the infection of secrecy and silence. Against the dictum in that case, moreover, may be set the opinion of Dwight, *C.*, in Mitchell v. Read,[1] where there is a dictum to the contrary. To say that a partner is free without restriction to buy in the reversion of the property where the business is conducted is to say in effect that he may strip the good will of its chief element of value, since good will is largely dependent upon continuity of possession. Equity refuses to confine within the bounds of classified transactions its precept of a loyalty that is undivided and unselfish. Certain at least it is that a "man obtaining his *locus standi*, and his opportunity for making such arrangements, by the position he occupies as a partner, is bound by his obligation to his copartners in such dealings not to separate his interest from theirs, but, if he acquires any benefit, to communicate it to them."[2] Certain it is also that there may be no abuse of special opportunities growing out of a special trust as manager or agent. If conflicting inferences are possible as to abuse or opportunity, the trier of the facts must make the choice between them. There can be no revision in this court unless the choice is clearly wrong. It is no answer for the fiduciary to say "that he was not bound to risk his money as he did, or to go into the enterprise at all." "He might have kept out of it altogether, but if he went in, he could not withhold from his employer the benefit of the bargain."[3] A constructive trust is, then, the remedial device through which preference of self is made subordinate to loyalty to others. Many and varied are its phases and occasions.

We have no thought to hold that Salmon was guilty of a conscious purpose to defraud. Very likely he assumed in all good faith that with the approaching end of the venture he might ignore his coadventurer and take the

---

[1] Reported in Volume 61 New York Reports 123, 143.

[2] *Cassels* v. *Stewart*, reported in Volume 6 Appeals Cases 64, 73 (Eng.).

[3] *Beatty* v. *Guggenheim Exploration Co.*, reported in Volume 225 New York Reports 380, 385.

extension for himself. He had given to the enterprise time and labor as well as money. He had made it a success. Meinhard, who had given money, but neither time nor labor, had already been richly paid. There might seem to be something grasping in his insistence upon more. Such recriminations are not unusual when coadventurers fall out. They are not without their force if conduct is to be judged by the common standards of competitors. That is not to say that they have pertinency here. Salmon had put himself in a position in which thought of self was to be renounced, however hard the abnegation. He was much more than a coadventurer. He was a managing coadventurer. For him and for those like him the rule of undivided loyalty is relentless and supreme. A different question would be here if there were lacking any nexus of relation between the business conducted by the manager and the opportunity brought to him as an incident of management. For this problem, as for most, there are distinctions of degree. If Salmon had received from Gerry a proposition to lease a building at a location far removed, he might have held for himself the privilege thus acquired, or so we shall assume. Here the subject-matter of the new lease was an extension and enlargement of the subject-matter of the old one. A managing coadventurer appropriating the benefit of such a lease without warning to his partner might fairly expect to be reproached with conduct that was underhand, or lacking, to say the least, in reasonable candor, if the partner were to surprise him in the act of signing the new instrument. Conduct subject to that reproach does not receive from equity a healing benediction.

A question remains as to the form and extent of the equitable interest to be allotted to the plaintiff. The trust as declared has been held to attach to the lease which was in the name of the defendant corporation. We think, it ought to attach at the option of the defendant Salmon to the shares of stock which were owned by him or were under his control. The difference may be important if the lessee shall wish to execute an assignment of the lease, as it ought to be free to do with the consent of the lessor. On the other hand, an equal division of the shares might lead to other hardships. It might take away from Salmon the power of control and management which under the plan of the joint venture he was to have from first to last. The number of shares to be allotted to the plaintiff should, therefore, be reduced to such an extent as may be necessary to preserve to the defendant Salmon the expected measure of dominion. To that end an extra share should be added to his half.

Subject to this adjustment, we agree with the Appellate Division that the plaintiff's equitable interest is to be measured by the value of half of the entire lease, and not merely by half of some undivided part. A single building covers the whole area. Physical division is impracticable along the lines of the Bristol site, the keystone of the whole. Division of interests and burdens is equally impracticable. Salmon, as tenant under the new lease, or as guarantor of the performance of the tenant's obligations, might well protest if Meinhard, claiming an equitable interest, had offered to assume a liability not equal to Salmon's, but only half as great. He might justly insist that the lease must be accepted by his coadventurer in such form as it had been given, and not constructively divided into imaginary fragments. What must be yielded to the one may be demanded by the other. The lease as it has been executed is single and entire. If confusion has resulted from the union of adjoining parcels, the trustee who consented to the union must bear the inconvenience.

Thus far, the case has been considered on the assumption that the interest in the joint venture acquired by the plaintiff in 1902 has been continuously his. The fact is, however, that in 1917 he assigned to his wife all his "right, title and interest in and to" the agreement with his coadventurer. The coadventurer did not object, but thereafter made his payments directly to the wife. There was a reassignment by the wife before this action was begun.

We do not need to determine what the effect of the assignment would have been in 1917 if either coadventurer had then chosen to treat the venture as dissolved. We do not even need to determine what the effect would have been if the enterprise had been a partnership in the strict sense with active duties of agency laid on each of the two adventurers. The form of the enterprise made Salmon the sole manager. The only active duty laid upon the other was one wholly ministerial, the duty of contributing his share of the expense. This he could still do with equal readiness, and still was bound to do, after the assignment to his wife. Neither by word nor by act did either partner manifest a choice to view the enterprise as ended. There is no inflexible rule in such conditions that dissolution shall ensue against the concurring wish of all that the venture shall continue. The effect of the assignment is then a question of intention.

Partnership Law, Section 53, subd. 1, is to the effect that "a conveyance by a partner of his interest in the partnership does not of itself dissolve the partnership, nor, as against the other partners in the absence of agreement, entitle the assignee, during the continuance of the partnership, to interfere in the management or administration of the partnership business or affairs, or to require any information or account of partnership transactions, or to inspect the partnership books; but it merely entitles the assignee to receive in accordance with his contract the profits to which the assigning partner would otherwise be entitled." This statute, which took effect October 1, 1919, did not indeed revive the enterprise if automatically on the execution of the assignment a dissolution had resulted in 1917. It sums up with precision, however, the effect of the assignment as the parties meant to shape it. We are to interpret their relation in the revealing light of conduct. The rule of the statute, even if it has modified the rule as to partnerships in general, is an accurate statement of the rule at common law when applied to these adventurers. The purpose of the assignment, understood by every one concerned, was to lower the plaintiff's tax by taking income out of his return and adding it to the return to be made by his wife. She was the appointee of the profits, to whom checks were to be remitted. Beyond that, the relation was to be the same as it had been. No one dreamed for a moment that the enterprise was to be wound up, or that Meinhard was relieved of his continuing obligation to contribute to its expenses if contribution became needful. Coadventurers and assignee, and most of all the defendant Salmon, as appears by his own letters, went forward on that basis. For more than five years Salmon dealt with Meinhard on the assumption that the enterprise was a subsisting one with mutual rights and duties, or so at least the triers of the facts, weighing the circumstantial evidence, might not unreasonably infer. By tacit, if not express approval, he continued and preserved it. We think it is too late now, when charged as a trustee, to come forward with the claim that it had been disrupted and dissolved.

The judgment should be modified by providing that at the option of the defendant Salmon there may be substituted for a trust attaching to the lease a trust attaching to the shares of stock, with the result that one-half of such shares together with one additional share will in that event be allotted to the defendant Salmon and the other shares to the plaintiff, and as so modified the judgment should be affirmed with costs.

POUND, CRANE and LEHMAN, *JJ.*, concur with CARDOZO, *Ch. J.*; ANDREWS, *J.*, dissents in opinion[1] in which KELLOGG and O'BRIEN, *JJ.*, concur.

[1]The dissent took the view that there was no direct appropriation of the expectancy of renewal because there was no offshoot of the original lease. Besides, there was merely a joint venture for a limited object, to end at a fixed time. The new lease was entirely different from the old.

"THE CITIZENRY MAY BE CALLED UPON TO ENFORCE THE JUSTICE OF THE STATE"

Babington v. *Yellow Taxi Corporation*, 250 N. Y. 14 (1929)

William Babington was driving a taxi-cab for the Yellow Taxi Corporation when a police-officer jumped on the running board and ordered him to pursue another car in order to arrest the occupant. The pursuit was well under way when suddenly a touring car cut across the path of the taxicab. Babington swerving to avoid hitting this automobile, crashed his cab into a trolley car with the result that he sustained injuries from which he died.

His widow commenced proceedings under the Workmen's Compensation Act to recover compensation for her husband's death. In order to sustain a recovery it was necessary to show that William Babington was acting in the performance of his duties as a cab-driver for his employer at the time the accident occurred. The lower court permitted recovery.

CARDOZO, C. J. * * *

"A person, who, after having been lawfully commanded to aid an officer in arresting any person, or in re-taking any person who has escaped from legal custody, or in executing any legal process, willfully neglects or refuses to aid such officer is guilty of a misdemeanor."[1] The duty goes back to the days of the hue and cry. "The main rule we think to be this," say the historians of our early law,[2] "that felons ought to be summarily arrested and put in gaol. All true men ought to take part in this work and are punishable if they neglect it." The law did not limit itself to imposing upon the manhood of the country a duty to pursue. To make pursuit effective, there were statutes in those early days whereby a man was subject to a duty to provide himself with instruments sufficient for the task. A typical illustration is the Statute of Winchester, 13 Edw. I, enacted in 1285. "Immediately upon such Robberies and Felonies committed, fresh Suit shall be made from Town to Town, and from Country to Country." Every man

---

[1]Penal Law, Section 1848.

[2]Pollack & Maitland, "History of English Law".

shall "have in his house Harness for to keep the Peace after the Antient Assise." The amount is to be proportioned to the quantity of lands and goods. Thus, for fifteen pounds of lands and goods there shall be kept "an Hauberke (a Breastplate) of Iron, a Sword, a Knife, and an Horse." We may be sure that the man who failed to use his horse, and who would only go afoot, would have had to answer to the king.

The horse has yielded to the motor car as an instrument of pursuit and flight. The ancient ordinance abides as an interpreter of present duty. Still, as in the days of Edward I, the citizenry may be called upon to enforce the justice of the state, not faintly and with lagging steps, but honestly and bravely and with whatever implements and facilities are convenient and at hand. The incorporeal being, the Yellow Taxi Corporation, would have been bound to respond in that spirit to the summons of the officer if it had been sitting in the driver's seat. In sending Babington upon the highway, it knew or is chargeable with knowledge that man and car alike would have to answer to the call. An officer may not pause to parley about the ownership of a vehicle in the possession of another when there is need of hot pursuit. In so far as the danger of pursuit was a danger incidental to the management of the car, it was one of the risks of the employment, an incident of the service, foreseeable, if not foreseen, and so covered by the statute.

We have preferred to place the ruling upon the broadest ground available. Others, though narrower, sustain it. Babington was in charge of the cab, and could not desert it without peril to his master's interests. The fact that, while protecting it for his master, he used it incidentally to preserve the public peace, was not such a departure from the course of duty as to constitute an abandonment of the employment, even if it be assumed that the direction of the officer was not a binding order. There is no evidence that the route was any different from the one that would otherwise have been followed, and none that the speed was so changed as to aggravate the danger. Causal connection there was none so far as the record has informed us, between the collision with the trolley car and the presence of the officer on the running board in pursuit of an offender.

The question is not here whether the employer would be liable to third persons injured in the chase, and, if so, to what extent. Negligence would certainly be relative to the need and the occasion; a speed too great at other times is proper in emergencies. Conceivably the employee would be deemed to have passed out of the service of his general employer and into the service of a special one. We leave that question open, not meaning to express, even by intimation, an opinion as to the answer. The general employer is still liable under the provisions of the statute.

The order should be affirmed with costs.

POUND, CRANE, ANDREWS and LEHMAN, *JJ.*, concur with CARDOZO, *Ch. J.;* O'BRIEN, *J.*, concurs in result; KELLOGG, *J.*, dissents in opinion.[1]

[1]Judge Kellogg contended that Babington acted as a member of the police department rather than as an employee of the defendant.

"THE ANTICS OF THE CLOWN ARE NOT THE PACES OF THE CLOISTERED CLERIC"

Murphy v. *Steeplechase Amusement Co. Inc.,* 250 N. Y. 479 (1929)

James Murphy and a group of friends went to the Amusement Park at Coney Island, maintained by the Steeplechase Amusement Company. One of the attractions at that park was known as "The Flopper." It consisted of a moving belt running upward on an inclined plane on which persons sit or stand at their option. The belt runs in a groove and is made to jerk backwards or sideways causing the customers to be thrown around. The walls around this attraction are padded on either side to a height of four feet and the floors beyond the walls are likewise padded. An electric motor supplies the needed power.

As Murphy put his foot upon the belt there was a sudden jerk and he was thrown to the floor. His friends who were also on the belt were thrown at the same time.

Murphy suffered a fracture of the kneecap and sought to hold the Steeplechase Amusement Company responsible for his injury, declaring in his complaint that the belt was dangerous to life and limb because it stopped and started violently and suddenly and was not properly equipped to prevent injuries to persons who were using it without knowledge of its dangers. He also maintained that it was not supplied with a proper railing or other device to prevent a fall. From a verdict in favor of Murphy which was affirmed in the Appellate Division, an appeal was taken to the Court of Appeals.

CARDOZO, C. J. * * *

Something more was here, as every one understood, than the slowly moving escalator that is common in shops and public places. A fall was foreseen as one of the risks of the adventure. There would have been no point to the whole thing, no adventure about it, if the risk had not been there. The very name, above the gate, "the Flopper," was warning to the timid. If the name was not enough, there was warning more distinct in the experience of others. We are told by the plaintiff's wife that the members of her party stood looking at the sport before joining in it themselves. Some aboard the belt were able, as she viewed them, to sit down with decorum or even to stand and keep their footing; others jumped or fell. The tumbling bodies and the screams and laughter supplied the merriment and fun. "I took a chance," she said when asked whether she thought that a fall might be expected.

Plaintiff took the chance with her, but, less lucky than his companions, suffered a fracture of a knee cap. He states in his complaint that the belt was dangerous to life and limb, in that it stopped and started violently and suddenly and was not properly equipped to prevent injuries to persons who were using it without knowledge of its dangers, and in a bill of particulars he adds that it was operated at a fast and dangerous rate of speed and was not supplied with a proper railing, guard, or other device to prevent a fall therefrom. No other negligence is charged.

We see no adequate basis for a finding that the belt was out of order. It was already in motion when the plaintiff put his foot on it. He cannot help himself to a verdict in such circumstances by the addition of the facile comment that it threw him with a jerk. One who steps upon a moving belt and finds his heels above his head is in no position to discriminate with nicety between the successive stages of the shock, between the jerk which is a cause and the jerk, accompanying the fall, as an instantaneous effect. There is evidence for the defendant that power was transmitted smoothly, and could not be transmitted otherwise. If the movement was spasmodic, it was an unexplained and, it seems, an inexplicable departure from the normal workings of the mechanism. An aberration so extraordinary, if it is to lay the basis for a verdict, should rest on something firmer than a mere descriptive epithet, a summary of the sensations of a tense and crowded moment. But the jerk, if it were established, would add little to the case. Whether the movement of the belt was uniform or irregular, the risk at greatest was a fall. This was the very hazard that was invited and foreseen.

Volenti non fit injuria. One who takes part in such a sport accepts the dangers that inhere in it so far as they are obvious and necessary, just as a fencer accepts the risk of a thrust by his antagonist or a spectator at a ball game the chance of contact with the ball. The antics of the clown are not the paces of the cloistered cleric. The rough and boisterous joke, the horseplay of the crowd, evokes its own guffaws, but they are not the pleasures of tranquillity. The plaintiff was not seeking a retreat for meditation. Visitors were tumbling about the belt to the merriment of onlookers when he made his choice to join them. He took the chance of a like fate, with whatever damage to his body might ensue from such a fall. The timorous may stay at home.

A different case would be here if the dangers inherent in the sport were obscure or unobserved, or so serious as to justify the belief that precautions of some kind must have been taken to avert them. Nothing happened to the plaintiff except what common experience tells us may happen at any time as the consequence of a sudden fall. Many a skater or a horseman can rehearse a tale of equal woe. A different case there would also be if the accidents had been so many as to show that the game in its inherent nature was too dangerous to be continued without change. The president of the amusement company says that there had never been such an accident before. A nurse employed at an emergency hospital maintained in connection with the park contradicts him to some extent. She says that on other occasions she had attended patrons of the park who had been injured at the Flopper, how many she could not say. None, however, had been badly injured or had suffered broken bones. Such testimony is not enough to show that the game was a trap for the unwary, too perilous to be endured. According to the defendant's estimate, 250,000 visitors were at the Flopper in a year. Some quota of accidents was to be looked for in so great a mass. One might as well say that a skating rink should be abandoned because skaters sometimes fall.

There is testimony by the plaintiff that he fell upon wood, and not upon a canvas padding. He is strongly contradicted by the photographs and by the witnesses for the defendant, and is without corroboration in the testimony of his companions who were witnesses in his behalf. If his observation was correct, there was a defect in the equipment, and one not obvious or known. The padding should have been kept in repair to break the force of any fall. The case did not go to the jury, however, upon any such theory of the defendant's liability, nor is the defect fairly suggested by the plaintiff's bill of particulars, which limits his complaint. The case went to the jury upon the theory that negligence was dependent upon a sharp and sudden jerk.

The judgment of the Appellate Division and that of the Trial Term should be reversed, and a new trial granted, with costs to abide the event.

POUND, CRANE, LEHMAN, KELLOGG, and HUBBS, *JJ.*, concur.

O'BRIEN, *J.*, dissents.

"UNCERTAINTY MUST BE SO RESOLVED THAT FORM SHALL BE ADAPTED AND MADE SUBORDINATE TO PURPOSE"

Sleicher v. *Sleicher,* 251 N. Y. 366 (1929)

Charles A. Sleicher and Harriet E. Sleicher were married in 1908. Fifteen years later they were separated and in a written separation agreement the husband promised to pay his wife for her support the sum of $400.00 a month from April, 1923 to June, 1924, and $300.00 monthly thereafter. It was further provided that should they be divorced the same allowance was to be paid her as long as she remained unmarried. In October of 1923 Harriet Sleicher obtained a judgment for divorce in Nevada, and the separation agreement was made part of the divorce judgment.

Less than a year later, in August, 1924, Harriet Sleicher married a Mr. Hannum. This second marriage was not a successful one, for shortly after it Mrs. Hannum brought suit to annul the marriage on the allegation that Mr. Hannum had fraudulently concealed from her the fact that at the time of the marriage he was insane. Judgment of annulment was granted on August 17, 1927. The alimony payments were stopped upon the second marriage.

In February, 1928, the former Mrs. Sleicher brought an action to recover from her first husband the unpaid installments under the separation agreement, claiming that her right to alimony revived when the second marriage was annulled, since the effect of the annulment was to declare the marriage void from the beginning. This in her opinion entitled her not only to the installments falling due from the time of the annulment but to those installments which had been withheld while the second marriage seemed to be in force. The Appellate Division had dismissed her complaint. The opinion of Chief Judge Cardozo, writing for the Court of Appeals, is as follows:

CARDOZO, C. J. * * *

We think the liability should be adjudged as to the future, but denied as to the past.

A marriage procured by fraud is voidable, not void. Even so, annulment when decreed, puts an end to it from the beginning. It is not dissolved as upon divorce. It is effaced as if it had never been. From then on, payments to either spouse may be demanded and must be made on the footing of its nullity. This is true, according to the holding of some courts, where bequests of income are to be paid until remarriage. It is true and for like reasons where installments of alimony are to be paid under a judgment. A marriage is unreal if procured by force or fraud.

The retroactive effect of rescission from the beginning is not, however, without limits, prescribed by policy and justice. These limits are not unknown even in controversies between parties or privies to the rescinded act, but they have their typical application to the rights and duties of a stranger. For the stranger, rescission from the beginning is a watchword to be heeded when an act to be thereafter done with reference to one or other of the parties may be governed or affected by the time or quality of the severance. It does not express a rule that reaches back into the past and lays upon innocence the opprobrium of guilt. The defendant, the first husband, must now comply with the mandate of the judgment of divorce and provide for his former wife as for one who has not remarried. This does not mean, as we view it, that he must provide for her during the years when the voidable remarriage was in force and unavoided.

"The doctrine of relation is a fiction of law adopted by the courts solely for the purposes of justice."[1] It becomes an instrument of injustice when used to change the quality of intervening acts or omissions by strangers to the controversy. The courts have shaped and restrained it in adaptation to its purpose. The defendant was not at fault when he failed to make his monthly payments of alimony from August 16, 1924, the date of the second marriage, to August 17, 1927, the date of the annulment. If the plaintiff had been unwilling to take advantage of the fraud, the second marriage might have continued while the parties to it were alive. The defendant could not know that it would ever be annulled, still less the time or cause. During all the years that it continued, or at least till action was begun, the second husband was chargeable with a duty of suit-

[1]*Gibson* v. *Chouteau* reported in Volume 13 Wall. (U. S.) 92, 101.

able support. There is a presumption, if nothing more, that the duty was fulfilled. To say that the judgment of annulment has put the defendant in default through the fiction of relation is to say that the plaintiff shall have support or equivalent from each of two men during the same period of time, and this by force of a fiction subservient to justice. Analogies of legal doctrine all point the other way.

The question in its last analysis is one as to the construction and effect of the judgment of the Nevada court. The defendant's duty is what that judgment made it and no more. The judgment, following the agreement, charged him with a duty which arose month by month, if it ever arose at all. Default there was none unless also default that was immediate. The meaning, as we view it, is not uncertain, but uncertainty, if any, must be so resolved that form shall be adapted and made subordinate to purpose. The purpose of an award of alimony is support for a divorced wife not otherwise supported. This purpose is perverted by imputing a dual obligation. In the case at hand, the wife might have waited to annul the marriage to her second husband till the first was in his grave. If that had been her choice, we cannot bring ourselves to believe that she could have recovered from his estate the installments accruing during life on the theory that by the fiction of relation he had been in default from the beginning. The test must be the same, however, whether the suit for installments overdue is brought during life or postponed till after death. We think a fair construction of the decree, in the light of the words to be interpreted and the purpose to be served, fits the duty month by month to the situation then existing, and declines to aggravate it later for defaults innocent when suffered. The duty is personal, and personal, not vicarious, is the wrong to be redressed. * * *

POUND, CRANE, LEHMAN and HUBBS, *JJ.*, concur with CARDOZO, *Ch. J.;* KELLOGG, *J.*, concurs in result in separate opinion in which O'BRIEN, *J.*, concurs.

"IF THE MORAL AND PHYSICAL FIBER OF ITS MANHOOD AND WOMANHOOD IS NOT A STATE CONCERN, WHAT IS?"

Adler v. *Deegan*, 251 N. Y. 467 (1929)

The New York State Constitution provides[1] that the state legislature shall not pass any law relating to the *property, affairs or government of cities which is special or local* in its terms or in its effect except on a message from the governor declaring that an emergency exists and then only with the concurrent action of two-thirds of the members of each house of the legislature. The legislature may, however, by a mere majority vote with the approval of the governor act in relation to the property, affairs or government of a city by a general law which in terms and effect applies alike to all cities.

In 1929 the Legislature by a majority vote passed the Multiple Dwelling Law, as a result of a study and report by a legislative commission created in 1927 to examine and revise the Tenement House Law. In effect its scope covered all types of structures in cities having a population of 800,000 or more (which meant only the City of New York) used for dwelling purposes except one-family and two-family homes, hospitals, asylums, public institutions, convents and monasteries. Provisions made set up certain minimum standards for fire-prevention, light, air and cleanliness. The law required larger yards, setting back of walls in certain instances, elimination of yard toilets, vertical ladder fire-escapes and rooms without windows in specified instances. Additional and new requirements were made for means of egress from and sanitary facilities in converted dwellings.

Although this law was limited in effect to the City of New York, other cities, towns and villages were authorized to adopt its provisions for the benefit of dwellings within their territory.

When William F. Deegan, the Tenement House Commissioner in the City of New York, attempted to enforce the provisions of this Multiple Dwelling Law, one Ernest N. Adler sought and obtained an injunction enjoining the Commissioner, on the ground that the act was not properly passed. The lower court decided that in accordance with the constitutional provisions hereinbefore set out the act should have been adopted by the action of two-thirds of both houses of the Legislature upon an emergency message of the

---

[1]Article 12, section 2.

governor since it related to the property, affairs or government of only the City of New York.

An appeal was taken. The appellants claimed that the act did not relate to the property, affairs or government of cities but with the affairs of the state itself. The meaning of "property, affairs or government of cities" became therefore, the determining factor upon this appeal. The Court of Appeals by a 5 to 2 vote, held with the appellants. Chief Judge Cardozo held with the majority in a concurring opinion.

CARDOZO, C. J. (concurring).

The Multiple Dwelling Act is aimed at many evils, but most of all it is a measure to eradicate the slum. It seeks to bring about conditions whereby healthy children shall be born, and healthy men and women reared, in the dwellings of the great metropolis. To have such men and women is not a city concern merely. It is the concern of the whole state. Here is to be bred the citizenry with which the state must do its work in the years that are to come. The end to be achieved is more than the avoidance of pestilence or contagion. The end to be achieved is the quality of men and women. Nothing herein contained says the statute[1] shall "restrict the powers of the legislature to pass laws regulating matters of state concern as distinguished from matters relating to the property, affairs or government of cities." If the moral and physical fiber of its manhood and its womanhood is not a state concern, the question is, what is? Till now the voice of the courts has not faltered for an answer.

A wide field remains for action by the city, and this, too, within the field of welfare legislation. Many welfare measures are city affairs solely. If a city lays out a park, or builds a recreation pier, or provides for public concerts, it is exercising the police power, and is acting for the welfare of its inhabitants, yet acting in a matter that is distinctively its own affair, a matter that is bound up with its own business, its own finances, its own corporate activities. The state may not say, by local law adopted by a majority vote, you must lay out a park in such a

[1]City Home Rule Law, Section 30.

place, or of such a size, or at such a time. The state may have its own parks, but that is another matter. Even in situations where the affair to be regulated does not involve a corporate activity of the city, is not a city affair in that sense, but is merely a matter of local interest or concern, the state, acting by local laws, and without an emergency message, must keep its hands off, unless a state concern is involved or affected, and this in some substantial measure. There may be difficulty at times in allocating interest to state or municipality, and in marking their respective limits when they seem to come together. If any one thing, however, has been settled in this realm of thought by unison of opinion, it is the state-wide extension of the interest in the maintenance of life and health. The advancement of that interest, like the advancement of education, is a function of the state at large. I do not know how many statutes we shall have to uproot, nor where we shall have to draw the line hereafter, nor what confusion we may be inviting, if we speak differently now.

The act is not a zoning resolution, nor the equivalent of one, though in it are provisions as to the height and area of buildings. A zoning resolution in many of its features is distinctively a city affair, a concern of the locality, affecting, as it does, the density of population, the growth of city life, and the course of city values. Whatever restraint in respect of height and area is imposed by this act upon the zoning power of the locality is incidental and subordinate. The power is left intact, except for the declaration of a minimum below which restriction may not fall, a minimum believed to be essential to healthful and decent living. If the minimum is maintained, ordinance and resolution may add to it at will.[1] A different question would be here, if the city were restrained from increasing the restriction in respect of height and area, as well as from reducing it. The concern of the state to protect the health and welfare of its inhabitants may not stand in the way of action by the city consistent with the ends envisaged by the state, but adding greater safeguards

[1]Multiple Dwelling Act, Section 365.

with reference to related ends that are municipal or urban. So the statute says. So, it may be argued, the law would say anyhow, if the statute had been silent. There can be no legitimate concern of the state, or none at least is now suggested, that would throw open Murray Hill[1] to industry and trade, if the city authorities were to hold fast to the belief that it should be preserved for residences only. We may say the like of other changes, whereby density of population would be magnified, with new pressure on streets and sewers and means of transportation, against the effort of the locality to distribute or reduce it. Interference in such a degree would be intrusion upon a concern or interest of the city, without a compensating offset in the advancement of a concern or interest of the state. So, at least, we may assume until something of the kind is threatened. It has not been threatened yet. The city may lay out its districts as it pleases. It may make the height of its tenements even lower, and their courtyards even larger. All that it may not do is to deny to its inhabitants the light and the air, the sanitary safeguards, and the protection against fire, without which healthy human beings cannot live to be the mainstay of the state, the source and the pledge of its prosperity and power.

The consequences of a different holding are indeed disquieting. By section 2 of the Home Rule article, the Legislature may not act with reference to the property, affairs or government of cities through the usual forms of legislation except by general laws, and by the same section a law is not general unless it applies to every city. A tenement law applicable to New York, Buffalo, and Rochester would not be a general law. A tenement law applicable to every city except Salamanca or Long Beach would not be a general law. If one were to go through the statute books, and pick out the acts relating to health or education or public order that apply to cities other than New York, or that apply to New York and not to other cities, acts passed since the adoption of the Home Rule Amendment and by a majority vote, the list would be

[1]Murray Hill is a small, select, residential area in mid-Manhattan, surrounded by shops, office-buildings and factories.

impressive. If all these acts are in truth invalid, we must submit to the inconvenience that would result from such a holding. It is not one to be invited. The very fact that by the City Home Rule Law, contemporaneous substantially with the amended Constitution, the Tenement House Law was excepted from the class of local statutes affecting the affairs of cities is evidence that it was understood by contemporaneous opinion to be matter of state concern, and not an affair of the locality. So, I think, it is, if matters of state concern are to have the meaning and effect that has been theirs throughout the years. The precedents of legislation, the decisions in other states where home rule cities have been organized, or at least their reasonable implications, as well as the judgment of the commentators, converge to that conclusion.

If the act is not in a prohibited sense an interference with municipal affairs, neither is it a change of municipal government. The same city officers who have been charged with the enforcement of the law regulating the construction and use of tenements are charged with it to-day. True, their duty is to enforce a different law, and one that they are without power to modify except to increase its restrictions. But this is not a change of government. If I am right in the meaning I have given to city and state affairs, there never has been a time when the power lodged in the city officers to regulate the form of tenements has been divorced from state control. The government of the city remains precisely what it was. The power was subject in its creation to the overriding action of the state, and subject to that action it continues unimpaired.

The case for the plaintiff is not helped because cities other than New York receive a grant of broader power. Such cities are left free to adopt the statute as their own by the passage of a local law, or to ignore it altogether. What is adopted by a local law may obviously be rejected or ended by a repeal of the local law. This enlargement, if such it be, of the powers of the other cities may or may not be ineffective as to them. The question is not here. If invalidity be assumed, the only consequence would be to invalidate the change, and not to eliminate the exception. We cannot fairly say that the Legislature would have refused to give its approval to the new system imposed by this act upon the city of New York if it had been informed that there was a flaw in the provision whereby the adoption of a like system was made optional for others. The regulation of buildings in the metropolis was manifestly its chief concern. We are warned by the statute to give effect to what is valid if there is invalidity in part. The Legislature held the view that housing conditions in the metropolis made sanitary and fire regulations imperative for the protection of life and health. It found in other cities no such pressing need and left the form of regulation there to the control of local officers. The measure of the need and the nature of the remedy may be marked by the Legislature through statutes local in operation and preferential in effect if the interest to be promoted is the welfare of the state.

I come back, then, to this, that the fundamental question to be determined is the line of division between city and state concerns. In every case, "it is necessary to inquire whether a proposed subject of legislation is a matter of State concern or of local concern."[1] If the former, the ordinary course of legislation may be followed. There are some affairs intimately connected with the exercise by the city of its corporate functions, which are city affairs only. Illustrations of these I have given, the laying out of parks, the building of recreation piers, the institution of public concerts. Many more could be enumerated. Most important of all, perhaps, is the control of the locality over payments from the local purse. There are other affairs exclusively those of the state, such as the law of domestic relations, of wills, of inheritance, of contracts, of crimes not essentially local (for example, larceny or forgery), the organization of courts, the procedure therein. None of these things can be said to touch the affairs that a city is organized to regulate, whether we have reference to history or to tradition or to the existing forms of charters.

[1]Fourth Report of Home Rule Commission, Legislative Documents, 1928, No. 55, p. 14.

Subjects such as these, not affecting the welfare of the inhabitants of the city *qua* inhabitants thereof, are not covered by the grant of power to regulate their conduct and make provision for their welfare, though the act or omission be within the municipal territory. A zone, however, exists where state and city concerns overlap and intermingle. The Constitution and the statute will not be read as enjoining an impossible dichotomy. The question to be faced is this: Has the state surrendered the power to enact local laws by the usual forms of legislation where subjects of state concern are directly and substantially involved, though intermingled with these, and perhaps identical with them, are concerns proper to the city? So far as judicial precedents in the courts of New York are available for guidance, they deal with the interpretation of the "affairs" of cities under the provisions of article 12 of the Constitution as it stood before its revision in 1923. They all point, however, to the holding that affairs, though concerns of a city, are subject, none the less, to regulation through the usual forms of legislation, if they are concerns also of the state. So far as legislative practice since the constitutional amendment is available for guidance, it points for the most part the same way.

Finally, these aids to construction are supplemental and confirmed by the basic principle that the power to adopt laws according to the usual forms of legislation resides with the Legislature, except in so far as it has been limited or surrendered, and that neither limitation nor surrender will be inferred unless intention is revealed with reasonable clarity.

"The provisions of this article shall not be deemed to restrict the power of the Legislature to enact laws relating to matters other than the property, affairs or government of cities."[1] Constitution, art. 12, Sec. 4. The reservation of the power is merely another way of saying that the Legislature is unfettered as to "matters of state concern." How great must be the infusion of local interest before fetters are imposed? There is concession even by the

[1]Constitution of the State of New York, Article 12, Section 4.

plaintiff that, if the subject be "predominantly" of state concern, the Legislature may act according to the usual forms. But predominance is not the test. The introduction of such a test involves comparisons too vague and too variable, too much a matter of mere opinion, to serve as an objective standard. To adopt it is to infect our legislation with the virus of uncertainty. The city has power under its charter to define the offense of disorderly conduct in its streets. The state, by a law applicable in the city of New York and nowhere else, defines disorderly conduct in other terms. The validity of the new definition has not been doubted, yet concerns, both state and local, are affected by the change. Who shall say in what proportion?

Consideration of "more or less" will lead us in such a case, and in many others, into a morass of indecision. The test is rather this: That, if the subject be in a substantial degree a matter of state concern, the Legislature may act, though intermingled with it are concerns of the locality. Measured by that test, this statute must prevail. I do not say that an affair must be one of city concern exclusively, to bring it within the scope of the powers conferred upon the municipality by section 3 of the Home Rule article and section 11 of the City Home Rule Law in cases where the state has not undertaken to occupy the field. I assume that, if the affair is partly state and partly local, the city is free to act until the state has intervened. As to concerns of this class there is thus concurrent jurisdiction for each in default of action by the other. The power of the city is subordinate at such times to the power of the state, but may be exerted without restraint to the extent that the two can work in harmony together.

The judgment should be reversed and the complaint dismissed.

CARDOZO, *Ch. J.*, and POUND, *J.*, in separate opinions, concur with CRANE, *J.;* KELLOGG and HUBBS, *JJ.*, concur in opinions of CRANE and POUND, *JJ.*, and of CARDOZO, *Ch. J.;* LEHMAN and O'BRIEN, *JJ.*, dissent in separate opinions.

"THERE ARE BREATHS OF HUMAN NATURE AT WHICH PRESUMPTIONS SHRINK AND WITHER"

In re Findlay, 253 N. Y. 1 (1930)

After twelve years of married life in England, Ann Brooks ran away from her husband Henry and three children in 1864, to live with James Findlay, her paramour. As a result of this latter union two more children, Walter and William, were born in England and Percy, the youngest, was born in the United States where Ann and her lover eventually came.

Ann and James were there joined by Albert, a legitimate son, who from then on assumed the name of John Findlay.

Henry Brooks, the abandoned husband, continuously remained in England until his death in 1906 at the age of seventy-nine. His marriage to Ann had never been dissolved.

John Findlay, the former Albert Brooks, had taken up his residence at Hempstead, Long Island and he there died a widower in 1926, without leaving a will. Thereupon William Findlay, the second son of Ann and James Findlay, claiming to be a legitimate brother of John, applied for letters of administration of "the goods, chattels and credits of John Findlay, deceased". Letters were issued accordingly in January 1927.

When Alfred Brooks, a legitimate son living in England, heard of this about six months later, he began proceedings to revoke the appointment of William Findlay upon the ground that the latter was not of legitimate kinship to the deceased. The Surrogate dismissed Alfred's petition upon the ground that the evidence was inadequate to overcome the presumption of William's legitimacy. And this despite the fact that William had acknowledged himself continuously as the son of Ann Aldridge and James Findlay. The Appellate Division unanimously affirmed the decision of the surrogate. Alfred Brooks appealed to the Court of Appeals.

CARDOZO, C. J. * * *

We have said that William had continuously acknowledged himself as the son of Ann Aldridge and James Findlay, and was so acknowledged by them. He did not retract this acknowledgment when testifying here. Placed on the stand as a witness for the petitioner, and asked the blunt question, "What was your father's name?" he answered bluntly "James Findlay." Cross-examined by his own counsel, he explained in effect that since his earliest infancy he had been brought up in that belief. Upbringing and belief must yield, we are told, to the presumption of legitimacy. If Ann Brooks, who ran away with James Findlay in 1864, did not come to America till 1875, the year of William's birth, there is a bare possibility that she was visited by her abandoned husband while she was living away from him in adultery, and that Walter and William and Percy, acknowledged by her and the adulterer as the fruit of the illicit union, were conceived at these clandestine meetings, unproven but presumed. Upon this possibility, and no more, the decree in controversy rests. The presumption of legitimacy will not bear so great a strain.

Potent, indeed, the presumption is one of the strongest and most persuasive known to the law, and yet subject to the sway of reason. Time was, the books tell us, when its rank was even higher. If a husband, not physically incapable, was within the four seas of England during the period of gestation, the court would not listen to evidence casting doubt on his paternity. The presumption in such circumstances was said to be conclusive, "on account of its absolute nonsense." Since then the presumption of legitimacy, like other presumptions, such as those of regularity and innocence, has been subject to be rebutted, though there have been varying statements of the cogency of the evidence sufficient to repel it.

At times the cases seemed to say that any possibility of access, no matter how violently improbable, would leave the presumption active as against neutralizing proof. A formula so inexorable has yielded with the years to one more natural and supple. There are survivals here and there of the rule of olden days. By and large, none the less, the courts are generally agreed that countervailing evidence may shatter the presumption though the possibility of access is not susceptible of exclusion to the point of utter demonstration. Issue will not be bastardized as the outcome of a choice between nicely balanced probabilities. They will not be held legitimate by a sacrifice of probabilities in a futile quest for certainty. Some of the books tell us that, to overcome the presumption, the evidence of non-access must be "clear and convincing"; others that it must lead to a conclusion that is "strong and irresistible"; others that it must be proof "beyond all reasonable doubt".

What is meant by these pronouncements, however differently phrased, is this, and nothing more, that the presumption will not fail unless common sense and reason are outraged by a holding that it abides. If husband and wife are living together in a conjugal relation, legitimacy will be presumed, though the wife has harbored an adulterer. It may even be presumed though the spouses are living apart if there is a fair basis for the belief that at times they may have come together. Whether such a basis exists in any given instance is to be determined, however, in the light of experience and reason. The presumption does not consecrate as truth the extravagantly improbable, which may be one, for ends juridical, with the indubitably false.

Illustration will be helpful to guide us to a choice. The beginning of the modern tendency can be marked in Goodright v. Saul.[1] The husband and the wife had separated, and a child born later had received a different name, and had been brought up by its mother while living with another man. The court held the presumption overcome, though there was a possibility of meetings between the separated spouses. The next case to be noted, Morris v. Davies,[2], is a judgment of the House of Lords. The mother was living in adultery when the child was born, its birth was concealed from the husband, it was baptized as a base-born child, and was recognized by the wife's paramour as the child of their union. Again the holding was that the presumption had been rebutted, though again there was a possibility, however remote, that the spouses had come together. Hawes v. Draeger[3] is another case where there was separation, with issue born thereafter, reared in the household of the paramour, and known by his name. Once more the presumption was held to have been shattered.

---

[1]Volume 4 Term Reports 356 (1791), English reports.
[2]Volume 5 Clark & Finnelly 163, 255 (1836) English reports.
[3]Law Reports, volume 23 Chancery Division 173.

We think the case at hand is ruled by these decisions. To apply to the facts before us the presumption of legitimacy, we must find in the first place that Ann Brooks was still in England in 1874 or 1875. This is very doubtful. On the one side, there is testimony that she left shortly after her elopement in 1864. On the other, there is William's statement, so haltingly expressed as to be hardly more than a suggestion, that by family tradition he had been brought to America while a babe in the arms. If we assume in his favor that his mother may be found on the strength of this statement to have been in England at his birth, other difficulties are left. There is no evidence that Henry Brooks was a man of perverted or indecent habits. He must have been this in shocking measure if he was continuing carnal commerce with his wife who had run away from his home and was living apart from him in unconcealed adultery. There is no evidence that Ann Brooks after her flight with James Findlay led a promiscuous or disordered life. On the contrary, the home that she established, so far as strangers could judge of it, was orderly and decent. There is thus at the outset a high degree of improbability in the hypothesis that covertly at intervals during a period of ten years she was lying with the husband whom she had abandoned for another.

This improbability, standing alone, might conceivably be insufficient to break the force of the presumption. It is reinforced by many others. The sons born to the mother after her desertion of her husband were recognized by the Findlays as their own and not another's. The eldest of the three, Walter, was a grown child of eight or ten when William came into the world. Each knew the other as his brother and the Findlays as his parents. Each was born into a family life maintained with all the signs of regularity and order. We presume a vileness and degradation so improbable as at least to border on extravagance when we infer without proof that the relation thus established, a relation of de facto marriage, was soiled by the disgrace of a clandestine connection between the separated spouses. The extravagance is more violent, it approaches an absurdity, when the presumption is upheld in the face of a lifetime of avowal by mother and paramour that the children, reared as their own, were their own in very truth. "When all the ends which the presumption of legitimacy is designed to conserve have been defeated by sordid facts, the courts must deal with the situation in a common sense way."[1] "Unless a case of this kind is to be dealt with otherwise than according to the ordinary rules of reason and probability, I think the burden of proof would be rather on those who might suggest that they did meet again than on those who suggest the contrary."[2] There are breaths of human nature at which presumptions shrink and wither.

Viewing the evidence before us in all its cumulative significance, we think it points with overwhelming force to one conclusion and one only. We have no thought to weaken the presumption of legitimacy by allowing its overthrow at the call of rumor or suspicion, or through inferences nicely poised. What we are now holding is in line with the historical development which has shorn the presumption of some of its follies and vagaries. Follies and vagaries by concession there have been. We have abandoned the "nonsense" of the rule of the four seas. We no longer adhere to Lord Campbell's dictum that a mulatto child born of a white mother must be ascribed to the white husband, and not to the black paramour, if the husband had access to his wife during the period of gestation. Extravagances hardly less violent there have been at other times in insisting upon the negation of every shadowy possibility. These and nothing more we are pruning from the law.

Another basis for the judgment suggested in the briefs of counsel must have a word of notice. The suggestion is put forward that there may have been a common-law marriage between James and Ann Findlay, and then, to meet the objection that such a marriage would have been bigamous, the court is asked to presume that the earlier mar-

---

[1]Burch, *J.*, in *Nolting* v. *Holt*, reported in Volume 113 Kansas Reports 495.

[2]Selborne, L. C., in The Aylesford Peerage Case, reported in (L. R.) Volume 11 Appeals Cases (England) 17.

riage, the one with Henry Brooks, was subject to some impediment, unknown and unproved, and may be disregarded now as void. In aid of a presumption that William is legitimate, there is to be an opposite presumption that the petitioner and the decedent, born of a ceremonial marriage, were, each of them, illegitimate. This is the presumption of legitimacy gone mad.

Ordered accordingly.

POUND, CRANE, LEHMAN, KELLOGG, O'BRIEN and HUBBS, *JJ.*, concur.

"A PERSONALITY CREATED BY LAW MAY CONTINUE UNIMPAIRED UNTIL LAW RATHER THAN MIGHT SHALL DECLARE IT AT AN END"

Petrogradsky Mejdumarodny Kommerchesky Bank v. *National City Bank of New York,* 253 N. Y. 23 (1930)

The plaintiff was a Russian bank originally chartered in 1869 by the Imperial Russian Government. It had deposit accounts with the National City Bank in New York, which were opened as far back as 1911, and at the time of the trial of this case had a balance to its credit in the sum of $66,749.45.

When the Soviet government took control in Russia in 1917, the assets of the bank in Russia were seized and the bank declared to be merged in the People's Bank. The directors were driven into exile. In January, 1920, the People's Bank was itself abolished since the Soviet government had determined that a banking system was not necessary to the economic life planned by the new government.

Under the terms of the plaintiff's charter, its governing body consisted of a directorate of seven members and three were to form a quorum. Of the seven directors who were living at the time of the confiscation of this bank, one was killed during the revolution and the other six set up their headquarters in Paris, holding meetings from time to time, doing such business as conditions would allow. At the time this action was begun (October, 1925) all six were still alive. The Soviet Government had not been recognized by the United States.

The efforts of these refugee directors were directed to bringing together the assets which the bank had outside the territorial limits of the Soviet Republic. They were successful in obtaining the assets existing in branch banks in London, Paris and Brussels, and were holding them for distribution as justice might require.

The directors attempted to collect the balance on deposit with the National City Bank in New York. They demanded payment. The New York bank refused to recognize their authority. They presented a check signed by the directors who in former years had been competent to draw checks, but the check was dishonored. Consequently, an action was commenced.

The National City Bank set up three main defenses. (1) That the Russian Bank had been dissolved and was no longer a juristic person. (2) That even if it be a juristic person, its former directors were no longer authorized to speak for it. (3) That the New York courts should decline jurisdiction in any event because a judgment against the National City Bank would leave it unprotected against subsequent conflicting claims.

The lower courts gave judgment in favor of the National City Bank and an appeal was taken to the Court of Appeals, which court in an opinion by Chief Judge Cardozo reversed the lower courts and directed judgment for the plaintiff. Judges Pound and O'Brien dissented without opinion.

CARDOZO, C. J. * * *

We think the plaintiff is not dissolved, but is still a juristic person with capacity to sue.

The decrees of the Soviet Republic nationalizing the Russian banks are not law in the United States, nor recognized as law. They are not pronouncements of authority. "Acts or decrees, to be ranked as governmental, must proceed from some authority recognized as a government de facto."[1] Exhibitions of power may be followed or attended by physical changes, legal or illegal. These we do not ignore, however lawless their origin, in any survey of the legal scene. They are a source at times of new rights and liabilities. *Ex facto jus oritur.* Exhibitions of power may couple the physical change with declarations of the jural consequences. These last we ignore, if the consequences, apart from the declaration, do not follow from the change itself. There may be exceptions to this as there are to most principles of equal generality. If so, it is only when "violence to fundamental principles of justice or to our own public policy might otherwise be done."[2] The every-day transactions of business or domestic life are not subject to impeachment, though the form may have been regulated by the command of the usurping government. To undo them would bring hardship or confusion to the helpless and the innocent without compensating benefit. On the other hand, there is no shelter in such exceptions for rapine or oppression. We do not recognize the decrees of Soviet

[1]*Sokoloff* v. *National City Bank,* reported in Volume 239 New York Reports 158.

[2]*Ibid.*

Russia as competent to divest the plaintiff of the title to any assets that would otherwise have the protection of our law. At least this must be so where the title thus divested is transferred to the very government not recognized as existent. For the same reason we do not admit their competence in aid of a like purpose to pass sentence of death on the expropriated owner. Death, if it has followed, is not death by act of law.

In saying this we assume, though we are not required to decide, that the decrees were intended to extinguish the life of the nationalized banks, and not merely to strip them of ownership or usufruct. Even so, the jural consequence of dissolution will not follow from what was said, unless, though nothing had been said, it would result from what was done. The dissolution of the banks was not "mere ordinary legislation, such as might have been had there been no war", but legislation closely interwoven with the overthrow of the old order and the creation of a new one. These and like circumstances have a bearing on the meed of recognition that is due in foreign lands. There is a distinction not to be ignored between the life of a human being and the life of a persona ficta, the creature of the state. When a human being dies, his death is equally a fact whether it is brought about legally or illegally, whether he has died of illness in his bed or has been murdered on the highway. The event is not conditioned by the juristic quality of the cause. But in respect of juristic beings, the quality of the cause may determine the event as well. The personality created by law may continue unimpaired until law rather than might shall declare it at an end. Conceivably, the law will declare it at an end when marauders have brought frustration to the purpose for which personality was given. That is another question. What is not to be lost sight of is that even so it is the law and not merely an assassin that must pronounce the words of doom.

Putting aside, then, as irrelevant the fiat of the Soviet government that the jural consequence shall be death, we are brought to the question whether the law of the Imperial government of Russia or of the later Provisional government would have ascribed the consequence of death to the supervening changes irrespective of the fiat. These changes in briefest summary are the loss of the Russian assets, the dispersion of the stockholders, and the exclusion of the directors as well as all subordinate agents from the soil of the old empire.

An answer to that question leads us to the contentious problem of the origin and nature of juristic personality. The theories, broadly speaking, are two, though subject to many variations within the main lines. The one is the concession theory, by which corporate personality is invariably the gift and creature of the state. "Corporate life and form," says Holdsworth,[1] "cannot exist without the permission of the state, express, presumed or implied." This is the prevailing theory in Anglo-American law, though rifts in its uniformity are visible here and there. The other is the theory that even in the absence of a charter or other token of the will of government there are groups so natural and spontaneous as to evoke legal recognition of a corporate existence. We are not advised by this record whether, by the law of Imperial Russia, the theory of a concession was exclusive of any other. Certain, however, it is that the theory was not unknown whether it be exclusive or concurrent. Here in this record are the legislative act and the charter or "statutes" formulated thereunder that bespeak the legislative gift. What the law itself has granted, the law must take away.

The corporation once existing, the burden was on the defendant to overthrow the presumption of continuance and to show that life had ceased. We cannot say upon this record that the burden has been borne. If we look to the analogies of our own law, the conclusion is not doubtful. Neither bankruptcy nor cessation of business, nor dispersion of stockholders, nor the absence of directors, nor all combined, will avail without more to stifle the breach of juristic personality. The corporation abides as an ideal creation, impervious to the shocks of these tem-

[1]Professor of the Laws of England in the University of Oxford and Benches of Lincoln's Inn. The quotation is from his "History of English Law", volume 9, page 48.

poral vicissitudes. Not even the sequestration of the assets at the hands of a receiver will terminate its being. "A corporation may by virtue of proceedings against it, or by reason of its pecuniary condition, cease to exist for all practical purposes, all the purposes for which it was created or for which a corporation may exist, but it cannot be held to be actually dissolved till so adjudged and determined, either by judicial sentence or the sovereign power."[1] "The appointment of a receiver to take and distribute among the creditors and stockholders all the property of a corporation may with sufficient accuracy be called, as it was by Chancellor Walworth in Verplanck v. Mercantile Insurance Co.,[2] 'a virtual dissolution of the corporation,' but it does not extinguish its franchise, terminate its legal existence, or render it incapable of being sued, at law or in equity."[3] A fortiori must that be true, if assets remain either in the domicile or elsewhere to be administered for the benefit of stockholders, known or unknown. In such a situation, there is no dissolution of any kind, either "virtual" or legal. The corporate life in that event does not serve an expropriated being, but one endowed with worldly goods, and in need of capacities adequate to protect them. Survival follows in such circumstances from the very concept of a corporation as it is known to our law. If there is anything in that concept at variance with the concept corporation as known to the law of Russia, the defendant, charged with the burden, has not informed us of the variance.

We are not unmindful of the witnesses who testified to an opinion that the plaintiff, as a result of all the changes it had experienced, was no longer a juristic person in the jurisdiction of its domicile. Their opinion, at least in part, was based on the assumption that the Soviet decrees were to be given the effect of law. It is not easy to disentangle what is left when that assumption is withdrawn. Prove, indeed, they did that the law of Imperial Russia would

---

[1] *Kincaid* v. *Dwinelle,* reported in Volume 59 New York Reports 552.

[2] Reported in Volume 2 Paige (New York) Reports 438, 452.

[3] Per Gray, *J.*, in *Folger* v. *Columbia Insurance Co.,* reported in Volume 99 Massachusetts Reports 267.

not suffer a bank to carry on the banking business while thus despoiled and crippled. This was far from proving that there would be a lack of corporate capacity to gather in the assets and repair the spoliation. In determining that capacity, we think away the physical impediments to the attainment of the corporate will, and ask, if these could be surmounted, whether the law would interpose new impediments of its own, would hold the struggle vain for want of a living victor to enjoy the tardy triumph. The statute does indeed prescribe that a bank shall be liquidated if it loses a quarter of its capital. The witnesses for the defendant concede that this provision does not execute itself and is unavailing ipso facto to terminate the corporate life. The statute prescribes visitation and control by the Minister of Finance. The witnesses for the defendant do not say that there is any law whereby the death of the Minister is the death of the corporations subject to his scrutiny. The statute prescribes the election of the directors on the expiration of their terms at the annual meeting of the shareholders. The witnesses do not say that the shareholders would be prohibited by anything in the pre-soviet law from coming together now and choosing a new board. The statute prescribes by implication, or so we may assume, that the directors shall meet at the principal office of the corporation, which in this instance was stated in the charter to be the city of Petrograd. The witnesses for the defendant do not point to any law whereby the directors would be without capacity to meet in Petrograd today if the new regime were overthrown or its vigilance eluded. The sum and substance of their testimony is this, and nothing more, that through the exercise of power without authority of law there has been a paralysis of action within the confines of the territory where the power is still dominant. They have yet to show that as a consequence of this paralysis of action the very law that has been flouted multiplies the misfortunes of the victim by taking back also the concession of juristic life. One of the witnesses was asked whether the plaintiff would be without corporate capacity if the revolutionary government were to be destroyed tomorrow and the empire re-established. He answered that capacity would fail because a new statute would be necessary to annul the Soviet decree that had nationalized the banks. Here, as often, interwoven into the statement of opinion even when formally disclaimed, is the notion that the Soviet decrees have the authority of law. Abstract that notion, and the structure fails.

We are told from time to time in text-book and decision that a finding of foreign law is a finding of fact, to be reviewed in subjection to the same restraints that apply to the review of findings of fact generally. True, of course, it is that there is no judicial notice of the law of foreign lands. This does not mean, however, that the mere opinion of a witness will control the judgment of a judge, except to the extent that it is a reasonable inference from statute or from precedent or from the implications of a legal concept, such as contract or testament or juristic personality. Unless it is this, the judge must use his own judgment and find the meaning of the foreign law as he would if the meaning to be ascertained were that of a deed or an agreement. This is as true upon appeal as it is upon a trial. At such times and for such inquiries, opinion has a significance proportioned to the sources that sustain it. Especially is that so where the problem to be solved is the measure of recognition that is due under a given legal system to the acts of another system that professes to displace and supersede it. There is little in the practice or training peculiar to a Russian lawyer that enables him to speak as to such matters with any special measure of assurance or authority. In the absence of any precedents supplied by Russian history, the tests to be applied are those of international law, as distinguished from any law that is municipal or local. The witnesses for the defendant believe that the corporation is no more, but the witness for the plaintiff believes that it survives. The fact is significant that there is no witness on either side who deduces his conclusion from any principle specifically Russian as to the continuance or destruction of juristic personality. Russian law is cited to show the rules that govern corporations during life. There is silence as to any rules for the ascertainment of the fact of death. In this conflict of opinion we are driven back upon the sources from which opinion must be derived if it is to have persuasion or validity. Statute and precedent and concept must be brought before the bar.

We find no statute or precedent that points with reasonable clarity to the conclusion that by the law of pre-Soviet Russia there has been an extinguishment of life as well as a suspension of activity. We find nothing in the Russian concept of juristic personality that leads to that conclusion, for there is nothing to show that the concept differs from our own. This being so, the presumption of continuance must tilt the balanced scales. The corporation survives in such a sense and to such a degree that it may still be dealt with as a *persona* in lands where the decrees of the Soviet Republic are not recognized as law. We think there is no substantial basis in the evidence for an opinion to the contrary.

The corporation surviving, the question must still be answered whether the former directors have authority to speak for it.

The concept of corporate personality is to be kept distinct in thought from that of authority or agency, though they are easily confused. It is one thing to say that there is still a corporation for whom directors, legally qualified, will be competent to act. It is another thing to say that directors, so qualified exist.

The defendant insists that at least for two reasons the former directors are not qualified today to represent the plaintiff corporation by suing in its name, even if corporate personality be assumed to have continued. One is that the directors, though lawfully elected, were chosen for terms which have expired, and that there has been no re-election since the Soviet revolution. The other is that meetings should have been held in Petrograd and nowhere else.

Neither objection, in our view, is sufficient to disprove authority.

The witnesses for the defendant state that there is no rule of Russian law whereby, in default of an annual meeting a director holds over until the choice of his successor. The plaintiff's witness says the contrary, and reinforces his opinion by the analogy of precedents in which the principle of holding over has been applied to fiduciaries of other kinds. One finds it incredible that automatically, upon the failure to hold a meeting of the shareholders before the expiration of the year at which an election is due, directors, not re-elected, are shorn of their powers, the corporation becoming a derelict without managers to guide it. Such a thing does not seem possible in an enlightened legal system. Taking the defendant's witnesses at their word, they do not go so far as to maintain that this chaos would ensue. The directors in their view would not hold over in the capacity of directors, but would be charged, none the less, with a special obligation of conservation and protection. That is merely to say in other words that they are directors de facto, whatever the title of the office, since there is no one other than themselves on whom the duty to manage is imposed. We think their authority is sufficient in default of other representatives to permit them to sue in our courts in the name and for the benefit of the corporation they represent. In saying this we are not unmindful that the shareholders, the equitable owners of the assets, are dispersed and to some extent unknown. Some of them, however, are known, though the complete list was destroyed upon the seizure of the Russian office. Others, if now unknown, may, not impossibly, be identified or discovered through inquiry and advertisement, or other forms of constructive service. The charter of the bank provides that "upon the death of a shareholder, his rights pass to his heirs at law or his testamentary heirs, but in no case can a share be split." It will be for the courts of the French Republic, if the fund is sent to France, to devise and apply the process and the remedies that will insure an administration of the assets in conformity to justice.

What has been said as to the consequences of a failure to re-elect the directors may be said with little variation as to the failure of the directors to hold their meetings at the banking house in Petrograd. The witnesses for the defendant assert that there was no authority to meet elsewhere. The witness for the plaintiff states the contrary. We may assume for present purposes that the principal banking house in Russia was the proper place of meeting, and that any director, not present, might refuse to be bound by action taken elsewhere. This does not mean of necessity that action might not be taken elsewhere by unanimous consent. Still less does it mean that action taken elsewhere by unanimous consent must be disregarded as a nullity if it was impossible by reason of vis major to hold the meeting at the home office. Fire, flood, or earthquake, as well as insurrection, might threaten death or ruin. One finds it incredible that at such a time a board would be driven by law to abandon the corporation to spoliation and destruction because unable to meet in Petrograd, though able to come together in some other part of Russia or across the Russian border. Testimony much more explicit and persuasive than any offered by the defendant would be necessary in order to lead us to the acceptance of a conclusion so grotesque. There is no suggestion of any rule of Russian law that so obstructs and cripples the life preserving power in the face of present peril. At the very least, a resolution thus adopted would have the force to be attributed to the action of de facto managers, speaking and acting for the corporation in an emergency too urgent to wait upon formality.

The possibility of adverse claims does not relieve the defendant from liability when sued in an action at law by a depositor who is successful in proving a title to the fund.

The defendant cites our decision in Russian Reinsurance Co. v. Stoddard,[1] as supporting its defense. The ruling is inapplicable to the situation now before us. There the subject of the controversy was a fund deposited in a bank to be held as trustee for a Russian insurance company, its stockholders and creditors. The company made demand that the res be returned by the trustee upon the ground that the purposes of the deposit had failed and that

---

[1]Reported in Volume 240 New York Reports 149.

the trust was at an end. The bank set up in defense the existence of an adverse claim of title by the Soviet Republic, and the danger that this claim might be upheld in France and in other countries where the Soviet decrees were recognized as law. We held that, in a suit in equity, there is discretion, if not duty, to refuse a decree whereby a trustee will be directed to make payment of the subject of the trust to one of two claimants unless there is power also by force of the same decree to protect against the rival. The rule is different altogether in actions of law. Here in the case before us the subject of the controversy is not property burdened with a trust to be administered in equity. The subject is an ordinary deposit in a bank to be sued for, if at all, in an action founded on the debt. In actions of that order, a refusal to pay when due is not sustained without more by the presence of an adverse claim. The defendant, if unable to interplead, must respond to the challenge, and defend as best it can.

The argument is pressed that the danger of double liability supplies the basis for an equitable defense, if not for any other. The danger is not imminent, as the course of events since our decision in Russian Reinsurance Co. v. Stoddard, supra, sufficiently attests. France recognizes the Soviet Republic as a member of the family of nations. Yet, till now at least, it has failed to give effect to title having their basis in decrees of confiscation. But in actions at law, the danger, whatever it may be, is no defense at all, whether equitable or legal. An equitable defense is one of such an order as would once have been enforced by the Court of Chancery through the remedy of an injunction restraining the prosecution of the remedy at law. The Court of Chancery did not enjoin the prosecution of a legal action because of the possibility of adverse claims unless the circumstances were such as to sustain a bill of interpleader. The defendant does not and cannot interplead the Soviet Republic. That being so, it must wage the battle for itself. Negligible is the risk that by any judgment in its domicile it will be compelled to pay again. Whatever risk it runs abroad, is one that it assumed as part of the business of a bank. "The chance of double payment is a common risk of life."[1]

The case comes down to this: A fund is in this state with title vested in the plaintiff at the time of the deposit. Nothing to divest that title has ever happened here or elsewhere. The directors who made the deposit in the name of the corporation or continued it in that name now ask to get it back. Either it must be paid to the depositor, acting by them, or it must be kept here indefinitely. Either they must control the custody, or for the present and the indefinite future it is not controllable by any one. The defendant expresses the fear that the money may be misapplied if the custody is changed. The fear has its basis in nothing more than mere suspicion. The directors, men of honor presumably, will be charged with the duties of trustees, and will be subject to prosecution, civil or criminal, if those duties are ignored. The defendant is not required to follow the money into their hands and see how they apply it. Its duty is to pay.

CRANE, LEHMAN, KELLOGG, and HUBBS, *JJ.*, concur.
POUND and O'BRIEN, *JJ.*, dissent.

---

[1] *Coler* v. *Corn Exchange Bank,* reported in Volume 250 New York Reports, 136, 145.

"THE COURT WILL STAND ASIDE WHEN BY INTERVENING IT WILL MAKE ITSELF AN INSTRUMENT OF INJUSTICE"

Graf v. *Hope Building Corp.*, 254 N. Y. 1 (1930)

The executors of Joseph L. Graf were the holders of a mortgage on a piece of real property owned by the Hope Building Corporation. The principal of the mortgage was $335,000 which was payable in quarter-annual instalments of $1,500 together with interest at the rate of 5¾% per annum until January 1, 1935 when the entire remaining unpaid balance ($276,500) was to be paid. A clause in this mortgage declared that if a default in the payment of any instalment of interest existed for 20 days the whole unpaid principal sum was to become due.

When David Herstein, the president and treasurer of the Hope Building Corporation who alone was authorized to sign its checks, prepared to go to Europe, in June 1927, he instructed his assistant to compute the interest which would be due on July first and to draw a check for that sum and one for $1,500 representing the instalment of the principal. Checks were drawn, Herstein signed them and then sailed away.

The interest check was drawn for $4,219.69, whereas it should have been $4,621.56, a difference of $401.87. Soon thereafter the error was discovered. The mortgagee was notified of the shortage and was informed that on Mr. Herstein's return from Europe the balance would be paid. On June 30 the checks signed by Mr. Herstein were forwarded to the mortgagee, deposited by the latter and paid.

Mr. Herstein returned to his office on July 5th. Through an omission in his office he was not informed of the default in the payment of interest. The sad discovery was made when the action to foreclose the mortgage was begun on July 22nd, only one day after the 20-day grace period expired. Promptly that same day the Hope Building Corporation tendered the interest sum due. The mortgagee refused the tender and insisted upon its rights to claim the entire unpaid balance due immediately under the acceleration clause above mentioned.

The Court of Appeals in the majority opinion written by O'Brien *J.* found that there was no defense to the foreclosure action. Graf might not be considered generous but the contract was definite and had to be enforced. Judges Pound, Crane and Hubbs agreed. Chief Judge Cardozo dissented in an opinion with which Judges Lehman and Kellogg concurred.

CARDOZO, C. J. (dissenting)

There is no undeviating principle that equity shall enforce the covenants of a mortgage, unmoved by an appeal *ad misericordiam*, however urgent or affecting. The development of the jurisdiction of a chancery is lined with historic monuments that point another course. Equity declines to treat a mortgage upon realty as a conveyance subject to a condition, but views it as a lien irrespective of its form. Equity declines to give effect to a covenant, however formal, whereby in the making of a mortgage, the mortgagor abjures and surrenders the privilege of redemption. Equity declines in the same spirit, to give effect to a covenant, improvident in its terms, for the sale of an inheritance, but compels the buyer to exhibit an involuntary charity if he is found to have taken advantage of the necessities of the seller. Equity declines to give effect to a covenant for liquidated damages if it is so unconscionable in amount as to be equivalent in its substance to a provision for a penalty. One could give many illustrations of the traditional and unchallenged exercise of a like dispensing power. It runs through the whole rubric of accident and mistake. Equity follows the law, but not slavishly nor always. If it did, there could never be occasion for the enforcement of equitable doctrine.

To all this, acceleration clauses in mortgages do not constitute an exception. They are not a class by themselves, removed from interference by force of something peculiar in their internal constitution. In general, it is true, they will be enforced as they are written. In particular this has been held of a covenant in a mortgage accelerating the maturity of the principal in default of punctual payment of an installment of the interest. If the quality of a penalty inheres in such a covenant at all, it is not there to such a degree as to call, in ordinary circumstances, for mitigation or repression. Less favor has been shown to a provision for acceleration of a mortgage in default of punctual payment of taxes or assessments. We have held that such a provision, though not a penalty in a strict or proper sense, is yet so closely akin thereto in view of the forfeiture of credit that equity will relieve against it if default has been due to mere venial inattention and if relief can be granted without damage to the lender. In the one case as in the other, in foreclosure for default of taxes just as in foreclosure for default of interest, the privilege of acceleration is absolute in the event of a default, if the privilege is to be measured by the language of the covenant. The distinction lies in this only, that the punctual payment of interest has an importance to the lender as affecting his way of life, perhaps the very means for his support, whereas the importance of payment of the taxes is merely as an assurance of security. The difference is not one of kind, for the provision is enforcible even as to taxes if the default is continuous or wilful; it is a difference merely of degree, the purpose of the payment being referred to as a test wherewith to gauge the measure of the hardship, the extent of the oppression.

There is neither purpose nor desire to impair the stability of the rule, which is still to be enforced as one of general application, that nonpayment of interest will accelerate the debt if the mortgage so provides. The rule is well understood, and is fair to borrower and lender in its normal operation. Especially is it fair if there is a period of grace (in this case twenty days) whereby a reasonable leeway is afforded to inadvertence and improvidence. In such circumstances, with one period of grace established by the covenant, only the most appealing equity will justify a court in transcending the allotted period and substituting another. There is a difference, however, between a denial of power, without heed to the hardship calling for its use, and a definition of hardship that will limit the occasions upon which power shall be exercised. In none of the cases cited as indicative of lack of power was there any need to determine the effect of accident or mistake apparent to a mortgagee who has preferred default to payment. Indeed, in the one case[1] in which there was even an approach to such a theme, what was said was merely obiter, the actual decision being that the borrower was not at fault. However

[1] *Noyes* v. *Anderson,* reported in Volume 124 New York Reports 175.

fixed the general rule and the policy of preserving it, there may be extraordinary conditions in which the enforcement of such a clause according to the letter of the covenant will be disloyalty to the basic principles for which equity exists. We have seen that this may happen where the default is one affecting the payment of the taxes, though the standard form of mortgage, now embodied in the statute, groups interest and taxes together in the clause that makes provision for the acceleration of the principal. The courts of sister states at times have been less liberal than ours, and have held that even in respect of taxes the covenant will be enforced as it has been written, irrespective of the hardship. For us the rule is settled otherwise, and not even in the prevailing opinion is there the expression of a purpose to recede from it. Having gone so far, however, we shall have difficulty in refusing to go farther. Already, in the spirit of our holding, there are decisions by other courts that relief may be granted in extraordinary conditions, though the default has relation to the payment of the interest. Thus, in a recent case in Connecticut, acceleration of the debt was refused where a check for the interest had miscarried after its deposit in the mails. The exercise of a dispensing power was deemed to be a branch of the jurisdiction of equity to relieve against the consequences of accident or mistake. "This does not mean that such provisions for accelerating payments are provisions for forfeitures. Fairly made and fairly enforced they are not." Even so, "a court of equity may intervene to prevent the creditor from taking an unconscionable advantage of the letter of his bargain."[1]

When an advantage is unconscionable depends upon the circumstances. It is not unconscionable generally to insist that payment shall be made according to the letter of a contract. It may be unconscionable to insist upon adherence to the letter where the default is limited to a trifling balance, where the failure to pay the balance is the product of mistake, and where the mortgagee indicates by his conduct that he appreciates the mistake and

[1]Beach, *J.*, in *Consolе* v. *Torchinsky*, reported in Volume 97 Connecticut Reports 353.

has attempted by silence and inaction to turn it to his own advantage. The holder of this mortgage must have understood that he could have his money for the asking. His silence, followed as it was, by immediate suit at the first available opportunity, brings conviction to the mind that he was avoiding any act that would spur the mortgagor to payment. What he did was almost as suggestive of that purpose as if he had kept out of the way in order to avoid a tender. Demand was, indeed, unnecessary to bring the debt to maturity at law. There is not a technical estoppel. The consequence does not follow that, in conditions so peculiar, the omission to make demand is without significance in equity. Significant it may be in helping the court to a determination whether the conduct of a suitor in taking advantage of a default, so easily averted and so plainly unintentional, is consistent with good conscience. True, indeed, it is that accident and mistake will often be inadequate to supply a basis for the granting or withholding of equitable remedies where the consequences to be corrected might have been avoided if the victim of the misfortune had ordered his affairs with reasonable diligence. The restriction, however, is not obdurate, for always the gravity of the fault must be compared with the gravity of the hardship. Let the hardship be strong enough, and equity will find a way, though many a formula of inaction may seem to bar the path.

Cases such as Klein v. New York Life Ins. Co., Wheeler v. Connecticut Mutual Life Ins. Co. and Whiteside v. North American Accident Ins. Co.[1] do not derogate from the doctrine that a postulant in equity for affirmative relief may be dismissed without a remedy where he is attempting as an actor in the lawsuit to make himself the beneficiary of accident or error. In those cases and in others like them there was an attempt to charge a defendant with a contractual liability in disregard of the conditions limiting its creation. The party insisting on the condition was before the court as a defendant resisting a liability which could only arise if the condition was a nullity.

[1]Reported respectively in Volume 104 United States Reports 88, Volume 82 New York Reports 543 and Volume 200 New York Reports 320.

Here, on the other hand, there is no endeavor by the owner of the property to charge the mortgagee with an obligation to do anything affirmative. The operation of the decree will be negative altogether. There is nothing more than a refusal to give active aid and countenance to one who seeks the aid of equity and is unwilling as a price to do equity himself. In equity as in mechanics, action and reaction are equal and opposite. The equity that one asks one must be ready to concede. The maxim applies "whatever be the nature of the controversy between two definite parties, and whatever be the nature of the remedy."[1] The court will stand aside when by intervening it will make itself an instrument of injustice. There is no occasion to define the situations in which it will be ready to go farther and stay the remedy at law. Enough for present purposes that it may withhold a remedy in equity. If justice exacts an acceptance of a tender, the relief to be granted will be subject to that condition, and the decree will be limited to the overdue installments, with costs accruing to the date of tender and refusal.

In this case, the hardship is so flagrant, the misadventure so undoubted, the oppression so apparent, as to justify a holding that only through an acceptance of the tender will equity be done. The omission to pay in full had its origin in a clerical or arithmetical error that accompanied the act of payment, the very act to be performed. The error was not known to the debtor except in a constructive sense, for the secretary, a subordinate clerk, omitted to do her duty and report it to her principal. The deficiency, though not so small as to be negligible within the doctrine of *de minimis,* was still slight and unimportant when compared with the payment duly made. The possibility of bad faith is overcome by many circumstances, of which not the least is the one that instantly upon the discovery of the error, the deficiency was paid, and this only a single day after the term of grace was at an end. Finally, there is no pretense of damage or even inconvenience ensuing to the lender. On the contrary, and this is the

---

[1]Pomeroy "Equity Jurisprudence".

vital point, the inference is inevitable that the lender appreciated the blunder and was unwilling to avert it. From his conduct on the day immediately succeeding the default, we can infer his state of mind as it existed the day before. When all these circumstances are viewed in their cumulative significance, the enforcement of the covenant according to its letter is seen to approach in hardship the oppression of a penalty, just as truly as in Noyes v. Anderson[1] there was unconscionable hardship in an insistence upon a default in the discharge of an assessment. Ninety-one per cent. of the interest had been paid when it matured. The other nine per cent. was paid as soon as the underpayment became known to an agent competent to act, and only a day too late. Equity declines to intervene at the instance of a suitor who after fostering the default would make the court his ally in an endeavor to turn it to his benefit.

---

[1]*Supra,* page 246.

"NEITHER PRINCIPLE NOR PRECEDENT SUPPORTS A DECREE OF ABSOLUTION GRANTED TO A WRONGDOER"

Evangelical Lutheran Church v. *Sahlem,* 254 N. Y. 161 (1930)

In September of 1923 a tract of land in the Village of Snyder, divided into 128 lots, was subjected to restrictions which allowed for the erection on any lot of only one single family dwelling.

Philip Sahlem bought two of these lots and had erected thereon a one-family house which he made his home. A few years thereafter the Evangelical Lutheran Church decided to purchase a few of these lots directly opposite those of Sahlem in order to erect a church edifice. Realizing that the plan was in violation of the restrictions, the Church applied to the lot-owners for permission to vary the restrictions. All the lot-owners except Sahlem were willing to permit the Church to be erected. He took the position that he had bought his lots for the purpose of a home and that his peace and comfort would be disturbed by the existence of a near-by Church with the parking of cars, the tooting of horns, and the general invasion of his privacy which necessarily would follow.

The Church, feeling perhaps that Sahlem himself a Lutheran, would eventually agree to its request, decided to take title and build despite his opposition. Sahlem immediately issued a warning that the Church would build at its peril. But title was taken, plans were filed and the excavation work commenced.

At this point another attempt was made to appease Sahlem. But nothing could be done with him. He would not budge from his stand.

The Church decided to invoke the aid of the courts before going any further with its building. It asked that the court declare the restrictive covenants affecting its lots to be no longer in effect. The court refused to declare that the covenants had spent their force and on the contrary, considered them valid, but on the ground that the damages occasioned to Sahlem would be slight and inconsequential in comparison to those occasioned to the Church if it were enjoined from erecting its edifice, held that Sahlem was not entitled to hinder the work of construction. He was to be limited to money damages.

This decision did not satisfy Sahlem and he appealed.

CARDOZO, C. J. * * *

The judgment rendered in its favor eviscerates the restrictive covenants while declaring them alive. It does this on the ground that the damages occasioned to the defendant by the building of a church will be "slight and inconsequential" in comparison to those occasioned to the plaintiff if the use shall be enjoined. There is neither finding nor proof that the character of the neighborhood has so changed as to defeat the object and purposes for which the restrictions were imposed. Business has moved to some extent into blocks not far away which once were used for dwellings. The tract subjected to these covenants remains, however, what it has been since the restrictions were established, a place for homes exclusively. Indeed, there is no claim by any one that the plaintiff is at liberty, ignoring the covenants altogether, to devote the land in its ownership to business uses generally. By concession, its immunity will end if its building is not a church. The basis of this judgment, denying to the defendant owner the aid of equitable remedies, is not the presence of changed conditions extracting from the covenants their original vitality and reducing them to barren archaisms. The covenants are as useful in preserving to this tract the quality of a home section as they were at the beginning. The basis of this judgment is a holding that an owner, anxious to improve his land in knowing violation of a covenant still subsisting, may have the judgment of a court of equity advising him in advance that, so far as equity is concerned, he may go forward with impunity if only on a balancing of losses the loss to the wrongdoer appears to be greater than his victim's.

By the settled doctrine of equity, restrictive covenants in respect of land will be enforced by preventive remedies while the violation is still in prospect, unless the attitude of the complaining owner in standing on his covenant is unconscionable or oppressive. Relief is not withheld because the money damage is unsubstantial or even none at all. "If the construction of the instrument be clear and the breach clear, then it is not a question of damage, but the mere circumstance of the breach of covenant affords sufficient ground for the Court to interfere by injunction."[1] "The parties had the right to determine for themselves in what way and for what purposes their lands should be occupied irrespective of pecuniary gain or loss, or the effect on the market value of the lots."[2] Inequity there may be in standing on the letter of a covenant when the neighborhood has so altered that the ends to be attained by the restriction have been frustrated by the years. Inequity there may be in a demand for a mandatory injunction that will tear a completed building down, when the builder has acted in good faith, the covenant is presently to expire, and the havoc wrought by demolition will be disproportionate, in a degree shocking to the conscience, to any corresponding benefit. Few formulas are so absolute as not to bend before the blast of extraordinary circumstances. In the award of equitable remedies there is often an element of discretion, but never a discretion that is absolute or arbitrary. In equity, as at law, there are signposts for the traveler, "Discretion * * * 'must be regulated upon grounds that will make it judicial'."[3]

Here, in the case at hand, no process of balancing the equities can make the plaintiff's the greater when compared with the defendant's, or even place the two in equipoise. The defendant, the owner, has done nothing but insist upon adherence to a covenant which is now as valid and binding as at the hour of its making. His neighbors are willing to modify the restriction and forego a portion of their rights. He refuses to go with them. Rightly or wrongly he believes that the comfort of his dwelling will be imperiled by the change, and so he chooses to abide by the covenant as framed. The choice is for him only. Neither at law nor in equity is it written that a license has been granted to religious corporations, by reason of the high purpose of their being, to set covenants at naught.

---

[1] *Tipping* v. *Eckersley,* reported in Volume 2 Kay and Johnson 264, 270 (English Reports).

[2] *Trustees of Columbia College* v. *Lynch,* reported in Volume 70 New York Reports 440.

[3] *Haberman* v. *Baker,* reported in Volume 128 New York Reports, 253, 256.

Indeed, if in such matters there can be degrees of obligation, one would suppose that a more sensitive adherence to the demands of plighted faith might be expected of them than would be looked for of the world at large. Other owners may consent. One owner, the defendant, satisfied with the existing state of things, refuses to disturb it. He will be protected in his refusal by all the power of the law.

If there is nothing in the defendant's conduct that should serve to banish him from equity, the question must still be met whether something in the plaintiff's conduct, some element of mistake or misadventure or even intolerable hardship, may work a like result. Nothing of the kind appears. Before taking a deed and even before signing the preliminary contract, the plaintiff knew of the restriction and knew that the defendant would not consent to any variance. It decided to ignore him. In the face of a covenant too plain to be misread, with conditions in the restricted tract the same as they had been when the covenant was made, it signed a contract with a builder for the construction of a parish house, reserving for the future the contract for the church, and dug some spadefuls of earth as a sign that building had begun. At this point it prudently desisted and invoked the blessing of the law. With the building still a project, it induced a court of equity to advise it that there would be no hindrance by injunction if operations were resumed. Destruction of the defendant's easements, or rights analogous to easements, would proceed with safety and in order.

Neither principle nor precedent supports the decree of absolution thus granted to a wrongdoer. Here is no case of irreparable hardship, shocking to the conscience, as where a mandatory injunction would destroy a finished building to vindicate a doubtful right. Here is a case where the building is yet a plan, the work on it preliminary, the outlay unsubstantial, the act to be absolved still waiting for the doer. His path has been made easy by a judicial declaration that the wrong may go on without annoying interference.

The judgments of the Appellate Division and the Special Term should be reversed, and judgment rendered in favor of the defendants declaring the restrictive covenants described in the complaint to be enforceable at law and in equity, with costs in all courts.

POUND, CRANE, LEHMAN, KELLOGG and HUBBS, *JJ.*, concur.

O'BRIEN, *J.*, dissents and votes for affirmance.

"A DEFENDANT STARTS HIS LIFE AFRESH WHEN HE STANDS BEFORE A JURY, A PRISONER AT THE BAR"

People v. *Zackowitz,* 254 N. Y. 192 (1931)

Joseph Zackowitz, age 24, and his 17 year old wife, Fluff, were going home from a dance shortly after midnight on November 10, 1929. As they neared their home, Zackowitz dropped behind his wife to buy some newspapers and she went on a block ahead of him. On the opposite side of the street four young men of whom Frank Copola was one, were at work repairing an automobile. When they saw the young woman walking alone across the street, one of them called out to her and she understood his words to be a request that she have intercourse with him for which he would pay her $2.00. When Zackowitz caught up to his wife he found her in tears, and she told him that she had been insulted though she did not then tell him what she thought had been said to her.

Zackowitz, still a little heated with liquor drunk at the dance, walked across the street to the four young men and in rather vile language threatened them that "if they did not get out of there in five minutes, he would come back and bump them all off." He then rejoined his wife and they went to their apartment house near by.

When the couple arrived at their apartment, Zackowitz induced his wife to tell him what the insulting words were. When she told him of this indecent proposal his anger was again aroused, and according to his statement later given to the police, he armed himself at the apartment with a .25 calibre automatic pistol, and went back to the scene of the insult and found the four young men still there.

When Zackowitz came up to the young men, words and blows quickly followed. Zachowitz kicked Copola in the stomach. Some evidence there was that Copola went at him with a monkey wrench. In any event, during the struggle, Zackowitz drew his pistol from his pocket and fired one shot which struck Copola in the lungs and soon caused his death.

Zackowitz ran from the scene, and at the corner met his wife who had followed him from their home, and they spent the rest of the night at the home of a friend. On the way Zackowitz threw his pistol into the river. About seven weeks later he was arrested.

Upon the trial evidence was placed before the jury by the prosecution which showed that at the time of the killing and his arrest, there were in Zackowitz's apartment three pistols and a tear gas gun, none of which, however, was used in the scuffle. The defendant despite a defense of self-defense, was convicted of murder in the first degree, and an appeal was automatically taken to the Court of Appeals where the court by a four to three decision reversed the conviction, holding that the admissibility of the weapons was a serious error. Judges Crane and Hubbs concurred in a dissenting opinion by Judge Pound. The dissenters approved the argument of the District Atorney that if Zackowitz had been arrested at the time of the killing and these weapons had been found on his person, the people would have been able to prove that fact, and they could not see why the fact that the weapons were near by in his apartment should make any difference. It was their argument that Zackowitz was presented to the jury as a man having dangerous weapons in his possession, making a selection therefrom and going forth to make good on his threats to kill, and not as a man of a dangerous disposition in general.

The majority opinion written by Chief Judge Cardozo follows:

CARDOZO, C. J. * * *

At the trial the vital question was the defendant's state of mind at the moment of the homicide. Did he shoot with a deliberate and premeditated design to kill? Was he so inflamed by drink or by anger or by both combined that, though he knew the nature of his act, he was the prey to sudden impulse, the fury of the fleeting moment? If he went forth from his apartment with a preconceived design to kill, how is it that he failed to shoot at once? How reconcile such a design with the drawing of the pistol later in the heat and rage of an affray? These and like questions the jurors were to ask themselves and answer before measuring the defendant's guilt. Answers consistent with guilt in its highest grade can reasonably be made. Even so, the line between impulse and deliberation is too narrow and elusive to make the answers wholly clear. The sphygmograph records with graphic certainty the fluctuations of the mind. At least, if such an instrument exists, it was not working at midnight in the Brooklyn street when Coppola and the defendant came together in a chance affray. With only the rough and ready tests supplied by their experience of life, the jurors were to look into the workings of another's mind, and discover its capacities and disabilities, its urges and inhibitions, in moments of intense excitement. Delicate enough and subtle is the inquiry, even in the most favorable conditions, with every warping influence excluded. There must be no blurring of the issues by evidence illegally admitted and carrying with it in its admission an appeal to prejudice and passion.

Evidence charged with that appeal was, we think, admitted here. Not only was it admitted, and this under objection and exception, but the changes were rung upon it by prosecutor and judge. Almost at the opening of the trial the people began the endeavor to load the defendant down with the burden of an evil character. He was to be put before the jury as a man of murderous disposition. To that end they were allowed to prove that at the time of the encounter and at that of his arrest he had in his apartment, kept there in a radio box, three pistols and a tear-gas gun. There was no claim that he had brought these weapons out at the time of the affray, no claim that with any of them he had discharged the fatal shot. He could not have done so, for they were all of different caliber. The end to be served by laying the weapons before the jury was something very different. The end was to bring persuasion that here was a man of vicious and dangerous propensities, who because of those propensities was more likely to kill with deliberate and premeditated design than a man of irreproachable life and amiable manners. Indeed, this is the very ground on which the introduction of the evidence is now explained and defended. The district attorney tells us in his brief that the possession of the weapons characterized the defendant as "a desperate type of criminal," a "person criminally inclined." The dissenting opinion, if it puts the argument less bluntly, leaves the substance of the thought unchanged. "Defendant was presented to the jury as a man having dangerous weapons in his possession, making a selection therefrom and going forth to put into execution his threats to kill." The weapons were not brought by the defendant to the scene of the encounter. They were left in his apartment where they were incapable of harm. In such circumstances, ownership of the weapons, if it has any relevance at all, has relevance only as indicating a general disposition to make use of them thereafter, and a general disposition to make use of them thereafter is without relevance except as indicating a "desperate type of criminal," a criminal affected with a murderous propensity.

We are asked to extenuate the error by calling it an incident; what was proved may have an air of innocence if it is styled the history of the crime. The virus of the ruling is not so easily extracted. Here was no passing reference to something casually brought out in the narrative of the killing, as if an admission had been proved against the defendant that he had picked one weapon out of several. Here in the forefront of the trial, immediately following the statement of the medical examiner, testimony was admitted that weapons, not the instruments of the killing had been discovered by the police in the apartment of the killer; and the weapons with great display were laid before the jury, marked as exhibits, and thereafter made the subject of animated argument. Room for doubt there is none that in the thought of the jury, as in that of the district attorney, the tendency of the whole performance was to characterize the defendant as a man murderously inclined. The purpose was not disguised. From the opening to the verdict, it was flaunted and avowed.

If a murderous propensity may be proved against a defendant as one of the tokens of his guilt, a rule of criminal evidence, long believed to be of fundamental importance for the protection of the innocent, must be first declared away. Fundamental hitherto has been the rule that character is never an issue in a criminal prosecution unless the defendant chooses to make it one. In a very real sense a defendant starts his life afresh when he stands before a jury, a prisoner at the bar. There has been a homicide in a public place. The killer admits the killing, but urges self defense and sudden impulse. Inflexibly the law has set its face against the endeavor to fasten guilt upon him by proof of character or experience predisposing to an act of crime. The endeavor has been often made, but always it has failed. At times, when the issue has been self defense, testimony has been admitted as to the murderous propensity of the deceased, the victim of the homicide but never of such a propensity on the part of the killer. The principle back of the exclusion is one, not of logic, but of policy. There may be cogency in the argument that a quarrelsome defendant is more likely to start a quarrel than one of milder type, a man of dangerous mode of life more likely than a shy recluse. The law is not blind to this, but equally it is not blind to the peril to the innocent if character is accepted as probative of crime. "The natural and inevitable tendency of the tribunal—whether judge or jury—is to give excessive weight to the vicious record of crime thus exhibited, and either to allow it to bear too strongly on the present charge, or to take the proof of it as justifying a condemnation irrespective of guilt of the present charge."[1]

A different question would be here if the pistols had been bought in expectation of this particular encounter. They would then have been admissible as evidence of preparation and design. A different question would be here if they were so connected with the crime as to identify the perpetrator, if he had dropped them, for example, at the scene of the affray. They would then have been admissible as tending to implicate the possessor (if identity was disputed), no matter what the opprobrium attached to his possession. Different, also, would be the question if the defendant had been shown to have gone forth from the apartment with all the weapons on his person. To be armed from head to foot at the very moment of an encounter may be a circumstance worthy to be considered, like acts of preparation generally, as a proof of preconceived design. There can be no such implication from the ownership of weapons which one leaves behind at home.

The endeavor was to generate an atmosphere of professional criminality. It was an endeavor the more unfair in that, apart from the suspicion attaching to the possession of these weapons, there is nothing to mark the defend-

---

[1]Wigmore, "Evidence," Volume 1, Section 194.

ant as a man of evil life. He was not in crime as a business. He did not shoot as a bandit shoots in the hope of wrongful gain. He was engaged in a decent calling, an optician regularly employed, without criminal record, or criminal associates. If his own testimony be true, he had gathered these weapons together as curios, a collection that interested and amused him. Perhaps his explanation of their ownership is false. There is nothing stronger than mere suspicion to guide us to an answer. Whether the explanation be false or true, he should not have been driven by the people to the necessity of offering it. Brought to answer a specific charge, and to defend himself against it, he was placed in a position where he had to defend himself against another, more general and sweeping. He was made to answer to the charge, persuasive and poisonous even if insidious and covert, that he was a man of murderous heart, of criminal disposition.

The argument is made that the evidence, if incompetent when admitted, became competent thereafter when the defendant took the stand. By taking the stand he subjected himself like any other witness to cross-examination designed to shake belief in his veracity by exhibiting his ways of life. Cross-examination brought out the fact that he had no license for a pistol. That fact disclosed, the prosecution was at liberty to prove the possession of the weapons in an attempt to impeach his credibility, since possession was a felony. All this may be true, but the evidence was not offered or admitted with such an end in view. It was received at a time when there was nothing to show that the defendant was without a license, and without suggestion that any such evidence would be brought into the case thereafter. The jury were not told that the possession of the weapons had significance only in so far as possession without a license had a tendency to cast a shadow on the defendant's character, and so to impair the faith to be given to his word. They were told in effect through the whole course and tenor of the trial that irrespective of any license, the mere possession of the weapons was evidence of a murderous disposition, which, apart from any bearing upon the defendant's credibility as a witness, was evidence of guilt. Here is no case of a mere technical departure from the approved order of proof. If the evidence had been received for the purpose of impeachment merely, the people would have been bound by the answer of the witness as to the time and purpose of the purchase, and would not have been permitted to contradict him. Here is a case where evidence offered and received as probative of an essential element of the crime, used for that purpose, and for no other, repeatedly throughout the trial, is now about to be viewed as if accepted at a later stage and accepted for a purpose unmentioned and unthought of. This is not justice in accordance with the forms of law. "The practice of calling out evidence for one purpose, apparently innocent, and using it for another, which is illegal, is improper; and, if it is clear and manifest that the avowed object is colorable merely, its admission is error."[1] Even more plainly is it a perversion to call out evidence for an avowed object manifestly illegal, and use it later on appeal as if admitted at another stage in aid of another purpose innocent and lawful.

The judgment of conviction should be reversed, and a new trial ordered.[2]

---

[1]*Coleman* v. *People,* reported in 55 New York Reports 81, 88.

[2]Upon the second trial, the defendant took a plea of guilty to the crime of manslaughter in the first degree and was sentenced to 10 to 20 years in prison.

"FRAUD INCLUDES THE PRETENSE OF KNOWLEDGE, WHEN KNOWLEDGE THERE IS NONE"

Ultramares Corporation v. *Touche,* 255 N. Y. 170 (1931)

Fred Stern & Co. Inc., a firm engaged in the importation and sale of rubber employed Touche, Nevin & Co., a firm of public accountants to prepare and certify a balance sheet showing the condition of its business as of the end of 1923. The accountants were aware of the fact that the corporation required extensive credit and that their balance sheet when certified would be exhibited by the Stern Company to banks, creditors, stockholders, customers and others who might advance credit, though the names of any specific persons to whom it would be shown were not known to them.

The audit was finished in February 1924 and a balance sheet made up. Assets were shown to be $2,550,671.88 and liabilities $1,479,956.62, showing thereby a net worth of $1,070,715.26. Attached to this balance sheet was a statement signed by Touche, Nevin & Co. which in substance declared that they had examined the accounts of Fred Stern & Co. Inc. for the year ending December 31, 1923, that the annexed balance sheet was in accordance therewith and with the information given them and certified the statement that in their opinion it was a correct view of the company's financial condition. Thirty-two duplicates were executed.

In March the Stern Company applied to the Ultramares Corporation for a loan. As a condition of any loans that corporation insisted that it receive a balance sheet certified by public accountants. Thereupon it was given one of the certificates signed by Touche, Nevins & Co. On the faith of that certificate many loans were advanced.

During all this time the Stern Company was insolvent and the balance sheet entirely false. Capital and surplus in reality did not exist. On January 2, 1925 the Stern Company was declared a bankrupt. The Ultramares Corporation sustained a heavy loss.

Suit was brought against the accountants. The principle relied upon for the imposition of liability was that if one undertakes to discharge any duty by which the conduct of others may be governed, he is bound to perform it in such a manner that those who are thus led to action relying on the proper discharge of that duty shall not suffer loss through improper performance or neglect in its execution. The complaint alleged loss through misrepresentations that were merely negligent and through misrepresentations charged to have been fraudulent.

The accountants maintained that they owed no duty to Ultramares Corporation, but that their obligation was contractual with the Stern Company. They also attempted to justify their balance sheet in the testimony they furnished by the way the figures were obtained. They showed the following: that when they commenced their audit in January 1924 they found that there had been no posting of the general ledger since the preceding April; that Romberg, who had charge of the accounts of the Stern Company, had added fictitious accounts receivables.

Siess, a junior accountant, supposed Romberg's entry to be correct and that since his work was merely to post the books, he left the verification for others who would do the auditing. The verification was never made either by Siess or by his superiors. The fact was that any examiner would have found that the entry by Romberg was not supported by any entry in the journal. The "debit memo book" from which the journal was made up would also not have supported the entry.

There did exist 17 invoices which did total to the added sum, but an examination of these would have disclosed suspicious features for they had neither shipping number nor customer's order number. The terms of credit on these invoices were also unusual.

There were other suspicious items. An item of over $113,000 alleged due from the Baltic Corporation received a not very convincing explanation from Stern and Romberg. Errors in large sums were discovered in the inventory but the accountants adjusted the balance sheets accordingly. There was ground for suspicion in the records of assigned accounts as inquiry of the creditors informed the accountants that the same accounts had been pledged to several banks at the same time. Though the latter fact did not diminish the assets, it showed that the business of the Stern Company was not being conducted on a high moral plane.

CARDOZO, C. J. * * *

We think the evidence supports a finding that the audit was negligently made, though in so saying we put aside for the moment the question whether negligence, even if it existed, was a wrong to the plaintiff.

If the defendants owed a duty to the plaintiff to act with the same care that would have been due under a contract of employment, a jury was at liberty to find a verdict of negligence upon a showing of a scrutiny so imperfect and perfunctory. No doubt the extent to which inquiry must be pressed beyond appearances is a question of judgment, as to which opinions will often differ. No doubt the wisdom that is born after the event will engender suspicion and distrust when old acquaintance and good repute may have silenced doubt at the beginning. All this is to be weighed by a jury in applying its standard of behavior, the state of mind, and conduct of the reasonable man. Even so, the adverse verdict, when rendered, imports an alignment of the weights in their proper places in the balance and a reckoning thereafter. The reckoning was not wrong upon the evidence before us, if duty be assumed.

We are brought to the question of duty, its origin and measure.

The defendants owed to their employer a duty imposed by law to make their certificate without fraud, and a duty growing out of contract to make it with the care and caution proper to their calling. Fraud includes the pretense of knowledge when knowledge there is none. To creditors and investors to whom the employer exhibited the certificate, the defendants owed a like duty to make it without fraud, since there was notice in the circumstances of its making that the employer did not intend to keep it to himself. A different question develops when we ask whether they owed a duty to these to make it without negligence. If liability for negligence exists, a thoughtless slip or blunder, the failure to detect a theft or forgery beneath the cover of deceptive entries, may expose accountants to a liability in an indeterminate amount for an indeterminate time to an indeterminate class. The hazards of a business conducted on these terms are so extreme as to enkindle doubt whether a flaw may not exist in the implication of a duty that exposes to these consequences. We put aside for the moment any statement in the certificate which involves the representation of a fact as true to the knowledge of the auditors. If such a statement was made, whether believed to be true or not, the defendants are liable for deceit in the event that it was false. The plaintiff does not need the invention of novel doctrine to help it out in such conditions. The case was submitted to the jury, and the verdict was returned upon the theory that, even in the absence of a misstatement of a fact, there is a liability also for erroneous opinion. The expression of an opinion is to be subject to a warranty implied by law. What, then, is the warranty, as yet unformulated, to be? Is it merely that the opinion is honestly conceived and that the preliminary inquiry has been honestly pursued, that a halt has not been made without a genuine belief that the search has been reasonably adequate to bring disclosure of the truth? Or does it go farther and involve the assumption of a liability for any blunder or inattention that could fairly be spoken of as negligence if the controversy were one between accountant and employer for breach of a contract to render services for pay?

The assault upon the citadel of privity is proceeding in these days apace. How far the inroads shall extend is now a favorite subject of juridical discussion. In the field of the law of contract there has been a gradual widening of the doctrine of Lawrence v. Fox[1] until today the beneficiary of a promise, clearly designated as such, is seldom left without a remedy. Even in that field, however, the remedy is narrower where the beneficiaries of the promise are indeterminate or general. Something more must then appear than an intention that the promise shall redound to the benefit of the public or to that of a class of indefinite extension. The promise must be such as to "bespeak the assumption of a duty to make reparation directly to the individual members of the public if the benefit is lost."[2] In the field of the law of torts a manufacturer who is negligent in the manufacture of a chattel in circumstances pointing to an unreasonable risk of serious bodily harm to those using it thereafter may be liable for negligence though privity is lacking between manufacturer and user. A force or instrument of harm having been launched with

[1]Reported in Volume 20 New York Reports 268. The doctrine of this case is to the effect that if A is indebted to B and a promise is made by C to A to do something for B, the *latter* may enforce C's promise even though the consideration for C's promise was given by A.

[2]*Moch Co.* v. *Rensselaer Water Co.,* reported in Volume 247 New York Reports 160, 164.

potentialities of danger manifest to the eye of prudence, the one who launches it is under a duty to keep it within bounds. Even so, the question is still open whether the potentialities of danger that will charge with liability are confined to harm to the person, or include injury to property. In either view, however, what is released or set in motion is a physical force. We are now asked to say that a like liability attaches to the circulation of a thought or a release of the explosive power resident in words.

Three cases in this court are said by the plaintiff to have committed us to the doctrine that words, written or oral, if negligently published with the expectation that the reader or listener will transmit them to another, will lay a basis for liability though privity be lacking. These are Glanzer v. Shepard, International Products Co. v. Erie, and Doyle v. Chatham & Phenix Nat. Bank.[1]

In Glanzer v. Shepard, the seller of beans requested the defendants, public weighers, to make return of the weight and furnish the buyer with a copy. This the defendants did. Their return, which was made out in duplicate, one copy to the seller and the other to the buyer, recites that it was made by order of the former for the use of the latter. The buyer paid the seller on the faith of the certificate which turned out to be erroneous. We held that the weighers were liable at the suit of the buyer for the moneys overpaid. Here was something more than the rendition of a service in the expectation that the one who ordered the certificate would use it thereafter in the operations of his business as occasion might require. Here was a case where the transmission of the certificate to another was not merely one possibility among many, but the "end and aim of the transaction," as certain and immediate and deliberately willed as if a husband were to order a gown to be delivered to his wife, or a telegraph company, contracting with the sender of a message, were to telegraph it wrongly to the damage of the person expected to receive it. The intimacy of the resulting nexus is attested by the fact that, after stating the case in terms

[1]These cases are reported in the New York reports Volume 233 at page 236, Volume 244 at page 331, and Volume 253 at page 369, respectively.

of legal duty, we went on to point out that viewing it as a phase or extension of Lawrence v. Fox, supra, we could reach the same result by stating it in terms of contract. The bond was so close as to approach that of privity, if not completely one with it. Not so in the case at hand. No one would be likely to urge that there was a contractual relation, or even one approaching it, at the root of any duty that was owing from the defendants now before us to the indeterminate class of persons who, presently or in the future, might deal with the Stern Company in reliance on the audit. In a word, the service rendered by the defendant in Glanzer v. Shepard was primarily for the information of a third person, in effect, if not in name, a party to the contract, and only incidentally for that of the formal promisee. In the case at hand, the service was primarily for the benefit of the Stern Company, a convenient instrumentality for use in the development of the business, and only incidentally or collaterally for the use of those to whom Stern and his associates might exhibit it thereafter. Foresight of these possibilities may charge with liability for fraud. The conclusion does not follow that it will charge with liability for negligence.

In the next of the three cases (International Products Co. v. Erie R. R. Co., supra) the plaintiff, an importer, had an agreement with the defendant, a railroad company, that the latter would act as bailee of goods arriving from abroad. The importer, to protect the goods by suitable insurance, made inquiry of the bailee as to the location of the storage. The warehouse was incorrectly named, and the policy did not attach. Here was a determinate relation, that of bailor and bailee, either present or prospective, with peculiar opportunity for knowledge on the part of the bailee as to the subject-matter of the statement and with a continuing duty to correct it if erroneous. Even the narrowest holdings as to liability for unintentional misstatement concede that a representation in such circumstances may be equivalent to a warranty. There is a class of cases "where a person within whose special province it lay to know a particular fact, has given an erroneous answer to an inquiry made with regard to it by a person desirous of ascertaining the fact for the purpose of determining his course accordingly, and has been held bound to make good the assurance he has given."[1] So in Burrowes v. Lock,[2] a trustee was asked by one who expected to make a loan upon the security of a trust fund whether notice of any prior incumbrance upon the fund had been given to him. An action for damages was upheld, though the false answer was made honestly in the belief that it was true.

In one respect the decision in International Products Co. v. Erie R. R. Co. is in advance of anything decided in Glanzer v. Shepard. The latter case suggests that the liability there enforced was not one for the mere utterance of words without due consideration, but for a negligent service, the act of weighing, which happened to find in the words of the certificate its culmination and its summary. This was said in the endeavor to emphasize the character of the certificate as a business transaction, an act in the law, and not a mere casual response to a request for information. The ruling in the case of the Erie Railroad shows that the rendition of a service is at most a mere circumstance and not an indispensable condition. The Erie was not held for negligence in the rendition of a service. It was held for words and nothing more. So in the case at hand. If liability for the consequences of a negligent certificate may be enforced by any member of an indeterminate class of creditors, present and prospective, known and unknown, the existence or non-existence of a preliminary act of service will not affect the cause of action. The service may have been rendered as carefully as you please, and its quality will count for nothing if there was negligence thereafter in distributing the summary.

Doyle v. Chatham & Phenix Nat. Bank, supra, the third of the cases cited, is even more plainly indecisive. A trust company was a trustee under a deed of trust to secure an issue of bonds. It was held liable to a subscriber for the

[1]Herschell, *L. C.*, in *Derry* v. *Peek,* reported in Volume 14 Appeals Cases, 337, 360.

[2]Reported in Volume 10 Ves. 470.

bonds when it certified them falsely. A representation by a trustee intended to sway action had been addressed to a person who by the act of subscription was to become a party to the deed and a cestui que trust.

The antidote to these decisions and to the overuse of the doctrine of liability for negligent misstatement may found in Jaillet v. Dow, Jones & Company.[1] In this case the defendant supplying ticker service to brokers was held not liable in damages to one of the broker's customers for the consequences of reliance upon a report negligently published on the ticker. If liability had been upheld, the step would have been a short one to the declaration of a like liability on the part of proprietors of newspapers. In the second the principle was clearly stated by Pound, *J.*, that "negligent words are not actionable unless they are uttered directly, with knowledge or notice that they will be acted on, to one to whom the speaker is bound by some relation of duty, arising out of public calling, contract or otherwise, to act with care if he acts at all."

From the foregoing analysis the conclusion is, we think, inevitable that nothing in our previous decisions commits us to a holding of liability for negligence in the circumstances of the case at hand, and that such liability, if recognized, will be an extension of the principle of those decisions to different conditions, even if more or less analogous. The question then is whether such an extension shall be made.

The extension, if made, will so expand the field of liability for negligent speech as to make it nearly, if not quite, coterminous with that of liability for fraud. Again and again, in decisions of this court, the bounds of this latter liability have been set up, with futility the fate of every endeavor to dislodge them. Scienter has been declared to be an indispensable element, except where the representation has been put forward as true of one's own knowledge, or in circumstances where the expression of opinion was a dishonorable pretense. Even an opinion, especially an opinion by an expert, may be found to be

---

[1]Reported in Volume 235 New York Reports 511.

fraudulent if the grounds supporting it are so flimsy as to lead to the conclusion that there was no genuine belief back of it. Further than that this court has never gone. Directors of corporations have been acquitted of liability for deceit, though they have been lax in investigation and negligent in speech. This has not meant, to be sure, that negligence may not be evidence from which a trier of the facts may draw an inference of fraud, but merely that, if that inference is rejected, or, in the light of all the circumstances, is found to be unreasonable, negligence alone is not a substitute for fraud. Many also are the cases that have distinguished between the willful or reckless representation essential to the maintenance at law of an action for deceit, and the misrepresentation, negligent or innocent, that will lay a sufficient basis for rescission in equity.[1] If this action is well conceived, all these principles and distinctions, so nicely wrought and formulated, have been a waste of time and effort. They have even been a snare, entrapping litigants and lawyers into an abandonment of the true remedy lying ready to the call. The suitors thrown out of court because they proved negligence, and nothing else, in an action for deceit, might have ridden to triumphant victory if they had proved the self-same facts, but had given the wrong another label, and all this in a state where forms of action have been abolished. So to hold is near to saying that we have been paltering with justice. A word of caution or suggestion would have set the erring suitor right. Many pages of opinion were written by judges the most eminent, yet the word was never spoken. We may not speak it now. A change so revolutionary, if expedient, must be wrought by legislation.

We have said that the duty to refrain from negligent representation would become coincident or nearly so with

---

[1]In the state of New York, an action for rescission will lie upon proof of a misrepresentation of a material fact which induced the other party to act to his damage. In this type of action each party is restored to his position as it existed before the contract was made. An action in deceit will lie upon proof of the same elements as in rescission plus the fact that the misrepresentation was intentional. Recovery in such case is the difference in value between what the plaintiff gave and what he actually received.

the duty to refrain from fraud if this action could be maintained. A representation, even though knowingly false, does not constitute ground for an action of deceit unless made with the intent to be communicated to the persons or class of persons who act upon it to their prejudice. Affirmance of this judgment would require us to hold that all or nearly all the persons so situated would suffer an impairment of an interest legally protected if the representation had been negligent. We speak of all "or nearly all," for cases can be imagined where a casual response, made in circumstances insufficient to indicate that care should be expected, would permit recovery for fraud if willfully deceitful. Cases of fraud between persons so circumstanced are, however, too infrequent and exceptional to make the radii greatly different if the fields of liability for negligence and deceit be figured as concentric circles. The like may be said of the possibility that the negligence of the injured party, contributing to the result, may avail to overcome the one remedy, though unavailing to defeat the other.

Neither of these possibilities is noted by the plaintiff in its answer to the suggestion that the two fields would be coincident. Its answer has been merely this, first, that the duty to speak with care does not arise unless the words are the culmination of a service, and, second, that it does not arise unless the service is rendered in the pursuit of an independent calling, characterized as public. As to the first of these suggestions, we have already had occasion to observe that given a relation making diligence a duty, speech as well as conduct must conform to that exacting standard. As to the second of the two suggestions, public accountants are public only in the sense that their services are offered to anyone who chooses to employ them. This is far from saying that those who do not employ them are in the same position as those who do.

Liability for negligence if adjudged in this case will extend to many callings other than an auditor's. Lawyers who certify their opinion as to the validity of municipal or corporate bonds, with knowledge that the opinion will be brought to the notice of the public, will become liable to the investors, if they have overlooked a statute or a decision, to the same extent as if the controversy were one between client and adviser. Title companies insuring titles to a tract of land, with knowledge that at an approaching auction the fact that they have insured will be stated to the bidders, will become liable to purchasers who may wish the benefit of a policy without payment of a premium. These illustrations may seem to be extreme, but they go little, if any, farther than we are invited to go now. Negligence, moreover, will have one standard when viewed in relation to the public. Explanations that might seem plausible, omissions that might be reasonable, if the duty is confined to the employer, conducting a business that presumably at least is not a fraud upon his creditors, might wear another aspect if an independent duty to be suspicious even of one's principal is owing to investors. "Every one making a promise having the quality of a contract will be under a duty to the promisee by virtue of the promise, but under another duty, apart from contract, to an indefinite number of potential beneficiaries when performance has begun. The assumption of one relation will mean the involuntary assumption of a series of new relations, inescapably hooked together."[1]

Our holding does not emancipate accountants from the consequence of fraud. It does not relieve them if their audit has been so negligent as to justify a finding that they had no genuine belief in its adequacy, for this again is fraud. It does no more than say that, if less than this is proved, if there has been neither reckless misstatement nor insincere profession of an opinion, but only honest blunder, the ensuing liability for negligence is one that is bounded by the contract, and is to be enforced between the parties by whom the contract has been made. We doubt whether the average business man receiving a certificate without paying for it, and receiving it merely as one among a multitude of possible investors, would look for anything more.

The second cause of action is yet to be considered.

---

[1]*Moch* v. *Rensselaer Water Co.*, reported in Volume 247 New York Reports 160.

The defendants certified as a fact, true to their own knowledge, that the balance sheet was in accordance with the books of account. If their statement was false, they are not to be exonerated because they believed it to be true. We think the triers of the facts might hold it to be false.

Correspondence between the balance sheet and the books imports something more, or so the triers of the facts might say, than correspondence between the balance sheet and the general ledger, unsupported or even contradicted by every other record. The correspondence to be of any moment may not unreasonably be held to signify a correspondence between the statement and the books of original entry, the books taken as a whole. If that is what the certificate means, a jury could find that the correspondence did not exist, and that the defendants signed the certificates without knowing it to exist and even without reasonable grounds for belief in its existence. The item of $706,000, representing fictitious accounts receivable, was entered in the ledger after defendant's employee Siess had posted the December sales. He knew of the interpolation, and knew that there was need to verify the entry by reference to books other than the ledger before the books could be found to be in agreement with the balance sheet. The evidence would sustain a finding that this was never done. By concession the interpolated item had no support in the journal, or in any journal voucher, or in the debit memo book, which was a summary of the invoices, or in anything except the invoices themselves. The defendants do not say that they ever looked at the invoices, seventeen in number, representing these accounts. They profess to be unable to recall whether they did so or not. They admit, however, that, if they had looked, they would have found omissions and irregularities so many and unusual as to have called for further investigation. When we couple the refusal to say that they did look with the admission that, if they had looked, they would or could have seen, the situation is revealed as one in which a jury might reasonably find that in truth they did not look, but certified the correspondence without testing its existence.

In this connection we are to bear in mind the principle already stated in the course of this opinion that negligence or blindness, even when not equivalent to fraud, is none the less evidence to sustain an inference of fraud. At least this is so if the negligence is gross.

* * *

The defendants attempt to excuse the omission of an inspection of the invoices proved to be fictitious by invoking a practice known as that of testing and sampling. A random choice of accounts is made from the total number on the books, and these, if found to be regular when inspected and investigated, are taken as a fair indication of the quality of the mass. The defendants say that about 200 invoices were examined in accordance with this practice, but they do not assert that any of the seventeen invoices supporting the fictitious sales were among the number so selected. Verification by test and sample was very likely a sufficient audit as to accounts regularly entered upon the books in the usual course of business. It was plainly insufficient, however, as to accounts not entered upon the books where inspection of the invoices was necessary, not as a check upon accounts fair upon their face, but in order to ascertain whether there were any accounts at all. If the only invoices inspected were invoices unrelated to the interpolated entry, the result was to certify a correspondence between the books and the balance sheet without any effort by the auditors, as to $706,000 of accounts, to ascertain whether the certified agreement was in accordance with the truth. How far books of account fair upon their face are to be probed by accountants, in an effort to ascertain whether the transactions back of them are in accordance with the entries, involves to some extent the exercise of judgment and discretion. Not so, however, the inquiry whether the entries certified as there, are there in very truth, there in the form and in the places where men of business training would expect them to be. The defendants were put on their guard by the circumstances touching the December accounts receivable to scrutinize with special care. A jury might find that, with suspicions thus awakened, they closed their eyes to the obvious, and blindly gave assent.

We conclude, to sum up the situation, that in certifying to the correspondence between balance sheet and accounts the defendants made a statement as true to their own knowledge, when they had, as a jury might find, no knowledge on the subject. If that is so, they may also be found to have acted without information leading to a sincere or genuine belief when they certified to an opinion that the balance sheet faithfully reflected the condition of the business.

Whatever wrong was committed by the defendants was not their personal act or omission, but that of their subordinates. This does not relieve them, however, of liability to answer in damages for the consequences of the wrong, if wrong there shall be found to be. It is not a question of constructive notice, as where facts are brought home to the knowledge of subordinates whose interests are adverse to those of the employer. These subordinates, so far as the record shows, had no interests adverse to the defendants', nor any thought in what they did to be unfaithful to their trust. The question is merely this, whether the defendants, having delegated the performance of this work to agents of their own selection, are responsible for the manner in which the business of the agency was done. As to that the answer is not doubtful.

POUND, CRANE, LEHMAN, KELLOGG, O'BRIEN and HUBBS, *JJ.*, concur.

"EQUITY DOES NOT ACT FOR EVERY SHADOWY OR UNSUBSTANTIAL WRONG"

Nann v. *Raimist,* 255 N. Y. 307 (1931)

The Amalgamated Food Workers and the Bakery & Confectionery Workers' International Union of America were two rival unions whose influence covered the bakers' and confectioners' trade. Each made its contracts with employers whereby the latter agreed to employ members of that particular union to the exclusion of all others. These contracts were not for fixed periods but were terminable at will.

The wage schedule fixed by the Amalgamated was much lower than that fixed by the International. The latter, however, established a "substitute system" under which every union member employed by the week was required to give up part of his time to a member out of a job. This shortened the work for some but decreased unemployment. This system did not find too much favor with employers, as it caused inconvenience and decreased efficiency and gradually the Amalgamated began to draw away employers who had previously given allegiance to the International.

Trouble was not long in coming. The International demanded that the Amalgamated merge or surrender. The demand was bluntly refused. Thereupon the International canvassed employers from shop to shop. Speakers on behalf of the International spoke from wagons on the street corners near Amalgamated shops and paraders carried placards down the streets, all denouncing its rival as a "fake" union, a collection of "scabs" and asserting that the International was the only regular or genuine union.

The Winthrop Baking Company had opened a new shop and had allied itself with the Amalgamated in August 1927, the very month during which these hostilities were started. When in addition to the aggravating remarks above mentioned the International representatives told passers-by that a strike was going on, the Winthrop Company sued for an injunction. The order merely restrained the International from marching up and down in front of the bakery with false or misleading signs and from making false or misleading statements, but it was not restrained from picketing. Followers of the International continued to loiter about the place, telling passers-by that a strike was in progress.

One afternoon (January 3, 1928) a Winthrop Company employee was set upon and beaten as he was leaving after the day's work. At noon the following day a fight ensued between rival members and in the conflict another Winthrop Company employee was beaten. A few days later, frightened by the goings-on, Scheffer & Edelstein, formerly of the International and now with the Amalgamated, signed a contract with the International.

On January 12, 1928 the Amalgamated, by Fred Nann, its president, commenced an action against Lasar Raimist, as treasurer of the International, to enjoin the International from destroying its existence by violent or illegal acts.

The lower court granted an injunction restraining the International and others from

(1) interfering with the conduct or business of any store, bakery or shop having a contract with the Amalgamated;
(2) threatening or intimidating any member of the Amalgamated or any one having a contract with it;
(3) from picketing, loitering or marching in front of or in the vicinity of any premises under contract with the Amalgamated;
(4) declaring that any business under contract with the Amalgamated is a "scab" or not a regular union shop or that the Amalgamated is a "scab" or not a regular union;
(5) declaring that the Amalgamated label is not a union label or that the head of the shops affiliated with the Amalgamated is not a union head;
(6) from persuading any employer having a contract with the Amalgamated to leave it or to discharge any member of the Amalgamated.

This injunction order was unanimously affirmed by the Appellate Division and an appeal was taken to the Court of Appeals.

CARDOZO, C. J. * * *

The plaintiff, if threatened in its business life by the violence of the defendant or by other wrongful acts, may have the aid of the court to preserve itself from disruption through recourse to these unlawful means. The remedy is not lost because the controversy is one between the members of rival unions, and not, as happens oftener, between unions and employers. On the other hand, the legality of the defendant's conduct is not affected by the fact that no strike is in progress in any of the plaintiff's shops. If the defendant believes in good faith that the policy pursued by the plaintiff and by the shops united with the plaintiff is hostile to the interests of organized labor, and is likely, if not suppressed, to lower the standards of living for workers in the trade, it has the privilege by the pressure of notoriety and persuasion to bring its own policy to triumph.

Upon the facts exhibited in this record the defendant went beyond the bounds of lawful conduct in conducting its campaign for the suppression of its rival. These acts were of such a nature as to justify some of the restraints imposed by the courts below, though they are insufficient to give support to others. The defendant does not complain of the injunction against acts of violence or intimidation or against causing crowds to gather or loitering in groups. Those provisions of the judgment may stand as they were written. What the defendant complains of is the injunction against picketing, against false and misleading signs and statements, and against peaceable persuasion.

"Where unlawful picketing has been continued, where violence and intimidation have been used, and where misstatements as to the employer's business have been distributed, a broad injunction prohibiting all picketing may be granted." * * * "The course of conduct of the strikers" is then "such as to indicate the danger of injury to property if any picketing whatever is allowed."[1]

Before this action was begun, the defendant had already been restrained in the suit by the Winthrop bakery from acts of violence or disorder, from picketing with false and misleading statements. These prohibitions it had violated, or so the trier of the facts has found. It had set upon and beaten innocent workmen. It had falsely asserted that a strike was in progress. By such falsehoods it had driven customers to other bakeries, had forced unwilling proprietors to succumb to its demands, and in so doing had threatened the prosperity and indeed the very existence of its rival.

---

[1] *Exchange Bakery & Restaurant* v. *Rifkin*, reported in Volume 245 New York Reports 269.

Whether the trial court, in view of this record of defiance, would give the defendant still another chance to picket peacefully and in order, was something to be determined in the exercise of a wise discretion. This court may not interfere except for manifest abuse. "It becomes a question for the judgment of the chancellor who has heard the witnesses, familiarized himself with the *locus in quo* and observed the tendencies to disturbance and conflict."[1] One chance the defendant had already been given. It had defied the mandate and abused the privilege. How many more chances was it to have before the court could intervene? An injunction does not issue in such circumstances as punishment for the past. Its only legitimate end is protection for the future. Not improbably a writ could have been framed whereby the desired end would have been attained by prohibitions less complete. We might have preferred such restraints if we had been exercising the powers of a chancellor. Sitting in this court we deal solely with defect of power or with abuse of discretion so gross as to be equivalent to defect of power. The injunction in such aspect is not to be sustained upon any theory that picketing per se is to be condemned as an illegal act. This court is committed to a contrary doctrine. The injunction is sustained upon the theory that the defendant, having been permitted to picket subject to conditions, violated those conditions, and in contempt of the existing mandate picketed with violence and with falsehood, spreading terror with a strong hand and a multitude of people. In the judgment of the trial court, "the (defendant's) course of conduct * * * has been such as to indicate the danger of injury to property if any picketing whatever is allowed." We cannot say that a basis for that belief is lacking altogether.

The injunction as written is not limited to the shops that had been the scenes of violence and intimidation, but extends to any others connected with the plaintiff's union. The defendant had threatened to go from one shop to an-

---

[1]*American Steel Foundries* v. *Tri-City Central Trades Council,* reported in Volume 257 United States Reports 184, 207.

other. A saving clause is necessary, however, to avoid misapprehension. The decree, perpetual in its operation, is broad enough to prohibit picketing for all time at any bakery or shop in alliance with the plaintiff, no matter what the grievance or the occasion of the controversy. This is too far-reaching. At some time in the future, a controversy unrelated to the dispute between the plaintiff and the defendant may arise between the defendant and a bakery or shop now protected by the judgment. The evidence is that 370 shops or bakeries are within the terms of the injunction. The restraint is to be interpreted as limited to acts done by the defendant in furtherance of its plan to exterminate the plaintiff union or in the course of the controversy that is the subject of the pending action.

The injunction as to false and misleading statements should be limited to one prohibiting the false announcement of a strike.

With picketing restrained, the plaintiff is in little need of protection by an injunction against words. The remedy when so applied is an exceptional one at best, and is to be reserved for those cases where the exigency is clear. Equity does not intervene to restrain the publication of words on a mere showing of their falsity. It intervenes in those cases where restraint becomes essential to the preservation of a business or of other property interests threatened with impairment by illegal combinations or by other tortious acts, the publication of the words being merely an instrument and incident.

In the case at hand most of the statements imputed to the defendant were well within its rights. This is true, for example, of the circulars and handbills. They amount to nothing more than praise of its own achievements, and criticism of the methods of its rival, with an appeal to the public for sympathy and preference. Warning is given that the International "is the only union that is on the lookout that its members should work under union conditions, which means like human beings and not like mules." Warning is given that "this Amalgamated organization, which calls itself a 'union,' is such a union that it is willing to ruin our conditions which were gained with your support." For those reasons and others the appeal is made to consumers to buy only "with this union label," a phrase followed by a reproduction of the label in use by the defendant. There is argument and entreaty, overcolored and hectic, involving perhaps at times the deduction from meager facts of debatable conclusions. There is no such malevolent distortion as to justify repression. Courts have enough to do in restraining physical disorder without busying themselves with logomachies in which the embattled words are the expression of the opinion of the writer or the speaker. If there is redress for such a wrong, unassociated with wrongful acts, the remedy is not in equity.

Other statements, not in the circulars and handbills, but testified to by witnesses, are closer to the border line. This is true of declarations that the plaintiff is a "scab" and not a regular union, and that any one dealing with its bakeries will not be buying union bread. Even these statements, however, are in essence expressions of opinion, dependent, in the main, upon an appraisal of methods and motives, and gaining much of their significance from context and occasion. Standing by themselves, the statements may be unduly broad. Heard or read in the light of the context or in the setting of the occasion, they may wear another aspect. They are then seen to be opinions merely. The opinion may be erroneous, but it does not follow that the defendant will be required to withdraw it under penalty of contempt. Indeed, there is a near approach to the ludicrous when a member of one union debating an industrial dispute with a member of another, is restrained by the solemn mandate of an injunction from stating his belief that the rival union is a "scab." An injunction might draw a distinction between one context and another, yet the dividing line is one that it would be hard to make manifest by words. Perhaps an attempt to draw it would be necessary if picketing were to continue. With picketing out, the danger, if any, is too slight, the zone of demarcation too nebulous, to turn the attempt into a duty. Equity does not act for every shadowy or unsubstantial wrong.

A genuine controversy exists between two competing groups as to the effectiveness and sincerity of the methods of one of them. By concession the form of a union has been adopted by each of the two bodies. Whether the spirit also is there, the spirit, that is to say, for which unions are created, is a question not susceptible of answer without heed being given to many imponderable elements. The plaintiff does not prevail by showing that the defendant's criticism is wrong, though even this it fails to do. What is wrong must be so clearly wrong that only "disinterested malevolence" or something close akin thereto can have supplied the motive power. If less than this appears, a court of equity will stand aside.

The other prohibitions are an impairment of the defendant's indubitable right to win converts over to its fold by recourse to peaceable persuasion, and to induce them by like methods to renounce allegiance to its rival. Recent decisions of this court have established that fundamental right too emphatically and forcefully to make further vindication needful. All these provisions must be expunged from the decree.

The judgment of the Appellate Division and that of the Special Term should be modified in accordance with this opinion, and as modified affirmed, without costs.

If the parties are unable to agree upon the form of the judgment, the form may be settled upon an application to the court.

POUND, CRANE, LEHMAN, KELLOGG, O'BRIEN, and HUBBS, *JJ.*, concur.

"OUR DUTY IS TO SAVE UNLESS IN SAVING WE PERVERT"

People v. *Mancuso,* 255 N. Y. 463 (1931)

Judge Francis X. Mancuso of the Court of General Sessions[1] and several others were directors of the City Trust Company, a moneyed corporation organized under the State Banking Law. The Company failed and the directors were indicted for participating as directors in the fraudulent insolvency of a moneyed corporation under Section 297 of the Penal Law, which read as follows:

> "Every director of a moneyed corporation who
>
> 1. In case of the fraudulent insolvency of such corporation shall have participated in such fraud; or,
>
> 2. Wilfully does any act as such director which is expressly forbidden by law, or wilfully omits to perform any duty imposed upon him as such director by law, is guilty of a misdemeanor, if no other punishment is prescribed therefor by law.
>
> The insolvency of a moneyed corporation is deemed fraudulent unless its affairs appear upon investigation to have been administered fairly, legally and with the same care and diligence that agents receiving a compensation for their services, are bound, by law, to observe."

Originally this section had at the end thereof a sentence which read "And it shall be incumbent on the directors and stockholders of every such insolvent corporation, to repel, by proof, the presumption of fraud," but this sentence was repealed in 1830.

Judge Mancuso and his co-defendants demurred[2] to the indictments and upon the authority of a decision of the United States Supreme Court in Manley v. Georgia[3] the demurrers were sustained.

The Supreme Court had before it in that case an act of Georgia in which it was declared that "every insolvency of a bank shall be

---

[1]The main business of this court is to sit in trial of felony cases occurring in the County of New York.

[2]The effect of a demurrer by a defendant is to state to the court that for the purpose of testing the sufficiency of the indictment the defendant admits all its allegations, but even when so admitted, the allegations do not set forth a crime.

[3]Reported in Volume 279 United States Reports 1.

deemed fraudulent, and the president and director shall be severally punished by imprisonment * * *; provided, that the defendant * * * may repel the presumption by showing that the affairs of the bank have been fairly and legally administered, etc." Under this act a director was convicted of fraudulent conspiracy. The court held that the presumption of fraud from the mere fact of insolvency was unreasonable and arbitrary and that the defendant could not lawfully be charged to repel it.

In his opinion in the Mancuso case, Chief Judge Cardozo distinguished the New York and Georgia acts. Judges Pound, Crane and Hubbs concurred. Judge Lehman concurred in a separate opinion. Judge Kellogg wrote a dissenting opinion concurred in by Judge O'Brien, stating as his conclusion that a declaration in a statute which forbade or required the doing of an act in terms so vague that even persons of common intelligence necessarily had to guess at its meaning and differ as to its application violated the first essential of due process of law.

CARDOZO, C. J. * * *

The defendants have been indicted for the crime of participating as directors in the fraudulent insolvency of a moneyed corporation in contravention of Penal Law, Sec. 297, subdivision 1.

"The insolvency of a moneyed corporation is deemed fraudulent unless its affairs appear upon investigation to have been administered fairly, legally and with the same care and diligence that agents receiving a compensation for their service are bound, by law, to observe." This provision is more than a presumption, if indeed it is that at all. It is also a definition. It defines the standard of conduct to be attained by directors if they are to avoid the imputation of sharing in a fraudulent insolvency. To the extent that it establishes a presumption in favor of the people, it is arbitrary and void. To the extent that it establishes a definition of a fraudulent insolvency, it is valid, unless the standard of conduct is too vague to give warning to directors of the rule to be obeyed.

The statute, as we read it, is not subject to that reproach. It appeals to common-law standards of diligence and duty, standards to which business men and fiduciaries have accommodated themselves for centuries. It gives warning to directors that they must manage the affairs of a moneyed corporation fairly and legally and with the same care and diligence that is owing from paid agents, and that if they fail to do this, and by reason of such omission insolvency supervenes, they will be guilty of a misdemeanor. "Fairly," we interpret as meaning "in good faith." If that branch of the definition is to be excluded as indefinite, there still is left enough to fix the meaning and the duty. The definition will not be suffered to fail as an entirety. "Legally," we interpret as referring to the statutes of the state, and particularly the statutes regulating the management of banks. Finally, supplementing the test of good faith and illegality, there is another test more definite, one that is capable of standing by itself if both others be rejected, the test of reasonable diligence. Here the duty is prescribed with clearness and precision. The test established by the statute, the diligence that is expected of agents in receipt of compensation for their services, is a legislative recognition of a standard of diligence long known to the common law. The diligent director is the one who exhibits in the performance of his trust "the same degree of care and prudence that men prompted by self-interest generally exercise in their own affairs."[1]

The act is not shorn of certainty of meaning by its reference to a standard of customary diligence. The power of the Legislature to make it a crime for banking officers to be so neglectful of their duties as to involve their banks in ruin is hardly to be doubted. The power existing, one is at a loss to imagine how the prohibited omissions could be more accurately stated, without a catalogue of particulars not susceptible of enumeration in advance of the event. "The law is full of instances where a man's fate depends on his estimating rightly, that is, as the jury subsequently estimates it, some matter of degree."[2] "The precise course of the line may be uncertain, but no one can come near it without knowing that he does so, if he thinks, and if he does so, it is familiar to the criminal law to make him take

---

[1]*Hun* v. *Cary,* reported in Volume 82 New York Reports 65, 71.

[2]*Nash* v. *United States,* reported in Volume 229 New York Reports 373.

the risk."[1] Much will depend on the distinction whether the standard is an old one, long recognized in law and life, or one novel and unfamiliar, not yet approaching certainty, at least in measurable degree, through habitude and example. On one side of the line is the standard of care or judgment exacted by the statute in supplying a working place or tools for servants, or in driving on a highway, or in the avoidance of a monopoly or of undue restraints on competition. In these and like instances "a great body of precedents on the civil side, coupled with familiar practice, make it comparatively easy for common sense to keep to what is safe."[2] On the other side is a statute imposing a penalty on any person who makes "any unjust or unreasonable rate or charge in handling or dealing in or with any necessaries," where neither accepted norms of conduct nor common-law traditions of customary diligence give definiteness and significance to the acts to be avoided. Not even a civil liability can rest upon a prohibition so vague and indeterminate. There is little analogy between this incoherence and the standard of behavior appropriate to the prudent and diligent fiduciary, bestowing upon the affairs of others care similar to that bestowed upon his own, a standard sanctioned and defined by centuries of precept and example.

Manley v. Georgia, supra, is not a ruling to the contrary. The decision in that case was not rendered on demurrer. There had been a judgment of conviction after a trial at which the statutory presumption had been applied in all its rigor. What was said in the opinion must be read in the light of the question to be answered. Not even by way of dictum, however, was there an intimation of a belief that the statute was too vague in its definition of care and diligence. At most, the intimation was that there was too much of uncertainty in the tests of good faith and illegality. No discrimination had been made in the conduct of the trial between one standard and another.

---

[1] *United States* v. *Wurzbach,* reported in Volume 280 United States Reports 396.

[2] *International Harvester Co.* v. *Kentucky,* reported in Volume 234 United States Reports 216.

In the statute now before us, the test of care and diligence would stand though those of good faith and illegality were rejected as indefinite. To what extent a severance of good from bad is permissible with a view to the preservation of a statute is a question of construction as to which the courts of the state, and not the federal courts, must speak with ultimate authority.

We have said that the definition of fraud implicit in the statute may be severed from any presumption whereby fraud must be repelled. Whether there was in truth a purpose to establish such a presumption is at least not free from doubt. Section 297 of the Penal Law is descended from section 604 of the Penal Code, enacted in 1881, which in turn derives from the Revised Statutes. One finds it hard to understand why the Legislature in re-enacting the Revised Statutes left out the old provision creating a presumption in terms too clear for misconstruction, if the purpose still was that the presumption should survive. Also one finds it hard to understand why, if such was the purpose, a provision should have been added that the defendant must be proved to have participated in the fraud. Much may be said in support of the contention that what was re-enacted in the new statute was meant to be a definition and no more. Where two meanings are reasonable, the preference is given to the one that sustains a statute rather than to the one that overturns it. If, however, this principle be disregarded, and the statute interpreted as continuing the old presumption, the result will not be changed. The act will then be read as if its provisions were as follows: "The insolvency of a moneyed corporation is fraudulent unless its affairs have been administered by its directors fairly, legally and with the same care and diligence that agents receiving a compensation for the services are bound, by law, to observe, and the burden of proof shall be on a director, when insolvency is proved, to show that it was not fraudulent, or that he did not participate in the fraud."

Plainly the presumption under a statute so framed is susceptible of severance from the accompanying definition. We think it is equally severable under the statute as enacted. Something more is here than "a mere speculation," whether the Legislature would have been willing to adopt the statute as remodeled. The failure to re-enact the original presumption in all its former length and breadth is in itself a token of the likely choice. It is persuasive evidence that whatever presumption may have been left surviving as the result of bungling phraseology was not thought of by the lawmakers as constituting the essence of the plan. We shall be laying "a doctrinaire emphasis on the possible rather than the probable" if we make a contrary assumption the basis of our ruling. The whole tendency during recent years, at least in this court, has been to apply the principle of severance with increasing liberality. "Severance," we have said,[1] "does not depend upon the separation of the good from the bad by paragraphs or sentences in the text of the enactment. The principle of division is not a principle of form. It is a principle of function." Our duty is to save, unless in saving we pervert.

The argument is made, however, that the definition itself, though it be severable from the presumption, must be severed once again into elements legal and illegal, and that this secondary severance exceeds the limits of our power. The suggested limitation to our thinking is without sufficient basis in reason or authority. For a secondary severance as for a primary one, the test remains the same. "The question is in every case whether the Legislature, if partial invalidity had been foreseen, would have wished the statute to be enforced with the invalid part exscinded, or rejected altogether."[2] The Legislature has said that insolvency shall be classified as fraudulent unless there shall be good faith and obedience to the law and reasonable diligence. The prosecution is not required to prove the absence of all these elements. If that were the requirement, a different conclusion would be necessary. The prosecution prevails (according to the letter of the statute) if it proves the absence of any one of them. This

[1] *People ex rel. Alpha Portland Cement Co.* v. *Knapp*, reported in Volume 230 New York Reports at page 60.

[2] *Ibid.*

being the definition, the only consequence of eliminating the element of good faith or even the element of compliance with the law is not to increase the defendant's burden but rather to reduce it. By the statute as enacted a threefold standard is prescribed. By the statute as divided the Legislature is deemed to say that if one or more of the standards be rejected as indefinite, the proof shall be confined to the one that satisfies the test of certainty. We are to figure the situation as it will exist at the conclusion of the trial. Let us assume that the people shall succeed in proving that the insolvency is the consequence of a failure on the part of the defendants to direct the affairs of the bank with reasonable diligence. Is it conceivable that the Legislature would have wished such a prosecution to fail because the jury must be told that if due diligence has been exercised, guilt may not be found for transgression of a vague command to run the business "fairly"? The question carries its own answer.

There is no occasion to consider whether certainty would be lacking if the Legislature had done something which it did not try to do, had prohibited participation in a "fraudulent insolvency" without definition of the term. Enough for present purposes that nothing of the kind was done.

We think the statute is not invalid. That objection failing, we think the negligent and illegal acts and omissions enumerated in the indictment are sufficiently stated to have been factors leading to insolvency and ruin.

Proof there must be of a causal connection between the wrong and the collapse before negligence will charge with a penal liability.

In brief, the insolvency of a moneyed corporation resulting from the failure to administer its affairs with reasonable care and diligence is a fraudulent insolvency within the definition of the statute, and a director participates in the fraud when he participates in the negligence with ruin as the consequence.

The order of the Appellate Division and that of the trial court should be reversed, and the demurrers overruled.[1]

POUND, CRANE and HUBBS, *JJ.*, concur with CARDOZO, *C.J.* LEHMAN, *J.*, concurs in result in separate opinion. KELLOGG, *J.*, dissents in opinion in which O'BRIEN, *J.*, concurs.

---

[1]After this decision was rendered, Mancuso and the other directors obtained permission to examine the grand jury minutes and upon a subsequent motion the indictment was dismissed because the records submitted failed to prove the insolvency of the bank. A new indictment was immediately voted. Upon the trial Mancuso was acquitted.

"THERE IS NO PRIVILEGE OF SILENCE WHEN RETICENCE IF TOLERATED WOULD THWART THE PUBLIC GOOD"

Matter of Edge Ho Holding Corporation, 256 N. Y. 374 (1931)

When several public-spirited citizens publicly complained that the prices paid by the city in condemnation proceedings were grossly excessive, the authorities in October, 1930 appointed Mr. Leonard M. Wallstein special assistant corporation counsel to conduct an investigation into the system of condemnation of real property for city purposes. The Commissioner of Accounts was also instructed by the Mayor to cooperate with Mr. Wallstein and to preside at any hearings which might be found appropriate.

The charter of the City of New York empowers the Commissioner of Accounts to examine the accounts of the various departments and officers of the City of New York, and for the purpose of ascertaining facts in connection with these examinations, he is given power to compel the attendance of witnesses, to administer oaths and to examine such persons as he may deem necessary. The Commissioner thereupon issued a subpoena directed to the Edge Ho Holding Corporation, its president and its secretary, requiring them to appear for an examination and to bring with them all documents relating to a sale of realty made by the Edge Ho Holding Corporation to another corporation in August, 1925, and by the latter corporation sold to the city through condemnation.

The persons so served immediately applied to the Supreme Court for an order vacating the process. The affidavit submitted by these witnesses in their application was made by their attorney who stated, upon information and belief, that the documents subpoenaed were not desired in good faith for the purpose of inquiry into the methods of any city department and were not pertinent thereto.

The Commissioner of Accounts in his answering affidavit asserted the good faith of the inquiry and maintained that it was entirely relevant and also important. The Supreme Court at Special Term denied the application to vacate the subpoenas but upon appeal to the Appellate Division, this determination was reversed, and the process vacated. An appeal was thereupon taken to the Court of Appeals.

CARDOZO, C. J. * * *

We think an inquiry as to the price paid to former owners for land condemned within a period of time not unreasonably remote is fairly related to an inquiry into the efficiency of the methods by which condemnation proceedings are conducted in the offices of the city government responsible therefor. In such proceedings as in lawsuits generally the courts must rest their determination on the evidence exhibited by counsel. They are helpless, except in rare instances, to speak the word of truth if the facts are not uncovered for them. It results that the efficiency of any system of awards for land condemned depends in no small measure upon the diligence and skill with which the case has been prepared. The inquisitor in the pending investigation has in mind to show that awards have been swollen in excess of the market values, and that this has been done without scrutiny of the cost and without attempt to prove it by witnesses easily available. We cannot say with fairness that such evidence is unrelated to an inquiry into the efficiency of official methods. It is directed to one of the things that an inquisitor, charged with a duty to investigate the existing system of condemnation, would not unnaturally wish to know. He would wish to know whether material information had been withheld or accessible witnesses ignored, whether preparation for trial had been painstaking and thorough or indifferent and lax. If indifference or laxity appeared to be serious or general, the conclusion might be drawn that there was something wrong in the methods of the office where these deficiencies prevailed. The deficiencies might point to the need of administrative reforms, or, if these should seem to be inadequate, to amendments of the statute.

The argument is made that the Commissioner is not at liberty to pursue an inquiry into the efficiency of governmental methods unless those methods have a direct relation to the system of accounts in the office or department subject to his scrutiny. We do not read so narrowly the statutory grant of power. The statute says that he may investigate the accounts and methods of the departments and offices of the city and of the counties embraced within it. This does not mean that both accounts and methods must be involved in every instance. Indeed it is hard to think of a situation in which incompetence or laxity so general as to amount to proof of method will not also have direct relation to the accounts of the department or office subject to the criticism, since the wages of the assistants are wastefully expended if reasonably efficient service is not rendered in return. We are not unmindful of the fact that this particular subpoena is directed to a single contract, and not to contracts generally. The Commissioner cannot reasonably be expected to prove everything at once. Only in its immediacy is his inquiry directed to a particular transaction as distinguished from a course of dealing. In its ultimate significance it seeks to uncover something typical of a practice or a method. We have held that investigation is not limited to a consideration of the methods actually in vogue. It may go beyond these into a consideration of what the methods ought to be. The inquiry now proposed is an attempt to probe into the past in the belief that discovery of its evils may bring correction in the future.

The argument is made that the witnesses are not employees of the city nor even claimants for an award, but merely former owners, and that they are exempt from a duty to make disclosure of their own affairs. We have held that the Commissioner's power to inquire is not limited to witnesses in the service of the city, and that there is no privilege of silence when reticence, if tolerated, would thwart the public good. Argument is made also that the subject matter of the contract described in the subpoena is the same as the subject matter of a proceeding for condemnation now pending in a court, and that inquiry by a court, though directed to a different end, displaces and supersedes inquiry by an administrative officer as to administrative methods. The law is settled to the contrary.

A final argument is built upon an analysis of motives. Nothing in the record gives fair support for the conclusion that the professed object of the inquiry into administrative methods is merely a cover and a sham. This being so, there is no occasion to consider whether the motives of the Commissioner are subject to judicial review when the subject of the inquiry is within his jurisdiction.

The powers devolved by the charter upon the Commissioner of Accounts are of great importance for the efficient administration of the huge machinery of government in the city of New York. They will be rendered to a large extent abortive if his subpoenas are to be quashed in advance of any hearing at the instance of unwilling witnesses upon forecasts of the testimony and nicely balanced arguments as to its probable importance. Very often the bearing of information is not susceptible of intelligent estimate until it is placed in its setting, a tile in the mosaic. Investigation will be paralyzed if arguments as to materiality or relevance, however appropriate at the hearing, are to be transferred upon a doubtful showing to the stage of a preliminary contest as to the obligation of the writ. Prophecy in such circumstances will step into the place that description and analysis may occupy more safely. Only where the futility of the process to uncover anything legitimate is inevitable or obvious must there be a halt upon the threshold.

The order of the Appellate Division should be reversed and that of the Special Term affirmed with costs in the Appellate Division and in this court.

POUND, CRANE, LEHMAN, KELLOGG, O'BRIEN and HUBBS, *JJ.*, concur.

"IMMUNITY MUST BE AS BROAD AS THE PRIVILEGE DESTROYED"

In the Matter of William F. Doyle, 257 N. Y. 244 (1931)

The Senate and Assembly of the State of New York by a joint resolution adopted March 23, 1931, created a legislative committee to investigate the administration and conduct of the various departments of the City of New York after charges had been lodged by citizens and by newspapers that corruption was rife.

One, William F. Doyle, a veterinarian, who had had marked success in a practice before the Board of Standards and Appeals involving changes in the zoning laws, was subpoenaed to attend before the committee. Other witnesses had declared that very large fees had been paid for his services, and the committee desired to be informed whether he had divided these fees with any political leaders or any public officers in furtherance of a concerted plan of bribery and corruption. In the course of his examination he refused to answer certain questions which were put to him on the ground that the answers thereto might tend to incriminate him. Some of the questions which were asked him and which he would not answer were as follows:

> You claim that you do no unlawful thing in dividing or splitting the fees which you obtained for your services before that board, do you not?
>
> I ask you whether you split those fees with anybody whether they were the Board of Standards and Appeals or whether they were not?
>
> Did you take those payments in cash rather than in checks because you were of the opinion that any disposition you made of them would be less easily traced?
>
> Did you give any of the proceeds of those fees to any political leader in the County of New York?
>
> Did you bribe any other public official?

After Dr. Doyle refused to answer these questions he was adjudged in contempt first, by a majority of the legislative committee and then by the Supreme Court.

It will be noted that as regards persons bribed the questions fell into two groups: first, whether the bribe takers were public officials, and second, whether they were not officials, particularly, political leaders.

Counsel for the legislative committee, Samuel Seabury, argued that the refusal to answer was not justified because the witness was entitled to complete immunity under Section 381 of the Penal Law and under Section 584 of the Penal Law. Attorneys for Dr. Doyle contended that the Legislature of the State of New York could not grant immunity merely by joint resolution; that Section 381 was not constitutional, and therefore, did not give any immunity; that Section 584 of the Penal Law was not applicable to testimony given before a legislative committee; and that the entire procedure was contrary to the constitution of the State since the committee sought to compel Dr. Doyle to be a witness against himself.

The Court of Appeals in the following opinion by Chief Judge Cardozo held that Section 381 directed a witness to answer in an investigation provided he testified to completed briberies and, therefore, the witness was not justified in refusing to answer questions concerning bribes offered to *and* accepted by *public officials.* It was further held, however, that Section 584 which dealt with immunity in cases of conspiracy with persons who were not public officials, did not give such immunity unless the testimony was given before a court, magistrate or referee, and since a legislative committee was neither of these three, the witness would not be receiving complete immunity and he was, therefore, not required to answer concerning the giving of any money to a person who was not a public official.

CARDOZO, C. J. * * *

We are to determine whether the refusal was contumacious or privileged.

The Constitution of the State provides that no person "shall be compelled in any criminal case to be a witness against himself."[1]

The privilege may not be violated because in a particular case its restraints are inconvenient or because the supposed malefactor may be a subject of public execration or because the disclosure of his wrongdoing will promote the public weal.

---

[1]New York State Constitution, Article 1, Section 6.

It is a barrier interposed between the individual and the power of the government, a barrier interposed by the sovereign people of the State; and neither legislators nor judges are free to overleap it.

The appellant is, therefore, privileged to refuse to answer questions that may tend to implicate him in a crime, unless by some act of amnesty or indemnity, or some valid resolution equivalent thereto, he has been relieved from the risk of prosecution for any felony or misdemeanor that his testimony may reveal. The immunity is not adequate if it does no more than assure him that the testimony coming from his lips will not be read in evidence against him upon a criminal prosecution. The clues thereby developed may still supply the links whereby a chain of guilt can be forged from the testimony of others. To force disclosure from unwilling lips, the immunity must be so broad that the risk of prosecution is ended altogether.

The respondent insists that immunity co-extensive with the requirements of this rule has been assured to the appellant by statute and resolution: by section 381 of the Penal Law as to the completed crime of bribery; by section 584 of the Penal Law as to the crime of conspiracy; and as to any and all crimes by the joint resolution of the two houses of the Legislature.

Penal Law, section 381, provides as follows: "A person offending against any provision of any section of this chapter relating to bribery and corruption, is a competent witness against another person so offending, and may be compelled to attend and testify upon any trial, hearing, proceeding, or investigation, in the same manner as any other person. But the testimony so given shall not be used in any prosecution or proceeding, civil or criminal, against the person so testifying. A person so testifying to the giving of a bribe *which has been accepted,* shall not thereafter be liable to indictment, prosecution, or punishment for that bribery, and may plead or prove the giving of testimony accordingly, in bar of such an indictment or prosecution."

An argument is made for the appellant that the immunity created by this section is in contravention of restrictions established by the Constitution of the State. The Constitution (Art. XIII, § 3) authorizes the exemption of the briber who testifies to the giving or offering of a bribe on the "prosecution" of a public officer for accepting it. The statute gives a like exemption to one who testifies to a like effect on "any trial, hearing, proceeding, or investigation." There is no denial by counsel for the committee that the immunity thus recognized is broader than the one that would be conferred by the Constitution if the statute were not here, since it extends to a legislative investigation designed, not to prosecute for crime, but to gather information for legislation in the future. The expansion may be conceded, and the validity of the statute will suffer no impairment. The purpose of the Constitution was to establish one immunity permanently in the fundamental law, but not to foreclose the Legislature from establishing additional ones thereafter.

Section 381 of the Penal Law is thus a valid statute, to be accepted at its face value. Whatever immunity it purports to give is the safe and sure possession of any witness who invokes it after being brought within its terms. But the immunity that it purports to give is limited and narrow. The witness is relieved of the risk of prosecution in one situation and one only: he must have testified to the offer or giving of a bribe which has been accepted. If there has been a conspiracy to bribe without evidence of acceptance, the supposed exemption fails. If there has been an offer without acceptance, it fails again. The purpose of this section of the statute, following in that respect the purpose of the Constitution (Art. XIII, § 3), is to reach the bribe-taker as the chief delinquent, and let the briber go if thereby the taker can be held. There is no token of a purpose that a like immunity shall follow when there has been a mere conspiracy to corrupt, or an offer of a bribe which has been rejected by the officer to whom the tender has been made. Immunity from prosecution for conspiracy or for an attempt not followed by acceptance must find some other basis, if immunity there is. The counsel for the committee, if we understand his argument aright, makes no contention to the contrary. Seeking another basis for immunity, he has found one, he believes, in another section of the same statute (Penal Law, § 584), in respect of any prosecution for a criminal conspiracy. He concedes that there is none against a prosecution for an attempt to bribe apart from a conspiracy, but the risk of such a prosecution he believes to be remote and unsubstantial.

We pass then to the question of the immunity offered to the witness against a prosecution for conspiracy.

The risk of such a prosecution is a real one unless a statute has removed it. Let us suppose that there is testimony by the witness that he split his fees with a political leader, or someone other than a public officer. Let us suppose that he did this under an agreement that the sharer of the fees would control by influence or by the payment of money the decisions of the Board of Standards and Appeals. Let us suppose further that there is no evidence establishing the acceptance of the money by any member of the Board or any one connected with it, no tracing of the bribe into the hands of any one invested with the functions of an office. Prosecution of a public officer for the crime of bribery or corruption will be impossible in such conditions. What *will* be possible will be a prosecution of the witness and his confederates for the crime of conspiracy to corrupt, or conceivably for an attempt to bribe. The risk that the prosecution will take the first of these forms is not remote or unsubstantial. We know from recent records of criminal trials that men charged with paying or receiving money as an inducement to official action have not been prosecuted for the completed crime of bribery or corruption, which would have been difficult to prove; they have been tried for conspiracy. The prosecutor may wish to make a like election here. If that shall be his choice, will section 584 of the Penal Law stand in the way of putting the choice into effect?

The section reads as follows: "No person shall be excused from attending and testifying, or producing any books, papers or other documents before any court, magistrate, or referee, upon any investigation, proceeding or trial, for a violation of any of the provisions of this article, upon the ground or for the reason that the testimony or evidence, documentary or otherwise, required of him may tend to convict him of a crime or to subject him to a penalty or for forfeiture; but no person shall be prosecuted or subjected to any penalty or forfeiture for or on account of any transaction, matter or thing concerning which he may so testify or produce evidence, documentary or otherwise, and no testimony so given or produced shall be received against him upon any criminal investigation, proceeding or trial."

The statute is not adequate to relieve the witness of his peril. It is limited to an investigation, proceeding or trial before a "court, magistrate or referee," and to such an investigation conducted for a violation of the "provisions of this article," *i. e.*, the article relating to conspiracy.

* * *

We think the conclusion is inescapable that the witness, if compelled to testify as to any act or agreement not amounting to the completed crime of bribery, will be subject to indictment for conspiracy, and that section 584 of the statute will not render him immune.

The suggestion is not ignored that conspiracy is a misdemeanor, not a felony, and that some of the inquiries have relation to acts or agreements more than two years old, as to which the Statute of Limitations may constitute a bar. A statute of limitations is equivalent to an act of amnesty when the crime erased by lapse of time is one standing by itself, and is not a clue to the commission of other crimes thereafter. Clearly it is no such equivalent when the crime is a continuing conspiracy, unaffected by any limitation till the combination is abandoned.

A witness is not required to show, in order to make his privilege available, that the testimony which he declines to give is certain to subject him to prosecution, or that it will prove the whole crime, unaided by testimony from others. It is enough, to wake the privilege into life, that there is a reasonable possibility of prosecution, and that the testimony, though falling short of proving the crime in its entirety, will prove some part or feature of it, will *tend* to a conviction when combined with proof of other circumstances which others may supply.

The privilege is not removed if there are loopholes in the tender of immunity through which a prosecutor can cut a way to indictment and conviction. The immunity must be as broad as the privilege destroyed.

What has been said as to the risks to which the witness is subjected applies to those questions and those only that are directed to a corrupt agreement between the witness and a confederate not occupying a public office, or to an agreement between the witness and an officer not affecting official action, or not consummated thereafter by payment of the bribe. Inquiry as to a consummated bribery stands upon a different footing. The witness may be compelled to state whether payments for corrupt purposes affecting official action were accepted by an officer, for in making proof of the acceptance he brings himself automatically within the indemnity secured by Penal Law, section 381, to one who testifies to a bribe which has been offered and accepted. There was, therefore, contempt of the committee when the witness after stating that he had never bribed any member of the Board of Standards and Appeals, declined to answer this question: "Did you bribe any other public official?" If the bribe is admitted, all the circumstances attending it may thereupon be explored, the name of the officer, the purpose of the payment, and the particulars of time and place.

The effect of the joint resolution of the two houses of the Legislature is still to be considered.

By the terms of the joint resolution creating the legislative committee, the Legislature has said: "Whenever in its judgment the public interest demands, the committee may determine that a person shall not be excused from attending and testifying before said committee * * * on the ground that the testimony * * * required of him may tend to incriminate him or to subject him to a penalty or forfeiture; but no person so attending and testifying * * * who has duly claimed excuse or privilege, which would be sufficient except for this provision of this resolution and which said excuse or privilege has been expressly denied by the committee, shall be subject to prosecution or to any penalty or forfeiture for or on account of the transaction, matter or thing concerning which he may as aforesaid testify * * * in obedience to its subpoena."

This resolution, if valid, is in effect an act of amnesty. It wipes out as to the witness whose claim of privilege has been denied the criminal statutes of the State with all their pains and penalties, and, like a pardon, makes him a new man. A pardon may be granted by the Governor after conviction of the crime. An act of amnesty may be passed, like any other bill, by the Legislature, acting separately in its two houses, with the approval of the Governor, or in the event of his veto, by a two-thirds vote thereafter. "Every bill which shall have passed the Senate and Assembly shall, before it becomes a law, be presented to the Governor; if he approve, he shall sign it; but if not, he shall return it with his objections to the house in which it shall have originated".[1] This resolution was never presented to the Governor. It never received his approval or his veto. It is not an act of amnesty; it is not an "act" at all.

There are precedents in the books for what is sometimes styled a legislative pardon. If they are scrutinized, they will be found in every instance to have been statutes in the usual form. They were acts of amnesty or indemnity adopted by the Legislature with the Governor's approval. Never has it been held that a Legislature alone may suspend the criminal law as to a person or a class of persons. In the constitution of that country from whose polity our own institutions derive to a large extent their origin and meaning, the rule is said to be that a resolution of the House of Commons is invalid and of no effect if in conflict with existing law. We cannot bring ourselves to believe that the efficacy of resolutions is any greater in New York.

---

[1]New York State Constitution, Article IV, Section 9.

The argument is made that a legislative body has inherent power to conduct an investigation for the discovery of abuses in the operations of government, and that the power to give immunity to witnesses and to suspend to that extent the general laws of the State, must be deemed to be a necessary incident of the power to investigate. But it is not such an incident. It may at times be a useful incident, but it is not a necessary one, necessary that is to say, in the sense of being a power so indispensable to the ordinary exercise of the investigating function that it must be taken as implied. Modern scholarship has traced back for centuries the capacity of a legislative body to equip itself for the task of legislation by discovery of the facts. If the power to suspend the laws in furtherance of the inquiry inheres in the inquirer without the aid of any statute, we can only regard it as extraordinary that so many investigations have been able to proceed without an attempt to use it. The parliamentary practice in Great Britain will be referred to later on. For the moment we confine ourselves to the practice in the United States. There is no record in the books of even a single instance, or none in any event has been brought to our attention, in which a witness, claiming privilege, has been compelled to reveal a crime upon the basis of an inherent power in the inquirer to relieve him from its consequences. Nor may we stop with Senate and Assembly if implication once begins. The power to suspend the laws, if attributed to these, must belong to others too. Local legislative bodies, such as boards of aldermen, have implied or inherent power to conduct investigations as to matters of local government. No one would be likely to assert that they have also the inherent power to give their witnesses immunity against the enforcement of the criminal law. The grand jury is an investigating body, but it has no power to pledge immunity to a witness who declines to answer. So is the Appellate Division when prosecuting an inquiry as to members of the bar or judges of the inferior courts. Even the Governor is at times an inquisitorial officer, as when examining in person or by deputy into the conduct of other officers or the administration of departments. If he is competent when so acting to give immunity to witnesses, the power must have its origin in the provisions of a statute.

The conclusion, we think, is inescapable that a power to suspend the criminal law by the tender of immunity is not an implied or inherent incident of a power to investigate. It may be necessary for fruitful results in a particular instance, but it is not so generally indispensable as to attach itself automatically to the mere power to inquire. Whether the good to be attained by procuring the testimony of criminals is greater or less than the evil to be wrought by exempting them forever from prosecution for their crimes is a question of high policy as to which the law-making department of the government is entitled to be heard. In the State of New York that department is not the Legislature alone, but the Legislature and the Governor, the one as much as the other an essential factor in the process. We beg the question when we argue that the Legislature may give immunity because the Legislature is the sole custodian of the legislative power. It is not the sole custodian of that power. The power is divided between the Legislature and the Governor. The Legislature can initiate, but without the action of the Governor it is powerless to complete. Not only do we beg the question when we infer the validity of the immunity from the possession by the Legislature of the full legislative power; we concede by implication that unless the legislative power has been thus committed without division, the immunity must fail. The argument, reduced to that basis, is seen to be self-destructive. The grant of an immunity *is* in very truth the assumption of a legislative power, and that is why the Legislature acting alone is incompetent to declare it. It is the assumption of a power to annul as to individuals or classes the statutory law of crimes, to stem the course of justice, to absolve the grand jurors of the county from the performance of their duties, and the prosecuting officer from his. All these changes may be wrought through the enactment of a statute. They may be wrought in no other way while the legislative structure of our government continues what it is.

The argument is made that the jurisdiction to grant immunity is an incident of the jurisdiction to punish for contempt. It is no more such an incident for a committee of the Legislature than it is for a court or judge. The punishment for contempt may be imposed for disobedience of a lawful mandate. The power thus to punish may not be used as an excuse for the issue of an unlawful mandate and the remission of the pains and penalties of crimes in consideration of obedience.

We have postponed to this stage the consideration of an argument that is drawn from the practice of the British Parliament.

The practice, instead of tending to give support to the validity of a resolution obliterating guilt, tends directly the other way.

The privilege against self-incrimination in so far as it exists in England does not derive its sanction from a written constitution, and is not binding upon the Houses of Parliament in a parliamentary inquiry. The privilege in New York applies to an investigation by a Legislature as fully as to a trial in court. The House of Lords does not compel an answer unless complete immunity is given. The House of Commons at times has been satisfied with less.

There is, however, an established practice whereby the members of the House of Commons, its officers, and shorthand writers are prohibited from making public in a court of justice or otherwise any testimony brought out upon a parliamentary inquiry without special leave of the house, which according to usage is not given if the testimony will expose to prosecution for a crime.

None the less, in the event that the testimony is published, whether in violation of the mandate of the house or not, the prosecuting authorities are free to prosecute the offender for the crime thereby revealed.

In other words, the prohibition, even in respect of disclosure by members of the house or persons in its service, is limited to the use as a confession of the very testimony given by the witness in the course of the inquiry, and does not relieve him from prosecution for the crime if a case can be proved without the use of the confession, though by following up its clues.

For this there is need of an act of indemnity which requires the concurrence of both houses and the approval of the Crown.

Far from sustaining the resolution, they show that in Great Britain the self-same question has arisen, and that the power of a House of Parliament has been limited to a restraint upon the disclosure of the testimony by members of the house or by others in its service, and has never been extended to the grant of an immunity co-extensive with the risk.

We do well to remember in weighing the significance of the English practice that publication of the proceedings of either of the Houses of Parliament, publication even of the debates, is a breach of privilege and a contempt unless the publication is by permission, tacit or express.

Nowhere in the United States does such a privilege exist.

A final argument is made that the risk of prosecution is unreal and unsubstantial, since it is not to be supposed that a District Attorney would prosecute a witness in the face of a solemn declaration of the will of two houses of the Legislature that the witness should go free. This argument ignores the provisions of article XIII, section 6, of the Constitution that "any district attorney who shall fail faithfully to prosecute a person charged with the violation in his county of any provision of this article which may come to his knowledge, shall be removed from office by the Governor, after due notice and an opportunity of being heard in his defense."

The witness is within his privilege in insisting that the basis for his immunity shall be something more substantial than the grace or favor of the prosecutor who may bring him to the bar of justice. To uphold a finding that his conduct amounted to a contempt it must appear that in refusing to answer he was violating a legal, and not merely a moral obligation. The immunity like the obligation must have its source and sanction in the law. An "equitable right to * * * clemency" a mere "gesture" of benevolence—is not a substitute for protection against indictment and conviction. Clemency may be refused and even if ultimately granted, must be postponed until conviction, the accused being subjected in the meantime to arrest and imprisonment. The King, like the President of the United States is free to pardon before conviction, and may thus intervene promptly for the relief of a witness to whom immunity has been promised by another department of the government, if mercy so inclines him. The Governor may not pardon until the offender has been tried and guilt has been established by the judgment of a court.

We put aside as remote and unsubstantial the supposed peril of exposure to prosecution for the making of false tax returns to State or Federal officers.

When upon the face of a question it would seem that to answer could not tend to implicate in crime, a court will exercise a discretion in determining whether to accept the mere conclusion of the witness that the tendency is present, though in every instance the conclusion is entitled to weight. On the other hand, when the obvious effect of the question is to call for the confession of criminality, when that indeed is its avowed purpose, immunity is not adequate unless the crime has been obliterated.

The upshot of the whole discussion is, therefore, this: The witness has immunity by force of Penal Law, section 381, sufficient to call for a response as to payments to public officers to affect their public acts. The witness has no immunity by force of section 584 or otherwise sufficient to call for a response as to a mere conspiracy to bribe, not followed or accompanied by payment, or as to any corrupt agreement halting at the stage of mere attempt.

The way to compel disclosure as to conspiracies and attempts is not obscure or devious. A grant of immunity similar to the one contained in the resolution may be embodied in a statute. The Legislature, when it convenes, may pass an act of amnesty with the approval of the Governor, an act of amnesty co-extensive with the privilege destroyed. The appellant as well as other witnesses will then be under a duty to declare the whole truth, irrespective of the number or the nature of the crimes exposed to view. Even if we were able to read a different meaning into the statutes now existing, the time in all likelihood would not be distant when there would be need of supplemental legislation to give immunity for other crimes, for crimes not covered by the sections dealing with conspiracy and bribery. A witness exposed to prosecution for larceny or extortion would be wholly without the pale of the immunity provisions in any statutes now existing, however liberally construed.

We are not unmindful of the public interests, of the insistent hope and need that the ways of bribers and corruptionists shall be exposed to an indignant world. Commanding as those interests are, they do not supply us with a license to palter with the truth or to twist what has been written in the statutes into something else that we should like to see. Historic liberties and privileges are not to bend from day to day "because of some accident of immediate overwhelming interest which appeals to the feelings and distorts the judgment",[1] are not to change their form and content in response to the "hydraulic pressure" exerted by great causes. A community whose judges would be willing to give it whatever law might gratify the impulse of the moment would find in the end that it had paid too high a price for relieving itself of the bother of awaiting a session of the Legislature and the enactment of a statute in accordance with established forms.

The order of the Appellate Division and that of the Special Term should be modified by directing that the appellant stand committed until he answers the question whether he has bribed any public officer, such imprisonment not to exceed the period of thirty days, and as so modified affirmed.

LEHMAN, KELLOGG, O'BRIEN and HUBBS, *JJ.* concur; CRANE, *J.*, concurs in separate opinion; POUND, *J.*, dissents in part.

---

[1]Holmes, *J.*, in *Northern Securities Co.* v. *United States*, reported in Volume 193 United States Reports at page 400.

"THERE IS NO INJURY TO THE AGENT WHEN THE PRINCIPAL CONSENTS"

People ex rel. Hastings v. *Hofstadter,* 258 N. Y. 425 (1932)

The joint resolution of the legislature discussed in the matter of Doyle[1] provided that the report of the committee was to be submitted not later than February 1, 1932. The resolution also provided that the committee might act "during the session of the legislature and during the recess or after adjournment thereof, with the same power and authority it would have were the legislature in session." This resolution was passed by the 1931 legislature and the terms of the members of the lower house (assembly) expired on December 31, 1931. The new members of the assembly were those who had been elected at the elections of November, 1931.

On January 4, 1932, a subpoena under the hand of the Vice Chairman of the committee was served upon John A. Hastings, a member of the Senate, requiring him to attend as a witness on that day and give certain testimony as to matters which were within the scope of the inquiry. Senator Hastings declined to appear maintaining that since he was a member of the Senate, the service of the subpoena could not properly be made upon him while the legislature was in session. He further argued that the jurisdiction of the committee had expired on December 31, 1931. He moved to vacate the subpoena, but his efforts were unsuccessful both in the Supreme Court and in the Appellate Division and he was condemned to imprisonment for thirty days. Senator Hastings appealed from the order of the Appellate Division, adjudging him in contempt, and the following opinion was rendered in the Court of Appeals by Chief Judge Cardozo and unanimously concurred in.

CARDOZO, C. J. * * *

"A member of the legislature shall be privileged from arrest in a civil action or proceeding other than for a forfeiture or breach of trust in public office or employment, while attending upon its session, and for fourteen days before and after each session, or while absent, for not more than fourteen days during the session with the leave

[1]See *ante* page 296.

of the house of which he is a member."[1] The appellant insists that the service of a subpœna requiring his attendance before a committee of the Legislature is a breach of the privilege thus secured to him by statute. Manifestly the letter of the privilege does not offer him exemption. A subpœna is not an arrest, though there are circumstances in which disobedience to its command may give rise to an arrest. If that infirmity in the claim of privilege were to be disregarded, others would remain. The execution by the sheriff of a warrant to apprehend a defaulting witness and bring him before the Legislature or one of its committees is not an arrest "in a civil action or proceeding." It is not in aid of a proceeding in a court of justice. It is in aid of a legislative function, the ascertainment of facts whereon to build the statutes of the future. The judge issuing the warrant is merely the implement of the Legislature, appointed by statute to act in its behalf. The sheriff executing the warrant is sheltered by a like consent. There is no privilege from arrest that can be asserted against the Legislature itself.

The same considerations answer the appellant's argument that the range of the privilege must be measured by the standards of parliamentary law and practice, and that so viewed the service of a subpœna is an arrest within the spirit of the statute, even if not within the letter. We do not need to determine whether this would be so if the service were in aid of a proceeding pending in a court. There is respectable authority for each of the opposing views. Choice may prudently be postponed until choice becomes essential. The decisive feature in this case is the origin of the mandate, the character of the governmental agency whence comes the summons to appear. The privilege dissolves when the member in asserting it is guilty of disloyalty to the duties of his membership. There is no injury to the agent when the principal consents.

The subpœna is assailed upon the ground that the life of the committee ended upon the final adjournment of the Legislature on April 10, 1931, or, at the latest, on Decem-

---

[1]Legislative Law, Section 2.

ber 31, 1931, with the end of the term of office for which one of the two houses had been chosen.

We have little difficulty in overruling this contention in so far as it has relation to the life of the committee during the months of adjournment and until the end of the year. The great weight of judicial authority sustains the power of the Legislature to invest its committees with power to function, though the session is over. A distinction has been drawn between a resolution by a single house and the joint action of the two houses, but the distinction is unimportant here where the resolution was concurrent. To the weight of judicial authority is to be added that of a practical interpretation ancient and unbroken. Many instances, brought together by the industry of counsel for the committee, are stated in the brief. A closer question arises when we ask ourselves whether a mere resolution may invest a committee with power when the year is at an end for which the Assembly was elected. Undoubtedly the members of the committee will be permitted to report, for to say that they may do this is to say little more than that the Legislature is at liberty to hear them if it will. This does not mean of necessity that a committee appointed in one year may exercise in a later year all the powers that belonged to it at the time of its creation, the power to disburse the appropriated moneys, the power to subpœna, and the power to punish for contempt. For many purposes, a newly elected house is deemed a newly created body, its life not continuous with that of the house that went before it. This is probably the reason why the rules of each house are adopted anew when a new house is elected, though the long-continued practice is to renew them without change. Accordingly, treatises of weight give support to the view that the authority of a legislative body may not be continued by resolution beyond the expiration of the term for which the body was elected, and that, if life is to be prolonged thereafter, the result must be attained by the adoption of a statute.

We leave the question open, for the record now before us does not require us to answer it. Statutory confirmation after a resolution has been adopted is as effective as statutory authority in advance of its adoption. Such confirmation is clearly visible when the course of legislation with reference to this committee is followed through the year. By chapter 637 of the Laws of 1931, which became a law April 22, 1931, there was appropriated in aid of this inquiry the sum of $250,000 to be added to a like sum included in the budget. The language of the act is that "the sum hereby appropriated shall be available for the use of the joint legislative committee appointed pursuant to joint resolution of the legislature, to investigate the affairs of the city of New York, and shall be payable only on audit of the comptroller, after approval by the speaker of the assembly and the president pro tempore of the senate and also by the chairman of the committee." The Legislature that passed this act must have known that the committee was to continue till February of the next year when its report would be presented. The conclusion is almost unthinkable that the appropriation was not to be available for the printing of the report and for other necessary disbursements during the weeks immediately preceding the date of presentation. If the committee could exercise its functions by drafts on the public purse, it could exercise them also by continuing to inquire. Even more significant are the provisions of a later act[1] adopted on August 28, 1931, the work of a special session called by the Governor for the declared purpose of supplying this committee with powers denied to it before. The statute begins with a declaration that "when used in this chapter 'committee' shall be deemed to refer to and mean the joint legislative committee of the senate and the assembly, appointed pursuant to the joint resolution adopted by the senate and the assembly on March 23, 1931, to investigate, inquire into and examine the administration and conduct of the various departments of the government of the city of New York, and of the counties, the state and local courts, and other agencies geographically included within said city." There is then a grant of authority to give

[1]Laws of 1931, Chapter 773.

immunity to witnesses who may be compelled to give testimony that would otherwise tend to expose them to punishment for crime. Here is an unmistakable recognition of the organization of the committee as established by the concurrent resolution and an unmistakable confirmation of its continuing validity. Mere incidents and details, not essential to the life of the investigating body, capacities, and functions capable of being divested without destroying its existence, will not be held to have been confirmed by the appropriation of a sum of money, nor even, it may be, by the later grant of added powers. On the other hand, those terms of the resolution that define the essential organization of the investigating body, its birth and life and death, must be deemed to have been ratified by acts of recognition so explicit and persuasive.

Holding, as we do, that the intention of the lawmakers was to confirm the existence of the committee as the concurring resolution had attempted to create it, there is left the question whether any rule of law exists whereby effect must be refused to the intention so declared. No such obstacle is disclosed to us by our examination of the precedents, nor does any become apparent from the principals that fix the limits of legislative power. No one would doubt the validity of a statute to the effect that, whenever a legislative committee has been appointed in one year, its members, if re-elected, shall continue to constitute the committee during the next year, unless and until their membership is otherwise revoked. What the Legislature may say in a statute applicable to legislative committees generally, it may say with the same validity in defining the life and the functions of a particular committee. Far from departing thereby from the principles and precedents of parliamentary procedure, it is following the very method to which consecrating usage has affixed the stamp of regularity.

* * *

The proper procedure is therefore this: A warrant shall issue to the sheriff of any county wherein the appellant may be found commanding the officer to apprehend the defaulting witness and bring him before the committee, or the subcommittee thereof before whom his attendance was required. If the witness when brought before such committee or subcommittee refuses to be examined, or to answer a legal and pertinent question, or to produce a book or paper, the court or a judge thereof, upon proof by affidavit of the facts, may by warrant commit the offender to jail, there to remain until he submits to do the act which he was so required to do or is discharged. The sentence of imprisonment at this stage of the inquiry must be held to be premature and thus illegally imposed. Whether imprisonment will become necessary hereafter, the sequel will decide.

The order denying the motion to vacate the subpoena should be affirmed.

The order adjudging the appellant in contempt and prescribing the remedies whereby the subpoena may be enforced should be modified in accordance with this opinion, and as modified affirmed.

POUND, CRANE, LEHMAN, KELLOGG, O'BRIEN, and HUBBS, *JJ.*, concur.

Ordered accordingly.

"THE FOURTEENTH AMENDMENT LAYS A DUTY UPON THE COURT TO LEVEL, BY ITS JUDGMENT, THE BARRIERS OF COLOR"

Nixon v. *Condon,* 286 United States Reports, 73 (1932)

L. A. Nixon, a negro living in Texas, brought this action to recover damages against the judges of election in Texas for their refusal to permit him to vote at a primary election. His claim was that he was refused this right by reason of his race or color.

This was not the first time that Nixon had found it necessary to apply to the Federal Courts for aid in his right to vote at a primary election. In 1924 he had been denied the right to vote as a member of the Democratic party. That denial was based upon the Texas statute which declared that a negro was not eligible to participate in a Democratic party primary election. At the suit of Nixon the statute was adjudged void by the Supreme Court.[1]

Promptly after the announcement of that decision the Legislature of Texas repealed the statute but it substituted another article by which it was provided that every political party in the State through its State Executive Committee shall have the power to prescribe the qualifications of its own members. The State Executive Committee of the Democratic party thereupon adopted a resolution limiting the right to vote to white Democrats. Nixon, who was otherwise qualified to vote, presented himself at the polls in July, 1928, in order to vote at the primaries, but the judges of election declined to furnish a ballot to him. This refusal was followed by an action for damages. The lower Courts decided against Nixon upon the ground that no State officer had discriminated against the petitioner. An appeal was taken to the Supreme Court of the United States and the case decided by a vote of 5 to 4, Mr. Justice Cardozo delivering the opinion of the Court.

MR. JUSTICE CARDOZO * * *

Barred from voting at a primary the petitioner has been, and this for the sole reason that his color is not white. The result for him is no different from what it was when his cause was here before. The argument for the respondents is, however, that identity of result has been attained through essential diversity of method. We are

[1]*Nixon* v. *Herndon,* reported in Volume 273 United States Reports 536.

reminded that the Fourteenth Amendment is a restraint upon the states and not upon private persons unconnected with a state. This line of demarcation drawn, we are told that a political party is merely a voluntary association; that it has inherent power like voluntary associations generally to determine its own membership; that the new article of the statute, adopted in place of the mandatory article of exclusion condemned by this court, has no other effect than to restore to the members of the party the power that would have been theirs if the lawmakers had been silent; and that qualifications thus established are as far aloof from the impact of constitutional restraint as those for membership in a golf club or for admission to a Masonic lodge.

Whether a political party in Texas has inherent power today without restraint by any law to determine its own membership, we are not required at this time either to affirm or to deny. The argument for the petitioner is that, quite apart from the article in controversy, there are other provisions of the Election Law whereby the privilege of unfettered choice has been withdrawn or abridged; that nomination at a primary is in many circumstances required by the statute if nomination is to be made at all; that parties and their representatives have become the custodians of official power; and that, if heed is to be given to the realities of political life, they are now agencies of the state, the instruments by which government becomes a living thing. In that view, so runs the argument, a party is still free to define for itself the political tenets of its member, but to those who profess its tenets there may be no denial of its privileges.

A narrower base will serve for our judgment in the cause at hand. Whether the effect of Texas legislation has been to work so complete a transformation of the concept of a political party as a voluntary association, we do not now decide. Nothing in this opinion is to be taken as carrying with it an intimation that the court is ready or unready to follow the petitioner so far. As to that, decision must be postponed until decision becomes necessary. Whatever our conclusion might be if the statute had remitted to the party the untrammeled power to prescribe the qualifications of its members, nothing of the kind was done. Instead, the statute lodged the power in a committee, which excluded the petitioner and others of his race, not by virtue of any authority originating or supposed to originate in the mandate of the law.

We recall at this point the wording of the statute invoked by the respondents. "Every political party in this State through its State Executive Committee shall have the power to prescribe the qualifications of its own members and shall in its own way determine who shall be qualified to vote or otherwise participate in such political party." Whatever inherent power a state political party has to determine the content of its membership resides in the State convention.

There platforms of principles are announced and the tests of party allegiance made known to the world. What is true in that regard of parties generally is true more particularly in Texas, where the statute is explicit in committing to the state convention the formulation of the party faith. The state executive committee, if it is the sovereign organ of the party, is not such by virtue of any powers inherent in its being. It is, as its name imports, a committee and nothing more, a committee to be chosen by the convention and to consist of a chairman and thirty-one members, one from each senatorial district of the state. To this committee the statute here in controversy has attempted to confide authority to determine of its own motion the requisites of party membership and in so doing to speak for the party as a whole. Never has the state convention made declaration of a will to bar negroes of the state from admission to the party ranks. Counsel for the respondents so conceded upon the hearing in this court. Whatever power of exclusion has been exercised by the members of the committee has come to them, therefore, not as the delegates of the state. Indeed, adherence to the statute leads to the conclusion that a resolution once adopted by the committee must continue to be binding upon the judges of election though the party in convention may have sought to override it, unless the committee, yielding to the moral force of numbers, shall revoke its earlier action and obey the party will. Power so intrenched is statutory, not inherent. If the state had not conferred it, there would be hardly color of right to give a basis for its exercise.

Our conclusion in that regard is not affected by what was ruled by the Supreme Court of Texas in Love v. Wilcox,[1] or by the Court of Civil Appeals in White v. Lubbock.[2]

The ruling in the first case was directed to the validity of the provision whereby neither the party nor the committee is to be permitted to make former political affiliations in the test of party regularity. There were general observations in the opinion as to the functions of parties and committees. They do not constitute the decision. The decision was merely this, that "the committee, whether viewed as an agency of the state or as a mere agency of the party, is not authorized to take any action which is forbidden by an express and valid statute". The ruling in the second case speaks of the exercise of the inherent powers of the party by the act of its proper officers. There is nothing to show, however, that the mind of the court was directed to the point that the members of a committee would not have been the proper officers to exercise the inherent powers of the party if the statute had not attempted to clothe them with that quality. The management of the affairs of a group already associated together as members of a party is obviously a very different function from that of determining who the members of the group shall be. If another view were to be accepted, a committee might rule out of the party a faction distasteful to itself, and exclude the very men who had helped to bring it into existence. In any event, the Supreme Court of Texas has not yet spoken on the subject with clearness or finality, and nothing in its pronouncements brings us to the belief that, in the absence of a statute or other express grant, it would recognize a mere committee as in-

[1]Reported in Volume 119 Texas Reports 256.
[2]Reported in Volume 30 Southwestern Reports, 2d series, 722.

vested with all the powers of the party assembled in convention. Indeed, its latest decision dealing with any aspect of the statute here in controversy, a decision handed down on April 21, 1932 (Love v. Buckner), describes the statute as constituting "a grant of power" to the state executive committee to determine who shall participate in the primary elections. What was questioned in that case was the validity of a pledge exacted from the voters that it was their bona fide purpose to support the party nominees. There is no suggestion in the opinion that the inherent power of the committee was broad enough (apart from legislation) to permit it to prescribe the extent of party membership, to say to a group of voters, ready as was the petitioner to take the statutory pledge, that one class should be eligible and another not. On the contrary, the whole opinion is instinct with the concession that pretensions so extraordinary must find their warrant in a statute. The most that can be said for the respondents is that the inherent powers of the committee are still unsettled in the local courts. Nothing in the state of the decisions requires us to hold that they have been settled in a manner that would be subversive of the fundamental postulates of party organization. The suggestion is offered that in default of inherent power or of statutory grant the committee may have been armed with the requisite authority by vote of the convention. Neither at our bar nor on the trial was the case presented on that theory. At every stage of the case the assumption has been made that authority, if there was any, was either the product of the statute or was inherent in the committee under the law of its creation.

* * * We do not impugn the competence of the Legislature to designate the agencies whereby the party faith shall be declared and the party discipline enforced. The pith of the matter is simply this, that, when those agencies are invested with an authority independent of the will of the association in whose name they undertake to speak, they become to that extent the organs of the state itself, the repositories of official power. They are then the gov-

ernmental instruments whereby parties are organized and regulated to the end that government itself may be established or continued. What they do in that relation, they must do in submission to the mandates of equality and liberty that bind officials everywhere. They are not acting in matters of merely private concern like the directors or agents of business corporations. They are acting in matters of high public interest, matters intimately connected with the capacity of government to exercise its functions unbrokenly and smoothly. Whether in given circumstances parties or their committees are agencies of government within the Fourteenth or the Fifteenth Amendment is a question which this court will determine for itself. It is not concluded upon such an inquiry by decisions rendered elsewhere. The test is not whether the members of the executive committee are the representatives of the state in the strict sense in which an agent is the representative of his principal. The test is whether they are to be classified as representatives of the state to such an extent and in such a sense that the great restraints of the Constitution set limits to their action.

With the problem thus laid bare and its essentials exposed to view, the case is seen to be ruled by Nixon v. Herndon, supra. Delegates of the state's power have discharged their official functions in such a way as to discriminate invidiously between white citizens and black. The Fourteenth Amendment, adopted as it was with special solicitude for the equal protection of members of the Negro race, lays a duty upon the court to level by its judgment these barriers of color.

The judgment below is reversed, and the cause remanded for further proceedings in conformity with this opinion.[1]

---

[1]A dissenting opinion was written by Mr. Justice McReynolds, and concurred in by Mr. Justice Van Devanter, Mr. Justice Sutherland and Mr. Justice Butler. The view of the dissent was that no Texas statute defined who shall be regarded as a party member in a political party. The party executive committeemen were not state officials and performed no governmental function. "White men may organize; blacks may do likewise. A woman's party may exclude males. This much is essential to free government."

"A DOUBLE REMEDY DURING LIFE IS NOT WITHOUT A RATIONAL OFFICE IF THE EFFECT OF THE DUPLICATION IS TO CARRY THE REMEDY FORWARD FOR OTHERS AFTER DEATH"

Cortes v. *Baltimore Insular Line,* 287 United States Reports 367 (1932)

Santiago was a seaman on a vessel of the Baltimore Insular Line, which was on its way from Florida to New York. During the voyage he fell ill of pneumonia and died in a hospital after reaching the home port. His administrator sued to recover damages for his death, which was charged to have been caused by the failure of the master of the ship to give him proper care. The Circuit Court of Appeals held that there could be no recovery because the seaman's right of action for negligent care was ended by his death, and did not accrue to the administrator.

Under the general maritime law a seaman is without a remedy for injury to his person suffered in the line of service with only two exceptions. These apply, first, if his injury has been suffered as a consequence of a defect in the ship or its equipment, and secondly, if the injury has been suffered through a breach of duty to provide him with maintenance and cure. But in all cases the remedy for the injury ends with death. The one exception to this latter rule exists under the Jones act, which gives a cause of action to the personal representative of a seaman who has suffered *personal injury* through the negligence of his employer and dies as a result of such an injury. The question raised on the appeal to the Supreme Court of the United States was whether death resulting from the failure to furnish care or cure, is death from *personal injury* within meaning of the Jones Act. The unanimous opinion of the Court was delivered by Mr. Justice Cardozo.

MR. JUSTICE CARDOZO * * *

The argument is pressed upon us that the care owing to a seaman disabled while in service is an implied term of his contract, and that the statute cannot have had in view the breach of a duty contractual in origin for which he had already a sufficient remedy under existing rules of law.

We think the origin of the duty is consistent with a remedy in tort, since the wrong, if a violation of a contract, is also something more. The duty, as already pointed out, is one annexed by law to a relation, and annexed as an inseparable incident without heed to any expression of the will of the contracting parties. For breach of a duty thus imposed, the remedy upon the contract does not exclude an alternative remedy built upon the tort. The passenger in a public conveyance who has been injured by the negligence of the carrier, may sue for breach of contract if he will, but also at his election in trespass on the case. The employee of an interstate carrier, injured through the omission to furnish him with safe and suitable appliances, may have a remedy under the Federal Employers' Liability Act § 1 or at times under the Safety Appliance Act, § 1 to 6, though the omission would not be actionable in the absence of a contract creating the employment. So, in the case at hand, the proper subject of inquiry is not the quality of the relation that gives birth to the duty, but the quality of the duty that is born of the relation. If the wrong is of such a nature as to bring it by fair intendment within the category of a "personal injury" that has been caused by the "negligence" of the master, it is not put beyond the statute because it may appropriately be placed in another category also.

We are thus brought to the inquiry whether "negligence" and "personal injury" are terms fittingly applied to the acts charged to the respondent. The case is helped by illustrations. Let us suppose the case of a seaman who is starved during the voyage in disregard of the duty of maintenance, with the result that his health is permanently impaired. There is little doubt that in the common speech of men he would be said to have suffered a personal injury, just as much as a child in an orphan's home who had been wronged in the same way. Let us suppose the case of a seaman slightly wounded through his own fault, but suffering grievous hurt thereafter as a consequence of septic poisoning brought about by lack of treatment. The common speech of men would give a like description to the wrong that he had suffered. The failure to provide maintenance or cure may be a personal injury or something else according to the consequences. If the seaman has been able to procure his maintenance and cure out of his own or his friends' money, his remedy is for the outlay, but personal injury there is none. If the default of the vessel and its officers has impaired his bodily or mental health, the damage to mind or body is none the less a personal injury because he may be free at his election to plead it in a different count. Nor is liability escaped by appeal to the distinction between acts of omission on the one hand and those of commission on the other. A division is sometimes drawn between the termination of a relation at a time when it is still executory or future, and its termination when performance has gone forward to such a point that abandonment of duty becomes an active agency of harm. The respondent is not helped though its treatment of the seaman be subjected to that test. Here performance was begun when the vessel started on her voyage with Santiago aboard and with care and cure cut off from him unless furnished by officers or crew. From that time forth withdrawal was impossible and abandonment a tort. Given a relation involving in its existence a duty of care irrespective of a contract, a tort may result as well from acts of omission as of commission in the fulfilment of the duty thus recognized by law.

We are told, however, that the personal injury from negligence covered by the statute must be given a narrow content, excluding starvation and malpractice, because for starvation and malpractice the seaman without an enabling act had a sufficient remedy before. The seaman may indeed have had such a remedy, but his personal representative had none if the wrong resulted in his death. While the seaman was still alive, his cause of action for personal injury created by the statute may have overlapped his cause of action for breach of the maritime duty of maintenance and cure, just as it may have overlapped his cause of action for injury caused through an unseaworthy ship. In such circumstances it was his privilege, in so far as the causes of action covered the same ground, to sue indifferently on any one of them. The overlapping is no reason for denying to the words of the statute the breadth of meaning and operation that would normally belong to them, at all events when a consequence of the denial is to withhold any remedy whatever from dependent next of kin. A double remedy during life is not without a rational office if the effect of the duplication is to carry the remedy forward for others after death. The argument for the respondent imputes to the lawmakers a subtlety of discrimination which they would probably disclaim. There was to be a remedy for the personal representative if the seaman was killed by the negligent omission to place a cover over a hatchway or to keep the rigging safe and sound. There was to be none, we are told, if he was killed for lack of food or medicine, though the one duty equally with the other was attached by law to the relation. This court has held that the act is to be liberally construed in aid of its beneficent purpose to give protection to the seaman and to those dependent on his earnings.[1] An assault by one member of the crew upon another with a view to hurrying up the work has been brought within the category of "negligence" and hence in a suit against the owner becomes an actionable wrong. Approaching the decision of this case in a like spirit of liberality, we put aside many of the refinements of construction that a different spirit might approve. The failure to furnish cure is a personal injury actionable at the suit of the seaman during life, and at the suit of his personal representative now that he is dead.

The judgment is reversed, and the cause remanded to the Court of Appeals for further proceedings in conformity with this opinion.

---

[1]*Jamussi* v. *Encarnacion*, reported in Volume 281 United States Reports 635.

"THERE IS A PERIL OF CORRUPTION IN THESE DAYS WHICH IS SURELY NO LESS THAN THE PERIL OF COERCION"

Clark v. *United States,* 289 United States Reports 1 (1933)

William B. Foshay, a leading citizen of Minnesota, was indicted in the Federal Court together with others, charged with the use of the mails in the furtherance of a scheme to defraud. One of the panel of the jurors summoned to attend was Mrs. Genevieve A. Clark. At first she tried to get excused from service, but when she learned that Foshay was to go on trial she stated to several women on the panel that for a special reason she wished to serve on the jury.

Upon being called to the jury box Mrs. Clark was questioned by the judge presiding. She was asked about her business and she replied that she had been a stenographer before her marriage, working for a banking concern, and for a real estate, insurance and automobile company, in succession. When asked whether she felt that her mind was free from bias she answered in the affirmative.

As a matter of fact she had formerly been employed for a few weeks by Foshay's company, though she did not know any of the defendants personally. She had also been employed in a bank of which her husband was president, and in which Foshay himself was a depositor and borrower. Her husband and Foshay were on very friendly terms, but there was no evidence anywhere that she herself had any personal acquaintance with Foshay or his associates.

During the deliberations of the jury after the case was finally submitted, she stubbornly refused to argue about the evidence. She insisted that Foshay was innocent. For a full week she held out and the final vote of the jury was 11 to 1 for conviction, the single vote for acquittal being cast by Mrs. Clark.

Thereupon the government hailed her before the court to answer a charge of criminal contempt, upon the ground that she willfully and corruptly, hindered and obstructed justice by her false statements and concealments in the jury box before the trial. The District Court and the Circuit Court of Appeals concluded that she was guilty and she was imprisoned and fined. She took an appeal to the Supreme Court of the United States.

MR. JUSTICE CARDOZO * * *

Concealment or misstatement by a juror upon a voir dire examination is punishable as a contempt if its tendency and design are to obstruct the processes of justice.

There was a concealment by the petitioner, and that willful and deliberate. She had been asked to state the kinds of work that she had been doing in other years. She counted off a few, and checked herself at the very point where the count, if completed, would be likely to bar her from the box. There is no room for the excuse of oversight or negligence. She had been warned that disclosure would lead to challenge and rejection. With her mind full of the warning she told the part truth that was useless, and held back the other part that had significance and value. Whether this was perjury or false swearing, there is no occasion to inquire. It was a deliberate endeavor to thwart the process of inquiry, and to turn a trial into a futile form.

Added to concealment there was positive misstatement. The petitioner stated to the court that her mind was free from bias. The evidence is persuasive that it was hostile to the government. Bias is to be gathered from the disingenuous concealment which kept her in the box. She was intruding into a relation for which she believed herself ineligible, and intruding with a motive. The only plausible explanation is a preconceived endeavor to uphold the cause of the defendants and save them from their doom. Bias, thus revealed at the beginning, is confirmed by everything that followed. While the trial was still in progress, she argued with her fellow jurors that Foshay was a hapless victim of circumstances too strong for him, and went outside the evidence, quoting statements in a newspaper to win them to her view. After the trial was over and deliberations had begun, she waived aside all argument and closed her ears to the debate. She had closed her mind to it before.

"An obstruction to the performance of judicial duty resulting from an act done in the presence of the court is * * * the characteristic upon which the power to punish for contempt must rest."[1] The petitioner is not condemned for concealment, though concealment has been proved. She is not condemned for false swearing, though false swearing has been proved. She is condemned for that she made use of false swearing and concealment as the means whereby to accomplish her acceptance as a juror, and under cover of that relation to obstruct the course of justice. There is a distinction not to be ignored between deceit by a witness and deceit by a talesman. A talesman when accepted as a juror becomes a part or member of the court. The judge who examines on the voir dire is engaged in the process of organizing the court. If the answers to the questions are willfully evasive or knowingly untrue, the talesman, when accepted, is a juror in name only. His relation to the court and to the parties is tainted in its origin; it is a mere pretense and sham. What was sought to be attained was the choice of an impartial arbiter. What happened was the intrusion of a partisan defender. If a kinsman of one of the litigants had gone into the jury room disguised as the complaisant juror, the effect would have been no different. The doom of mere sterility was on the trial from the beginning.

The books propound the question whether perjury is contempt, and answer it with nice distinctions. Perjury by a witness has been thought to be not enough where the obstruction to judicial power is only that inherent in the wrong of testifying falsely.

For offenses of that order the remedy by indictment is appropriate and adequate. On the other hand, obstruction to judicial power will not lose the quality of contempt though one of its aggravations be the commission of perjury. We must give heed to all the circumstances, and of these not the least important is the relation to the court of the one charged as a contemnor. Deceit by an attorney may be punished as a contempt if the deceit is an abuse of the functions of his office, and that apart from its punishable quality if it had been the act of some one else. A talesman, sworn as a juror, becomes, like an attorney, an

---

[1]White, *C.J.*, in *Ex parte Hudgings,* reported in 249 United States Supreme Court 378.

officer of the court, and must submit to like restraints. The petitioner blurs the picture when she splits her misconduct into parts, as if each were a separate wrong to be separately punished. What is punished is misconceived unless conceived of as a unit; the abuse of an official relation by concealment and deceit. Some of her acts or none of them may be punishable as crimes. The result is all one as to her responsibility here and now. She has trifled with the court of which she was a part, and made its processes a mockery. This is contempt, whatever it may be besides.

The admission of testimony as to the conduct of the petitioner during the deliberations of the jury was not a denial or impairment of any lawful privilege.

The books suggest a doctrine that the arguments and votes of jurors, the *media concludendi,* are secrets, protected from disclosures unless the privilege is waived. What is said upon the subject in the adjudicated cases is dictum rather than decision. Even so, the dicta are significant because they bear with them the implications of an immemorial tradition. For the origin of the privilege we are referred to ancient usage, and for its defense to public policy. Freedom of debate might be stifled and independence of thought checked if jurors were made to feel that their arguments and ballots were to be freely published to the world. The force of these considerations is not to be gainsaid. But the recognition of a privilege does not mean that it is without conditions or exceptions. The social policy that will prevail in many situations may run foul in others of a different social policy, competing for supremacy. It is then the function of a court to mediate between them, assigning, so far as possible, a proper value to each, and summoning to its aid all the distinctions and analogies that are the tools of the judicial process. The function is the mere essential where a privilege has its origin in inveterate but vague tradition, and where no attempt has been made either in treatise or in decisions to chart its limits with precision.

Assuming that there is a privilege which protects from impertinent exposure the arguments and ballots of a juror while considering his verdict, we think the privilege does not apply where the relation giving birth to it has been fraudulently begun or fraudulently continued. Other exceptions may have to be made in other situations not brought before us now. It is sufficient to mark the one that is decisive of the case at hand. The privilege takes as its postulate a genuine relation, honestly created and honestly maintained. If that condition is not satisfied, if the relation is merely a sham and a pretense, the juror may not invoke a relation dishonestly assumed as a cover and cloak for the concealment of the truth. In saying this we do not mean that a mere charge of wrongdoing will avail without more to put the privilege to flight. There must be a showing of a prima facie case sufficient to satisfy the judge that the light should be let in. Upon that showing being made, the debates and ballots in the jury room are admissible as corroborative evidence, supplementing and confirming the case that would exist without them. Let us assume for illustration a prosecution for bribery. Let us assume that there is evidence, direct or circumstantial, that money has been paid to a juror in consideration of his vote. The argument for the petitioner, if accepted, would bring us to a holding that the case for the people must go to the triers of the facts without proof that the vote has been responsive to the bribe. This is paying too high a price for the assurance to a juror of serenity of mind.

We turn to the precedents in the search for an analogy, and the search is not in vain. There is a privilege protecting communications between attorney and client. The privilege takes flight if the relation is abused. A client who consults an attorney for advice that will serve him the commission of a fraud will have no help from the law. He must let the truth be told. There are early cases apparently to the effect that a mere charge of illegality, not supported by any evidence, will set the confidences free. But this conception of the privilege is without support in later rulings. "It is obvious that it would be absurd to say that the privilege could be got rid of merely by making a charge of fraud." To drive the privilege away, there must be "something to give colour to the charge"; there must be "prima facie evidence that it has some foundation in fact."[1] When that evidence is supplied, the seal of secrecy is broken. Nor does the loss of the privilege depend upon the showing of a conspiracy, upon proof that client and attorney are involved in equal guilt. The attorney may be innocent, and still the guilty client must let the truth come out.

With the aid of this analogy, we recur to the social policies competing for supremacy. A privilege surviving until the relation is abused and vanishing when abuse is shown to the satisfaction of the judge has been found to be a workable technique for the protection of the confidences of client and attorney. Is there sufficient reason to believe that it will be found to be inadequate for the protection of a juror? No doubt the need is weighty that conduct in the jury room shall be untrammeled by the fear of embarrassing publicity. The need is no less weighty that it shall be pure and undefiled. A juror of integrity and reasonable firmness will not fear to speak his mind if the confidences of debate are barred to the ears of mere impertinence or malice. He will not expect to be shielded against the disclosure of his conduct in the event that there is evidence reflecting upon his honor. The chance that now and then there may be found some timid soul who will take counsel of his fears and give way to their repressive power is too remote and shadowy to shape the course of justice. It must yield to the overmastering need, so vital in our polity, of preserving trial by jury in its purity against the inroads of corruption.

Nothing in our decision impairs the authority of Bushell's Case[2] with its historic vindication of the privilege of jurors to return a verdict freely according to their conscience. There had been a trial of Penn and Mead on a charge of taking part in an unlawful assembly. The jurors found a verdict of acquittal, though in so doing they refused to follow the instructions of the court. For this

---

[1] *O'Rourke* v. *Darbishire* (1920) English Appeal Cases 581.

[2] Reported in Vaughan's Cases, page 135 (1670).

they were fined and imprisoned, but were discharged on habeas corpus, Vaughan, C. J., pronouncing "that memorable opinion which soon ended the fining of jurors for their verdicts, and vindicated their character as judges of fact." Bushell's Case was born of the fear of the Star Chamber and of the tyranny of the Stuarts. It stands for a great principle, which is not to be whittled down or sacrificed. On the other hand, it is not to be strained and distorted into fanciful extensions. There is a peril of corruption in these days which is surely no less than the peril of coercion. What was said and done in the jury room is not the gist of her wrongdoing. What was said and done in the jury room is no more than confirmatory evidence of her state of mind before. One could urge with as much reason that she would be subjected to coercion if she had been indicted and tried for bribery and the same evidence had been accepted in support of the indictment.

In the record now before us the evidence of guilt is ample, without the happenings in the jury room, to break down the claim of privilege, and thus let in the light. There is the evidence of the concealment of the petitioner's unemployment with all its sinister implications. There is the evidence of her arguments with the jurors while the trial was going on. There is even the evidence of her vote, for the fact that she had voted for acquittal had been stated in her answer, and to the extent of the voluntary disclosure the privilege had been waived. Indeed what happened in the jury room added so little to the case that the error, if there had been any, in permitting it to be proved, would have to be regarded as unsubstantial and without effect on the result. No one can read the findings of the triers of the facts and hesitate in concluding that even with this evidence omitted there would have been an adjudication of contempt. In considering with all this fullness the merits of the ruling, we have been moved by the desire to build securely for the future.

The judgment of the Circuit Court of Appeals is affirmed.

"THE CERTAINTY OF A DESCRIPTION IS ALSO A MATTER OF DEGREE"

Cooper v. *Dasher,* 290 United States Reports 106 (1933)

During the night immediately following the filing of a bankruptcy petition, R. F. Dasher, the president of the bankrupt concern, took most of the merchandise belonging to that concern and lodged it in a place known only to himself. Part of the merchandise was found but nearly $20,000.00 worth could not be located. The merchandise had no identifying marks so that they could not be recognized unless pointed out by someone familiar with them. The referee in bankruptcy after giving Dasher an opportunity to return the merchandise, ordered its return. The order described the goods as follows: "balance of merchandise in the hands of R. F. Dasher at the time of the bankruptcy at a cost price value of $19,157.66, of a class of merchandise shown to have been purchased on the credit of the bankrupt corporation, and delivered to it, and as such a class of merchandise as is usually carried and sold in a retail drug store . . .". This order was reversed by the court for indefiniteness. The trustee in bankruptcy brought the case to the Supreme Court of the United States which unanimously decided as follows:

MR. JUSTICE CARDOZO * * *

The respondent has made away with goods belonging to the estate and defiantly withholds them. So the referee has found upon evidence not in the return and hence presumably sufficient. The process of computation and inference outlined in his report and leading up to his conclusion has support in many cases. The abstraction of the merchandise being evidenced by clear and convincing proof, there is no doubt about the jurisdiction of the court to direct a summary return. The respondent seeks to thwart the exercise of this conceded jurisdiction by the objection that the merchandise is not sufficiently described. He says that instead of the general description in the findings and the order there should be an inventory of items. The drugs, the perfumery, the surgical appliances, and the many miscellaneous articles that make up the stock in trade of a modern drug store should be set forth, he insists, in particular schedules. Only thus, we are told, will the respondent be in a position to understand the mandate to which obedience is due.

Misunderstanding of the mandate is upon the facts in this record an illusory peril. The order gives the only description that the nature of the case allows. The respondent, and no one else, is in a position to supply a better one. The mandate is addressed to him, and to him its meaning is definite, however indefinite to others. If it is clear enough to be understood, it is clear enough to be obeyed. "All evidence," said Lord Mansfield,[1] "is to be weighed according to the proof which it was in the power of one side to have produced and in the power of the other side to have contradicted." The validity of this order is to be subjected to a kindred test. Words after all are symbols, and the significance of the symbols varies with the knowledge and experience of the mind receiving them. The certainty of a description is always a matter of degree. "In every case the words used might be translated into things and facts by parol evidence."[2] How many identifying tokens we are to exact the reason and common sense of the situation must tell us. There are times when a restraining order enjoins the commission of acts that are not within the peculiar knowledge of the one to be enjoined. In that event the requirement of definiteness assumes a new importance, and failure to give heed to it may even make the order void. No doubt it is wise, irrespective of the knowledge of the parties, to make the terms of the order as definite as possible. The findings of the referee show that this is what was done. To insist upon more would be to sacrifice the substance of the right to the magic of a formula. In the ensuing war of words the wrongdoer would be enabled to slip away from his pursuers and take advantage of his wrong.

---

[1] *Blatch* v. *Archer,* reported in Cowper's Report, at page 65.

[2] Holmes, *J.,* in *Doherty* v. *Hill,* reported in Volume 144 Massachusetts Reports 465.

An argument is based upon embarrassments that may clog the enforcement of other remedies hereafter. The respondent, it is said, may refuse to comply with the order and may be sent to jail till he obeys. If later he repents and tenders a stock of goods to the trustee, the marshal will not know whether the tender is complete and will be unable to determine whether to hold him or to let him go. Embarrassments such as these, contingent and imaginary, will be resolved when they develop. The description of the merchandise might be much more definite than it is without enabling a marshal to identify a stock in trade, unaided by the advice of those acquainted with the business. Besides, the court is always in reserve, with capacity to act when the dispute becomes acute. If the respondent makes a genuine effort to restore the secreted goods, there will probably be little difficulty in determining whether the tender is sufficient. At present, the marshal is not before us praying for instructions, nor is the respondent yet in jail. We are not to presume that the order will be flouted. Let the respondent yield obedience to a mandate intelligible to him, and his liberty is then assured. The law will not be overpatient with his protest that if he persists in his defiance, he may be caught in his own snares.

The form of turnover orders in bankruptcy proceedings has been much considered in the federal courts. It has provoked a difference of opinion. In accord with the decisions of the court below are decisions of the Court of Appeals for the ninth circuit and the first. The contrary view has been taken in the fourth circuit and the second. Many orders not unlike the one in question have been upheld *sub silentio* in the absence of objection.

The order should be reversed and the cause remanded to the District Court with instructions to proceed in accordance with this opinion.

Reversed.

"CITIZENSHIP IS A PRIVILEGE NOT DUE OF COMMON RIGHT"

Morrison v. *People of State of California,* 291 United States Reports 82 (1934)

George Morrison and H. Doi were indicted in California, charged with *conspiring* to place Doi in the possession of agricultural land. It was further charged that this possession was obtained and that Doi was an alien Japanese, ineligible to citizenship. Such acts if committed, make out a criminal conspiracy under the California Statute.

On the trial the State proved Doi's agreement with Morrison, and that Doi had gone upon the land and used it, but it did not even try to prove that Doi was not a citizen of the United States, or that he was ineligible for citizenship. The reason for not attempting to prove this was Section 9a of the California Alien Land Law, which provided that in any civil or criminal action brought by the State of California, when the proof introduced by the State establishes the acquisition, possession, use or transfer of any real property, and the complaint or indictment alleges that the defendant is an alien and ineligible to United States citizenship, the burden proving the citizenship or eligibilty falls upon the defendant.

Upon the trial Morrison and Doi contended that this law was in effect a denial of due process under the 14th Amendment of the Constitution of the United States. This contention was overruled and the defendants were convicted. An appeal followed to the Supreme Court. The following unanimous opinion was rendered:

MR. JUSTICE CARDOZO * * *

A person of the Japanese race is a citizen of the United States if he was born within the United States. He is a citizen, even though born abroad, if his father was a citizen, provided, however, that this privilege shall not exist unless the father was at some time a resident of the United States as well as a citizen, and provided also such a child, who continues to reside abroad, shall, in order to receive the protection of this government, be required upon reaching the age of eighteen years to record at an American consulate his intention to become a resident and remain a citizen of the United States, and shall be further required to take the oath of allegiance to the United States upon attaining his majority. But a person of Japanese race, if not born a citizen, is ineligible to become a citizen, *i.e.,* to be naturalized. The privilege of naturalization is confined to aliens who are "free white persons, and to aliens of African nativity and to persons of African descent". "White persons", within the meaning of the statute, are members of the Caucasian race, as Caucasian is defined in the understanding of the mass of men. The term excludes the Chinese, the Japanese, the Hindus, the American Indians, and the Filipinos, though Indians and Filipinos who have done military or naval service may be entitled to special privileges. Nor is the range of the exclusion limited to persons of the full blood. The privilege of naturalization is denied to all who are not white (unless the applicants are of African nativity or African descent); and men are not white if the strain of colored blood in them is a half or a quarter, or, not improbably, even less, the governing test always being that of common understanding. * * *

There is a Treaty between the United States and Japan[1] by which the Japanese may own or lease houses, manufactories, warehouses, and shops, and may lease land for residential and commercial purposes. The treaty does not confer a privilege to own or use land for the purposes of agriculture. * * * There is nothing in the statute whereby unlawful occupation of land by an alien ineligible for citizenship is declared to be a crime unless the occupation has been acquired by force of a conspiracy.

This court in Morrison v. California[2] passed upon a controversy as to the validity of section 9b of the California Alien Land Law, which, though akin to section 9a, has important elements of difference. This section (9b) provides in substance that, when it has been proved that the defendant has been in the use or occupation of real

---

[1]Dated February 21, 1911.
[2]Reported in Volume 288 United States Reports 591.

property, and when it has also been proved that he is a member of a race ineligible for citizenship under the naturalization laws of the United States, the defendant shall have the burden of proving citizenship as a defense. We sustained that enactment when challenged as invalid under the Fourteenth Amendment of the Federal Constitution. The state had given evidence with reference to the defendant, the occupant of the land, that by reason of his race he was ineligible to be made a citizen. With this evidence present, we held that the burden was his to show that by reason of his birth he was a citizen already, and thus to bring himself within a rule which has the effect of an exception. In the vast majority of cases, he could do this without trouble if his claim of citizenship was honest. The people, on the other hand, if forced to disprove his claim, would be relatively helpless. In all likeliness his life history would be known only to himself and at times to relatives or intimates unwilling to speak against him.

The ruling was not novel. The decisions are manifold that within limits of reason and fairness the burden of proof may be lifted from the state in criminal prosecutions and cast on a defendant. The limits are in substance these, that the state shall have proved enough to make it just for the defendant to be required to repel what has been proved with excuse or explanation, or at least that upon a balancing of convenience or of the opportunities for knowledge the shifting of the burden will be found to be an aid to the accuser without subjecting the accused to hardship or oppression. Special reasons are at hand to make the change permissible when citizenship vel non is the issue to be determined. Citizenship is a privilege not due of common right. One who lays claim to it as his, and does this in justification or excuse of an act otherwise illegal, may fairly be called upon to prove his title good. In accord with that view are decisions of this court in proceedings under the acts of Congress for the deportation of aliens. A Chinaman by race resisted deportation on the ground that, though a Chinaman, he had been born in the United States. The ruling was that as to the place of birth the burden was upon the alien, and not upon the government. The ruling also was that the imposition of that burden did not deprive the alien of his constitutional immunities. "The inestimable heritage of citizenship is not to be conceded to those who seek to avail themselves of it under pressure of a particular exigency, without being able to show that it was ever possessed."[1] We adhered to that principle in Morrison v. California, supra. Upon that basis, we approved the ruling of the Supreme Court of California[2] that section 9b of the Alien Land Law casting upon a Japanese defendant the burden of proving citizenship after proof of his race had been given by the state was not an impairment of his immunities under the Federal Constitution. No point was made in the statement of jurisdiction or the supporting brief that the crime was conspiracy, and that one of the defendants belonged to the white race. The case was submitted as if both were Japanese.

The question is now as to section 9a. Obviously there is a wide difference between the scope of the two sections. Possession of agricultural land by one not shown to be ineligible for citizenship is an act that carries with it not even a hint of criminality. To prove such possession without more is to take hardly a step forward in support of an indictment. No such probability of wrongdoing grows out of the naked fact of use or occupation as to awaken a belief that the user or occupier is guilty if he fails to come forward with excuse or explanation. "The legislature may go a good way in raising (a presumption) or in charging the burden of proof, but there are limits." What is proved must be so related to what is inferred in the case of a true presumption as to be at least a warning signal according to the teachings of experience. "It is not within the province of a legislature to declare an individual guilty

[1] *Chin Bak Kaw* v. *United States,* reported in Volume 186 United States Reports 193.

[2] This ruling was enunciated in *People* v. *Osaki* reported in Volume 209 California Reports 169.

or presumptively guilty of a crime."[1] There are, indeed, "presumptions that are not evidence in a proper sense but simply regulations of the burden of proof." Even so, the occasions that justify regulations of the one order have a kinship, if nothing more, to those that justify the others. For a transfer of the burden, experience must teach that the evidence held to be inculpatory has at least a sinister significance, or, if that at times be lacking, there must be in any event a manifest disparity in convenience of proof and opportunity for knowledge, as, for instance, where a general prohibition is applicable to every one who is unable to bring himself within the range of an exception. The list is not exhaustive. Other instances may have arisen or may develop in the future where the balance of convenience can be redressed without oppression to the defendant through the same procedural expedient. The decisive considerations are too variable, too much distinctions of degree, too dependent in last analysis upon a common sense estimate of fairness or of facilities of proof, to be crowded into a formula. One can do no more than adumbrate them; sharper definition must await the specific case as it arises.

We turn to this statute and endeavor to assign it to its class. In the law of California there is no general prohibition of the use of agricultural lands by aliens, with special or limited provisos or exceptions. To the contrary, it is the privilege that is general, and only the prohibition that is limited and special. Without preliminary proof of race, occupation of the land is not even a suspicious circumstance. The inquiry must therefore be whether occupants so situated may be charged with the burden of proving themselves eligible and thus establishing their innocence.

First. The indictment is for conspiracy and, indeed, the Alien Land Law creates no other crime. Morrison and Doi are charged to have conspired, but Doi alone is charged to be ineligible for citizenship. One might suppose from

[1]*McFarland* v. *American Sugar Co.,* reported in Volume 241 United States Reports 79.

a reading of the statute that the burden of proof, even if shifted to him, would be unaffected as to Morrison. The California courts, however, have cast the same burden upon both; and both have been convicted. None the less, in applying the presumption, we must keep before us steadily the quality of their crime. It is impossible in the nature of things for a man to conspire with himself. In California as elsewhere conspiracy imports a corrupt agreement between not less than two with guilty knowledge on the part of each.

Now, plainly as to Morrison, an imputation of knowledge is a wholly arbitrary presumption. He may never have seen Doi before the transfer of possession or afterwards. He may have made his agreement, by an agent or over the telephone or by writings delivered through the mails. Even if lessor and lessee came together face to face, there is nothing to show whether Doi was a Japanese of the full blood, whose race would have been apparent to any one looking at him. Moreover, if his race was apparent, he may still have been a citizen, for anything that was known to Morrison or others. The statute does not make it a crime to put a lessee into possession without knowledge or inquiry as to race and place of birth. The statute makes it a crime to put an ineligible lessee into possession as the result of a willful conspiracy to violate the law. Nothing in the people's evidence gives support to the inference that Morrison had knowledge of the disqualifications of his tenant or could testify about them. What was known to him, so far as the evidence discloses, was known also to the people, and provable with equal ease. Only an arbitrary mandate could charge him with guilty knowledge as an inference of law if it were proved that Doi was not a citizen or eligible to become one. Still less can he be charged with such knowledge when Doi's disqualification is itself a mere presumption. In such circumstances the conviction of Morrison because he failed to assume the burden of disproving a conspiracy was a denial of due process that vitiates the judgment as to him. Nor is that the only consequence. Doi was not a conspirator, however guilty his own state of mind, unless Morrison had shared in the guilty knowledge and design. The joinder was something to be proved, for it was of the essence of the crime. Without it there was a civil wrong, but not a criminal conspiracy, the only crime denounced. The conviction failing as to the one defendant must fail as to the other.

Second. The result will not be changed if we view the case on the assumption that possession by one ineligible, when it is the product of agreement, may be criminal as to the tenant who holds with guilty knowledge, though innocent as to the landlord who believes that all is lawful.

We have pointed out before that a lease of agricultural land, unaccompanied by evidence of the race of the lessee, conveys no hint of criminality. For the moment we assume, without intending to decide, that strong considerations of convenience, if they existed, might cast upon the tenant the burden of proving his qualifications and thus disproving guilt. The question will then be whether the normal burden of proof will so thwart or hamper justice as to create a practical necessity, without preponderating hardship to the defendant, for a departure from the usual rule.

In the vast majority of cases the race of a Japanese or a Chinaman will be known to any one who looks at him. There is no practical necessity in such circumstances for shifting the burden to the defendant. Not only is there no necessity; there is only a faint promotion of procedural convenience. The triers of the facts will look upon the defendant sitting in the courtroom and will draw their own conclusions. If more than this is necessary, the people may call witnesses familiar with the characteristics of the race, who will state his racial origin. The only situation in which the shifting of the burden can be of any substantial profit to the state is where the defendant is of mixed blood, the white or the African so preponderating that there will be no external evidence of another. But in such circumstances the promotion of convenience from the point of view of the prosecution will be outweighed by the probability of injustice to the accused. One whose racial origins are so blended as to be not discoverable at sight will often be unaware of them. If he can state nothing but his ignorance, he has not sustained the burden of proving eligibility, and must stand condemned of crime.

Reflection will satisfy that the chance of this injustice is not remote or shadowy. Let us assume a charge that agricultural land has been occupied by Filipinos not born in the United States, and not entitled to the privilege growing out of service in the army. They are then ineligible for citizenship, and subject to indictment under the laws of California if they have gone into possession in aid of a conspiracy. But Filipinos have intermarried with many other peoples. They have intermarried with whites and with Negroes and mulattos. A laborer, born in Canada, his parents apparently mulattos, but one of his grandparents a Filipino, according to the charge in an indictment, would be ignorant in many cases whether he was a Filipino or an African. The admixture of oriental blood might be too slight for his race to be apparent to the eye, and family traditions are not always well preserved, especially when the descendants are men and women of humble origin, remote from kith and kin. The same possibility of injustice would be present where the occupant of the land is a descendant of Mexicans and Indians, or an Eurasian, his ancestors partly European and partially Asiatic.

The probability is thus apparent that the transfer of the burden may result in grave injustice in the only class of cases in which it will be of any practical importance. The statute does not say that the defendant shall be acquitted if he does not know his racial origin and is unable to make proof of it. What the effect of such a law would be, we are not required to consider. To the contrary, the statute says in substance that, unless he can and does prove it, he will have failed to discharge his burden, and will therefore be found guilty. Moreover, if he were to profess ignorance, and ignorance were an excuse, the trier of the facts might refuse to credit him.

There can be no escape from hardship and injustice, outweighing many times any procedural convenience, unless the burden of persuasion in respect of racial origin is cast upon the people.

What has been written applies only to those provisions of the statute that prescribe the rule for criminal causes. Other considerations may or may not apply where the controversy is civil. We leave that question open.

The judgment is reversed, and the cause remanded for further proceedings not inconsistent with this opinion.

It is so ordered.

"JUSTICE, THOUGH DUE TO THE ACCUSED, IS DUE TO THE ACCUSER ALSO"

Snyder v. *Commonwealth of Massachusetts,* 291 United States Reports 97 (1934)

Herman Snyder and two others murdered one, Kiley, at a gasoline station in Massachusetts, for the purpose of effectuating a robbery. One of the three confessed and turned state's evidence, and there was abundant evidence to establish the guilt of the other two beyond a reasonable doubt. The main point of the appeal from the conviction was that the trial judge had refused to permit the defendant Snyder to be present while the jury viewed the premises where the murder occurred. He claimed that this was a denial of due process of law under the Fourteenth Amendment of the Federal Constitution. The request that the jury be directed to view the scene of the crime was made by the district attorney. The attorneys for the defendants did go along with the jury. Counsel for Snyder's co-defendant asked that he be permitted to go there with his client after the jury viewed the premises, but no request was made that his client be present with the jury. Counsel for Snyder moved that his client be permitted to view the scene with the jury, but this motion was denied.

The jury were taken around the gasoline station where the murder occurred, as well as through the adjacent streets, and various observations were made both by the district attorney and by Snyder's counsel.

The appeal was carried to the Supreme Court of the United States and by a vote of 5 to 4 the conviction of murder was upheld. The majority opinion was written by Mr. Justice Cardozo.

MR. JUSTICE CARDOZO * * *

The commonwealth of Massachusetts is free to regulate the procedure of its courts in accordance with its own conception of policy and fairness, unless in so doing it offends some principle of justice so rooted in the traditions and conscience of our people as to be ranked as fundamental. Its procedure does not run foul of the Fourteenth Amendment because another method may seem to our thinking to be fairer or wiser or to give a surer promise of protection to the prisoner at the bar. Consistently with that amendment, trial by jury may be abolished. Indictments by a grand jury may give way to informations by a public officer. The privilege against self-incrimination may be withdrawn and the accused put upon the stand as a witness for the state. What may not be taken away is notice of the charge and an adequate opportunity to be heard in defense of it.

We assume in aid of the petitioner that in a prosecution for a felony the defendant has the privilege under the Fourteenth Amendment to be present in his own person whenever his presence has a relation, reasonably substantial, to the fullness of his opportunity to defend against the charge. Thus, the privilege to confront one's accusers and cross-examine them face to face is assured to a defendant by the Sixth Amendment in prosecutions in the federal courts, and in prosecutions in the State courts is assured very often by the Constitutions of the states. For present purposes we assume that the privilege is reinforced by the Fourteenth Amendment, though this has not been squarely held. Again, defense may be made easier if the accused is permitted to be present at the examination of jurors or the summing up of counsel, for it will be in his power, if present, to give advice or suggestion or even to supersede his lawyers altogether and conduct the trial himself. No doubt the privilege may be lost by consent or at times even by misconduct. Our concern is with its extension when unmodified by waiver, either actual or imputed.

In all the cases thus assumed the presence of the defendant satisfies the test that was put forward a moment ago as basic and decisive. It bears, or may fairly be assumed to bear, a relation, reasonably substantial, to his opportunity to defend. Nowhere in the decisions of this court is there a dictum, and still less a ruling that the Fourteenth Amendment assures the privilege of presence when presence would be useless, or the benefit but a shadow. What has been said, if not decided, is distinctly to the contrary. The underlying principle gains point and precision from the distinction everywhere drawn between proceedings at the trial and those before and after. Many motions before trial are heard in the defendant's absence, and many motions after trial or in the prosecution of appeals. Confusion of thought will result if we fail to mark the distinction between requirements in respect of presence that have their source, either expressly or by implication, in the Federal Constitution. Confusion will result again if the privilege of presence be identified with the privilege of confrontations, which is limited to the stages of the trial when there are witnesses to be questioned. "It was intended to prevent the conviction of the accused upon depositions or ex parte affidavits, and particularly to preserve the right of the accused to test the recollection of the witness in the exercise of the right of cross-examination".[1] So far as the Fourteenth Amendment is concerned, the presence of a defendant is a condition of due process to the extent that a fair and just hearing would be thwarted by his absence, and to that extent only.

We are thus brought to an inquiry as to the relation between the defendant's presence at a view and the fundamental justice assured to him by the Constitution of the United States.

At the outset, we consider a bare inspection and nothing more, a view where nothing is said by any one to direct the attention of the jury to one feature or another. The Fourteenth Amendment does not assure to a defendant the privilege to be present at such a time. There is nothing he could do if he were there, and almost nothing he could gain. The only shred of advantage would be to make certain that the jury had been brought to the right place and had viewed the right scene. If he felt any doubt about this, he could examine the bailiffs at the trial and learn what they had looked at. The risk that they would lie is no greater than the risk that attaches to testimony about anything. "Constitutional law, like other mortal

[1]*Dowdell* v. *United States,* reported in Volume 221 United States Reports 325, 330.

contrivances, has to take some chances."[1] Here the chance is so remote that it dwindles to the vanishing point. If the bailiffs were to bear false witness as to the place they had shown, the lie would be known to the jury. There is no immutable principle of justice that secures protection to a defendant against so shadowy a risk. The argument is made that conceivably the place might have been changed and in a way that would be material. In that event the fact could be brought out by appropriate inquiry. There could be inquiry of witnesses in court and of counsel out of court. Description would disclose the conditions at the view, and the defendant or his witnesses could prove what the conditions were before. He could do nothing more though he had been there with the jury. Indeed, the record makes it clear that upon request he would have been allowed to go there afterwards in company with his counsel. Opportunity was ample to learn whatever there was need to know.

If the risk of injustice to the prisoner is shadowy at its greatest, it ceases to be even a shadow when he admits that the jurors were brought to the right place and shown what it was right to see. That, in substance, is what happened here. On the trial, photographs and diagrams of the scene of the homicide were put in evidence by the commonwealth and placed before the jury. There was no suggestion by the defendant or his counsel that these photographs and diagrams did not truly represent the place that had been seen upon the view. There was no suggestion of any change except the one that was conceded. The defendant took the stand and admitted that he was at the gasoline station at the time of the crime. He tried to reduce the grade of his wrongdoing by testifying that the shot had been fired by his codefendant, Donnellon, and that larceny, not robbery, was the aim of the conspiracy.[2] In the course of his testimony, he described

[1]*Blinn* v. *Nelson,* reported in Volume 222 United States Reports 1, 7.

[2]Under the law of Massachusetts, a homicide committed with deliberately premeditated malice aforethought, or in the commission or attempted commission of a crime punishable with imprisonment for life, is murder in the first degree. Robbery while armed with a dangerous weapon, is so punishable. Not so with larceny.

his own and Donnellon's movements with the aid of the diagram in evidence. At the end of the trial he made a brief statement to the jury, supplementing the argument that had been made by his counsel. "I am sorry," he said, "that I had any part in the crime. I am sorry for the grief I have caused. But I did not fire the fatal shot. That is all." Nowhere is there a suggestion of any doubt as to the place. Like concessions are implicit in the summing up of counsel. His argument reminds the jurors of what they had seen upon the view, and of the dimensions of the building, which are shown also on the diagram. The place is undisputed.

If it be true that there is no denial of due process as the result of a bare inspection in the absence of a defendant, the question remains whether such a denial results where counsel are permitted, without any statement of the evidence, to point out particular features of the scene and to request the jury to observe them. The courts of Massachusetts hold that statements, thus restricted, are proper incidents of a view. The rule in Massachusetts is that these acts are permissible, though the defendant is not present, and though he is kept away under protest. We are to determine whether the Fourteenth Amendment prescribes anything to the contrary.

Obviously the difference between a view at which every one is silent and a view accompanied by a request to note this feature or another is one of degree, and nothing more. The mere bringing of a jury to a particular place, whether a building or a room or a wall with a bullet hole, is in effect a statement that this is the place which was the scene of the offense, and a request to examine it. When the tacit directions are made explicit, the defendant is not wronged unless supplement of words so transforms the quality of the procedure that injustice will be done if the defendant is kept away. Statements to the jury pointing out the specific objects to be noted have been a traditional accompaniment of a view for about two centuries, if not longer. The Fourteenth Amendment has not displaced the procedure of the ages.

As early as 1747 there is the record of a precedent that exhibits the remedy in action. The practice then was to place the jury in the charge of "showers", who were sworn to lead them to the view.

When the scene is explained by showers who are not the counsel for the parties, a defendant gains nothing by being present at a view any more than he gains where there is only a bare inspection without an explanatory word. He has no privilege in such circumstances, and certainly no constitutional privilege, to speak to the showers and give suggestions or advice. "We do not see what good the presence of the prisoner would do, as he could neither ask nor answer questions, nor in any way interfere with the acts, observations or conclusions of the jury."[1] If they fail to point out anything material, he may prove the fact upon the trial and ask for another view. He had the same privilege here, for there was a stenographic transcript of all that was said and done. Never, at any stage of the proceeding, has there been a suggestion by the defendant or his counsel that there was need of something more.

The situation is not changed to his prejudice because the showers in this instance were the counsel for the parties. The choice of counsel for that purpose has its roots in ancient practice. Far from being harmful, it supplies an additional assurance that nothing helpful to either side will be overlooked upon the view. True, indeed, it is that, when counsel are the showers, the defendant may be able, if he is present, to give suggestion or advice, or so at least we may assume. Constitutional immunities and privileges do not depend upon the accidents. The Fourteenth Amendment does not say that showers are at liberty in the absence of the defendant, to point out the things to be viewed if the showers are not counsel, but are not at liberty to do so if they happen to be counsel. The least a defendant must do, if he would annul the practice upon a view which the Commonwealth has approved by the judgment of its courts, is to show that in the particular case in

[1]*People* v. *Bonney,* reported in Volume 19 California Reports 426, 446.

which the practice is exposed to challenge there is a reasonable possibility that injustice has been done. No one can read what was said at this view in the light of the uncontroverted facts established at the trial, and have even a passing thought that the presence of Snyder would have been an aid to his defense.

There is an approach to the subject from the viewpoint of history that clarifies the prospect. We may assume that the knowledge derived from an inspection of the scene may be characterized as evidence. Even if this be so, a view is not a "trial" nor any part of a trial in the sense in which a trial was understood at common law. This is seen from two circumstances. In the first place, the judge is not required to be present at a view, though he may go there if he will. In the second place, the practice for many years was to have a committee of the jurors, the usual number being six, attend at the view to represent the whole body. We have no thought to suggest that a view by a part of a jury is permissible to-day. That question is not before us. There is significance, none the less, in the fact that it was permissible in England, the home of the principle that a defendant charged with felony has the privilege of confronting his accusers and of being present at his trial. Certain it is that in the land where these maxims had their genesis and from which they were carried to our shores the proceeding known as a trial was thought of as something very different from the proceeding known as a view. To transfer to a view the constitutional privileges applicable to a trial is to be forgetful of our history.

A fertile source of perversion in constitutional theory is the tyranny of labels. Out of the vague precepts of the Fourteenth Amendment a court frames a rule which is general in form, though it has been wrought under the pressure of particular situations. Forthwith another situation is placed under the rule because it is fitted to the words, though related faintly, if at all, to the reasons that brought the rule into existence. A defendant in a criminal case must be present at a trial when evidence is offered, for the opportunity must be his to advise with his counsel, and cross-examine his accusers. Let the words "evidence" and "trial" be extended but a little, and the privilege will apply to stages of the cause at which the function of counsel is mechanical or formal and at which a scene and not a witness is to deliver up its message. In such circumstances the solution of the problem is not to be found in dictionary definitions of evidence or trials. It is not to be found in judgments of the courts that at other times or in other circumstances the presence of a defendant is a postulate of justice. There can be no sound solution without an answer to the question whether in the particular conditions exhibited by the record the enforced absence of the defendant is so flagrantly unjust that the Constitution of the United States steps in to forbid it. What we are subjecting to revision is not the action of a Legislature excluding a defendant from a view at all times or in all conditions. What is here for revision is the action of the judicial department of a state excluding the defendant in a particular set of circumstances, and the justice or injustice of that exclusion must be determined in the light of the whole record. Discretion has not been abdicated. To the contrary, the record makes it clear that discretion has been exercised. Much is made of a supposed analogy between a view and a photograph, but the analogy, whatever its superficial force, is partial and misleading. The photograph, to be admissible, should be verified by the oath of the photographer, who must be subject to cross-examination as to the manner of its taking. It is common knowledge that a camera can be so placed, and lights and shadows so adjusted, as to give a distorted picture of reality. Nor is there need for us to hold that conditions can never arise in which justice will be outraged if there is a view in the defendant's absence. Enough for present purposes that they have not arisen here. Due process of law requires that the proceedings shall be fair, but fairness is a relative, not an absolute, concept. It is fairness with reference to particular conditions or particular results. "The due process clause does not impose upon the states a duty to establish ideal systems for the administration of justice, with every modern improvement and with provision against every possible hardship that may befall." What is fair in one set of circumstances may be an act of tyranny in others. This court has not yet held that even upon a trial in court the absence of a defendant for a few moments while formal documents are marked in evidence will vitiate a judgment. But we do not need to dwell upon the measure of the privilege at such a time or in such conditions. Whatever it may be, not even an intimation will be found in our decisions that there is a denial of due process if the accused be excluded from a view, though present at every stage of the proceedings in the court. It is one thing to say that the prevailing practice is to permit the accused to accompany the jury, if he express such a wish. It is another thing to say that the practice may not be changed without a denial of his privileges under the Constitution of the United States.

We find it of no moment that the judge in this case described the view as evidence. The Supreme Judicial Court of Massachusetts has said of a view that "its chief purpose is to enable the jury to understand better the testimony which has or may be introduced." Even so, its inevitable effect is that of evidence, no matter what label the judge may choose to give it. Such is the holding of many well-considered cases. To say that the defendant may be excluded from the scene if the court tells the jury that the view has no other function than to give them understanding of the evidence, but that there is an impairment of the constitutional privileges of a defendant thus excluded if the court tells the jury that the view is part of the evidence—to make the securities of the constitution depend upon such quiddities is to cheapen and degrade them.

The law, as we have seen, is sedulous in maintaining for a defendant charged with crime whatever forms of procedure are of the essence of an opportunity to defend. Privileges so fundamental as to be inherent in every concept of a fair trial that could be acceptable to the thought of reasonable men will be kept inviolate and inviolable, however crushing may be the presssure of incriminating proof. But justice, though due to the accused, is due to the accuser also. The concept of fairness must not be strained till it is narrow, fairness must not be strained till it is narrowed to a filament. We are to keep the balance true.

The Constitution and statutes and judicial decisions of the commonwealth of Massachusetts are the authentic forms through which the sense of justice of the people of that commonwealth expresses itself in law. We are not to supersede them on the ground that they deny the essentials of a trial because opinions may differ as to their policy or fairness. Not all the precepts of conduct precious to the hearts of many of us are immutable principles of justice, acknowledged *semper ubique et ab omnibus,* wherever the good life is a subject of concern. There is danger that the criminal law will be brought into contempt—that discredit will even touch the great immunities assured by the Fourteenth Amendment—if gossamer possibilities of prejudice to a defendant are to nullify a sentence pronounced by a court of competent jurisdiction in obedience to local law, and set the guilty free.

The judgment is affirmed. Mr. Justice ROBERTS, Mr. Justice BRANDEIS, Mr. Justice SUTHERLAND and Mr. Justice BUTLER dissenting.[1]

---

[1]Mr. Justice Roberts wrote the dissenting opinion and took the view that our traditions, the Bill of Rights, and the decisions of the Courts all declare for the privilege of the accused to be present throughout his trial. He did not approve of the argument that this privilege was for no other purpose than to safeguard his opportunity to cross-examine adverse witnesses. He argued that if the accused may be excluded from a view, it logically followed that he can be excluded from the court room while documentary and physical evidence are proffered to and examined by the jury. If knowledge gained by a view is to play its part with oral documentary and written evidence, that view is part of the trial. Furthermore, it would be a dangerous precedent to place the right of the defendant to be present at all times, upon the amount of harm that may be done to him if kept away.

"STANDARDS OF PRUDENT CONDUCT ARE DECLARED AT TIMES BY COURTS, BUT THEY ARE TAKEN OVER FROM THE FACTS OF LIFE"

Pokora v. *Wabash Ry. Co.,* 292 United States Reports 98 (1934)

John Pokora, an ice dealer drove his truck across a railway grade crossing in Springfield, Illinois, when he was struck by a train and injured. Just before reaching the tracks he looked and listened for approaching trains. A string of box cars a short distance away cut off almost his entire view. He heard neither bell nor whistle. The train that hit him came from the north at a speed of about 30 miles an hour. The lower courts held against Pokora because of a ruling in a former case[1] which required a driver who wasn't sure whether a train was dangerously near, to stop his car and get out of the vehicle to look. An appeal was taken by Pokora to the Supreme Court of the United States.

MR. JUSTICE CARDOZO * * *

The question, we think, was for the jury whether reasonable caution forbade his going forward in reliance on the sense of hearing, unaided by that of sight. No doubt it was his duty to look along the track from his seat, if looking would avail to warn him of the danger. This does not mean, however, that if vision was cut off by obstacles, there was negligence in going on, any more than there would have been in trusting to his ears if vision had been cut off by the darkness of the night. Pokora made his crossing in the daytime, but like the traveler by night he used the faculties available to one in his position. A jury, but not the court, might say that with faculties thus limited he should have found some other means of assuring himself of safety before venturing to cross. The crossing was a frequented highway in a populous city. Behind him was a line of other cars, making ready to follow him. To some extent, at least, there was assurance in the thought that the defendant would not run its train as such a time and

[1] *B. & O. R. Co.* v. *Goodman,* reported in Volume 275 United States Reports 66.

place without sounding bell or whistle. Indeed, the statutory signals did not exhaust the defendant's duty when to its knowledge there was special danger to the traveler through obstructions on the roadbed narrowing the field of vision. All this the plaintiff, like any other reasonable traveler, might fairly take into account. All this must be taken into account by us in comparing what he did with the conduct reasonably to be expected of reasonable men.

The argument is made, however, that our decision in B. & O. R. Co. v. Goodman, is a barrier in the plaintiff's path, irrespective of the conclusion that might commend itself if the question were at large. There is no doubt that the opinion in that case is correct in its result. Goodman, the driver, traveling only five or six miles an hour, had, before reaching the track, a clear space of eighteen feet within which the train was plainly visible. With that opportunity, he fell short of the legal standard of duty established for a traveler when he failed to look and see. This was decisive of the case. But the court did not stop there. It added a remark, unnecessary upon the facts before it, which has been a fertile source of controversy. "In such circumstances it seems to us that if a driver cannot be sure otherwise whether a train is dangerously near he must stop and get out of his vehicle, although obviously he will not often be required to do more than to stop and look."

There is need at this stage to clear the ground of brushwood that may obscure the point at issue. We do not now inquire into the existence of a duty to stop, disconnected from a duty to get out and reconnoitre. The inquiry, if pursued, would lead us into the thickets of conflicting judgments. Some courts apply what is often spoken of as the Pennsylvania rule, and impose an unyielding duty to stop, as well as to look and listen, no matter how clear the crossing or the tracks on either side. Other courts, the majority, adopt the rule that the traveler must look and listen, but that the existence of a duty to stop depends upon the circumstances, and hence generally, even if not invariably, upon the judgment of the jury. The subject has been less considered in this court, but in none of its opinions is there a suggestion that at any and every crossing the duty to stop is absolute, irrespective of the danger. Not even in B. & O. R. Co. v. Goodman, which goes farther than the earlier cases, is there support for such a rule. To the contrary, the opinion makes it clear that the duty is conditioned upon the presence of impediments whereby sight and hearing become inadequate for the traveler's protection.

Choice between these diversities of doctrine is unnecessary for the decision of the case at hand. Here the fact is not disputed that the plaintiff did stop before he started to cross the tracks. If we assume that by reason of the box cars, there was a duty to stop again when the obstructions had been cleared, that duty did not arise unless a stop could be made safely after the point of clearance had been reached. For reasons already stated, the testimony permits the inference that the truck was in the zone of danger by the time the field of vision was enlarged. No stop would then have helped the plaintiff if he remained seated on his truck, or so the triers of the facts might find. His case was for the jury, unless as a matter of law he was subject to a duty to get out of the vehicle before it crossed the switch, walk forward to the front, and then, afoot, survey the scene. We must say whether his failure to do this was negligence so obvious and certain that one conclusion and one only is permissible for rational and candid minds.

Standards of prudent conduct are declared at times by courts, but they are taken over from the facts of life. To get out of a vehicle and reconnoitre is an uncommon precaution, as everyday experience informs us. Besides being uncommon, it is very likely to be futile, and sometimes even dangerous. If the driver leaves his vehicle when he nears a cut or curve, he will learn nothing by getting out about the perils that lurk beyond. By the time he regains his seat and sets his car in motion, the hidden train may be upon him. Often the added safeguard will be dubious though the track happens to be straight, as it seems that this one was, at all events as far as the station, about five blocks to the north. A train travelling at a speed of thirty miles an hour will cover a quarter of a mile in the space of thirty seconds. It may thus emerge out of obscurity as the driver turns his back to regain the waiting car, and may then descend upon him suddenly when his car is on the track. Instead of helping himself by getting out, he might do better to press forward with all his faculties alert. So a train at a neighboring station, apparently at rest and harmless, may be transformed in a few seconds into an instrument of destruction. At times the course of safety may be different. One can figure to oneself a road-bed so level and unbroken that getting out will be a gain. Even then the balance of advantage depends on many circumstances and can be easily disturbed. Where was Pokora to leave his truck after getting out to reconnoitre? If he was to leave it on the switch, there was the possibility that the box cars would be shunted down upon him before he could regain his seat. The defendant did not show whether there was a locomotive at the forward end, or whether the cars were so few that a locomotive could be seen. If he was to leave his vehicle near the curb, there was even stronger reason to believe that the space to be covered in going back and forth would make his observations worthless. One must remember that while the traveler turns his eyes in one direction, a train or a loose engine may be approaching from the other.

Illustrations such as these bear witness to the need for caution in framing standards of behavior that amount to rules of law. The need is the more urgent when there is no background of experience out of which the standards have emerged. They are then, not the natural flowerings of behavior in its customary forms, but rules artificially developed, and imposed from without. Extraordinary situations may not wisely or fairly be subjected to tests or regulations that are fitting for the commonplace or normal. In default of the guide of customary conduct, what is suitable for the traveler caught in a mesh where the ordinary safeguards fail him is for the judgment of a jury. The opinion in Goodman's Case has been a source of confusion in the federal courts to the extent that it imposes a standard for application by the judge, and has had only wavering support in the courts of the states. We limit it accordingly.

The judgment should be reversed, and the cause remanded for further proceedings in accordance with this opinion.

It is so ordered.

"ONE DOES NOT PROVE BY HIS MARTYRDOM THAT HE HAS KEPT WITHIN THE LAW"

Hamilton v. *Regents of the University of California*, 293 United States Reports 245 (1934)

The University of California is a land grant college in that State. Congress donated public lands to it for the purpose of supporting a college where the leading object was to be the teaching of branches of learning related to agriculture and the mechanical arts without excluding other scientific and classical studies and including military tactics. Under the California Law any resident of California with proper requirements may become a student in the University. Because of the donations of Congress, the students were able to obtain an education at a fee lower than that prevailing at other universities in the state.

A law of California required the students of the University of California to take a course in military science and tactics. One Albert W. Hamilton, together with others who were students at this University, petitioned the school authorities for exemption from such military training upon the ground of their religious and conscientious objections to war and military training. The regents of the University refused to exempt these students. Thereupon, and solely because of their religious and conscientious objections the students declined to take the prescribed course. Shortly thereafter they received formal notification from the Regents suspending them from the University, but with leave to apply for readmission at any time, conditioned upon their ability and willingness to comply with all applicable regulations of the University governing the attendance of students. The main opinion of the Supreme Court upholding the Regents was written by Mr. Justice Butler.

MR. JUSTICE CARDOZO (concurring). * * *

Concurring in the opinion, I wish to say an extra word.

I assume for present purposes that the religious liberty protected by the First Amendment against invasion by the nation is protected by the Fourteenth Amendment against invasion by the states.

Accepting that premise, I cannot find in the respondents' ordinance an obstruction by the state to "the free exercise" of religion as the phrase was understood by the founders of the nation, and by the generations that have followed.

There is no occasion at this time to mark the limits of governmental power in the exaction of military service when the nation is at peace. The petitioners have not been required to bear arms for any hostile purpose, offensive or defensive, either now or in the future. They have not even been required in any absolute or peremptory way to join in courses of instruction that will fit them to bear arms. If they elect to resort to an institution for higher education maintained with the state's moneys, then and only then they are commanded to follow courses of instruction believed by the state to be vital to its welfare. This may be condemned by some as unwise or illiberal or unfair when there is violence to conscientious scruples, either religious or merely ethical. More must be shown to set the ordinance at naught. In controversies of this order, courts do not concern themselves with matters of legislative policy, unrelated to privileges or liberties secured by the organic law. The First Amendment, if it be read into the Fourteenth, makes invalid any state law "respecting an establishment of religion, or prohibiting the free exercise thereof." Instruction in military science is not instruction in the practice or tenets of a religion. Neither directly nor indirectly is government establishing a state religion when it insists upon such training. Instruction in military science, unaccompanied here by any pledge of military service, is not an interference by the state with the free exercise of religion when the liberties of the Constitution are read in the light of a century and a half of history during days of peace and war.

The meaning of those liberties has striking illustration in statutes that were enacted in colonial times and later. From the beginnings of our history, Quakers and other conscientious objectors have been exempted as an act of grace from military service, but the exemption, when granted, has been coupled with a condition, at least in many instances, that they supply the Army with a substitute or with the money necessary to hire one. This was done in Virginia in 1738 and in 1782 in Massachusetts; in North Carolina, and in New York. A like practice has been continued in the Constitutions of many of the states. For one opposed to force, the affront to conscience must be greater in furnishing men and money wherewith to wage a pending contest than in studying military science without the duty or the pledge of service. Never in our history has the notion been accepted, or even, it is believed, advanced, that acts thus indirectly related to service in the camp or field are so tied to the practice of religion as to be exempt, in law or in morals, from regulation by the state. On the contrary, the very lawmakers who were willing to give release from warlike acts had no thought that they were doing anything inconsistent with the moral claims of an objector, still less with his constitutional immunities, in coupling the exemption with these collateral conditions.

Manifestly a different doctrine would carry us to lengths that have never yet been dreamed of. The conscientious objector, if his liberties were to be thus extended, might refuse to contribute taxes in furtherance of a war, whether for attack or for defense, or in furtherance of any other end condemned by his conscience as irreligious or immoral. The right of private judgment has never yet been so exalted above the powers and the compulsion of the agencies of government. One who is a martyr to a principle—which may turn out in the end to be a delusion or an error—does not prove by his martyrdom that he has kept within the law.

I am authorized to state that Mr. Justice BRANDEIS and Mr. Justice STONE join in this opinion.

"IN THE LONG RUN PROSPERITY AND SALVATION ARE IN UNION AND NOT DIVISION"

Baldwin v. *G. A. F. Seelig, Inc.*, 294 United States Reports 511 (1935)

The New York Milk Control Act set up a system of minimum prices to be paid by milk dealers to producers. The inhabitants of the City of New York and vicinity obtain about 70% of the milk needed for their use from the farms of New York State. In order to keep the price level free from competition from outside the State, the act provided that the prices were to be extended to that part of the supply coming from other States. The statute in substance declared that there shall be no sale within New York of milk obtained from outside the state unless the price paid to the producers was one that would be lawful upon a similar transaction in New York. The statute controlling prices in the State of New York had been held valid prior to the dispute here involved.

The Seelig Corporation was a milk dealer in the City of New York, and it bought its milk from a creamery in Vermont. The milk was distributed to consumers in New York. Title to the purchased milk passed from the creamery to the purchaser in Vermont. The milk was bought in Vermont at a price lower than the minimum provided for in the New York statute. A license was refused the Seelig Corporation to transact its business unless it signed an agreement to conform to the New York statute. This the Seelig Corporation refused to do. Whereupon, the Commissioner of Farms and Markets announced his intent to prosecute for trading without a license and to recover heavy penalties. This suit was brought to restrain the commissioner upon the ground that the statute violated the constitutional rights of Seelig Corporation. The District Court granted a decree restraining the enforcement of the act in so far as sales were concerned while the milk was in the cans or in the original package in which it was brought from Vermont into New York but refused a restriction as to the milk taken out of the cans for bottles and thereafter sold, in bottles. Both sides took an appeal. The unanimous opinion of the court follows.

MR. JUSTICE CARDOZO * * *

First. An injunction was properly granted restraining the enforcement of the act in its application to sales in the original packages.

New York has no power to project its legislation into Vermont by regulating the price to be paid in that state for milk acquired there. So much is not disputed. New York is equally without power to prohibit the introduction within her territory of milk of wholesome quality acquired in Vermont, whether at high prices or at low ones. This again is not disputed. Accepting those postulates, New York asserts her power to outlaw milk so introduced by prohibiting its sale thereafter if the price that has been paid for it to the farmers of Vermont is less than would be owing in like circumstances to farmers in New York. The importer in that view may keep his milk or drink it, but sell it he may not.

Such a power, if exerted, will set a barrier to traffic between one state and another as effective as if customs duties, equal to the price differential, had been laid upon the thing transported. Imposts or duties upon commerce with other countries are placed, by an express prohibition of the Constitution, beyond the power of a state, "except what may be absolutely necessary for executing its inspection Laws." Imposts and duties upon interstate commerce are placed beyond the power of a state, without the mention of an exception, by the provision committing commerce of that order to the power of the Congress. "It is the established doctrine of this court that a state may not, in any form or under any guise, directly burden the prosecution of interstate business."[1] Nice distinctions have been made at times between direct and indirect burdens. They are irrelevant when the avowed purpose of the obstruction, as well as its necessary tendency, is to suppress or mitigate the consequences of competition between the states. Such an obstruction is direct by the very terms of the hypothesis. We are reminded in the opinion below that a chief occasion of the commerce clauses was "the mutual jealousies and aggressions of the States, taking form in customs barriers and other economic retaliation." If New York, in order to promote

---

[1]*International Text Book Co.* v. *Pigg,* reported in Volume 217 United States Reports 91.

the economic welfare of her farmers, may guard them against competition with the cheaper prices of Vermont, the door has been opened to rivalries and reprisals that were meant to be averted by subjecting commerce between the states to the power of the nation.

The argument is pressed upon us, however, that the end to be served by the Milk Control Act is something more than the economic welfare of the farmers or of any other class or classes. The end to be served is the maintenance of a regular and adequate supply of pure and wholesome milk; the supply being put in jeopardy when the farmers of the state are unable to earn a living income. Price security, we are told, is only a special form of sanitary security; the economic motive is secondary and subordinate; the state intervenes to make its inhabitants healthy, and not to make them rich. On that assumption we are asked to say that intervention will be upheld as a valid exercise by the state of its internal police power, though there is an incidental obstruction to commerce between one state and another. This would be to eat up the rule under the guise of an exception. Economic welfare is always related to health, for there can be no health if men are starving. Let such an exception be admitted, and all that a state will have to do in times of stress and strain is to say that its farmers and merchants and workmen must be protected against competition from without, lest they go upon the poor relief lists or perish altogether. To give entrance to that excuse would be to invite a speedy end of our national solidarity. The Constitution was framed under the dominion of a political philosophy less parochial in range. It was framed upon the theory that the peoples of the several states must sink or swim together, and that in the long run prosperity and salvation are in union and not division.

We have dwelt up to this point upon the argument of the state that economic security for farmers in the milk shed may be a means of assuring to consumers a steady supply of a food of prime necessity. There is, however, another argument which seeks to establish a relation between the well-being of the producer and the quality of the product. We are told that farmers who are underpaid will be tempted to save the expense of sanitary precautions. This temptation will affect the farmers outside New York as well as those within it. For that reason, the exclusion of milk paid for in Vermont below the New York minimum will tend, it is said, to impose a higher standard of quality and thereby promote health. We think the argument will not avail to justify impediments to commerce between the states. There is neither evidence nor presumption that the same minimum prices established by order of the board for producers in New York are necessary also for producers in Vermont. But apart from such defects of proof, the evils springing from uncared for cattle must be remedied by measures of repression more direct and certain than the creation of a parity of prices between New York and other states. Appropriate certificates may be exacted from farmers in Vermont and elsewhere; milk may be excluded if necessary safeguards have been omitted; but commerce between the states is burdened unduly when one state regulates by indirection the prices to be paid to producers in another, in the faith that augmentation of prices will lift up the level of economic welfare, and that this will stimulate the observance of sanitary requirements in the preparation of the product. The next step would be to condition importation upon proof of a satisfactory wage scale in factory or shop, or even upon proof of the profits of the business. Whatever relation there may be between earnings and sanitation is too remote and indirect to justify obstructions to the normal flow of commerce in its movement between states. One state may not put pressure of that sort upon others to reform their economic standards. If farmers or manufacturers in Vermont are abandoning farms or factories, or are failing to maintain them properly, the Legislature of Vermont and not that of New York must supply the fitting remedy.

Many cases from our reports are cited by counsel for the state. They do not touch the case at hand. The line of division between direct and indirect restraints of commerce involves in its marking a reference to considerations of degree. Even so, the borderland is wide between the restraints upheld as incidental and those attempted here. Subject to the paramount power of the Congress, a state may regulate the importation of unhealthy swine or cattle. Things such as these are not proper subjects of commerce, and there is no unreasonable interference when they are inspected and excluded. So a state may protect its inhabitants against the fraudulent substitution, by deceptive coloring or otherwise, of one article for another. It may give protection to travelers against the dangers of overcrowded highways and protection to its residents against unnecessary noises. None of these statutes—inspection laws, game laws, laws intended to curb fraud or exterminate disease—approaches in drastic quality the statute here in controversy which would neutralize the economic consequences of free trade among the states.

Second. There was error in refusing an injunction to restrain the enforcement of the act in its application to milk in bottles to be sold by the importer.

The test of the "original package," is not inflexible and final for the transactions of interstate commerce, whatever may be its validity for commerce with other countries. There are purposes for which merchandise, transported from another state, will be treated as a part of the general mass of property at the state of destination though still in the original containers. This is so, for illustration, where merchandise so contained is subjected to a nondiscriminatory property tax which it bears equally with other merchandise produced within the state. There are other purposes for which the same merchandise will have the benefit of the protection appropriate to interstate commerce, though the original packages have been broken and the contents subdivided. "A state tax upon merchandise brought in from another state or upon its sales, whether in original packages or not, after it has reached its destination and is in a state of rest, is lawful only when the tax is not discriminating in its incidence against the merchandise because of its origin in another state."[1] In brief, the test of the original package is not an ultimate principle. It is an illustration of a principle. It marks a convenient boundary, and one sufficiently precise save in exceptional conditions. What is ultimate is the principle that one state in its dealings with another may not place itself in a position of economic isolation. Formulas and catchwords are subordinate to this overmastering requirement. Neither the power to tax nor the police power may be used by the state of destination with the aim and effect of establishing an economic barrier against competition with the products of another state or the labor of its residents. Restrictions so contrived are an unreasonable clog upon the mobility of commerce. They set up what is equivalent to a rampart of customs duties designed to neutralize advantages belonging to the place of origin. They are thus hostile in conception as well as burdensome in result. The form of the packages in such circumstances is immaterial, whether they are original or broken. The importer must be free from imposts framed for the very purpose of suppressing competition from without and leading inescapably to the suppression so intended.

The statute here in controversy will not survive that test. A dealer in milk buys it in Vermont at prices there prevailing. He brings it to New York, and is told he may not sell it if he removes it from the can and pours it into bottles. He may not do this for the reason that milk in Vermont is cheaper than milk in New York at the regimented prices, and New York is moved by the desire to protect her inhabitants from the cut prices and other consequences of Vermont competition. To overcome that competition a common incident of ownership, the privilege of sale in convenient receptacles, is denied to one who has bought in interstate commerce. He may not sell on any terms to any one, whether the orders were given in advance or came to him thereafter. The decisions of this court as to the significance of the original package in

---

[1]*Sonneborn Bros.* v. *Cureton,* reported in Volume 262 United States Reports 516.

interstate transactions were not meant to be a cover for retortion or suppression.

It is one thing for a state to exact adherence by an importer to fitting standards of sanitation before the products of the farm or factory may be sold in its markets. It is a very different thing to establish a wage scale or a scale of prices for use in other states, and to bar the sale of the products, whether in the original packages or in others, unless the scale has been observed.

"DEFENDANTS CHARGED WITH CRIME ARE AS SLOW AS ARE MEN GENERALLY TO BORROW TROUBLE OF THE FUTURE"

Herndon v. *State of Georgia,* 295 United States Reports 441 (1935)

Angelo Herndon was sentenced to a term of imprisonment after conviction by a jury in a Georgia Court of an attempt to incite insurrection by trying to induce others to join in combined resistance to the authority of the state, to be accomplished by violence. This conviction was affirmed by the highest Court of Georgia. Herndon attempted to appeal to the Supreme Court of the United States, upon the ground that the statute violated the due process clause of the Fourteenth Amendment of the Federal Constitution. He claimed that the statute was so indefinite in its definition of "insurrection" that it constituted an unconstitutional restraint upon freedom of speech.

Before the Supreme Court of the United States, the state urged that the Federal courts could not take jurisdiction because no Federal question was seasonably raised in the State courts or passed upon by the State courts. The fact of the matter was that a preliminary attack upon the indictment on the ground of unconstitutionality had been made and the contention was overruled but according to the majority opinion of the Supreme Court this adverse action of the trial court was not preserved by proper exception or raised as error in the record of appeal as the rules of practice in Georgia required. Under these circumstances the highest court of Georgia had declined to reverse that ruling of the trial court.

It was Herndon's contention that the raising of the constitutional question before the Supreme Court of the United States was the first opportunity he had had to do so before any appellate court. The trial court had instructed the jury that the evidence would not be sufficient to convict Herndon if it did not indicate that his advocacy would be acted upon *immediately.* When the highest court in Georgia passed upon the evidence it interpreted the statute as not requiring that an insurrection should follow instantly, or at any given time, but that it would be sufficient if the defendant intended it to happen *at any time* as a result of his activities, and upon that construction the Georgia appellate court determined the sufficiency of the evidence against Herndon. Since it was from the latter construction that the present appeal was taken, the defendant claimed he could not have known of this until after the ruling had been handed down.

The majority of the Supreme Court of the United States admitted that under that reasoning, the defendant would be right but it pointed out that several months before the highest court of Georgia had spoken in this case the court of Georgia in another case had interpreted the statute in the same way as it did in the present instance. Consequently Herndon could not plead ignorance of the attitude of the court and was therefore bound to anticipate the probability of a similar ruling in his own case.

Four judges of the court did not agree with the majority contention that Herndon had failed to raise the Federal question at the first opportunity. The opinion of the minority (concurred in by Mr. Justice Brandeis and Mr. Justice Stone) was written by Mr. Justice Cardozo.

MR. JUSTICE CARDOZO (dissenting) * * *

I hold the view that the protection of the Constitution was seasonably invoked and that the court should proceed to an adjudication of the merits. Where the merits lie I do not now consider, for in the view of the majority the merits are irrelevant. My protest is confined to the disclaimer of jurisdiction. The settled doctrine is that when a constitutional privilege or immunity has been denied for the first time by a ruling made upon appeal, a litigant thus surprised may challenge the unexpected ruling by a motion for rehearing, and the challenge will be timely. Within that settled doctrine the cause is rightly here.

Though the merits are now irrelevant, the controversy must be so far explained as to show how a federal question has come into the record. The appellant insists that words do not amount to an incitement to revolution, or to an attempt at such incitement, unless they are of such a nature and are used in such circumstances as to create "a clear and present danger" of bringing the prohibited result to pass. He insists that without this limitation a statute so lacking in precision as the one applied against him here is an unconstitutional restraint upon historic liberties of speech. For present purposes it is unimportant whether his argument be sound or shallow. At least it has color of support in words uttered from this bench, and uttered with intense conviction. The court might be unwilling, if it were to pass to a decision of the merits, to fit the words so uttered within the framework of this case. What the appellant is now asking of us is an opportunity to be heard. That privilege is his unless he has thrown it away by silence and acquiescence when there was need of speech and protest.

We are told by the state that the securities of the Constitution should have been invoked upon the trial. The presiding judge should have been warned that a refusal to accept the test of clear and present danger would be a rejection of the restraints of the Fourteenth Amendment. But the trial judge had not refused to accept the test proposed; on the contrary, he had accepted it and even gone a step beyond. In substance he had charged that even a present "danger" would not suffice, if there was not also an expectation, and one grounded in reason, that the insurrection would begin at once. It is novel doctrine that a defendant who has had the benefit of all he asks, and indeed of a good deal more, must place a statement on the record that if some other court at some other time shall read the statute differently, there will be a denial of liberties that at the moment of the protest are unchallenged and intact. Defendants charged with crime are as slow as are men generally to borrow trouble of the future.

We are told, however, that protest, even if unnecessary at the trial, should have been made by an assignment of error or in some other appropriate way in connection with the appeal, and this for the reason that by that time, if not before, the defendant was chargeable with knowledge as a result of two decisions of the highest court of Georgia that the statute was destined to be given another meaning. The decisions relied upon are Carr v. State (No. 1), and Carr v. State (No. 2).[1] The first of these cases was decided in November, 1932, before the trial of the appellant, which occurred in January, 1933. The second was decided in March, 1933, after the appellant had been convicted, but

---

[1]Both cases are reported in Volume 176 of the Georgia Reports. The first is at page 55 and the second at page 747.

before the denial or submission of his motion for a new trial. Neither is decisive of the question before us now.

Carr v. State, No. 1, came up on demurrer to an indictment. The prosecution was under section 58 of the Penal Code, which makes it a crime to circulate revolutionary documents. All that was held was that upon the face of the indictment there had been a wilful incitement to violence, sufficient, if proved, to constitute a crime. The opinion contains an extract covering about four pages from the opinion of this court in Gitlow v. New York. Imbedded in that long quotation are the words now pointed to by the state as decisive of the case at hand. They are the words of Sanford, J., writing for this court.[1] "The immediate danger is none the less real and substantial, because the effect of a given utterance cannot be accurately foreseen." A state "cannot reasonably be required to defer the adoption of measures for its own peace and safety until the revolutionary utterances lead to actual disturbances of the public peace or imminent and immediate danger of its own destruction; but it may, in the exercise of its judgment, suppress the threatened danger in its incipiency."

To learn the meaning of these words in their application to the Georgia statute we must read them in their setting. Sanford, J., had pointed out that the statute then before him, the New York criminal anarchy act, forbade the teaching and propagation by spoken word or writing of a particular form of doctrine, carefully defined and after such definition denounced on reasonable grounds as fraught with peril to the state. There had been a determination by the state through its legislative body that such utterances "are so inimical to the general welfare and involve such danger of substantive evil that they may be penalized in the exercise of its police power." In such circumstances "the question whether any specific utterance coming within the prohibited class is likely, in and of itself, to bring about the substantive evil, is not open to consideration. It is sufficient that the statute itself be

[1]Reported in Volume 268 United States Reports 652. The quotations are at page 669 et seq.

constitutional and that the use of the language comes within its prohibition." In effect the words had been placed upon an expurgatory index. At the same time the distinction was sharply drawn between statutes condemning utterances identified by a description of their meaning and statutes condemning them by reference to the results that they are likely to induce. "It is clear that the question in such cases [i. e. where stated doctrines are denounced] is entirely different from that involved in those cases where the statute merely prohibits certain acts involving the danger of substantive evil, without any reference to language itself, and it is sought to apply its provisions to language used by the defendant for the purpose of bringing about the prohibited results."

The effect of all this was to leave the question open whether in cases of the second class, in cases, that is to say, where the unlawful quality of words is to be determined not upon their face but in relation to their consequences, the opinion in Schenck v. United States,[1] supplies the operative rule. The conduct charged to this appellant —in substance an attempt to enlarge the membership of the Communist party in the city of Atlanta—falls, it will be assumed, within the second of these groupings, but plainly is outside the first. There is no reason to believe that the Supreme Court of Georgia, when it quoted from the opinion in Gitlow's case, rejected the restraints which the author of that opinion had placed upon his words. For the decision of the case before it there was no need to go so far. Circulation of documents with intent to incite to revolution had been charged in an indictment. The state had the power to punish such an act as criminal, or so the court had held. How close the nexus would have to be between the attempt and its projected consequences was matter for the trial.

Carr v. State, No. 2 like the case under review, was a prosecution under Penal Code, § 56 (not § 58), and like Carr v. State, No. 1, came up on demurrer. All that the

[1]Reported in Volume 249 United States Reports 47. "The question in every case is whether the words * * * create a clear and present danger that they will bring about the substantive evils that Congress has a right to prevent."

court held was that when attacked by demurrer the indictment would stand. This appears from the headnote, drafted by the court itself. After referring to this headnote, the court states that it may be "useful and salutary" to repeat what it had written in Carr v. State, No. 1. Thereupon it quotes copiously from its opinion in that case including the bulk of the same extracts from Gitlow v. New York. The extracts show upon their face that they have in view a statute denouncing a particular doctrine and prohibiting attempts to teach it. They give no test of the bond of union between an idea and an event.

What has been said as to the significance of the opinions in the two cases against Carr has confirmation in what happened when appellant was brought to trial. The judge who presided at that trial had the first of those opinions before him when he charged the jury, or so we may assume. He did not read it as taking from the state the burden of establishing a clear and present danger that insurrection would ensue as a result of the defendant's conduct. This is obvious from the fact that in his charge he laid that very burden on the state with emphasis and clarity. True, he did not have before him the opinion in prosecution No. 2, for it had not yet been handed down, but if he had seen it, he could not have gathered from its quotation of the earlier case that it was announcing novel doctrine.

From all this it results that Herndon, this appellant, came into the highest court of Georgia without notice that the statute defining his offense was to be given a new meaning. There had been no rejection, certainly no unequivocal rejection, of the doctrine of Schenck v. United States, which had been made the law of the case by the judge presiding at his trial. For all that the record tells us, the prosecuting officer acquiesced in the charge, and did not ask the appellate court to apply a different test. In such a situation the appellant might plant himself as he did on the position that on the case given to the jury his guilt had not been proved. He was not under a duty to put before his judges the possibility of a definition less favorable to himself, and make an argument against it, when there had been no threat of any change, still less any forecast of its form or measure. He might wait until the law of the case had been rejected by the reviewing court before insisting that the effect would be an invasion of his constitutional immunities. If invasion should occur, a motion for rehearing diligently pressed thereafter would be seasonable notice. It is the doctrine that must prevail if the great securities of the Constitution are not to be lost in a web of procedural entanglements.

New strength is given to considerations such as these when one passes to a closer view of just what the Georgia court did in its definition of the statute. We have heard that the meaning had been fixed by what had been held already in Carr v. State, and that thereby the imminence of the danger had been shown to be unrelated to innocence or guilt. But if that is the teaching of those cases, it was discarded by the very judgment now subjected to review. True, the Georgia court, by its first opinion in the case at hand, did prescribe a test that, if accepted, would bar the consideration of proximity in time. "It is immaterial whether the authority of the state was in danger of being subverted or that an insurrection actually occurred or was impending." "Force must have been contemplated, but * * * the statute does not include either its occurrence or its imminence as an ingredient of the particular offense charged." It would not be "necessary to guilt that the alleged offender should have intended that an insurrection should follow instantly or at any given time, but it would be sufficient that he intended it to happen at any time, as a result of his influence, by those whom he sought to incite." On the motion for a rehearing the Georgia court repelled with a little heat the argument of counsel that these words were to be taken literally, without "the usual reasonable implications." "The phrase 'at any time' as criticized in the motion for rehearing was not intended to mean at any time in the indefinite future, or at any possible later time, however remote." "On the contrary, the phrase 'at any time' was necessarily intended, and should have been understood, to mean within a reasonable time; that is, within such time as one's persuasion or other adopted means might reasonably be expected to be directly operative in causing an insurrection." "Under the statute as thus interpreted, we say, as before, that the evidence was sufficient to authorize the conviction."

Here is an unequivocal rejection of the test of clear and present danger, yet a denial also of responsibility without boundaries in time. True, in this rejection, the court disclaimed a willingness to pass upon the question as one of constitutional law, assigning as a reason that no appeal to the Constitution had been made upon the trial or then considered by the judge. Such a rule of state practice may have the effect of attaching a corresponding limitation to the jurisdiction of this court where fault can fairly be imputed to an appellant for the omission to present the question sooner. No such consequence can follow where the ruling of the trial judge has put the Constitution out of the case and made an appeal to its provisions impertinent and futile. In such circumstances, the power does not reside in a state by any rule of local practice to restrict the jurisdiction of this court in the determination of a constitutional question brought into the case thereafter. If the rejection of the test of clear and present danger was a denial of fundamental liberties, the path is clear for us to say so.

What was brought into the case upon the motion for rehearing was a standard wholly novel, the expectancy of life to be ascribed to the persuasive power of an idea. The defendant had no opportunity in the state court to prepare his argument accordingly. He had no opportunity to argue from the record that guilt was not a reasonable inference, or one permitted by the Constitution, on the basis of that test any more than on the basis of others discarded as unfitting. The argument thus shut out is submitted to us now. Will men "judging in calmness" say of the defendant's conduct as shown forth in the pages of this record that it was an attempt to stir up revolution through the power of his persuasion and within the time when that persuasion might be expected to endure? If men so judging will say yes, will the Constitution of the United States uphold a reading of the statute that will lead to that response? Those are the questions that the defendant lays before us after conviction of a crime punishable by death in the discretion of the jury. I think he should receive an answer.

Mr. Justice BRANDEIS and Mr. Justice STONE join in this opinion.[1]

---

[1]After this decision by the majority, Herndon sought a writ of habeas corpus. The Georgia courts then considered and disposed of the defendant's claim based upon the Federal Constitution. This gave the Federal courts jurisdiction. Thus when the highest Georgia court refused him a discharge upon habeas corpus, Herndon once again went into the Supreme Court of the United States. The Supreme Court held by a vote of 5 to 4 (the dissenters were Justices Van Devanter, McReynolds, Sutherland and Butler) that the Georgia statute under which the defendant was convicted, was so vague and indeterminate in the standard of guilt therein prescribed—the statute defined the crime of attempting to incite insurrection—that it violated the freedom of speech and assembly protected by the Fourteenth Amendment. The majority opinion was written by Mr. Justice Roberts. This case is reported in Volume 301 United States Reports 242.

"RECKLESSNESS AND DECEIT DO NOT AUTOMATICALLY EXCUSE THEMSELVES BY NOTICE OF REPENTANCE"

Jones v. *Securities and Exchange Commission,* 298 United States Reports 1 (1936)

The Securities Exchange Act of 1934 provided that before certain types of stock issues could be floated for public subscription, the issuer was to file with the Securities and Exchange Commission certain designated information with respect to the stock and the assets supporting such stock. Penalties were to be enforced for willful violations of any of the provisions of the act or of the regulations promulgated by the commission. The commission was given the power to administer oaths, subpoena witnesses, take evidence and require the production of books and papers.

On May 4, 1935, J. Edward Jones filed with the commission a registration statement covering a proposed issue of trustee certificates. This statement under the terms of the act was to become effective twenty days later. On the nineteenth day the commission notified Jones that his statement appeared to be untrue and that it omitted material facts required and in addition a date in June was fixed for a hearing at the office of the commission. A few days before this date arrived a subpoena was issued commanding Jones to appear before the commission to testify with respect to his registration statement and bring with him certain records dealing with the proposed issue. Thereupon Jones wrote to the commission formally withdrawing his application for registration and his counsel asked for an order from the commission, permitting this withdrawal and dismissing the registration proceeding. The commission refused to grant this order and began proceedings in the Federal Court to require Jones to appear before the Commission to give evidence with respect to his registration statement. The District Court and Circuit Court of Appeals both sustained the request of the commission. Jones took an appeal to the Supreme Court of the United States. The latter court by a decision of 6 to 3, Mr. Justice Sutherland writing for the majority, reversed the lower Courts upon the ground that the power of the commission can be no greater than that of a court, and that consequently Jones had, as he would have in an ordinary action, an unqualified right to have his proceeding terminated in the absence of proof that legal prejudice would result to others by such termination. In this case, said the court, there was no possibility of prejudice to the public or investors. The dissenting opinion was written by

Mr. Justice Cardozo, and concurred in by Mr. Justice Brandeis, and Mr. Justice Stone.

MR. JUSTICE CARDOZO (dissenting):

I am unable to concur in the opinion of the court. * * *

Recklessness and deceit do not automatically excuse themselves by note of repentance. Under section 24 of the Act, 15, there is the possibility, at times the likelihood, of penal liability. A statement willfully false or willfully defective is a penal offense to be visited, upon conviction, with fine or imprisonment. Under section 12, there is the possibility, if not the likelihood, of liability for damages. The statement now in question had been effective for over twenty days, and the witness did not couple his notice of withdrawal with an affidavit or even a declaration that securities had not been sold. Nor is the statute lacking in machinery with which to set these liabilities in motion upon appropriate occasion. There will be only partial attainment of the ends of public justice unless retribution for the past is added to prevention for the future. But the opinion of the court teaches us that however flagrant the offense and however laudable the purpose to uncover and repress it, investigations will be thwarted on the instant when once the statement of the registrant has been effectively withdrawn. If that is so, or even indeed if the effect of the retraction is to embarrass the inquiry—to cloud the power to continue—the fairness of the rule is proved out of the mouths of its accusers. If such consequences are inherent in a privilege of withdrawal indiscriminately bestowed, there is need of some restraint upon the power of the wrongdoer to mitigate the penalties attaching to his wrong. Shall the truth be shown forth or buried in the archives? The commission is to determine in the light of all the circumstances, including its information as to the conduct of the applicant, whether the public interest will be prompted by forgetting and forgiving.

The objection is inadequate that an investigation directed to the discovery of a crime is one not for the commission, but for the prosecuting officer. There are times when the functions of the two will coincide or overlap. Congress had made it plain that any inquiry helpful in the enforcement of the statute may be pursued by the commission, though conduct punishable as a crime may thereby be uncovered. Indeed, the act is explicit, that a witness is not excused from testifying on the ground that the testimony required of him may tend to incriminate him or expose him to a penalty or forfeiture. He may, however, claim his privilege, and if then compelled to testify, may not be prosecuted thereafter for any matter thus revealed. All this is far from proving that there can be no practical advantage in keeping the proceeding open. Aside from the possibility of civil liability, the offender may not choose to claim the privilege, and even if he does and is then excused from testifying, other witnesses may be available, for example, employes, who are not implicated in the offense and who can bring the facts to view. Moreover, amnesty for one offender may mean conviction for another, an associate in the crime. Inquiry by the commission is thus more penetrating and efficient than one by a grand jury where there is no statutory grant of amnesty to compel confederates to speak. More important still, the enforcement of the act is aided when guilt is exposed to the censure of the world, though the witness in the act of speaking may make punishment impossible. It is no answer to all this that upon the record now presented a crime has not been proved or even definitely charged. An investigator is not expected to prove or charge at the beginning the offenses which he has reason to suspect will be uncovered at the end. The petition in behalf of the commission enumerates one by one the false statements and the omissions imputed to the registrant. Some at least are of such a nature that if chargeable to him at all, they can hardly have been made otherwise than with criminal intent. To give the investigating officer an opportunity to reach down into the hidden wells of knowledge and the more hidden wells of motive is the very purpose of the regulation by which the proceeding is kept open after the registrant has tried to end it.

The opinion of the court reminds us of the dangers that wait upon the abuse of power by officialdom unchained. The warning is so fraught with truth that it can never be untimely. But timely too is the reminder, as a host of impoverished investors will be ready to attest, that there are dangers in untruths and half truths, designed to be passed on for the guidance of confiding buyers, are to be ranked as peccadillos, or even perhaps as part of the amenities of business. When wrongs such as these have been committed or attempted, they must be dragged to light and pilloried. To permit an offending registrant to stifle an inquiry by precipitate retreat on the eve of his exposure is to give immunity to guilt; to encourage falsehood and evasion; to invite the cunning and unscrupulous to gamble with detection. If withdrawal without leave may check investigation before securities have been issued, it may do as much thereafter, unless indeed consistency be thrown to the winds, for by the teaching of the decision withdrawal without leave is equivalent to a stop order, with the result that forthwith there is nothing to investigate. The statute and its sanctions become the sport of clever knaves.

Appeal is vaguely made to some constitutional immunity, whether express or implied is not stated with distinctness. It cannot be an immunity from the unreasonable search or seizure of papers or effects: the books and documents of the witness are unaffected by the challenged order. It cannot be an immunity from impertinent intrusion into matters of strictly personal concern: the intimacies of private business lose their self-regarding quality after they have been spread upon official records to induce official action. If the immunity rests upon some express provision of the Constitution, the opinion of the court does not point us to the article or section. If its source is to be found in some impalpable essence, the spirit of the Constitution or the philosophy of government favored by the Fathers, one may take leave to deny that there is anything in that philosophy or spirit whereby the signer of a statement filed with a regulatory body to induce official action is protected against inquiry into his own purpose to deceive. The argument for immunity lays hold of strange analogies. A commission which is without coercive powers, which cannot arrest or amerce or imprison though a crime has been uncovered or even punish for contempt, but can only inquire and report, the propriety of every question in the course of the inquiry being subject to the supervision of the ordinary courts of justice, is likened with denunciatory fervor to the Star Chamber of the Stuarts. Historians may find hyperbole in the sanguinary simile.

The rule now assailed was wisely conceived and lawfully adopted to foil the plans of knaves intent upon obscuring or suppressing the knowledge of their knavery.

The witness was under a duty to respond to the subpoena.

"A GREAT PRINCIPLE OF CONSTITUTIONAL LAW IS NOT SUSCEPTIBLE OF COMPREHENSIVE STATEMENT IN AN ADJECTIVE"

Carter v. *Carter Oil Co.,* 298 United States Reports 238 (1936)

In 1935 the Bituminous Coal Conservation Act was passed in order to stabilize the bituminous coal mining industry, and to promote its interstate commerce. The act provided for cooperative marketing of such coal, and one of its purposes was to conserve the natural resources. Bituminous coal was declared to be affected with a national public interest. The statute also included provisions covering minimum wages, wage agreements, maximum hours of labor, and collective bargaining powers of employees. It also provided for a price fixing arrangement.

A proceeding was brought to enjoin the federal officials from proceeding under the act and the Supreme Court majority held as follows: that the affirmation in the act that distribution of bituminous coal was of a national interest affecting the general welfare of the nation and interstate commerce was not conclusive upon the court; that beneficent aims, however well directed, can never serve in place of constitutional power; that the powers exercised in the act exceeded the powers which the general government is permitted to exercise under the Federal Constitution; that the internal affairs of state governments were wrongfully affected; that the labor provisions were unconstitutional as interfering with personal liberty and private property; that the valid parts of the act were so interwoven with the invalid, that as a matter of statutory construction the whole statute had to fall.

The views of the majority as expressed by Mr. Justice Sutherland were strongly opposed by four justices of the Court: Chief Justice Hughes, and Justices Cardozo, Brandeis, and Stone. One dissenting opinion was written by the Chief Justice and the other by Mr. Justice Cardozo. The latter opinion follows:

MR. JUSTICE CARDOZO (dissenting) * * *

My conclusions compendiously stated are these:

(a) Part 2 of the statute sets up a valid system of price-fixing as applied to transactions in interstate commerce and to those in intrastate commerce where interstate commerce is directly or intimately affected. The prevailing opinion holds nothing to the contrary.

(b) Part 2, with its system of price-fixing, is separable from part 3, which contains the provisions as to labor considered and condemned in the opinion of the Court.

(c) Part 2 being valid, the complainants are under a duty to come in under the code, and are subject to a penalty if they persist in a refusal.

(d) The suits are premature in so far as they seek a judicial declaration as to the validity or invalidity of the regulations in respect of labor embodied in part 3. No opinion is expressed either directly or by implication as to those aspects of the case. It will be time enough to consider them when there is the threat or even the possibility of imminent enforcement. If that time shall arrive, protection will be given by clear provisions of the statute (section 3) against any adverse inference flowing from delay or acquiescence.

(e) The suits are not premature to the extent that they are intended to avert a present wrong, though the wrong upon analysis will be found to be unreal.

The complainants are asking for a decree to restrain the enforcement of the statute in all or any of its provisions on the ground that it is a void enactment, and void in all its parts. If some of its parts are valid and are separable from others that are or may be void, and if the parts upheld and separated are sufficient to sustain a regulatory penalty, the injunction may not issue and hence the suits must fail. There is no need when that conclusion has been reached to stir a step beyond. Of the provisions not considered, some may never take effect, at least in the absence of future happenings which are still uncertain and contingent. Some may operate in one way as to one group and in another way as to others according to particular conditions as yet unknown and unknowable. A decision in advance as to the operation and validity of separable provisions in varying contingencies is premature and hence unwise. "The Court will not 'anticipate a question of constitutional law in advance of the necessity of deciding it.' It is not the habit of the court to decide questions of a constitutional nature unless absolutely necessary to a decision of the case."[1] The moment we perceive that there are valid and separable portions, broad enough to lay the basis for a regulatory penalty, inquiry should halt. The complainants must conform to whatever is upheld, and as to parts excluded from the decision, especially if the parts are not presently effective, must make their protest in the future when the occasion or the need arises.

First. I am satisfied that the act is within the power of the central government in so far as it provides for minimum and maximum prices upon sales of bituminous coal in the transactions of interstate commerce and in those of intrastate commerce where interstate commerce is directly or intimately affected. Whether it is valid also in other provisions that have been considered and condemned in the opinion of the Court, I do not find it necessary to determine at this time. Silence must not be taken as importing acquiescence. Much would have to be written if the subject, even as thus restricted were to be explored through all its implications, historical and economic as well as strictly legal. The fact that the prevailing opinion leaves the price provisions open for consideration in the future makes it appropriate to forego a fullness of elaboration that might otherwise be necessary. As a system of price fixing, the act is challenged upon three grounds: (1) Because the governance of prices is not within the commerce clause; (2) because it is a denial of due process forbidden by the Fifth Amendment; and (3) because the standards for administrative action are indefinite, with the result that there has been an unlawful delegation of legislative power.

(1) With reference to the first objection, the obvious and sufficient answer is, so far as the act is directed to interstate transactions, that sales made in such conditions

---

[1]Per Brandeis, *J.*, in *Ashwander* v. *Tennessee Valley Authority*, reported in Volume 297 United States Reports 288, 346.

constitute interstate commerce, and do not merely "affect" it. To regulate the price for such transactions is to regulate commerce itself, and not alone its antecedent conditions or its ultimate consequences. The very act of sale is limited and governed. Prices in interstate transactions may not be regulated by the states. They must therefore be subject to the power of the Nation unless they are to be withdrawn altogether from governmental supervision. If such a vacuum were permitted, many a public evil incidental to interstate transactions would be left without a remedy. This does not mean, of course, that prices may be fixed for arbitrary reasons or in an arbitrary way. The commerce power of the Nation is subject to the requirement of due process like the police power of the states. Heed must be given to similar considerations of social benefit or detriment in marking the division between reason and oppression. The evidence is overwhelming that congress did not ignore those considerations in the adoption of this act. What is to be said in that regard may conveniently be postponed to the part of the opinion dealing with the Fifth Amendment.

Regulation of prices being an exercise of the commerce power in respect of interstate transactions, the question remains whether it comes within that power as applied to intrastate sales where interstate prices are directly or intimately affected. Mining and agriculture and manufacture are not interstate commerce considered by themselves, yet their relation to that commerce may be such that for the protection of the one there is need to regulate the other. Sometimes it is said that the relation must be "direct" to bring that power into play. In many circumstances such a description will be sufficiently precise to meet the needs of the occasion. But a great principle of constitutional law is not susceptible of comprehensive statement in an adjective. The underlying thought is merely this, that "the law is not indifferent to considerations of degree."[1] It cannot be indifferent to them with-

[1]*Schechter Poultry Corporation* v. *United States,* reported in Volume 295 United States Reports 495, 554.

out an expansion of the commerce clause that would absorb or imperil the reserved powers of the states. At times, the waves of causation will have radiated so far that their undulatory motion, if discernible at all, will be too faint or obscure, too broken by cross-currents, to be heeded by the law. In such circumstances the holding is not directed at prices or wages considered in the abstract, but at prices or wages in particular conditions. The relation may be tenuous or the opposite according to the facts. Always the setting of the facts is to be viewed if one would know the closeness of the tie. Perhaps, if one group of adjectives is to be chosen in preference to another, "intimate" and "remote" will be found to be as good as any. At all events, "direct" and "indirect," even if accepted as sufficient, must not be read too narrowly. A survey of the cases shows that the words have been interpreted with suppleness of adaptation and flexibility of meaning. The power is as broad as the need that evokes it.

One of the most common and typical instances of a relation characterized as direct has been that between interstate and intrastate rates for carriers by rail where the local rates are so low as to divert business unreasonably from interstate competitors. In such circumstances Congress has the power to protect the business of its carriers against disintegrating encroachments. To be sure, the relation even then may be characterized as indirect if one is nice or over-literal in the choice of words. Strictly speaking, the intrastate rates have a primary effect upon the intrastate traffic and not upon any other, though the repercussions of the competitive system may lead to secondary consequences affecting interstate traffic also. What the cases really mean is that the casual relation in such circumstances is so close and intimate and obvious as to permit it to be called direct without subjecting the word to an unfair or excessive strain. There is a like immediacy here. Within rulings the most orthodox, the prices for intrastate sales of coal have so inescapable a relation to those for interstate sales that a system of regulation for transactions of the one class is necessary to give adequate protection to the system of regulation adopted for the other. The argument is strongly pressed by intervening counsel that this may not be true in all communities or in exceptional conditions. If so, the operators unlawfully affected may show that the act to that extent is invalid as to them. Such partial invalidity is plainly an insufficient basis for a declaration that the act is invalid as a whole.

What has been said in this regard is said with added certitude when complainants' business is considered in the light of the statistics exhibited in the several records. The Carter Company has its mines in West Virginia; the mines of the other companies are located in Kentucky. In each of those states, moreover, coal from other regions is purchased in large quantities, and is thus brought into competition with the coal locally produced. Plainly, it is impossible to say either from the statute itself or from any figures laid before us that interstate sales will not be prejudicially affected in West Virginia and Kentucky if intrastate prices are maintained on a lower level. If it be assumed for present purposes that there are other states or regions where the effect may be different, the complainants are not the champions of any rights except their own.

(2) The commerce clause being accepted as a sufficient source of power, the next inquiry must be whether the power has been exercised consistently with the Fifth Amendment. In the pursuit of that inquiry, Nebbia v. New York,[1] lays down the applicable principle. There a statute of New York prescribing a minimum price for milk was upheld against the objection that price-fixing was forbidden by the Fourteenth Amendment. We found it a sufficient reason to uphold the challenged system that "the conditions or practices in an industry make unrestricted competition an inadequate safeguard of the consumer's interests, produce waste harmful to the public, threaten ultimately to cut off the supply of a commodity

[1]Reported in Volume 291 United States Reports 502.

needed by the public, or portend the destruction of the industry itself."

All this may be said, and with equal, if not greater force, of the conditions and practices in the bituminous coal industry, not only at the enactment of this statute in August, 1935, but for many years before. Overproduction was at a point where free competition had been degraded into anarchy. Prices had been cut so low that profit had become impossible for all except a lucky handful. Wages came down along with prices and with profits. There were strikes, at times nation-wide in extent, at other times spreading over broad areas and many mines, with the accompaniment of violence and bloodshed and misery and bitter feeling. The sordid tale is unfolded in many a document and treatise. During the twenty-three years between 1913 and 1935, there were nineteen invstigations or hearings by Congress or by specially created commissions with reference to conditions in the coal mines. The hope of betterment was faint unless the industry could be subjected to the compulsion of a code. In the weeks immediately preceding the passage of this act the country was threatened once more with a strike of ominous proportions. The plight of the industry was not merely a menace to owners and to mine workers, it was and had long been a menace to the public, deeply concerned in a steady and uniform supply of a fuel so vital to the national economy.

Congress was not condemned to inaction in the face of price wars and wage wars so pregnant with disaster. Commerce had been choked and burdened; its normal flow had been diverted from one state to another; there had been bankruptcy and waste and ruin alike for capital and for labor. The liberty protected by the Fifth Amendment does not include the right to persist in this anarchic riot. "When industry is grievously hurt, when producing concerns fail, when unemployment mounts and communities dependent upon profitable production are prostrated, the wells of commerce go dry."[1] The free competition so

[1] *Appalachian Coals, Inc.* v. *United States,* reported in Volume 288 United States Reports 344, 372.

often figured as a social good imports order and moderation and a decent regard for the welfare of the group. There is testimony in these records, testimony even by the assailants of the statute, that only through a system of regulated prices can the industry be stabilized and set upon the road of orderly and peaceful progress. If further facts are looked for, they are narrated in the findings as well as in Congressional Reports and a mass of public records. After making every allowance for difference of opinion as to the most efficient cure, the student of the subject is confronted with the indisputable truth that there were ills to be corrected, and ills that had a direct relation to the maintenance of commerce among the states without friction or diversion. An evil existing, and also the power to correct it, the lawmakers were at liberty to use their own discretion in the selection of the means.

(3) Finally, and in answer to the third objection to the statute in its price-fixing provisions, there has been no excessive delegation of legislative power. The prices to be fixed by the district boards and the commission must conform to the following standards: They must be just and equitable; they must take account of the weighted average cost of production for each minimum price area; they must not be unduly prejudicial or preferential as between districts or as between producers within a district; and they must reflect as nearly as possible the relative market value of the various kinds, qualities, and sizes of coal, at points of delivery in each common consuming market area; to the end of affording the producers in the several districts substantially the same opportunity to dispose of their coals on a competitive basis as has heretofore existed. The minimum for any district shall yield a return, per net ton, not less than the weighted average of the total costs per net ton of the tonnage of the minimum price area; the maximum for any mine, if a maximum is fixed, shall yield a return not less than cost plus a reasonable profit. Reasonable prices can as easily be ascertained for coal as for the carriage of passengers or property under the Interstate Commerce Act

or for the services of brokers in the stockyards, or for the use of dwellings under the Emergency Rent Laws, adopted at a time of excessive scarcity, when the laws of supply and demand no longer gave a measure for the ascertainment of the reasonable. The standards established by this act are quite as definite as others that have had the approval of this court. Certainly a bench of judges, not experts in the coal business, cannot say with assurance that members of a commission will be unable, when advised and informed by others experienced in the industry, to make the standards workable, or to overcome through the development of an administrative technique many obstacles and difficulties that might be baffling or confusing to inexperience or ignorance.

Second. The next inquiry must be whether section 4, part 1 of the statute which creates the administrative agencies, and part 2 which has to do in the main with the price-fixing machinery, as well as preliminary sections levying a tax or penalty, are separable from part 3 which deals with labor relations in the industry with the result that what is earlier would stand if what is later were to fall.

The statute prescribes the rule by which construction shall be governed. "If any provision of this Act [chapter], or the application thereof to any person or circumstances, is held invalid, the remainder of the Act [chapter] and the application of such provisions to other persons or circumstances shall not be affected thereby." The rule is not read as an inexorable mandate. It creates a "presumption of divisibility," which is not applied mechanically or in a manner to frustrate the intention of the law-makers. Even so, the burden is on the litigant who would escape its operation. Here the probabilities of intention are far from overcoming the force of presumption. They fortify and confirm it. A confirmatory token is the formal division of the statute into "parts" separately numbered. Part 3 which deals with labor is physically separate from everything that goes before it. But more convincing than the evidences of form and structure, the division into chapters and sections and paragraphs, each with its proper subject matter, are the evidences of plan and function. Part 2, which deals with prices, is to take effect at once, or as soon as the administrative agencies have finished their administrative work. Part 3 in some of its most significant provisions, the section or sub-division in respect of wages and the hours of labor, may never take effect at all. This is clear beyond the need for argument from the mere reading of the statute. The maximum hours of labor may be fixed by agreement between the producers of more than two-thirds of the annual national tonnage production for the preceding calendar year and the representatives of more than one-half of the mine workers. Wages may be fixed by agreement or agreements negotiated by collective bargaining in any district or group of two or more districts between representatives of producers of more than two-thirds of the annual tonnage production of such districts or each of such districts in a contracting group during the preceding calendar year, and representatives of the majority of the mine workers therein. It is possible that none of these agreements as to hours and wages will ever be made. If made, they may not be completed for months or even years. In the meantime, however, the provisions of part 2 will be continuously operative, and will determine prices in the industry. Plainly, then, there was no intention on the part of the framers of the statute that prices should not be fixed if the provisions for wages or hours of labor were found to be invalid.

Undoubtedly the rules as to labor relations are important provisions of the statute. Undoubtedly the law-makers were anxious that provisions so important should have the force of law. But they announced with all the directness possible for words that they would keep what they could have if they could not have the whole. Stabilizing prices would go a long way toward stabilizing labor relations by giving the producers capacity to pay a living wage. To hold otherwise is to ignore the whole history of mining. All in vain have official committees inquired and reported in thousands of printed pages if this lesson has been lost. In the face of that history the Court is now holding that Congress would have been unwilling to give the force of law to the provisions of part 2, which were to take effect at once, if it could not have part 3, which in the absence of agreement between the employers and the miners would never take effect at all. Indeed, the prevailing opinion goes so far, is seems, as to insist that if the least provision of the statute in any of the three chapters is to be set aside as void, the whole statute must go down, for the reason that everything from end to end, or everything at all events beginning with section 4, is part of the Bituminous Coal Code, to be swallowed at a single draught, without power in the commission or even in the court to abate a jot or tittle. One can only wonder what is left of the "presumption of divisibility" which the lawmakers were at pains to establish later on. Codes under the National Recovery Act[1] are not a genuine analogy. The Recovery Act made it mandatory that every code should contain provisions as to labor, including wages and hours, and left everything else to the discretion of the codifiers. Wages and hours in such circumstances were properly described as "essential features of the plan, its very bone and sinew" which taken from the body of a code would cause it to collapse. Here on the face of the statute the price provisions of one part and the labor provisions of the other (the two to be administered by separate agencies) are made of equal rank.

What is true of the sections and subdivisions that deal with wages and the hours of labor is true also of the other provisions of the same chapter of the act. Employees are to have the right to organize and bargain collectively through representatives of their own choosing, and shall be free from interference, restraint, or coercion of employers, or their agents, in the designation of such representatives, or in self-organization or in other concerted activities for the purpose of collective bargaining or other

[1]Volume 15 United States Code Annotated, Section 707a.

mutual aid or protection, and no employee and no one seeking employment shall be required as a condition of employment to join any company union. No threat has been made by any one to do violence to the enjoyment of these immunities and privileges. No attempt to violate them may be made by the complainants or indeed by any one else in the term of four years during which the act is to remain in force. By another subdivision employees are to have the right of peaceable assemblage for the discussion of the principles of collective bargaining, shall be entitled to select their own check-weighman to inspect the weighing or measuring of coal, and shall not be required as a condition of employment to live in company houses or to trade at the store of the employer. None of these privileges or immunities has been threatened with impairment. No attempt to impair them may ever be made by any one.

Analysis of the statute thus leads to the conclusion that the provisions of part 3, so far as summarized, are separable from parts 1 and 2, and that any declaration in respect of their validity or invalidity under the commerce clause of the Constitution or under any other section will anticipate a controversy that may never become real. This being so, the proper course is to withhold an expression of opinion until expression becomes necessary. A different situation would be here if a portion of the statute, and a portion sufficient to uphold the regulatory penalty, did not appear to be valid. If the whole statute were a nullity, the complainants would be at liberty to stay the hand of the tax-gatherer threatening to collect the penalty, for collection in such circumstances would be a trespass, an illegal and forbidden act. It would be no answer to say that the complainants might avert the penalty by declaring themselves code members (section 3) and fighting the statute afterwards. In the circumstances supposed there would be no power in the national government to put that constraint upon them. The act by hypothesis being void in all its parts as a regulatory measure, the complainants might stand their ground, refuse to sign anything, and resist the onslaught of the collector as the aggression of a trespasser. But the case as it comes to us assumes a different posture, a posture inconsistent with the commission of a trespass either present or prospective. The hypothesis of complete invalidity has been shown to be unreal. The price provisions being valid, the complainants were under a duty to come in under the code, whether the provisions as to labor are valid or invalid, and their failure to come in has exposed them to a penalty lawfully imposed. They are thus in no position to restrain the acts of the collector, or to procure a judgment defeating the operation of the statute, whatever may be the fate hereafter of particular provisions not presently enforceable. The right to an injunction failing, the suits must be dismissed. Nothing more is needful—no pronouncement more elaborate—for a disposition of the controversy.

A last assault upon the statute is still to be repulsed. The complainants take the ground that the act may not coerce them through the imposition of a penalty into a seeming recognition or acceptance of the code, if any of the code provisions are invalid, however separable from others. I cannot yield assent to a position so extreme. It is one thing to impose a penalty for refusing to come in under a code that is void altogether. It is a very different thing if a penalty is imposed for refusing to come in under a code invalid at the utmost in separable provisions, not immediately operative, the right to contest them being explicitly reserved. The penalty in those circumstances is adopted as a lawful sanction to compel submission to a statute having the quality of law. A sanction of that type is the one in controversy here. Finally, the adequacy of the remedial devices is made even more apparent when one remembers that the attack upon the statute in its labor regulations assumes the existence of a controversy that may never become actual. The failure to agree upon a wage scale or upon maximum hours of daily or weekly labor may make the statutory scheme abortive in the very phases and aspects that the court has chosen to condemn. What the code will provide as to wages and hours of labor, or whether it will provide anything, is still in the domain of prophecy. The opinion of the Court begins at the wrong end. To adopt a homely form of words, the complainants have been crying before they are really hurt.

My vote is for affirmance.

I am authorized to state that Mr. Justice BRANDEIS and Mr. Justice STONE join in this opinion.

"EVEN SOVEREIGNS MAY CONTRACT WITHOUT DEROGATING FROM THEIR SOVEREIGNTY"

Steward Machine Co. v. *Davis,* 301 United States Reports 548 (1937)

In 1935 there was enacted the Social Security Act, consisting of eleven separate titles, of which titles IX and III, are related to this case. Under title IX, an employer employing 8 persons or more was to pay in each calendar year, a certain percentage of the wages paid by him, and the proceeds when collected were to go into the treasury of the United States without being earmarked in any way. If the tax payer had made contributions to any unemployment fund under a state law he might credit such contributions against the federal tax up to 90% of the tax against which it is credited. This allowance was permitted if the state involved paid all contributions to the state fund to the Secretary of the Treasury who invested in government securities such portion not required to meet current withdrawals. The Secretary of the Treasury was authorized to pay out of the fund to any competent state agency such sums as it might duly requisition from the amount standing to its credit.

Title III authorized the appropriations of monies for the purpose of helping the states in the administration of their unemployment compensation laws and an annual maximum was fixed. The authority covered only needed future appropriations, the act itself not providing for any present appropriation. Provisions were included in the statute designed to give assurance to the Federal Government that the monies granted by it would not be expended for any purposes alien to the grant but would be used in the administration of genuine employment compensation laws.

The Charles C. Steward Machine Co. of Alabama assailed the tax on the ground that it was not an excise tax; that it was not uniform throughout the United States; that it violated the Fifth Amendment; that its purpose was not revenue but an unlawful invasion of the reserved powers of the state and in fact compelled a surrender of their governmental functions. The lower courts held the act valid. An appeal was taken.

MR. JUSTICE CARDOZO * * *

The objections will be considered seriatim with such further explanation as may be necessary to make their meaning clear.

First: The tax, which is described in the statute as an excise, is laid with uniformity throughout the United States as a duty, an impost, or an excise upon the relation of employment.

1. We are told that the relation of employment is one so essential to the pursuit of happiness that it may not be burdened with a tax. Appeal is made to history. From the precedents of colonial days, we are supplied with illustrations of excises common in the colonies. They are said to have been bound up with the enjoyment of particular commodities. Appeal is also made to principle or the analysis of concepts. An excise, we are told, imports a tax upon a privilege; employment, it is said, is a right, not a privilege, from which it follows that employment is not subject to an excise. Neither the one appeal nor the other leads to the desired goal.

As to the argument from history: Doubtless there were many excises in colonial days and later that were associated, more or less intimately, with the enjoyment or the use of property. This would not prove, even if no others were then known, that the forms then accepted were not subject to enlargement. But in truth other excises were known, and known since early times. Thus in 1695 Parliament passed an act which granted "to His Majesty certain Rates and Duties upon Marriages, Births and Burials," all for the purpose of "carrying on the War against France with Vigour." No commodity was affected there. The industry of counsel has supplied us with an apter illustration where the tax was not different in substance from the one now challenged as invalid. In 1777, before our Constitutional Convention, Parliament laid upon employers an annual "duty" of 21 shillings for "every male Servant" employed in stated forms of work. The point is made as a distinction that a tax upon the use of male servants was thought of as a tax upon a luxury. It did not touch employments in husbandry or business. This is to throw over the argument that historically an excise is a tax upon the enjoyment of commodities. But the attempted distinction, whatever may be thought of its validity, is inapplicable to a statute of Virginia passed in 1780. There a tax of 3 pounds, 6 shillings, and 8 pence was to be paid for every male tithable above the age of twenty-one years (with stated exceptions), and a like tax for "every white servant whatsoever, except apprentices under the age of twenty-one years." Our colonial forbears knew more about ways of taxing than some of their descendants seem to be willing to concede.

The historical prop failing, the prop or fancied prop of principle remains. We learn that employment for lawful gain is a "natural" or "inherent" or "inalienable" right, and not a "privilege" at all. But natural rights, so called, are as much subject to taxation as rights of less importance. An excise is not limited to vocations or activities that may be prohibited altogether. It is not limited to those that are the outcome of a franchise. It extends to vocations or activities pursued as of common right. What the individual does in the operation of a business is amenable to taxation just as much as what he owns, at all events if the classification is not tyrannical or arbitrary. Indeed, ownership itself, as we had occasion to point out the other day, is only a bundle of rights and privileges invested with a single name. "A state is at liberty, if it pleases, to tax them all collectively, or to separate the faggots and lay the charge distributively."[1] Employment is a business relation, if not itself a business. It is a relation without which business could seldom be carried on effectively. The power to tax the activities and relations that constitute a calling considered as a unit is the power to tax any of them. The whole includes the parts.

The subject-matter of taxation open to the power of the Congress is as comprehensive as that open to the power of the states, though the method of apportionment may at times be different. "The Congress shall have Power to lay and collect Taxes, Duties, Imposts and Excises."[2] If the tax is a direct one, it shall be apportioned according

---

[1]*Henneford* v. *Silas Mason Co.,* reported in Volume 57 Supreme Court Reporter 524.

[2]Article 1, section 8, of the Constitution of the United States.

to the census or enumeration. If it is a duty, impost, or excise, it shall be uniform throughout the United States. Together, these classes include every form of tax appropriate to sovereignty. Whether the tax is to be classified as an "excise" is in truth not of critical importance. If not that, it is an "impost". A capitation or other "direct" tax it certainly is not. "Although there have been, from time to time, intimations that there might be some tax which was not a direct tax, nor included under the words 'duties, imposts, and excises,' such a tax, for more than 100 years of national existence, has as yet remained undiscovered, notwithstanding the stress of particular circumstances has invited thorough investigation into sources of revenue."[1] There is no departure from that thought in later cases, but rather a new emphasis of it. At times taxpayers have contended that the Congress is without power to lay an excise on the enjoyment of a privilege created by state law. The contention has been put aside as baseless. Congress may tax the transmission of property by inheritance or will, though the states and not Congress have created the privilege of succession. Congress may tax the enjoyment of a corporate franchise, though a state and not Congress has brought the franchise into being. The statute books of the states are strewn with illustrations of taxes laid on occupations pursued of common right. We find no basis for a holding that the power in that regard which belongs by accepted practice to the Legislatures of the states, has been denied by the Constitution to the Congress of the nation.

2. The tax being an excise, its imposition must conform to the canon of uniformity. There has been no departure from this requirement. According to the settled doctrine, the uniformity exacted is geographical, not intrinsic.

Second: The excise is not invalid under the provisions of the Fifth Amendment by force of its exemptions.

---

[1]*Pollock* v. *Farmers' Loan & Trust Co.*, reported in Volume 157 United States Reports 429, 557.

The statute does not apply, as we have seen, to employers of less than eight. It does not apply to agricultural labor, or domestic service in a private home or to some other classes of less importance. Petitioner contends that the effect of these restrictions is an arbitrary discrimination vitiating the tax.

The Fifth Amendment unlike the Fourteenth has no equal protection clause. But even the states, though subject to such a clause, are not confined to a formula of rigid uniformity in framing measures of taxation. They may tax some kinds of property at one rate, and others at another, and exempt others altogether. They may lay an excise on the operations of a particular kind of business, and exempt some other kind of business closely akin thereto. If this latitude of judgment is lawful for the states, it is lawful, a fortiori, in legislation by the Congress, which is subject to restraints less narrow and confining.

The classifications and exemptions directed by the statute now in controversy have support in considerations of policy and practical convenience that connot be condemned as arbitrary.

Third: The excise is not void as involving the coercion of the states in contravention of the Tenth Amendment or of restrictions implicit in our federal form of government.

The proceeds of the excise when collected are paid into the Treasury at Washington, and thereafter are subject to appropriation like public moneys generally. No presumption can be indulged that they will be misapplied or wasted. Even if they were collected in the hope or expectation that some other and collateral good would be furthered as an incident, that without more would not make the act invalid. This indeed is hardly questioned. The case for the petitioner is built on the contention that here an ulterior aim is wrought into the very structure of the act, and what is even more important that the aim is not only ulterior, but essentially unlawful. In particular, the 90 per cent. credit is relied upon as supporting that conclusion. But before the statute succumbs to an assault upon these lines, two propositions must be made out by the assailant. There must be a showing in the first place that separated from the credit the revenue provisions are incapable of standing by themselves. There must be a showing in the second place that the tax and the credit in combination are weapons of coercion, destroying or impairing the autonomy of the states. The truth of each proposition being essential to the success of the assault, we pass for convenience to a consideration of the second, without pausing to inquire whether there has been a demonstration of the first.

To draw the line intelligently between duress and inducement, there is need to remind ourselves of facts as to the problem of unemployment that are now matters of common knowledge. The relevant statistics are gathered in the brief of counsel for the government. Of the many available figures a few only will be mentioned. During the years 1929 to 1936, when the country was passing through a cyclical depression, the number of the unemployed mounted to unprecedented heights. Often the average was more than 10 million; at times a peak was attained of 16 million or more. Disaster to the breadwinner meant disaster to dependents. Accordingly the roll of the unemployed, itself formidable enough, was only a partial roll of the destitute or needy. The fact developed quickly that the states were unable to give the requisite relief. The problem had become national in area and dimensions. There was need of help from the nation if the people were not to starve. It is too late today for the argument to be heard with tolerance that in a crisis so extreme the use of the moneys of the nation to relieve the unemployed and their dependents is a use for any purpose narrower than the promotion of the general welfare. The nation responded to the call of the distressed. Between January 1, 1933, and July 1, 1936, the states (according to statistics submitted by the government) incurred obligations of $689,291,802 for emergency relief; local subdivisions an additional $775,675,366. In the same period the obligations for emergency relief incurred by the national government were $2,929,307,125, or twice the obligations of states and local agencies combined. According to the President's budget message for the fiscal year 1938, the national government expended for public works and unemployment relief for the three fiscal years 1934, 1935, and 1936, the stupendous total of $8,681,000,000. The *parens patriae* has many reasons—fiscal and economic as well as social and moral—for planning to mitigate disasters that bring these burdens in their train.

In the presence of this urgent need for some remedial expedient, the question is to be answered whether the expedient adopted has overlept the bounds of power. The assailants of the statute say that its dominant end and aim is to drive the state Legislatures under the whip of economic pressure into the enactment of unemployment compensation laws at the bidding of the central government. Supporters of the statute say that its operation is not constraint, but the creation of a larger freedom, the states and the nation joining in a co-operative endeavor to avert a common evil. Before Congress acted, unemployment compensation insurance was still, for the most part, a project and no more. Wisconsin was the pioneer. Her statute was adopted in 1931. At times bills for such insurance were introduced elsewhere, but they did not reach the stage of law. In 1935, four states (California, Massachusetts, New Hampshire, and New York) passed unemployment laws on the eve of the adoption of the Social Security Act, and two others did likewise after the federal act and later in the year. The statutes differed to some extent in type, but were directed to a common end. In 1936, twenty-eight other states fell in line, and eight more the present year. But if states had been holding back before the passage of the federal law, inaction was not owing, for the most part, to the lack of sympathetic interest. Many held back through alarm lest in laying such a toll upon their industries, they would place themselves in a position of economic disadvantage as compared with neighbors or competitors.[1] Two consequences ensued. One was that the freedom of a state to contribute its fair share to the solution of a national problem was paralyzed by fear. The other was that in so far as there was failure by the states to contribute relief according to the measure of their capacity, a disproportionate burden, and a mountainous one, was laid upon the resources of the government of the nation.

The Social Security Act is an attempt to find a method by which all these public agencies may work together to a common end. Every dollar of the new taxes will continue in all likelihood to be used and needed by the nation as long as states are unwilling, whether through timidity or for other motives, to do what can be done at home. At least the inference is permissible that Congress so believed, though retaining undiminished freedom to spend the money as it pleased. On the other hand, fulfillment of the home duty will be lightened and encouraged by crediting the taxpayer upon his account with the Treasury of the nation to the extent that his contributions under the laws of the locality have simplified or diminished the problem of relief and the probable demand upon the resources of the fisc. Duplicated taxes, or burdens that approach them are recognized hardships that government, state or national, may properly avoid. If Congress believed that the general welfare would better be promoted by relief through local units than by the system then in vogue, the co-operating localities ought not in all fairness to pay a second time.

Who then is coerced through the operation of this statute? Not the taxpayer. He pays in fulfillment of the mandate of the local legislature. Not the state. Even now she does not offer a suggestion that in passing the un-

[1]The attitude of Massachusetts is significant. Her act became a law August 12, 1935, two days before the federal act. Even so, she prescribed that its provisions should not become operative unless the federal bill became a law, or unless eleven of the following states (Alabama, Connecticut, Delaware, Georgia, Illinois, Indiana, Iowa, Maine, Maryland, Michigan, Minnesota, Missouri, New Hampshire, New Jersey, New York, North Carolina, Ohio, Rhode Island, South Carolina, Tennessee, Vermont) should impose on the employers burdens substantially equivalent. St. of 1935, c. 479, p. 655. Her fear of competition is thus forcefully attested.

employment law she was affected by duress. For all that appears, she is satisfied with her choice, and would be sorely disappointed if it were now to be annulled. The difficulty with the petitioner's contention is that it confuses motive with coercion. "Every tax is in some measure regulatory. To some extent it interposes an economic impediment to the activity taxed as compared with others not taxed."[1] In like manner every rebate from a tax when conditioned upon conduct is in some measure a temptation. But to hold that motive or temptation is equivalent to coercion is to plunge the law in endless difficulties. The outcome of such a doctrine is the acceptance of a philosophical determinism by which choice becomes impossible. Till now the law has been guided by a robust common sense which assumes a freedom of the will as a working hypothesis in the solution of its problems. The wisdom of the hypothesis has illustration in this case. Nothing in the case suggests the exertion of a power akin to undue influence, if we assume that such a concept can ever be applied with fitness to the relations between state and nation. Even on that assumption the location of the point at which pressure turns into compulsion, and ceases to be inducement, would be a question of degree, at times, perhaps, of fact. The point had not been reached when Alabama made her choice. We cannot say that she was acting, not of her unfettered will, but under the strain of a persuasion equivalent to undue influence, when she chose to have relief administered under laws of her own making, by agents of her own selection, instead of under federal laws, administered by federal officers, with all the ensuing evils, at least to many minds, of federal patronage and power. There would be a strange irony, indeed, if her choice were now to be annulled on the basis of an assumed duress in the enactment of a statute which her courts have accepted as a true expression of her will. We think the choice must stand.

---

[1] *Sonzinsky* v. *United States,* reported in Volume 57 Supreme Court Reporter 554.

In ruling as we do, we leave many questions open. We do not say that a tax is valid, when imposed by act of Congress, if it is laid upon the condition that a state may escape its operation through the adoption of a statute unrelated in subject-matter to activities fairly within the scope of national policy and power. No such question is before use. In the tender of this credit Congress does not intrude upon fields foreign to its function. The purpose of its intervention, as we have shown, is to safeguard its own treasury and as an incident to that protection to place the states upon a footing of equal opportunity. Drains upon its own resources are to be checked; obstructions to the freedom of the states are to be leveled. It is one thing to impose a tax dependent upon the conduct of the taxpayers, or of the state in which they live, where the conduct to be stimulated or discouraged is unrelated to the fiscal need subserved by the tax in its normal operation, or to any other end legitimately national. It is quite another thing to say that a tax will be abated upon the doing of an act that will satisfy the fiscal need, the tax and the alternative being approximate equivalents. In such circumstances, if in no others, inducement or persuasion does not go beyond the bounds of power. We do not fix the outermost line. Enough for present purposes that wherever the line may be this statute is within it. Definition more precise must abide the wisdom of the future.

* * * *

Fourth: The statute does not call for a surrender by the states of powers essential to their quasi sovereign existence.

Argument to the contrary has its source in two sections of the act. One section defines the minimum criteria to which a state compensation system is required to conform if it is to be accepted by the Board as the basis for a credit. The other section rounds out the requirement with complementary rights and duties. Not all the criteria or their incidents are challenged as unlawful. We will speak of them first generally, and then more specifically in so far as they are questioned.

A credit to taxpayers for payments made to a state under a state unemployment law will be manifestly futile in the absence of some assurance that the law leading to the credit is in truth what it professes to be. An unemployment law framed in such a way that the unemployed who look to it will be deprived of reasonable protection is one in name and nothing more. What is basic and essential may be assured by suitable conditions. The terms embodied in these sections are directed to that end. A wide range of judgment is given to the several states as to the particular type of statute to be spread upon their books. For anything to the contrary in the provisions of this act they may use the pooled unemployment form, which is in effect with variations in Alabama, California, Michigan, New York, and elsewhere. They may establish a system of merit ratings applicable at once or to go into effect later on the basis of subsequent experience. They may provide for employee contributions as in Alabama and California, or put the entire burden upon the employer as in New York. They may choose a system of unemployment reserve accounts by which an employer is permitted after his reserve has accumulated to contribute at a reduced rate or even not at all. This is the system which had its origin in Wisconsin. What they may not do, if they would earn the credit, is to depart from those standards which in the judgment of Congress are to be ranked as fundamental. Even if opinion may differ as to the fundamental quality of one or more of the conditions, the difference will not avail to vitiate the statute. In determining essentials, Congress must have the benefit of a fair margin of discretion. One cannot say with reason that this margin has been exceeded, or that the basic standards have been determined in any arbitrary fashion. In the event that some particular condition shall be found to be too uncertain to be capable of enforcement, it may be severed from the others, and what is left will still be valid.

We are to keep in mind steadily that the conditions to be approved by the Board as the basis for a credit are not provisions of a contract, but terms of a statute, which may be altered or repealed. The state does not bind itself to keep the law in force. It does not even bind itself that the moneys paid into the federal fund will be kept there indefinitely or for any stated time. On the contrary, the Secretary of the Treasury will honor a requisition for the whole or any part of the deposit in the fund whenever one is made by the appropriate officials. The only consequence of the repeal or excessive amendment of the statute, or the expenditure of the money, when requisitioned, for other than compensation uses or administrative expenses, is that approval of the law will end, and with it the allowance of a credit, upon notice to the state agency and an opportunity for hearing.

These basic considerations are in truth a solvent of the problem. Subjected to their test, the several objections on the score of abdication are found to be unreal.

Thus, the argument is made that by force of an agreement the moneys when withdrawn must be "paid through public employment offices in the State or such other agencies as the Board may approve." But in truth there is no agreement as to the method of disbursement. There is only a condition which the state is free at pleasure to disregard or to fulfill. Moreover, approval is not requisite if public employment offices are made the disbursing instruments. Approval is to be a check upon resort to "other agencies" that may perchance, be irresponsible. A state looking for a credit must give assurance that her system has been organized upon a base of rationality.

There is argument again that the moneys when withdrawn are to be devoted to specific uses, the relief of unemployment, and that by agreement for such payment the quasi-sovereign position of the state has been impaired, if not abandoned. But again there is confusion between promise and condition. Alabama is still free, without breach of an agreement to change her system over night. No officer or agency of the national government can force a compensation law upon her or keep it in existence. No officer or agency of that government, either by suit or other means, can supervise or control the application of the payments.

Finally and chiefly, abdication is supposed to follow from section 904 of the statute and the parts of section 903 that are complementary thereto. By these the Secretary of the Treasury is authorized and directed to receive and hold in the Unemployment Trust Fund all moneys deposited therein by a state agency for a state unemployment fund and to invest in obligations of the United States such portion of the fund as is not in his judgment required to meet current withdrawals. We are told that Alabama in consenting to that deposit has renounced the plenitude of power inherent in her statehood.

The same pervasive misconception is in evidence again. All that the state has done is to say in effect through the enactment of a statute that her agents shall be authorized to deposit the unemployment tax receipts in the Treasury at Washington. The consent may be revoked. The deposits may be withdrawn. The moment the state commission gives notice to the depositary that it would like the moneys back, the Treasurer will return them. To find state destruction there is to find it almost anywhere. With nearly as much reason one might say that a state abdicates its functions when it places the state moneys on deposit in a national bank.

There are very good reasons of fiscal and governmental policy why a state should be willing to make the Secretary of the Treasury the custodian of the fund. His possession of the moneys and his control of investments will be an assurance of stability and safety in times of stress and strain. A report of the Ways and Means Committee of the House of Representatives, develops the situation clearly. Nor is there risk of loss or waste. The credit of the Treasury is at all times back of the deposit, with the result that the right of withdrawal will be unaffected by the fate of any intermediate investments, just as if a checking account in the usual form had been opened in a bank.

The inference of abdication thus dissolves in thinnest air when the deposit is conceived of as dependent upon a statutory consent, and not upon a contract effective to create a duty. By this we do not intimate that the conclusion would be different if a contract were discovered. Even sovereigns may contract without derogating from their sovereignty. The states are at liberty, upon obtaining the consent of Congress, to make agreements with one another. We find no room for doubt that they may do the like with Congress if the essence of their statehood is maintained without impairment. Alabama is seeking and obtaining a credit of many millions in favor of her citizens out of the Treasury of the nation. Nowhere in our scheme of government—in the limitations express or implied of our Federal Constitution—do we find that she is prohibited from assenting to conditions that will assure a fair and just requital for benefits received. But we will not labor the point further. An unreal prohibition directed to an unreal agreement will not vitiate an act of Congress, and cause it to collapse in ruin.

Fifth: Title III of the act is separable from title IX, and its validity is not at issue.

The essential provisions of that title have been stated in the opinion. As already pointed out, the title does not appropriate a dollar of the public moneys. It does no more than authorize appropriations to be made in the future for the purpose of assisting states in the administration of their laws, if Congress shall decide that appropriations are desirable. The title might be expunged, and title IX would stand intact. Without a severability clause we should still be led to that conclusion. The presence of such a clause makes the conclusion even clearer.

The judgment is affirmed.[1]

* * * *

[1]Mr. Justice McReynolds criticized the above opinion, taking the position that the decision of the majority opened the way for practical annihilation of the doctrine that the states remain free to exercise governmental powers not delegated to the federal government nor prohibited by the con-

stitution to the states. He added that "no cloud of words or ostentatious parade of irrelevant statistics should be permitted to obscure that fact." He felt that the door was opened for similar experiments which would enable the Federal Government to tax the states and thus destroy their genuine independence of action. Mr. Justice Sutherland agreed with most of what was said in the opinion of Mr. Justice Cardozo. He concurred that the pay roll tax levied was an excise within the power of Congress; that the devotion of not more than 90% of it to the credit of employers in states requiring the payment of a similar tax was not an unconstitutional use of the Federal tax; that the provision which made the adoption by the state of a certain type of unemployment law a condition precedent to the credit of the tax did not render the law invalid; and that the states were not thus forced to adopt unemployment legislation. He felt however, that the administrative provisions invaded the powers of the states reserved by the 10th amendment. Under the enactment here involved a state was surrendering its share in the execution of a governmental power to the Federal Government. That was contrary to our principles of government. Mr. Justice Van Devanter joined in this opinion. Another dissenting opinion was written by Mr. Justice Butler who approved of the objections of both dissenting opinions. He argued that since the grant by the federal government to the state depended upon state compliance with conditions prescribed by federal authorities, and since the amounts to be given were within the discretion of Congress, the federal government was able to effectively influence state policy, standards and details of administration. For if it failed to adopt a plan acceptable to federal authorities the full burden of the federal government would fall upon the state.

The following month there was argued before the Court an attack upon Title VIII and II of the Social Security act. Title VIII laid another excise upon employers in addition to the one imposed by Title IX, though with different exemptions. It also laid a special income tax upon employees, to be deducted from their wages and paid by the employers. Title II provided for the payment of Old Age Benefits. The tax under Title VIII was measured by wages, a certain percentage every year being deducted. The proceeds of both taxes were to be paid into the Federal Treasury, and were not to be earmarked in any way. Penalties for non-payment were provided for. A shareholder of the Edison Electric Illuminating Co. of Boston brought suit to restrain the Corporation from making any payments or deducting any wages called for by the act which was declared to be void under the Constitution of the United States. The Supreme Court of the United States in an opinion by Mr. Justice Cardozo (Mr. Justice McReynolds and Mr. Justice Butler dissenting) held that the act was valid. In the opinion (reported in Volume 301 United States Reports 619) the following passages are particularly worthy of note:

"Nor is the concept of general welfare static. Needs that were narrow or parochial a century ago may be interwoven in our day with the well-being of the nation. What is critical or urgent changes with the times.

The purge of nation-wide calamity that began in 1929 has taught us many lessons. Not the least is the solidarity of interests that may once have seemed to be divided. Unemployment spreads from state to state, the hinterland now settled that in pioneer days gave an avenue of escape. Spreading from state to state, unemployment is an ill not particular but general, which may be checked, if Congress so determines, by the resources of the nation. If this can have been doubtful until now, our ruling today in the case of the Steward Machine Co., supra, has set the doubt at rest. But the ill is all one or at least not greatly different whether men are thrown out of work because there is no longer work to do or because the disabilities of age make them incapable of doing it. Rescue becomes necessary irrespective of the cause. The hope behind this statute is to save men and women from the rigors of the poor house as well as from the haunting fear that such a lot awaits them when journey's end is near.

The number of persons in the United States 65 years of age or over is increasing proportionately as well as absolutely. What is even more important the number of such persons unable to take care of themselves is growing at a threatening pace. More and more our population is becoming urban and industrial instead of rural and agricultural. The evidence is impressive that among industrial workers, the younger men and women are preferred over the older. In times of retrenchment the older are commonly the first to go, and even if retained, their wages are likely to be lowered. The plight of men and women at so low an age as 40 is hard, almost hopeless, when they are driven to seek for reemployment.

The problem is plainly national in area and dimensions. Moreover, laws of the separate states cannot deal with it effectively. Congress, at least, had a basis for that belief. States and local governments are often lacking in the resources that are necessary to finance an adequate program of security for the aged. Apart from the failure of resources, states and local governments are at times reluctant to increase so heavily the burden of taxation to be borne by their residents for fear of placing themselves in a position of economic disadvantage as compared with neighbors or competitors. A system of old age pensions has special dangers of its own, if put in force in one state and rejected in another. The existence of such a system is a bait to the needy and dependent elsewhere, encouraging them to migrate and seek a haven of repose. Only a power that is national can serve the interests of all.

Whether wisdom or unwisdom resides in the scheme of benefits set forth in Title II, it is not for us to say. The answer to such inquiries must come from Congress, not the Courts. Our concern here as often is with power, not with wisdom. Counsel for respondent has recalled to us the virtues of self-reliance and frugality. There is a possibility, he says, that aid from a paternal government may sap those sturdy virtues and breed a race of weaklings. If Massachusetts so believes and shapes her laws in that conviction, must her breed of sons be changed, he asks, because some other philosophy of government finds favor in the halls of Congress? But the answer is not doubtful. One might ask with equal reason whether the system of protective tariffs is to be set aside at will in one state or another whenever local policy prefers the rule of laissez faire. The issue is a closed one. It was fought out long ago.

When money is spent to promote the general welfare, the concept of welfare or the opposite is shaped by Congress, not the states. So the concept be not arbitrary, the locality must yield.

"JUSTICE WOULD NOT PERISH IF THE ACCUSED WERE SUBJECT TO A DUTY TO RESPOND TO ORDERLY INQUIRY"

Palko v. *State of Connecticut,* 58 Supreme Court Reporter 149 (1937)

Frank Palko was indicted in Connecticut for the crime of murder in the first degree. The jury found him guilty of murder in the second degree and he was sentenced to life imprisonment. The laws of Connecticut permitted the state with the permission of the presiding judge to appeal from the rulings and decisions upon all questions of law arising on the trial of criminal cases, in the same manner as allowed to the accused. After this conviction the State of Connecticut with the permission of the judge presiding served its notice of appeal, claiming errors in law upon the trial to the prejudice of the state. The defendant was brought to trial again and before the jury was impaneled he made the objection that the effect of the new trial was to place him twice in jeopardy for the same offense. The objection was overruled, the trial proceeded and the jury rendered a verdict of murder in the first degree after which the defendant was sentenced to the punishment of death. The highest court of Connecticut affirmed the judgment and the case came to the Supreme Court of the United States on the question of "double jeopardy."

MR. JUSTICE CARDOZO * * *

We do not find it profitable to mark the precise limits of the prohibition of double jeopardy in federal prosecutions. The subject was much considered in Kepner v. United States,[1] by a closely divided court. The view was there expressed for a majority of the court that the prohibition was not confined to jeopardy in a new and independent case. It forbade jeopardy in the same case if the new trial was at the instance of the government and not upon defendant's motion. All this may be assumed for the purpose of the case at hand, though the dissenting opinions show how much was to be said in favor of a different ruling. Right-minded men, as we learn from those opinions, could reasonably, even if mistakenly, believe that a

[1]Reported in Volume 195 United States Reports 100.

second trial was lawful in prosecutions subject to the Fifth Amendment, if it was all in the same case. Even more plainly, right-minded men could reasonably believe that in espousing that conclusion they were not favoring a practice repugnant to the conscience of mankind. Is double jeopardy in such circumstances, if double jeopardy it must be called, a denial of due process forbidden to the States? The tyranny of labels must not lead us to leap to a conclusion that a word which in one set of facts may stand for oppression or enormity is of like effect in every other.

We have said that in appellant's view the Fourteenth Amendment is to be taken as embodying the prohibitions of the Fifth. His thesis is even broader. Whatever would be a violation of the original bill of rights if done by the federal government is now equally unlawful by force of the Fourteenth Amendment if done by a state. There is no such general rule.

The Fifth Amendment provides, among other things, that no person shall be held to answer for a capital or otherwise infamous crime unless on presentment or indictment of a grand jury. This court has held that, in prosecutions by a state, presentment or indictment by a grand jury may give way to informations at the instance of a public officer.[1] The Fifth Amendment provides also that no person shall be compelled in any criminal case to be a witness against himself. This court has said that, in prosecutions by a state, the exemption will fail if the state elects to end it.[2] The Sixth Amendment calls for a jury trial in criminal cases and the Seventh for a jury trial in civil cases at common law where the value in controversy shall exceed $20. This court has ruled that consistently with those amendments trial by jury may be modified by a state or abolished altogether.

---

[1]*Hurtudo* v. *California,* reported in Volume 110 United States Reports 516, and in *Gaines* v. *Washington,* reported in Volume 277 United States Reports 81.

[2]*Twining* v. *New Jersey,* reported in Volume 211 United States Reports 78.

On the other hand, the due process clause of the Fourteenth Amendment may make it unlawful for a state to abridge by its statutes the freedom of speech which the First Amendment safeguards against encroachment by the Congress or the like freedom of the press, or the free exercise of religion, or the right of peaceable assembly, without which speech would be unduly trammeled, or the right of one accused of crime to the benefit of counsel. In these and other situations immunities that are valid as against the federal government by force of the specific pledges of particular amendments have been found to be implicit in the concept of ordered liberty, and thus, through the Fourteenth Amendment, become valid as against the states.

The line of division may seem to be wavering and broken if there is a hasty catalogue of the cases on the one side and the other. Reflection and analysis will induce a different view. There emerges the perception of a rationalizing principle which gives to discreet instances a proper order and coherence. The right to trial by jury and the immunity from prosecution except as the result of an indictment may have value and importance. Even so, they are not of the very essence of a scheme of ordered liberty. To abolish them is not to violate a "principle of justice so rooted in the traditions and conscience of our people as to be ranked as fundamental."[1] Few would be so narrow or provincial as to maintain that a fair and enlightened system of justice would be impossible without them. What is true of jury trials and indictments is true also, as the cases show, of the immunity from compulsory self-incrimination. This too might be lost, and justice still be done. Indeed, today as in the past there are students of our penal system who look upon the immunity as a mischief rather than a benefit, and who would limit its scope, or destroy it altogether. No doubt there would remain the need to give protection against torture, physical or mental. Justice, however, would not perish if the accused were

---

[1]*Snyder* v. *Massachusetts,* reported in Volume 291 United States Reports 97, 105. See *supra,* page 345.

subject to a duty to respond to orderly inquiry. The exclusion of these immunities and privileges from the privileges and immunities protected against the action of the States has not been arbitrary or casual. It has been dictated by a study and appreciation of the meaning, the essential implications, of liberty itself.

We reach a different plane of social and moral values when we pass to the privileges and immunities that have been taken over from the earlier articles of the Federal Bill of Rights and brought within the Fourteenth Amendment by a process of absorption. These in their origin were effective against the federal government alone. If the Fourteenth Amendment has absorbed them, the process of absorption has had its source in the belief that neither liberty nor justice would exist if they were sacrificed. This is true, for illustration, of freedom of thought and speech. Of that freedom one may say that it is the matrix, the indispensable condition, of nearly every other form of freedom. With rare aberrations a pervasive recognition of that truth can be traced in our history, political and legal. So it has come about that the domain of liberty, withdrawn by the Fourteenth Amendment from encroachment by the states, has been enlarged by latter-day judgments to include liberty of the mind as well as liberty of action. The extension became, indeed, a logical imperative when once the notion was abandoned, as long ago it was, that liberty is something more than exemption from physical restraint, and that even in the field of substantive rights and duties the legislative judgment, if oppressive and arbitrary, may be overridden by the courts. Fundamental too in the concept of due process, and so in that of liberty, is the thought that condemnation shall be rendered only after trial. The hearing, moreover, must be a real one, not a sham or a pretense. For that reason, ignorant defendants in a capital case were held to have been condemned unlawfully when in truth, though not in form, they were refused the aid of counsel. The decision did not turn upon the fact that the benefit of counsel would have been guaranteed to the defendants by the provisions of the Sixth Amendment if they had been prosecuted in a federal court. The decision turned upon the fact that in the particular situation laid before us in the evidence the benefit of counsel was essential to the substance of a hearing.

Our survey of the cases serves, we think, to justify the statement that the dividing line between them, if not unfaltering throughout its course, has been true for the most part to a unifying principle. On which side of the line the case made out by the appellant has appropriate location must be the next inquiry and the final one. Is that kind of double jeopardy to which the statute has subjected him a hardship so acute and shocking that our polity will not endure it? Does it violate those "fundamental principles of liberty and justice which lie at the base of all our civil and political institutions"? The answer surely must be "no." What the answer would have to be if the state were permitted after a trial free from error to try the accused over again or to bring another case against him, we have no occasion to consider. We deal with the statute before us and no other. The state is not attempting to wear the accused out by a multitude of cases with accumulated trials. It asks no more than this, that the case against him shall go on until there shall be a trial free from the corrosion of substantial legal error. This is not cruelty at all, nor even vexation in any immoderate degree. If the trial had been infected with error adverse to the accused, there might have been review at his instance, and as often as necessary to purge the vicious taint. A reciprocal privilege, subject at all times to the discretion of the presiding judge, has now been granted to the state. There is here no seismic innovation. The edifice of justice stands, its symmetry, to many, greater than before.

The judgment is affirmed.

Mr. Justice BUTLER dissents.

QUOTATIONS FROM OTHER OPINIONS

To enforce one's rights when they are violated is never a legal wrong, and may often be a moral duty. It happens in many instances that the violation passes with no effort to redress it—sometimes from praiseworthy forbearance, sometimes from weakness, sometimes from mere inertia. But the law, which creates a right, can certainly not concede that an insistence upon its enforcement is evidence of a wrong.[1]

•

It is not now, and never has been the law that a man assailed in his own dwelling is bound to retreat. If assailed there, he may stand his ground, and resist the attack. He is under no duty to take to the fields and the highways, a fugitive from his own home. * * * Flight is sanctuary and shelter, and shelter, if not sanctuary, is in the home.[2]

•

Faith in the honesty of trusted friends and relatives is seldom negligence.[3]

•

The law does not force its ministers of justice to abet a criminal project to set the law at naught.[4]

•

Courts are not to shut their eyes to the realities of business life.[5]

•

The law has outgrown its primitive stage of formalism when the precise word was the sovereign talisman, and every slip was fatal. It takes a broader view today.[6]

---

[1]*Mornington* v. *Lafayette Hotel Co.*, reported in volume 211 New York Reports at p. 468.

[2]*People* v. *Tomlins*, reported in Volume 213 New York Reports at p. 243.

[3]*People's Trust Co.* v. *Smith*, reported in Volume 215 New York Reports at p. 492.

[4]*People* v. *Schmidt*, reported in Volume 216 New York Reports at p. 341.

[5]*Barkin Construction Co.* v. *Goodman*, reported in Volume 221 New York Reports at p. 161.

[6]*Wood* v. *Lady Duff Gordon*, reported in Volume 222 New York Reports at p. 91.

The proper legal meaning, however, is not always the meaning of the parties. Surrounding circumstances may stamp upon a contract a popular or looser meaning. The words "loans" and "discounts" are not so clear and certain that circumstances may not broaden them to include renewals. They often have that meaning in the language of business life. In the thought of business men, to renew a loan or discount is to make it over again, but none the less to make it. Especially is that so where, as here, a new note is given at each renewal, and interest is paid. The triers of the facts must fix the sense in which the words were used in the contract now before us. To take the primary or strict meaning is to make the whole transaction futile. To take the secondary or loose meaning is to give it efficacy and purpose. In such a situation the genesis and aim of the transaction may rightly guide our choice.[1]

•

If a foreign statute gives the right, the mere fact that we do not give a like right is no reason for refusing to help the plaintiff in getting what belongs to him. We are not so provincial as to say that every solution of a problem is wrong because we deal with it otherwise at home.[2]

•

We must see the whole picture. For the purpose of this appeal, it is enough that the defendant is not exonerated as of course, because the man at the helm was not his servant. One cannot let oneself be driven at breakneck speed through city streets, and charge the whole guilt upon the driver who has done one's tacit bidding.[3]

•

There is to be no traffic in the privilege of invoking the public justice of the state. One may press a charge or withhold it as one will. One may not make action or

[1] *Utica City Natl. Bank* v. *Gunn,* reported in Volume 222 New York Reports at p. 208.

[2] *Loucks* v. *Standard Oil Co.,* reported in Volume 224 New York Reports at pp. 110, 111.

[3] *Dowler* v. *Johnson,* reported in Volume 225 New York Reports at p. 43.

inaction dependent on a price. The state has, indeed, no interest to be promoted by the prosecution of the innocent * * * The state has an interest, however, in preserving to complainants the freedom of choice, the incentives to sincerity, which are the safeguards and the assurance of the prosecution of the guilty * * * Innocence will strangely multiply when the accuser is the paid defender. In such matters, the law looks beyond the specific instance where the evil may be small or nothing. It throttles a corrupting tendency.[1]

•

Error of judgment there may have been, but error is not inconsistent with fault. The standard of diligence exacted is that of the typical prudent man. The individual must answer for the consequences when he falls below that norm.[2]

•

We think the unexcused omission of the statutory signals (lighted headlights on automobiles at night) is more than some evidence of negligence. It *is* negligence in itself. Lights are intended for the guidance and protection of other travelers on the highway. By the very terms of the hypothesis, to omit, wilfully or heedlessly, the safeguards prescribed by law for the benefit of another that he may be preserved in life or limb, is to fall short of the standard of diligence to which those who live in organized society, are under a duty to conform. That, we think, is now the established rule in this state.[3]

•

Mistakes with corporations as with men, are often paid for in shortened lives. But error is not suicide.[4]

---

[1] *Union Exchange Bank* v. *Joseph,* reported in Volume 231 New York Reports at pp. 253, 254.

[2] *Pellegrino* v. *Smith,* reported in Volume 226 New York Reports at p. 167.

[3] *Martin* v. *Herzog,* reported in Volume 228 New York Reports at p. 168.

[4] *Assets Realization Co.* v. *Roth,* reported in Volume 228 New York Reports at p. 377.

The supreme rule of the road is the rule of mutual forbearance.[1]

•

One who stands by and induces the belief that he assents will not thereafter be heard to complain of the act that another might have sustained from, if dissent had been announced.[2]

•

Courts are slow to say that promises, bearing upon their face the outward or formal tokens of a contract with mutual obligations, shall be set at naught on the assumption that the parties were oblivious of the advantages and burdens of their reciprocal engagements.[3]

•

Acts in furtherance of a criminal project do not reach the stage of an attempt unless they carry the project forward within dangerous proximity to the criminal end to be attained.[4]

•

There is little room for misapprehension as to the ends to be achieved by the safeguards surrounding the process of amendment. The integrity of the basic law is to be preserved against hasty or ill-considered changes, the fruit of ignorance or passion.[5]

•

When an article of the Constitution has been ratified by popular vote, after acceptance by two Legislatures, separately chosen, the courts would be discrediting constitutional government rather than supporting it if they were to hold that limitations read into the text of the Constitution by dubious construction could nullify the mandate of the people and the people's representatives.[6]

---

[1]*Ward* v. *Clark,* reported in Volume 232, New York Reports at p. 198.

[2]*Giles Dyeing Machine Co.* v. *Klauder-Weldon,* reported in Volume 233 New York Reports at p. 477.

[3]*Walton Water Co.* v. *Village of Walton,* reported in Volume 238 New York Reports at p. 51.

[4]*People* v. *Werblow,* reported in Volume 241 New York Reports at p. 61.

[5]*Browne* v. *City of New York,* reported in Volume 241 New York Reports at p. 109.

[6]*Ibid.* at p. 112.

Metaphors in law are to be narrowly watched, for starting as devices to liberate thought, they end often by enslaving it. We say at times that the corporate entity will be ignored when the parent corporation operates a business through a subsidiary which is characterized as an "alias" or a "dummy." All this is well enough if the picturesqueness of the epithets does not lead us to forget that the essential term to be defined is the act of operation.[1]

•

Aviation is today an established method of transportation. The future, even the near future will make it still more general. The city that is without the foresight to build the ports for the new traffic may soon be left behind in the race of competition. Chalcedon was called the city of the blind, because its founders rejected the nobler sight of Byzantium lying at their feet. The need for vision of the future in the governance of cities has not lessened with the years. The dweller within the gates, even more than the stranger from afar, will pay the price of blindness.[2]

•

The wrongdoer will be left in the toils of his duplicity.[3]

•

If literalness is sheer absurdity, we are to seek some other meaning whereby reason will be instilled and absurdity avoided.[4]

•

Many things that are defamatory may be said with impunity through the medium of speech. Not so, however, when the speech is caught upon the wing and transmuted into print. What gives the sting to the writing is its permanence of form. The spoken word dissolves, but the written one abides and "perpetuates the scandal."[5]

---

[1]*Berkey* v. *Third Avenue Ry. Co.,* reported in Volume 244 New York Reports at pp. 84, 94.

[2]*Hesse* v. *Rath,* reported in Volume 249 New York Reports at p. 437.

[3]*American Surety Co.* v. *Connor,* reported in Volume 251 New York Reports at p. 10.

[4]*Outlet Embroidery Co.* v. *Derwent,* reported in Volume 254 New York Reports at p. 183.

[5]*Ostrowe* v. *Lee,* reported in Volume 256 New York Reports at p. 39.

The soundness of a conclusion may not infrequently be tested by its consequences.[1]

•

To learn what the law was, we must try to ascertain what the colonists of those days believed it to be, and to learn what they believed it to be, we must try to discover what they did.[2]

•

A system of procedure is perverted from its proper function when it multiplies impediments to justice without the warrant of clear necessity.[3]

•

Expediency may tip the scales when arguments are nicely balanced.[4]

•

One does not hold the dying to the observance of all the niceties of speech to which conformity is exacted from a witness on the stand.

It is for ordinary minds, and not for psychoanalysts, that our rules of evidence are framed. They have their source very often in considerations of administrative convenience, of practical expediency, and not in rules of logic. When the risk of confusion is as great as to upset the balance of advantage, the evidence goes out.[5]

•

Liberty of contract is not an absolute concept. It is relative to many conditions of time and place and circumstance. The Constitution has not ordained that the forms of business shall be cast in imperishable moulds.[6]

•

Discretion is not unconfined and vagrant. It is canalized within banks that keep it from overflowing. * * * The

---

[1] *Ibid.*

[2] *Beers* v. *Hotchkiss,* reported in Volume 256 New York Reports at p. 58.

[3] *Reed* v. *Allen,* reported in Volume 286 United States Reports at p. 209.

[4] *Woolford Realty Co.* v. *Rose,* reported in Volume 286 United States Reports at p. 330.

[5] *Shepard* v. *United States,* reported in Volume 290 United States Reports at p. 96.

[6] *Hartford Accident & I. Co.* v. *N. O. Nelson,* reported in Volume 291 United States Reports at p. 360.

separation of powers between Executive and Congress is not a doctrinaire concept to be made use of with pedantic rigor. There must be sensible approximation, there must be elasticity of adjustment, in response to the practiced necessities of government, which cannot foresee today the developments of tomorrow in their nearly infinite variety.[1]

•

But prophecy, however honest, is generally a poor substitute for experience.[2]

•

Due process is a growth too sturdy to succumb to the infection of the least ingredient of error.[3]

•

When the task that is set before one is that of cleaning house, it is prudent as well as usual to take counsel of the dwellers.[4]

•

Motion at the outer rim is communicated perceptibly, though minutely, to recording instruments at the center. * * * The law is not indifferent to considerations of degree. Activities local in their immediacy do not become interstate and national because of distant repercussions. What is near and what is distant may at times be uncertain. * * * If centripetal forces are to be isolated to the exclusion of the forces that oppose and counteract them, there will be an end to our federal system.[5]

•

One must see the controversy in its setting before the implications of a ruling can be prefigured with assurance.[6]

---

[1]*Panama Refining Co.* v. *Ryan,* reported in Volume 293 United States Reports at p. 440.

[2]*West Ohio Gas Co.* v. *Public Utilities Commission,* reported in Volume 294 United States Reports at p. 82.

[3]*Roberts* v. *City of New York,* reported in Volume 295 United States Reports at p. 278.

[4]*A. L. A. Schechter Poultry Corp.* v. *United States,* reported in Volume 295 United States Reports at p. 552.

[5]*Ibid.* p. 554.

[6]*Lowden* v. *Northwestern National Bank,* reported in Volume 298 United States Reports at p. 163.

A decision balancing the equities must await the exposure of a concrete situation with all its qualifying incidents. What we disclaim at the moment is a willingness to put the law into a straitjacket by subjecting it to a pronouncement of needless generality.[1]

•

We must be on our guard against depriving the processes of justice of their suppleness of adaptation to varying conditions. Especially in cases of extraordinary public moment, the individual may be required to submit to delay not immoderate in extent and not oppressive in its consequences if the public welfare or convenience will thereby be promoted.[2]

•

---

[1]*Ibid.* at p. 166.

[2]*Landis* v. *North American Co.,* reported in Volume 299 United States Reports at p. 248.

QUOTATIONS FROM "THE NATURE OF THE JUDICIAL PROCESS"[1]

The persuasion that one's own infallibility is a myth leads by easy stages and with somewhat greater satisfaction to a refusal to ascribe infallability to others.[2]

•

The judge who moulds the law by the method of philosophy may be satisfying an intellectual craving for symmetry of form and substance. But he is doing something more. He is keeping the law true in its response to a deep-seated and imperious sentiment.[3]

•

Life casts the moulds of conduct, which will some day become fixed as law. Law preserves the moulds, which have taken form and shape from life.[4]

•

The final cause of law is the welfare of society. The rule that misses its aim cannot permanently justify its existence.[5]

•

Logic and history and custom have their place. We will shape the law to conform to them when we may; but only within bounds. The end which the law serves will dominate them all.[6]

•

A constitution states or ought to state not rules for the passing hour, but principles for an expanding future. In so far as it deviates from that standard, and descends into details and particulars, it loses its flexibility, the scope of interpretation contracts, the meaning hardens. While it is true to its function, it maintains its power of adaptation, its suppleness, its play.[7]

---

[1]Reprinted from *Cardozo: The Nature of the Judicial Process* (1922) by permission of Yale University Press.
[2]*Ibid.* p. 30.
[3]*Ibid.* p. 35.
[4]*Ibid.* p. 64.
[5]*Ibid.* p. 66.
[6]*Ibid.* p. 66.
[7]*Ibid.* pp. 83, 84.

We do not pick our rules of law full-blossomed from the trees.[1]

•

Law is, indeed, an historical growth, for it is an expression of customary morality which develops silently and unconsciously from one age to another.[2]

•

My analysis of the judicial process comes then to this, and little more: logic, and history, and custom, and utility, and the accepted standards of right conduct, are the forces which singly or in combination shape the progress of the law. Which of these forces shall dominate in any case, must depend largely upon the comparative importance or value of the social interests that will be thereby promoted or impaired.[3]

•

But symmetrical development may be bought at too high a price. Uniformity ceases to be a good when it becomes uniformity of oppression. The social interest served by symmetry or certainty must then be balanced against the social interest served by equity and fairness or other elements of social welfare.[4]

•

But I am ready to concede that the rule of adherence to precedence, though it ought not to be abandoned, ought to be in some degree relaxed. I think that when a rule, after it has been duly tested by experience, has been found to be inconsistent with the sense of justice or with the social welfare, there should be less hesitation in frank avowal and full abandonment.[5]

•

If judges have wofully misinterpreted the mores of their day, or if the mores of their day are not longer those

---

[1]*Ibid.* p. 103.
[2]*Ibid.* pp. 104, 105.
[3]*Ibid.* p. 112.
[4]*Ibid.* pp. 112, 113.
[5]*Ibid.* p. 150.

of ours, they ought not to tie, in helpless submission, the hands of their successors.[1]

•

I was much troubled in spirit, in my first years upon the bench, to find how trackless was the ocean on which I had embarked. I sought for certainty. I was oppressed and disheartened when I found that the quest for it was futile. I was trying to reach land, the solid land of fixed and settled rules, the paradise of a justice that would declare itself by tokens plainer and more commanding than its pale and glimmering reflections in my own vacillating mind and conscience. I found with the voyagers in Browning's "Paracelsus" that the real haven was always beyond.[2]

•

The spirit of the age, as it is revealed to each of us, is too often only the spirit of the group in which the accidents of birth or education or occupation or fellowship have given us a place. No effort or revolution of the mind will overthrow utterly and at all times the empire of these subconscious loyalties.[3]

•

I sometimes think that we worry ourselves overmuch about the enduring consequences of our errors. They may work a little confusion for a time. In the end, they will be modified or corrected or their teachings ignored. The future takes care of such things. In the endless process of testing and retesting, there is a constant rejection of the dross, and a constant retention of whatever is pure and sound and fine.[4]

---

[1] *Ibid.* p. 152.
[2] *Ibid.* p. 166.
[3] *Ibid.* pp. 174, 175.
[4] *Ibid.* p. 179.

QUOTATIONS FROM "THE GROWTH OF THE LAW"[1]

Law as a guide to conduct is reduced to the level of mere futility if it is unknown and unknowable.[2]

•

In our worship of certainty, we must distinguish between the sound certainty and the sham, between what is gold and what is tinsel; and then, when certainty is attained, we must remember that it is not the only good; that we can buy it at too high a price; that there is danger in perpetual quiescence as well as in perpetual motion; and that a compromise must be found in a principle of growth.[3]

•

We must have the courage to unmask pretense if we are to reach a peace that will abide beyond the fleeting hour. The law's uncertainties are to be corrected, but so also are its deformities.[4]

•

Existing rules and principles can give us our present location, our bearings, our latitude and longitude. The inn that shelters for the night is not the journey's end. The law, like the traveler, must be ready for the morrow. It must have a principle of growth.[5]

•

The theorist has a hard time to make his way in an ungrateful world.[6]

•

Of the lot of all theorists, that of the philosopher is the sorriest.[7]

---

[1]Reprinted from *Cardozo: The Growth of the Law* (1924) by permission of Yale University Press.
[2]*Ibid.* p. 3.
[3]*Ibid.* pp. 16, 17.
[4]*Ibid.* p. 18.
[5]*Ibid.* pp. 19, 20.
[6]*Ibid.* p. 21.
[7]*Ibid.* p. 22.

* * * law, like other branches of social science, must be satisfied to test the validity of its conclusions by the logic of probabilities rather than the logic of certainty.[1]

•

Judgments themselves have importance for the student so far, and so far only, as they permit a reasonable prediction that like judgments will be rendered if like situations are repeated. The study of the law is thus seen to be the study of principles of order revealing themselves in uniformities of antecedents and consequents."[2]

•

We shall unite in viewing as law that body of principle and dogma which with a reasonable measure of probability may be predicted as the basis for judgment in pending or in future controversies. When the predicition reaches a high degree of certainty or assurance, we speak of the law as settled, though, no matter how great the apparent settlement, the possibility of error in the prediction is always present. When the prediction does not reach so high a standard, we speak of the law as doubtful or uncertain. Farther down is the vanishing point where law does not exist, and must be brought into being, if at all, by an act of free creation.[3]

•

Judges march at times to pitiless conclusions under the prod of a remorseless logic which is supposed to leave them no alternative. They deplore the sacrificial rite. They perform it, none the less, with averted gaze, convinced as they plunge the knife that they obey the bidding of their office. The victim is offered up to the gods of jurisprudence on the altar of regularity.[4]

•

Not logic alone, but logic supplemented by the social sciences becomes the instrument of advance.[5]

---

[1] *Ibid.* p. 33.
[2] *Ibid.* p. 37.
[3] *Ibid.* p. 44.
[4] *Ibid.* p. 66.
[5] *Ibid.* p. 73.

The truth is not always to be reached by looking back to the beginning and deducing from the source. The end may be frustrated unless we look forward to the goal.[1]

•

When the legislature has spoken, and declared one interest superior to another, the judge must subordinate his personal or subjective estimate of value to the estimate thus declared. He may not nullify or pervert a statute because convinced that an erroneous axiology is reflected in its terms. Even when the legislature has not spoken, he is to regulate his estimate of values by objective rather than subjective standards, by the thought and will of the community rather than by his own idiosyncrasies of conduct and belief.[2]

•

An appeal to origins will be futile, their significance perverted, unless tested and illuminated by an appeal to ends.[3]

•

There are times when we can learn whether a rule functions well or ill by comparison with a standard of justice or equity, known, or capable of being known, to us all through a scrutiny of consicence or through appeal to everyday experience.[4]

•

The student does not need to be warned against fertilizing law with the teachings of philosophy. The warning must rather be to be on the watch for the philosophy which, disguised or unavowed, is latent in existing law, to extricate it when it is hidden, to test its truth and value, and to be ready to correct or discard it when it is defective or outworn.[5]

---

[1]*Ibid.* pp. 73, 74.
[2]*Ibid.* pp. 94, 95.
[3]*Ibid.* pp. 106, 107.
[4]*Ibid.* pp. 122, 123.
[5]*Ibid.* p. 131.

Justice is not to be taken by storm. She is to be wooed by slow advances.[1]

•

Law is the expression of a principle of order to which men must conform in their conduct and relations as members of society, if friction and waste are to be avoided among the units of the aggregate, the atoms of the mass.[2]

---

[1] *Ibid.* p. 133.
[2] *Ibid.* pp. 140, 141.

QUOTATIONS FROM "THE PARADOXES OF LEGAL SCIENCE"[1]

We have the claims of stability to be harmonized with those of progress. We are to reconcile liberty with equality, and both of them with order. The property rights of the individual we are to respect, yet we are not to press them to the point at which they threaten the welfare or the security of the many. We must preserve to justice its universal quality, and yet leave to it the capacity to be individual and particular.[2]

•

Violent breaks with the past must come, indeed, from legislation, but manifold are the occasions when advance or retrogression is within the competence of judges as their competence has been determined by practice and tradition.[3]

•

The moral code of each generation, this amalgam of custom and philosophy and many an intermediate grade of conduct and belief, supplies a norm or standard of behavior which struggles to make itself articulate in law.[4]

•

Law accepts as the pattern of its justice the morality of the community whose conduct it assumes to regulate. * * * The law will not hold the crowd to the morality of saints and seers. It will follow, or strive to follow, the principle and practice of the men and women of the community whom the social mind would rank as intelligent and virtuous.[5]

•

Justice as a jural norm is not a fixed or determinate phase of the totality of moral conduct in a given situation. On the other hand, it is not morality as a whole, even objectively considered. It is so much of morality as the thought and practice of a given epoch shall conceive to

---

[1]Reprinted from *Cardozo: The Paradoxes of Legal Science* (1928) by permission of Columbia University Press.

[2]*Ibid.* p. 5.

[3]*Ibid.* pp. 7, 8.

[4]*Ibid.* p. 17.

[5]*Ibid.* p. 37.

be appropriately invested with a legal sanction, and thereby marked off from morality in general.[1]

•

We gather together our principles and precedents and analogies, even at times our fictions, and summon them to yield the energy that will best attain the jural end. If our wand has the divining touch, it will seldom knock in vain. So it is that the conclusion, however deliberate and labored, has often the aspect in the end of nothing but a lucky find.[2]

•

A fruitful parent of injustice is the tyranny of concepts.[3]

•

The tendency of principle and rule to conform to moral standards, which is a true avenue of growth for law, is not to be confounded with the suspension of all principle and rule and the substitution of sentiment or unregulated benevolence, which, pushed to an extreme, is the negation of all law.[4]

•

There are topics where the law is still unformed and void. Some hint of premonition of coming shapes and moulds, it betrays amid the flux, yet it is so amorphous, so indeterminate, that formulation, if attempted, would be the prophecy of what is to be rather than the statement of what is.[5]

•

Liberty as a legal concept contains an underlying paradox. Liberty in the most literal sense is the negation of law, for law is restraint, and the absence of restraint is anarchy. On the other hand, anarchy by destroying restraint would leave liberty the exclusive possession of the strong or the unscrupulous.[6]

•

In delimiting the field of liberty, courts have professed for the most part to go about their work empirically and

---

[1]*Ibid.* pp. 41, 42.
[2]*Ibid.* p. 60.
[3]*Ibid.* p. 61.
[4]*Ibid.* p. 68.
[5]*Ibid.* p. 76.
[6]*Ibid.* p. 94.

have rather prided themselves on doing so. They have said, we will not define due process of law. We will leave it to be "pricked out" by a process of inclusion and exclusion in individual cases. That was to play safely, and very likely at the beginning to play wisely. The question is how long we are to be satisfied with a series of ad hoc conclusions. It is all very well to go on pricking the lines, but the time must come when we shall do prudently to look them over, and see whether they make a pattern or a medley of scraps and patches.[1]

•

What is personal and arbitrary in mandate and restraint does not gain rationality and coherence because it takes the form of statute. The legislature does not speak with finality as to the measure of its own powers. The final word is for the courts.[2]

•

The world has a certain stock of knowledge which has been garnered through the toil of centuries. The value of this stock has been so tested and verified by successive generations that to shut the young out from the opportunity of sharing in it would be to shut them out from the opportunity of pushing the bounds of knowledge farther. If private schools do not reach a level of reasonable competence, the state may insist that the young shall be trained in its own schools till this level is attained.[3]

•

Our statutes against monopoly and against combinations in restraint of trade bear witness to the underlying assumption of our law that liberty can be pushed to a point at which liberty is destroyed. The lesson, of course, is that in fixing the content of the constitutional immunity, we must test the validity of statutes with our eyes ever on the concrete fact. We must know how men work, and how they live, before we can say whether liberty will be increased or diminished by regulations affecting the manner of their living.[4]

---

[1]*Ibid.* p. 96.
[2]*Ibid.* p. 99.
[3]*Ibid.* p. 111.
[4]*Ibid.* p. 120.

The urge of selfish groups, or more rarely passion or indifference, may drive the lawmaker at times to forgetfulness or disregard of interests more permanent and essential than those exalted by his statute. It is the theory of our policy that beneath the transitory flux the judge may be expected to discern the deeper principle, and to rescue it from submergence in what is passing and particular.[1]

•

The complexities of modern life are so great that in the absence of fuller information than is commonly available to judges, the significance of apparent limitations upon liberty is likely to be lost. The result is the treatment of liberty as something static and predetermined.[2]

•

The presumption of validity should be more than a pious formula, to be sanctimoniously repeated at the opening of an opinion and forgotten at the end.[3]

•

Often a liberal antidote of experience supplies a sovereign cure for a paralyzing abstraction built upon a theory. Many a statutory innovation that would seem of sinister or destructive aspect if it were considered in advance, has lost its terror with its novelty.[4]

•

If reasoning is vitiated at times by adhering to abstractions, it is vitiated also by starting with a prepossession and finding arguments to sustain it. The weakness is inherent in the judicial process.[5]

•

The bundle of power and privileges to which we give the name of ownership is not constant through the ages. The faggots must be put together and rebound from time to time.[6]

---

[1] *Ibid.* p. 124.
[2] *Ibid.* pp. 124, 125.
[3] *Ibid.* p. 125.
[4] *Ibid.* pp. 125, 126.
[5] *Ibid.* pp. 126, 127.
[6] *Ibid.* p. 129.

QUOTATIONS FROM "LAW AND LITERATURE"[1]

The picture cannot be painted if the significant and the insignificant are given equal prominence. One must know how to select. All these generalities are as easy as they are obvious, but, alas! the application is an ordeal to try the souls of men.[2]

•

The development of law is conceived of, more and more, as a process of adaptation and adjustment. The pronouncements of its ministers are timid and tentative approximations, to be judged through their workings, by some pragmatic test of truth.[3]

•

Most of us are so uncertain of our strength, so beset with doubts and difficulties, that we feel oppressed with the need of justifying every holding by analogies and precedents and an exposure of the reasons.[4]

•

Comparatively speaking at least, the dissenter is irresponsible. The spokesman of the court is cautious, timid, fearful of the vivid word, the heightened phrase. He dreams of an unworthy brood of scions, the spawn of careless dicta, disowned by the *ratio decidendi,* to which all legitimate offspring must be able to trace their lineage. The result is to cramp and paralyze. One fears to say anything when the peril of misunderstanding puts a warning finger to the lips. Not so, however, the dissenter. He has laid aside the role of the hierophant, which he will be only too glad to resume when the chances of war make him again the spokesman of the majority. For the moment, he is the gladiator making a last stand against the lions.[5]

•

---

[1]Reprinted from *Cardozo: Law and Literature* (1931) by permission of Harcourt, Brace and Company, Inc.

[2]*Ibid.* p. 8.

[3]*Ibid.* p. 15.

[4]*Ibid.* p. 16.

[5]*Ibid.* p. 34

The prophet and the martyr do not see the hooting throng. Their eyes are fixed on the eternities.[1]

•

Sometimes the inroads upon justice are subtle and insidious. A spirit or a tendency, revealing itself in a multitude of little things, is the evil to be remedied. No one of its manifestations is enough, when viewed alone, to spur the conscience to revolt. The mischief is the work of a long series of encroachments. Examples are many in the law of practice and procedure.[2]

•

We have put away the blood feud, the vendetta, the other forms of private war but in the framing of our penal codes we have not forgotten the passions that had their outlet and release in pursuit and retribution. I do not say that it is wise to forget them altogether. The thirst for vengeance is a very real, even if it be a hideous thing; and states may not ignore it till humanity has been raised to greater heights than any that have yet been scaled in all the long ages of struggle and ascent.[3]

•

Human nature, like human life, has complexities and diversities too many and too intricate to be compressed within a formula. I would not shut the door of hope on any one, though classified in some statistical table as defective or recidivist, so long as scientific analysis and study of his mental and physical reactions after the state had taken him in hand held out the promise of redemption. Neither in punishment nor in any other form of judging shall we ever rid ourselves altogether of the heartbreaking burden of individual adjustment.[4]

•

Perhaps the whole business of the retention of the death penalty will seem to the next generation, as it seems to many even now, an anachronism too discordant to be

---

[1]*Ibid.* p. 36.
[2]*Ibid.* pp. 52, 53.
[3]*Ibid.* pp. 87, 88.
[4]*Ibid.* p. 92.

suffered, mocking with grim reproach all our clamorous professions of the sanctity of life.[1]

•

The law falters and averts her face and sheaths her own sword when pronouncing judgment upon creatures of flesh and blood thus goaded by the Furies.[2]

•

The lesson for legal science is that the structure depends on the foundations; that the fundamental conceptions of the law breed others in their image, and that the progeny will be mis-shapen or distorted, unless the parent conceptions are sound and pure and clear, as only accurate analysis can make us certain that they are.[3]

•

Those of us whose lives have been spent on the bench or at the bar have learned caution and reticence, perhaps even in excess. We know the value of the veiled phrase, the blurred edge, the uncertain line. Well, I am strong for them even now, at least in their proper places, or rather, I ought to say, for reservations and limitations which will preserve whatever of value there may be in impressionistic forms and phrases.[4]

o

The seductions of a dinner were thought to have a tendency to mollify convictions and stimulate with the gastric juices a tendency to compromise. The tendency may be admitted, but, nowadays at least, men are seldom sure enough of their convictions to be willing to put inflexibility in the forefront of the virtues and compromise behind it.[5]

o

The heroic hours of life do not announce their presence by drum and trumpet, challenging us to be true to our-

[1]*Ibid.* pp. 93, 94.
[2]*Ibid.* p. 114.
[3]*Ibid.* pp. 131, 132.
[4]*Ibid.* p. 137.
[5]*Ibid.* p. 158.

selves by appeals to the martial spirit that keeps the blood at heat. Some little, unassuming, unobtrusive choice presents itself before us slyly and craftily, glib and insinuating, in the modest garb of innocence. To yield to its blandishments is so easy. The wrong, it seems, is venial. Only hyper-sensitiveness, we assure ourselves, would call it a wrong at all. These are moments when you will need to remember the game that you are playing. Then it is that you will be summoned to show the courage of adventurous youth. There are some unquenchable spirits who never lose it, though the calendar may say that they have left youth behind and reached manhood or old age.[1]

[1]*Ibid.* pp. 170, 171.

www.ingramcontent.com/pod-product-compliance
Lightning Source LLC
LaVergne TN
LVHW100133061126
851857LV00010B/67
9781616195038